The Original
Bible Restored

by

Ernest L. Martin, Ph.D.

PUBLICATIONS

From the cowardice that shrinks from new truth,
From the laziness that is content with half-truths,
From the arrogance that thinks it knows all truth,

O God of Truth, deliver us.

-- Ancient Prayer

Publications
P.O. Box 25000, Portland, Oregon 97225, USA

THE ORIGINAL BIBLE RESTORED (SECOND EDITION)

Copyright © Ernest L. Martin, 1991

ISBN 0-945657-89-7

CONTENTS

The Reason for Writing this Book
The Guessing Game of Scholars

All scholars love to guess. I also love to guess, especially when I feel that I am on the right road toward being correct. And in the case of the canonization of the Old and the New Testaments all people are in the guessing game. The only trouble is, with many scholars they will not inform the general public that they are guessing when they write about how the books of the Bible came to be accepted as proper and right. Almost all have guessed that the various books of the New Testament were apparently found in various church congregations scattered around the Mediterranean and the Mesopotamian and Persian areas and that gradually, without any official canonization by top New Testament authorities, the books just seemed to come together out of the clear blue sky to form a canon and that by the fourth century most churches had come to accept the 27 books that now make up our New Testament.

This guessing is based purely on assumption. All admit, when questioned, that this assumption has not the slightest evidence to support it in a pragmatic sense, yet it is so accepted as being proper by most theologians, preachers, priests, evangelists, heads of denominations, etc. that it is considered to be the height of absurdity to question its legitimacy. But why should such guessing be accepted as proper when there are other explanations that are far better?

This book approaches the question from a different point of view, and it is, as I see it, the correct one. We start with the belief that God the Father and Christ Jesus were the ones who decided what the canon of the Old and New Testaments should be, and that they gave deliberate authority to certain men to accomplish the task of canonization. This book presents new and refreshing evidence to show that the biblical books in the basic Protestant canon are the proper and authoritative ones. We do show, however, that the books were arranged differently and placed in seven major divisions that are different from those today and that we ought to return to the original manuscript arrangement of the biblical books. This book shows what the original Bible was like when it first left the hands of the authoritative canonizers. It provides the proper evidence to assure ourselves that we now have "The Original Bible Restored."

Introduction

There is no doubt that the world has the complete Bible in its midst. One of them is the beloved King James' Version published in 1611. There have been many other complete versions produced over the last 100 years. So, why do we need "The Original Bible Restored"? The fact is, there needs to be a drastic revision within all Bible translations and versions (and that means *all* Bibles in existence no matter in what languages they have been published). Truly, there is not a Bible on the market today which follows the arrangement of the earliest manuscripts. One might think that such a state of affairs could not exist, but *it does*. Publishers have assiduously neglected to produce a complete Bible which positions the books in the correct manuscript order. The outcome has been a mass of Bible translations and versions which are literally topsy-turvy in their design and arrangement.

One might at first glance dismiss this infraction as being of minor consequence. But this represents a prime misjudgment when anyone looks seriously at the issue. In truth, the Bible of the manuscripts has all its divisions, parts and order of books in a symmetrical balance which shows a harmonious story-flow from beginning to end. But publishers have abandoned all attempts to restore *this* Bible to the general public.

Look at it this way. Suppose you bought a novel containing 49 chapters which introduced the various characters and plot in a progressive way from start to finish. Would it not be difficult to understand what the plot was all about if chapter 16 followed immediately after chapter 6, and especially if the chapters were not properly numbered? What then if chapter 22 were placed after chapter 7, chapter 22 before 21, chapter 14 after 21, chapters 12 and 13 followed 14, chapter 18 positioned after 13, chapter 17 followed 8 and 9, chapter 20 after 10, and finally chapter 11 after chapter 20? This would represent utter confusion. But if one reckons the *chapters* of our hypothetical novel as being the *books* of the Old Testament, this is the exact sequence we are saddled with in our present Bibles.

Let's not stop with the Old Testament. Look at what has happened to the 27 New Testament books. Return once more to the illustration of our novel. It means that chapters 23 to 27 follow immediately after chapter 11. Chapters 28 to 34 are found after chapter 44, while chapter 44 itself follows chapter 48, and chapters 35 to 43 are positioned after chapter 27. This is further confusion.

Some might say, however, that a comparison of the Bible with a novel is not proper. But this is exactly where the first mistake is made in appreciating the manuscript order of the biblical books. It will be shown in this book that there is a definite weaving together of a single story theme through the biblical books. And it is a remarkably consistent account which often amazes people when they see it for the first time. The only reason that such a homogeneous narrative has not been recognized by most people today is because none of our published Bibles has the books of the Old and New Testaments in the original manuscript order. When the proper design is restored, a marvelous and revealing series of connected subjects is seen running through the Bible which illustrates a compatible and coherent account from beginning to end. This book will reveal some of those amazing relationships which exist between and among the various books. This information may well prove to be an eye-opener to many students of the Bible — facts that have never been realized before.

Other matters are considered in the body of this book. It will be seen that the responsibility for canonizing the New Testament fell to the apostles themselves. It was they who had the authority to write and collect the various books of the New Testament, and that two apostles in particular were given the special assignment of formulating the New Testament into a complete and final book. It will also be shown that the original number of both the Old and New Testament books should be reckoned as 49 — not the 66 that we have in our modern Bibles. The present enumeration reflects a numerical pattern which is very unlike the original. Indeed, some Bibles even have an extra eleven (or fourteen) books included in their contents. This divergency represents an abandonment of the original number and arrangement of the books.

The subject of this book is almost like an adventure story — a story of re-discovery. Yet, in actual fact, this book contains not *one bit of new evidence* (regarding the manuscript order of the biblical books) that has not been known by New Testament textual scholars for over a century and a half. It is an incredible circumstance that most readers of the Bible are totally unaware of this evidence. Such proof has long been in the hands of scholars but not one attempt has been made to provide the English speaking world with a complete Bible which follows the manuscripts. And it is a rare occasion indeed that the introductions to any English version even deem it necessary to inform the general public what the manuscript order really is, and even then it is usually a brief and inconsequential reference that the reader would hardly think important.

It is time that the world be presented with "The Manuscript Version of the Bible." Publishing such a work would provide a proper *canon* of the Bible. The word "canon" means *rule* or *standard.* There is no version being published today that resembles the canonical Bible of the manuscripts. But why not? Should not Christians want to perpetuate the biblical canon devised by the men who formed it? In this book we provide a great deal of internal evidence from the Bible itself which goes a long way in showing that the early manuscript order of the books is not only correct, it is an essential factor which helps to emphasize some significant biblical themes. There is one which is most important. If the books of the Old and New Testaments are restored to their manuscript arrangement, *the center books* of the whole Bible are the five New Testament books which describe the life and times of Jesus Christ. In a word, Jesus Christ is featured as the *focal point* (the *fulcrum*) of all Scripture. But only the manuscript order is able to demonstrate this.

In this book we stress the importance of letting the Bible itself speak about its own origin and arrangement of books. It is now being recognized in the scholarly world that such internal evidence is a valuable tool in understanding canonical matters. We provide a considerable amount of information on this internal evidence that is often overlooked by many students of the Scripture.

When people allow the Bible itself to be its own interpreter to show the proper doctrinal principles that govern the whole issue of canonization, we find that much of the guessing that scholars have had to resort to up to now can be replaced with sensible and reasonable information that those who love the biblical revelation can rely on with confidence. That is what this book is all about.

In this book the emphasis is placed upon what the Bible itself teaches about its own rules that govern canonization. This is a refreshing research study which will put in people's hands, for the first time in modern times, the proper tools to decide properly which books belong in the canon and which ones do not. This biblical research will show why the original manuscript order of the divine canon (which differs remarkably with the versions and translations we are saddled with today) also gives the correct order and arrangement of the *real* Holy Scriptures that left the hands of the prophets and apostles.

What is beneficial from this research is the fact that all teachings in the Bible become clearer and plainer when the 49 biblical books are placed back in their correct and divine order. It is truly amazing what the books of the Bible have to tell us when we read the Holy Scriptures in the context that was first intended by those who officially canonized the Bible.

It is time that the world, for the first time in over 1600 years, be given the *real* Bible of the official and authoritative canonizers. Thankfully, as of 1991, some top theological scholars now realize the need to reproduce for the first time in modern history "the original Bible." Within the next five years this proper version should be available and in bookstores around the world. It will show what the original Bible was like when it was first canonized.

This present book leads the way in showing the need for this return to the proper Bible of the prophets and apostles. The information in the following pages of this book will demonstrate in the clearest of ways why this modern world needs "The Original Bible Restored."

1

The Original Bible Restored

It can be demonstrated in a clear and positive way that no popular version of the Bible in modern times has followed the ancient manuscripts in the arrangement of the biblical books. It is almost unbelievable that such a situation could exist, especially in our highly critical age, yet publishers in their quest to print numerous versions of the Bible have been led to avoid the actual manuscript positioning of the biblical books in favor of a later ecclesiastical order which has no justification from early Hebrew and Greek texts.

Let us look at the New Testament first. When the textual scholars of the last century printed their final results of surveying the early New Testament manuscripts, they *all* without exception placed the resultant arrangement of the books in the same order. They felt compelled to do this because of the overwhelming evidence from the manuscripts. Scrivener, after surveying over 4000 manuscripts, said:

> "Whether copies contain the whole or a part of the sacred volume, the general order of the books is the following: Gospels, Acts, Catholic Epistles, Pauline Epistles, Apocalypse" (*Introduction to the Criticism of the New Testament*, vol.I,p.72).

The fact is, *all* textual scholars who led the pioneering work in the evaluation of New Testament manuscripts consistently recorded the proper manuscript order of the books in their editions intended for biblical scholars. They placed the seven Catholic Epistles (James, I & II Peter, I,II & III John and Jude) *before* the fourteen of the apostle Paul. This is a very significant feature of the early manuscripts. (It ought to be stated that the word "Catholic" in this instance does not refer to any Christian denomination. It only means that the epistles

6

themselves are "Universal" or "General.")

> "This is the position [of the Catholic Epistles] assigned them in
> the critical editions of Lachmann, Tischendorf, Tregelles, West-
> cott and Hort" (Hastings, *Dict. of the Bible*, vol.I,p.360).

The early manuscripts which most textual critics uphold as the best
in existence (notably the *Vaticanus, the Alexandrinus* and the
Ephraem) position the seven Catholic Epistles before those of Paul.
There can be little doubt that this is where they belong. But in our
modern versions, the translators have abandoned this order and
adopted an ecclesiastical one which most will admit is provincial and
sectarian and one that cannot represent the original arrangement of
the New Testament books. This, on the other hand, was not the case
with the ancient scholars and leaders of the church.

Early Christian Beliefs

Almost all the Greek speaking ecclesiastical authorities from the
areas of Palestine, Syria, Asia Minor, and Greece refer to the books of
the New Testament in the manuscript arrangement mentioned
above.

Athanasius said the order was "the four Gospels; the Acts of the
Apostles; the seven Catholic Epistles; the fourteen epistles of St.
Paul; and the Revelation of John" (Horne, *Introduction.* vol.IV,p.253).

Leontius of Byzantium mentioned the order as "Matthew, Mark,
Luke, John; the Acts of the Apostles; the seven Catholic Epistles; the
Epistles of Paul; and the Apocalypse" (*ibid.*).

Philastris was even bold in his statement that the seven Catholic
Epistles must be positioned before Paul's because in Galatians 1:17
Paul said that the Jewish apostles were "before me" (Moffatt,
Introduction to the Literature of the N.T., p.13).

The normal manuscript order was also advocated by the clerics at
the eastern Church Council of Laodicea (Canon LX, *NPNF*, vol.XIV.
p.159) and it was further maintained by Cyril, Bishop of Jerusalem,
(Catechetical Lectures 4.36, *NPNF*, vol.VII,pp.27,28).

John of Damascus (born 675 A.D.) — author of the standard
textbook on *Dogmatic Theology* for the Greek Church — referred to

the manuscript order of the books as the proper one. Without qualification he stated that the seven Catholic Epistles must be placed right after the Book of Acts (Lardner, *Credibility*, vol.V,p.147).

Further names could be cited in support of this prevelant view among eastern churchmen. These included Cassiodorus, Nicephorus and also the Peshitta Version of the New Testament (Moffatt, p.14). These were followed by the *Stoichiometry* from Cotelerius (806 A.D.) and Oecumenius (950 A.D) the Bishop of Thessaly who wrote a short copy of verse on the New Testament in the proper manuscript order (Lardner, vol.V,pp.89,154,155).

This order (with the Catholic Epistles positioned before those of Paul) was even recognized by Jerome, the translator of the Latin Vulgate Version of the Bible. However, when Jerome wrote a personal letter to his friend Paulinus, he followed an order peculiar to Epiphanius who even placed Paul's letters right after the four Gospels (Lardner, vol.IV,pp.437,438). This order is also found in the *Sinaiticus* manuscript.

But what about the order of New Testament books which we find in our Bibles today? This arrangement had its origin in the areas of Rome and Carthage and came essentially from Latin speaking ecclesiastical authorities. The western fathers were prone to place Paul's epistles immediately after the Book of Acts, thus violating the early Greek manuscript arrangement. This re-adjustment (from the western point of view) had the advantage of placing the epistles of Paul (the apostle to the Gentiles) into a first rank position over and above the "Jewish" apostles. It especially was fortuitous because it elevated the Book of Romans (the first epistle in Paul's collection) to first rank above all other epistles of the New Testament. The upshot of this re-positioning by western authorities provided a supposed biblical sanction for advancing the jurisdiction of the Roman church into a position of first rank over all other church areas. Let me state at the outset that this evaluation of mine is not intended as a censure of the Church at Rome. But it is a simple fact of history that the "authority" arguments which were going on in the third and fourth centuries played a major role in the re-designing of the New Testament books by those in the western (and Gentile) sections of Christendom.

The reason for the western advancement of Paul (and Rome) over the seven Catholic epistles (which were considered "Jewish") was given in the last century by M'Clintock and Strong:

> "The Western Church . . . as represented by Jerome and Augustine, and their successors, gave priority of position to the Pauline epistles. The tendency of the Western Church to recognize Rome as the center of authority may perhaps, in part, account for this departure from the custom of the East. The order in the Alexandrian, Vatican and Ephraem manuscripts gives precedence to the Catholic Epistles, and as this is also recognized by the Council of Laodicea, Cyril of Jerusalem and Athanasius, it would appear to have been characteristic of the Eastern churches" (*CBTEL*, vol.I,p.800).

It is really easy to see that the "western re-arrangement" (which we find in our Bibles today) was an attempt to exalt the political position of the western church over early Christendom. It put Rome ahead of the churches of the East.

A reflection of this type of re-designing is found in the writings of the Latin theologian Rufinus, born about 330 A.D., a churchman of the "western school" (Lardner, vol.IV,pp.483,484). The western arrangement was also advocated by the Third Council of Carthage (*ibid.* p.487). Innocent of Rome did the same (*ibid.* p.586) and so did Gelasius, Bishop of Rome (492 A.D.) (*ibid.* vol.V, p.76). These wanted Rome (not Jerusalem or eastern cities) in top authority among the Christian churches.

There were even two easterners who followed the western order. One was Gregory of Nazianzus. This might be expected with Gregory because he championed a universal orthodoxy for both the eastern and western sections of the church against the doctrines of eastern Arianism. Associated with him was Amphilochius, Bishop of Iconium (*ibid.* vol.IV,pp.292,293).

There is no doubt that the main reason for the westerners' replacement of Paul's epistles to a position before those of James, Peter, John, and Jude, was to exalt Paul (the Gentile apostle) over the Jewish apostles, which in turn helped to elevate the later western ecclesiastical authorities of the third and fourth centuries into a supreme political position within Christendom. There was, however, a major problem with the exaltation of Paul because it put Peter (whom most people felt was the first Bishop of Rome) into an inferior position. This may have been an embarrassment, but it was avoided by pointing out that the two epistles of Peter were written to Jews, not Gentiles as the Romans were. So even the first "Pope" got put into a last position.

In spite of these sectarian reasons for placing Paul's letters before the seven Catholic Epistles, the proper order of the New Testament books was well known and maintained by the majority of early Greek manuscripts. And this is exactly how the New Testament books should be positioned today. Professor Gregory, who devoted his life to the study of the manuscripts, summed up the real order of the New Testament books.

> "The order in which we place the books of the New Testament is not a matter of indifference. Every Christian should be familiar with these books, and should know precisely where to find each book. Every New Testament should have the books in precisely the same order, the order of the Greek Church, which in this case is of right the guardian of this ancient literature. The proper order is, I think: First, the Four Gospels: Matthew, Mark, Luke, and John. Second, the Book of Acts. Third, the Catholic Epistles: James, First and Second Peter, First, Second, and Third John, and Jude. Fourth, the Epistles of Paul: Romans, First and Second Corinthians, Galatians, Ephesians, Philippians, Colossians, First and Second Thessalonians, Hebrews, First and Second Timothy, Titus, Philemon. And fifth, the Book of Revelation. . . The Greek order is that which places the Epistle to the Hebrews between Thessalonians and Timothy, *and that is the order to which we should hold.* The Latin order places Hebrews after Philemon. But *we must keep to the old order* or we shall have the New Testament turned upside down in connection with every fancied discovery as to authorship and date of books" (*Canon and Text of the New Testament,* pp.467-469, italics mine).

There can be no question that Professor Gregory was right in his scholarly evaluation. Indeed, in the critical edition of Westcott and Hort (two of the top textual critics of modern times) they printed their Greek New Testament in the order that Professor Gregory stated was correct. It is time that New Testament scholars and also the publishers of Bibles return to the proper order and inform the general public about the original disposition of the New Testament books. The rewards for restoring the manuscript order can afford us with a much better understanding of the messages of the New Testament. And when both the Old and New Testaments *are returned* to their original designs (and combined together) a brand new appreciation of the Bible could be the result.

The Old Testament

The books of the Old Testament also need to be re-positioned to accord with the manuscripts maintained by the Jewish authorities. Our Christian Old Testament follows an order of books which had its origin in Egypt in the second and third centuries A.D. This was finally accomplished about 200 years after Christ when the codex form for producing books became popular (this is the type of book with which we are familiar today). Before this was done, however, it was customary to use scrolls for the reproduction of books and in Egypt there was no standardization of book arrangement for most of the Old Testament books. Their positioning and design did not seem important to those in Egypt as long as the Old Testament books were in scroll form.

There was, on the other hand, an early interest among the Egyptians in the sacred writings of the Jews. As early as the third century before Christ, the Egyptians were having parts of the Old Testament translated into Greek. By the time of Christ we can be reasonably assured that all the Old Testament was translated into Greek. The apostles were accustomed to refer to these Greek translations from Egyptian sources. They were called the Septuagint (from the belief that seventy—LXX—elders of the Jews began the translations over two and a half centuries before the birth of Christ).

Though all the books of the Old Testament were able to be consulted in the Greek by the time of Christ, still *the order of those books* was not established until the invention of the codex form of book. As stated before, this is the kind of *book* that we are familiar with today. In ancient times (and even throughout the early period of the apostles) it was common to read documents from scrolls — from rolled up pieces of papyrus or animal skins. But the codex form of producing books was brought into existence in the latter part of our first century. It was about 200 years later that the Septuagint Version of the Old Testament was finally assembled together into our modern codex form. This codexing of the Old Testament books had the effect of standardizing the Egyptian order for the Gentile Christians who could only read the sacred books in the Greek. This caused the later Christians in Egypt to abandon the Jewish arrangement which was maintained in Palestine. But, the Old Testament, reckoned as official by the Jews for their synagogue services, is the proper and original one. The arrangement can be shown to be in existence at least back to the second century B.C. It is this order that all Christian Bibles should retain — not the ecclesiastical (and traditional) one which had its origin at the time the Septuagint was codexed in Egypt. The Palestinian design needs to be restored! When it is, there will emerge some revealing and important teachings which will go a long way in showing that we have the complete and proper Old Testament today.

The manuscript order of the Hebrew canon is as follows:

I THE LAW (TORAH)
1) Genesis
2) Exodus
3) Leviticus
4) Numbers
5) Deuteronomy

II THE PROPHETS
6) Joshua and Judges
7) The Book of Kingdoms (Samuel and Kings)
8) Isaiah
9) Jeremiah
10) Ezekiel
11) The Twelve (Hosea to Malachi)

III THE HOLY WRITINGS (or THE PSALMS)
12) Psalms
13) Proverbs
14) Job
15) Song of Songs

16) Ruth
17) Lamentations
18) Ecclesiastes
19) Esther
20) Daniel
21) Ezra-Nehemiah
22) The Book of Chronicles

These 22 books of the Old Testament (and their arrangement as indicated above) should be the standard followed by every version of the Bible today. They represent the exact number which are presently in our King James Version but, as one can observe, they are arranged and enumerated differently.

Notice also that the Old Testament was divided into three parts called "The Tripartite Divisions." These divisions were maintained among the original Temple scrolls and reproduced for particular use in synagogue services. Christ himself referred to these official Tripartite Divisions as the Law of Moses, the Prophets, and the Psalms (Luke 24:44,45). (His reference to "the Psalms" was, as we will show, to all the eleven books of the Third Division which got its title from the book which introduced the division.) Remarkably, Christ designated these Tripartite Divisions as "*the* Scriptures" (verse 45). This recognition by Christ of the three divisions of the Old Testament is the only place in the New Testament where the Old Testament revelation is defined. This provides the highest possible authority for the retention of those three divisions.

When these features are restored to modern Bibles there will be an amazing relationship to be seen between all the books of the Old and New Testaments. The Bible would become interesting to most people, and a great deal of important information about the Bible would come on the scene that people have not realized before.

A Numerical Summary

The standard manuscript disposition of the Old and New Testament books shows a symmetrical balance between the divisions and parts that is truly inspiring and instructive. We will look at the significance of this matter later on in this book, but as a preliminary synopsis, note that the original Scriptures had exactly 49 books: 22 in the Old Testament and 27 in the New. This number is, of course, 7 times 7, and *seven* represents the symbolic number of *completion* or *finalization.* One could spend many pages giving biblical references to the significance of the number *seven.* But as a simple illustration of its symbolic meaning, look at the basic features of the Jewish calendar. The Hebrews recognized that the seventh day of the week *completed* the week. The seven weeks of grain harvest (the 49 days from Passover to Pentecost) *completed* the firstfruits harvest. The first seven months of the Hebrew calendar contained the times for the seven annual festivals commanded by Moses. In a sense it could be said that the festival year of Moses was seven months long, and those seven months contained and *completed* the holyday schedule for the Israelites. And let us not forget that every seventh year was reckoned a Sabbatical Year and it commemorated the *completion* of six years of agricultural activity for the Hebrews in Palestine. After seven of those Sabbatical Years were *completed* (a period of 49 years), the Year of Jubilee was reached—which was supposed to be a time of agricultural and financial rejuvenation for all Israelites in Palestine. This was the time when all social and economic activities were supposed to return to the same condition as at the beginning of the previous 49 years.

Why are these sevens and multiples of sevens important? They show that it was no accident that the total number of Old and New Testament books came to 49 in number in the enumeration maintained by the early Jewish and Christian authorities. But there is more to it than that. There are also three divisions to the . Old Testament: 1) The Law, 2) The Prophets, and 3) The Writings' (the Psalms) Division. To these can be added the four divisions of the New Testament: 1) The Historical Books (Gospels and Acts), 2) The seven General (or Catholic) Epistles, 3) The fourteen (2 times 7) epistles of Paul, and 4) the final Book of Revelation. When one adds the three divisions of the Old with the four of the New, we arrive at seven divisions to the complete Bible. This was no happenstance matter either.

Throughout this book will be shown many more numerical relationships within and among the various books of the Bible involving the number *seven.* The divine Scripture is truly a marvelously arranged book and it has a message from those numerical patterns that will help enhance one's comprehension of the biblical revelation. For the general public to appreciate this fact, however, the first thing that ought to be done is for publishers of Bibles, biblical scholars, and modern preachers of the Gospel to abandon the sectarian arrangement of the biblical books (which had its origin some two or three hundred years after Christ) and return to the early manuscript order as maintained by the Jews and Greeks. This would be a major undertaking of revision because every version combining the Old and New Testaments being published in the world today is in error and should be adjusted. It would also be an enormous task to re-educate people to accept the original manuscript divisions and arrangement of the biblical books. The biggest problem of all is to change people's minds from the apathy that is presently expressed over the issue, and get them excited about a return to the original Bible. We must not forget that there could be a resistance to any change because it might rekindle the doctrinal arguments of the third and fourth centuries regarding the place where proper authority rests within Christendom. If one accepts the retention of our present catalog of books, then some might imagine that the Roman church has credentials for a top position. But if one returns to the original manuscript order and restores the seven Catholic Epistles to their rightful position in the New Testament canon (and placing the Book of Hebrews after II Thessalonians), this would tend to exalt the "Jewish apostles" over the apostle Paul and the Gentile section of the Christian Church. This is clearly the proper thing to do. Even the apostle Paul said that the message of Christian salvation should go to "the Jew first" (Rom.2:10; 3:1,2). And in Paul's personal evaluation of his rank in the Christian Church, he admitted that the pillars in the Church were James, Peter, and John at Jerusalem (Gal.2:9) and that they were apostles "before me" (Gal.1:17). Indeed, the apostle Paul even considered himself the "least of the apostles" (I Cor.15:9), and that he was a person "who am less than the least of all saints" (Eph.3:8). There can be no question that if the apostle Paul himself would have had a say in the positioning of his own fourteen epistles, he would not have insisted they be placed *before* the pillar apostles.

The actual fact is, there is no need to lessen any church's jurisdiction when the world returns to the manuscript order of the

Old and New Testament books. Such authority is based on a host of other considerations, not simply the positioning of the canonical books. Indeed the apostle Peter (the first recorded Bishop of Rome) would then assume his rightful classification of rank ahead of the apostle Paul who considered himself to be "the least of the apostles."

The original arrangement of the New Testament books is what we could call today "the Jewish order of the books" (even though all the canonical books of the New Testament are written in the Greek tongue). Our present arrangement which can be traced predominantly to the influence of Jerome in the early fifth century is really an attempt to exalt the Gentiles over the Jews, even in matters dealing with the canonization of the New Testament.

But our "Gentile order of the books" is not in accord with the original manuscripts nor (as we will abundantly show in this book) the biblical principles of authority which are found in all parts of the Bible. In a word, the Bible, including the New Testament itself, is really "a Jewish book" in every way. Though much of its writings went to Gentile peoples, its authors were Jewish Christians (even Luke, though a Gentile, wrote under the auspices of the apostle Paul who was Jewish).

Our present arrangement actually exalts "Rome" and the Gentiles as being in authority over Christian affairs rather than "Jerusalem" and the early Jewish apostles whom Christ Jesus selected to teach the basic doctrines of Christianity to the world. The proper manuscript arrangement truly exalts the proper authority as being "Jerusalem" and the Jewish apostles of Christ, not Rome, Athens, London, Moscow, Berlin, New York, or any other city or any other persons on earth. The order of the books is not the only reason for showing authority in Christian affairs, but it plays its part in directing people to the proper principles for solving the authority issue. Certainly, our modern world is entitled to have the versions of their Bibles (in their own languages) in the same manner in which the early Christians had theirs. We think that a new appreciation for the Holy Bible will be the result.

2

The Biblical Keys
to Canonization

This book on the design and development of the Old and New Testaments differs substantially from studies made over the last hundred and fifty years. In this work, a principle has been adopted which has the potential for solving a great number of perplexing problems now confronting scholarly investigation in the field of biblical canonization. It is a proper procedure which should be used to evaluate any historical account, but strangely, in major studies involving scripture canonization it has not been emphasized as a main guideline. Its lack of use is especially apparent in matters concerning the original design and development of the Holy Scriptures. In this book, however, the principle will be placed in prime position for interpretation. The results can be a satisfying and stimulating advance towards a real understanding of what books belong in the Holy Bible and in what order they ought to appear.

The method of which we speak involves a recognition of the environmental elements which governed the social, political, and religious conduct of the people who formulated the Bible. It is a well-known fact that people find it psychologically difficult, if not impossible, to keep from absorbing the social concepts which permeate the environment in which they live and function. When the external surroundings influencing the canonizers are recognized, and those factors are employed in the interpretation of their writings, a fuller comprehension of what the Bible teaches can be the result.

The Religious Environment for Canonization

The age in which the New Testament was written and canonized was very different from that of modern times. This is especially true when one compares our present world with the religious atmosphere of the peoples who once existed in the Roman and Parthian Empires. Preeminent among all others in their desire to promote religious teachings were the Jewish people. Their society was dominated by scriptural teachings and interpretations maintained by the rabbis and priests. There has never been a communal existence more regulated by rigorous biblical customs and philosophies than that of first century Jews. And though their reliance on Old Testament standards may seem unreasonable to many moderns, early Jewish mentality regarded the performance of their religious duties as normal and natural. They were most interested in keeping the Laws of Moses. In actual fact, they even went beyond the strictness of Moses (Matt.23: 1-3), and created a hide-bound religious community which the apostle Paul called a state of bondage (Gal.4:25). Peter and the other apostles agreed (Acts 15:10).

Nevertheless, that uncompromising religious system and the principles that governed it played a profound role in the canonization of the New Testament. Without a comprehension of its major features (to which all the apostles were subjected) is a prime reason why some scholars are at a loss to explain how or why the books of the New Testament were selected and positioned within the canon.

In this chapter we wish to describe some of the important aspects of that first century Jewish environment. It will help to show why the manuscript order of the Old and New Testament writings is proper.

Seven Environmental Factors

The first of seven social factors which influenced all historical periods covered by the Bible is that involving the recognition and respect for *eldership*. Let me explain the importance of this concept. It simply means that anyone *older* than someone else was accorded a superior respect in all matters concerning the social graces. And though this principle could be put aside if someone younger was of more political or religious importance, the general feeling of all ancient people was that those who were older in age were given a position of prestige and honor.

A good example of this is the account of Elihu (in the Book of Job) when he desired to give his opinion on why Job had suffered misfortunes. The Bible is clear that the younger man Elihu waited until the older and supposedly more wiser men had their opportunities to instruct the patriarch Job. Only after their discourses were completed did Elihu speak (Job 32:1-9).

This concept of elders having the first chance to be heard is one which monopolizes all historical narratives of the Bible from beginning to end. Are we to imagine that the canonizers of the Bible would disallow this principle of elder supremacy when they thought of positioning the books of the Bible? It would seem highly unlikely. And, in fact, when one looks at the arrangement of the biblical books, it is obvious that they held to the concept in a definite way.

Let us first look at the order of the books in the New Testament. Notice the books which followed the four Gospels and the Book of Acts. The ancient manuscripts have: James, I & II Peter, I,II & III John, Jude. These seven epistles were placed before the fourteen assigned to the apostle Paul. But why? For one reason, the four men who wrote these seven books were men who heard Christ teach while he was in the flesh, and they were ordained to preach the Gospel *before* the apostle Paul was converted on the road to Damascus. Simply put, they were elders of Paul. The apostle Paul recognized this fact and said that they were ministers "before me" (Gal.1:17). Paul even considered himself as the "least of the apostles" (I Cor.15:9). Indeed, he even demoted himself to being "less than the least of all saints" (Eph.3:8).

If one had to rely solely upon the statements of Paul (and comprehending the principle of eldership predominance) then the writings of those men who were apostles *before* Paul should have their teachings positioned *before* those of Paul. Interestingly, this is exactly the position in which we find them in the early manuscript order of the New Testament books. There can be no doubt that the advancement of the seven epistles of these early apostles *before* the fourteen of the apostle Paul is the correct procedure.

There is a *second* environmental principle which must be taken into consideration, and it is akin to the first. This is the deference afforded those who were in high positions of government or those who occupied august religious offices, no matter what their ages might be. A notable example of this is found in the actions of the apostle Paul. The New Testament shows that Paul was at one time extremely critical of the decisions advocated by one of his persecutors. But when he found out that the person was the High Priest (who was probably not wearing his pontifical robes at the time), Paul respected his rank and apologized for speaking to him abusively (Acts 23:1-5). Many such examples of esteem for authorities (no matter if they were good or evil) can be cited throughout Scripture. Even today in Jewish circles, if a member of a synagogue possesses a name associated with the priesthood (Cohen, Kahn, Conn, etc.), that person has the inalienable right to read the lessons before anyone else. This rule also applies to Jews having Levitical names (Levi, Levine, etc.) — they are only a step removed from priesthood positions in rank of importance. However, if no one attending the synagogue has names of sacerdotal significance, then any Israelite male today can assume the duties of reading the scriptural lessons. This courtesy to administrational rank is sustained consistently throughout all parts of the Old and New Testaments. An example of this is found in the order of the three divisions which make up the Old Testament. The first section are the five books of the Law written by Moses. (Moses was the highest ranking man of the Old Testament, followed by his brother Aaron who was the first High Priest.) The second section are the six books titled "the Prophets." This part was called "the Prophets" because it was written by men of prophetical rank. The third section of eleven books was called "the Writings." We will later see that these books were composed by or written about kings, queens, statesmen. It came to be called "the Royal Division."

Now note this. In matters of rank, Moses and the Law which he was commissioned to write were head and shoulders above all succeeding prophets, priests, or kings. All Israelites were expected to be subservient to Moses. But, on the other hand, all kings and rulers were inferior in rank to the prophets (most of whom were priests). Recall that Nathan the prophet had authority over David (II Sam.12:1-15), and that Elijah and Elisha were in supreme power over Gentile as well as Israelitish rulers as far as the teaching of the Bible is concerned (II Kings 5:1-19). And this rank of authority (Moses over prophets and prophets ahead of rulers) is shown in the order of the three divisions of the Old Testament. First comes "the Law of Moses," then "the Prophets," and finally "the Royal Division" (the last eleven books).

For a further example of this recognition of rank, note that the apostle Paul's name *always* follows that of Barnabas (who was a Levite — Acts 4:36) until Paul later took over the apostolic leadership at Antioch of Pisidia (Acts 13:14,46). Paul's primacy is then upheld, except when he and Barnabas were in the presence of the "pillar" apostles, for among those in Jerusalem the Levitical rank of Barnabas reassumed its elevated position (Acts 15:12).

It is also a fact that Peter's name always precedes that of John in contexts involving both apostles (Luke 22:8; Acts 3:1, etc.), simply because Peter was given a higher rank than John (Matt.16:18,19). And when the "pillar" apostles are mentioned together, it is James (the Lord's brother, and leader of the Jerusalem church) who precedes Peter and John (Gal.2:9).

This positioning of names in the New Testament is both a conscious and unconscious attempt to show honor and respect to the ranks of the men involved. Such a procedure represents the normal concepts of protocol in Middle Eastern societies. What is important to our present study is the fact that this principle was one which prevailed in the psychological make-up of the men who wrote and canonized the books of the Bible. Note, again, that the seven general epistles of James, Peter, John, and Jude precede the fourteen of the apostle Paul's in the original manuscript order of the books. And even within the positioning of the seven epistles, James is placed before Peter, while Peter appears before John, and John is before Jude. The arrangement of these books is precisely as one would expect *if* the ranks of the men were being considered. And recall that even the apostle Paul, when referring to the three Jerusalem apostles, mentioned them in the order of their positions of authority in the Jerusalem church, "James, Cephas (Peter), and John, who seemed to be pillars" (Gal.2:9). This courtesy of mentioning the apostles in this fashion was no arbitrary incident. It had deliberate and conscious significance as anyone studying the customs of the biblical periods would realize. The order of the scriptural books echoes the use of this formality.

There is yet a *third* principle that must be considered. There was in the first century among the Jewish community (of which the apostles were a part) a distinct belief that those who could claim a connection with the race of Israel had a special relationship with God that no other people had. The apostle Paul shared this belief. He stated most assuredly that only Israelites possessed the sonship, the shekinah glory, the personal covenants, the Mosaic law, the right to perform the Temple services, and the only ones in the world who had the promises of salvation (Rom.9:4). Paul insisted that before the introduction of Christianity, all other races were completely cut off from "the commonwealth of Israel, and strangers from the covenants of promise, having no hope, and without God in the world" (Eph.2:12).

There is no doubt that this recognition of a special association with God was the universal belief among Jews of the early first century, and even Gentiles who wanted to be in covenant with God also felt the need to join the society of Israel. And though in Christ, Paul taught that all peoples were on an equal status with Israel (Gal.3:28), the spiritual ascendancy of the favored nation over all Gentiles was never forgotten by the apostles — including Paul himself. Notice what he said to the Gentile Romans.

> "What advantage then hath the Jew? or what profit is there in circumcision? Much every way: chiefly because that unto them were committed the oracles of God" (Rom.3:1,2).

The Old Testament had been placed in the hands of the Jewish people. This gave the Jews a superior position. This covenant relationship with God was never diminished in the eyes of the apostle Paul (nor among the other apostles who at first were commissioned to preach only to Jews). Paul readily acknowledged the principle that the Jews were to have *first choice* in receiving the Gospel. They were in a legal position ahead of the Gentiles.

> "Glory, honour, and peace, to every man that worketh good, *to the Jew first,* and also to the Gentile" (Rom.2:10).

This first rank for the Jewish people was always given, even in matters of judgment (Rom.2:9). And in regard to Christ's salvation, Paul was adamant that the message should go to the Jews *first.*

> "For I am not ashamed of the gospel of Christ: for it is the power of God unto salvation to every one that believeth; *to the Jew first,*

and also to the Greek" (Rom.1:16).

The apostle Paul never deviated from his belief in the Jews having first position to receive the Gospel. In fact, he had been commissioned by Christ to preach both to Israelites and Gentiles (Acts 9:15) and he never shirked his responsibility of going to the Jews first. Note Paul's example.

When Paul went to the Gentile island of Cyprus, he spoke first to the Jews (Acts 13:5). When he went to the central area of Galatia, he first preached in the synagogues of the Jews (Acts 13:14) — and only secondarily did he speak to the Gentiles (Acts 13:42). This was also the case at Iconium (Acts 14:1), later in Macedonia (Acts 16:1-13; 17:1,10), at Corinth (Acts 18:4), Ephesus (Acts 19:8), and even Rome itself (Acts 28:17-27). It was only at places where the Jewish community almost totally rejected him did Paul turn exclusively to the Gentiles (Acts 13:46; 18:6; 28:28).

It is also shown in the Book of Acts that the Gospel of Christ went *first* to the Jews at Jerusalem, and then progressively it finally got to the Gentiles at Rome. Jerusalem was *first* and Rome was *last*. Indeed, for the first few years the Gospel was taught "to Jews only" (Acts 11:19) without a thought that the Gentiles themselves would one day be graced with the Gospel message. And even when it became clear that the Gentiles were meant to receive the Gospel, Paul said: "*It was necessary* that the word of God should *first* have been spoken to you [Jews]" (Acts 13:46). This was of prime importance to the apostles.

This fact of apostolic history is also reflected within the design of the New Testament canon. This is because the psychological motives dominating the thinking of the apostles demanded that the Gospel of salvation must, in all cases, be presented to the Jewish people first. This is just another reason why the canonizers of the New Testament followed the conviction that first position among the 27 Christian books within the divine library must be awarded to the books designed primarily for the Jews. This is why the seven general epistles of James, Peter, John, and Jude (who were commissioned to preach to the Jews—Gal.2:7-9) should logically precede the fourteen of the apostle Paul who was the apostle to the Gentiles (II Tim.1:11). There can be no doubt that the early Christian apostles (when presented with the responsibility of forming a New Testament from the available writings) would have placed the apostles specially assigned to the Jews *before* those of Paul who was the apostle to the Gentiles. All knew that the Gospel was to the Jew *first*. And interestingly, that *is exactly* how the majority of early manuscripts of the New Testament have the books arranged.

The *fourth* principle which motivated the thinking of the biblical writers and canonizers was their perception of the manner in which people attained to a proper religious conversion. Nothing is more important to people with deep religious persuasions than recognizing the methods by which individuals are able to reach a proper relationship with God. And in the New Testament we have the methodology clearly deliniated. The step-by-step procedure by which Christian conversion is accomplished is found in the Book of Hebrews. The author records the stages that will lead a person into a full, adult relationship with Christ. There were seven phases which direct a person to a complete salvation in Christ. These are shown in a harmonious story-flow from beginning to end.

The seventh and final stage was considered as having a priority position. This conclusion to the salvation process — which is the attainment of *perfection* (Heb.6:1) — is followed by the step by step means by which salvation is reached. The most important factor is mentioned first. Then is shown in sequence the six primary steps of doctrinal accomplishment which have to be executed before a person can reach that final and seventh stage called *perfection*. When one fulfills the first requirement, then one can proceed to the second, the third, and progressively to the seventh. Let us notice those seven levels of development. They are 1) a *repentance* from dead works (v.1), 2) having *faith* toward God (v.1), 3) understanding the doctrine of *baptisms* (v.2), 4) the *laying on of hands* (for receiving the Holy Spirit) (v.2), 5) doctrines concerning the *resurrection* from the dead (v.2), 6) a recognition of matters concerning the *judgment* (rewards) from God (v.2), and finally one is taught the last phase of Christian attainment which is 7) the desired *perfection* — which represents salvation (v.1).

The foregoing procedure for acquiring redemption under the New Covenant was so a part of the psychological make-up of those who wrote and canonized the Bible that we find it cropping up in a stage-by-stage fashion in the theological books of the New Testament. This seven-fold doctrinal attainment provides the sequence of Paul's subjects which he discussed in the Book of Romans. The information in Hebrews 6:1,2 constituted the *outline* for the logical presentation of Paul's theological teachings.

Notice that the first subject Paul speaks about in Romans is *repentance* (see the first chapter of Romans leading up to Romans 2:4 — "the goodness of God leadeth thee to *repentance*"). The second topic dovetails with the second in Hebrews, *faith*. And Paul's discussion on *faith* in Romans occupies all of chapters 3 to 5. Then Paul in Romans 6 and 7 (and right in the sequence of Hebrews 6) proceeds with a discourse on *baptism* and its spiritual consequences. The author of Hebrews then follows with the mention of "the laying on of hands." This concerned factors associated with the Holy Spirit and its functions. And remarkably, the Book of Romans continues with the same sequential theme — a major discourse on the attributes and role of the Holy Spirit (Romans 8). The fifth and sixth subjects in Hebrews concerned the *resurrection* and *judgment*, and in Romans 9 through 11 Paul presented his account of how Israel, though temporarily cast aside, will experience a thorough salvation and a judgment (their allotted rewards) when Christ finally returns to rescue them. This redemption will lead to what the Book of Hebrews, seventhly, calls *perfection*, and what Paul in Romans corresponds to the prophesied salvation which will be extended to all Israel (Rom.11:25).

The progressive doctrinal theme of Hebrews 6:1,2 is seen also in First Corinthians. Whereas the Book of Romans concentrates primarily on the first three subjects of 1) repentance, 2) faith, and 3) baptism (with lesser emphasis on the Holy Spirit, the resurrection, judgment, and perfection), the Book of First Corinthians reverses the order with only scant attention to those first three topics but fully elaborates with major discussions on the doctrines of 4) the Holy Spirit (chapters 12 to 14), 5) and the resurrection (chapter 15). In First Corinthians Paul, like in Romans, touches upon the subjects of 6) judgment and 7) perfection, but these matters are more thoroughly treated in the later books of Ephesians, Philippians, Colossians, and (of course) Hebrews ("leaving the principles of the doctrine of Christ, let us go on to *perfection*" — Hebrews 6:1).

When one looks at the canonical order of the books of Romans and

First Corinthians (followed by the remainder of Paul's letters), it will be seen that all the sequential doctrinal subjects (which Hebrews calls the elementary teachings) are dealt with in orderly fashion.

This procedure is seen in the positioning of all the New Testament books. The four Gospels give the basic teaching of Christianity (and we will later observe that Matthew gives the Jewish approach, while Mark presents the Jewish/Gentile, Luke the Gentile/Jewish, and John gives a thoroughly Gentile or universal one). The design is to give teaching which progresses from the physical (the expected Jewish kingdom of the Messiah) to the real spiritual one (the universal, heavenly Kingdom of God). The Gospels and Acts are followed by the seven general epistles. The subjects discussed in those seven books are primarily non-theological, and are intended to give an introduction to the fourteen epistles of Paul where the subjects of repentance, faith, baptism, the Spirit, resurrections, judgment, and perfection are rehearsed in detail. The Book of Revelation ends the canon with a prophetic account of eschatological events concerning Christ's second advent which will usher in the hopes and promises which were mentioned in the preceding books of the New Testament.

What we find in the manuscript order of the New Testament books is a progressive account of doctrinal teaching. If the books are left in the order that the canonizers intended, the matter of doctrine would be understood much better. But our modern Bibles have misplaced books, which were intended to give elementary (and preliminary) teaching, into a later position and elevated the epistles of Paul (which are more doctrinally mature) into a location ahead of the introductory ones. This causes confusion. We feel that it is far better to leave the books in the order that the majority of manuscripts have them.

There was a *fifth* principle which pervaded the consciousness of the writers of the Bible, particularly with those of the New Testament. Though there are many virtues of the Holy Spirit mentioned in the Bible, the apostle Paul mentioned three prime ones (stated in order of importance): *faith, hope, and love* (I Cor.13:13). And note this! The first eight chapters of Romans essentially cover the matter of *faith*, while chapters 9 to 11 emphasize the *hope* of Israel, and the final chapters (12 to 16) focus on the concept of love — to mankind in general, the brotherhood in particular, and to God especially. But it doesn't stop there. In the canonical order of the epistles of James, Peter and John, it will be seen that the first emphasizes *true faith and religion* (James), the second *hope in suffering* (Peter), and the third underlines *love for the brotherhood* (John). The positioning of those books in this way is not an indiscriminate affair. There appears to be a conscious design in operation relative to the order of the books. It reflects a method of teaching in which the important attributes of the Holy Spirit are progressively mentioned and emphasized. We will have more to say about this type of design within the books of the Bible as we progress through this book.

The *sixth* principle which dominated the thinking of the men of the Bible (and this certainly applied to those who wrote and formulated the New Testament) concerns the proper methods for teaching. It is well-known that the best way to teach is to begin with the elementary aspects of a subject and proceed to the more advanced. We certainly find this principle very much in action in the arrangement of the biblical books. We find that the writings were placed to give the "kindergarten" teaching first, followed by "grade school, high school, college, and then post-graduate studies."

This can be easily demonstrated by the writings of the apostle Paul. His first book in the canonical order is Romans. This book clearly represents the ABC's of Christian doctrine on a level for those not having heard much about the plan of salvation. Recall that Paul had never been to Rome before. He wrote the book for people who were needing to be established (Rom.1:11). In the Book of Romans, Paul proceeded to give them the elementary doctrinal teachings of Christianity. This is why the Book of Romans comes first in the canonical epistles of Paul.

This book is followed by First Corinthians. Though some progress was being made in doctrinal understanding (Paul had taught the Corinthians for 18 months, unlike the Romans whom he had never taught), Paul's emphasis in Corinthians was on corrective measures and shows how new and immature the Corinthians were in the Christian faith. In fact, Paul made the plain statement that they were still spiritual babes in the faith.

> "And I brethren, could not speak unto you as unto spiritual, but
> as unto carnal, *even as unto babes in Christ.* I have fed you with

milk: for hitherto you were not able to bear it, neither yet now are ye able" (I Cor.3:1,2).

The Corinthians were only capable of receiving elementary teachings from Paul. Not only were they acting like "children" (see a further reference in I Cor.14:20), but their spiritual performances were more like baptized heathens. Paul demanded that they grow up and behave like mature Chirstians. Thankfully, the Corinthians learned some vital lessons by the time Paul wrote his second epistle, but in spite of their progress, Paul still said in Second Corinthians: "I speak unto you as children" (II Cor.6:13).

As for the Galatians (the next book in the canonical order), Paul was upset with them for returning so quickly to an "infancy" in Christ and resorting to the rule of the "schoolmaster" (the Mosaic law) (Gal.3:24-29; 4:1-10). The Galatians were reinstituting "elementary" teachings (Gal.4:9). They were going back to a "grade school" type of instruction in Christ. They were returning to the lowest level of Christian development—the keeping of the Law. The Galatians were retreating into Mosaic rules (observing weekly and annual sabbath days, new moons and months, and sabbatical years). These doctrines were intended for spiritual children who were in "grade school," and not (as Paul looked at it) befitting mature Christians.

Thus, the epistles of Paul to the Romans, Corinthians, and Galatians (in our regular canonical order) were designed for those just coming into a knowledge of Christ. And note: the message in the Book of Romans was for people that Paul had never instructed before, while his teaching to the Corinthians was for those whom he had taught for 18 months, and that to the Galatians was designed for those who had been taught the Gospel for more than four years! Yet in all of these first four epistles, the messages of Paul were intended for spiritual *children*.

But when it comes to the next three epistles of Paul in the New Testament canon (Ephesians, Philippians, and Colossians), they were designed to give instruction to mature and fully developed Christians! In Ephesians the subjects are directed to those who are "no more children." These teachings of Paul were advanced doctrinal discourses:

"For the perfecting [maturing] of the saints, for the work of the ministry, for the edifying of the body of Christ: till we all come in the unity of the faith, and of the knowledge of the Son of God, unto a perfect man [a fully mature man], unto the measure of the stature of the fulness of Christ: that we henceforth be *no more children* tossed to and fro, and carried about with every wind of doctrine" (Eph.4:12-14).

There could hardly be any plainer teaching. The readers of these latter epistles were far advanced in spiritual knowledge than the early Romans, Corinthians, and Galatians. Paul was even able to write the latter three epistles in very sophisticated language.

Paul's letters to the first three churches were arranged to provide information from the ABC's of doctrinal teaching, to the XYZ's of knowledge with the latter three. These are followed in the manuscripts by the epistles to a *seventh* church — that of the Thessalonians. And what is the subject matter of those two epistles? It is teaching about the appearance of the Man of Sin, the second advent of Christ back to this earth, and the resurrection from the dead which will accompany Christ's advent. The number *seven* (as is evident) has the ring of completion and *finality* in its symbolic meaning. Thus, the seventh church epistles discuss the *end of the age* and the completion of the church age. While the first six churches had epistles which described the doctrines of the church (and how one must walk in the Christian life), the seventh church had two epistles which have information about the conclusion of the church age and the attainment of the promises which the previous epistles talked about.

REV. 10:7

The next book in the manuscript order is Hebrews. It is very mature teaching. "Leaving the principles of the doctrine of Christ, let us go on to perfection" (Heb.6:1,2). Its commentary explains how the Temple and physical rituals were types of things to come, but how the reality is found in Christ. It discusses the true kingdom of God which is to appear on earth. Emphasis is given to "the sabbath to come" (Heb.4:9) and the new Jerusalem (Heb.12:22,23).

In the Book of Hebrews the author says that the elementary doctrines of repentance, faith, baptisms, laying on of hands, the resurrection, and the judgment (which Paul discussed thoroughly in Romans, Corinthians, and Galatians) were to be left behind, and only subjects dealing with *perfection* were then appropriate (Heb.5:11-14; 6:1-3).

The remaining four books in Paul's canon were instructions for the pastoral duties of ministers. Obviously, these later teachings are most mature — after all, they were written from one professional minister to other professionals. The teaching contained in them was hardly for spiritual infants. And, finally, the manuscripts have the Book of Revelation last of all. This covers all aspects of the end of the age — and its contents pertain to the whole world, not only to the Christian church (as the two to the Thessalonians do). It is the most mature and difficult book to understand. It comes last. And it is a fitting conclusion not only to the New Testament but to the Bible as a whole.

When we get further into the body of this book, we will find that the subjects of the various books of the Bible, plus the arrangement of the books in relationship to one another, echo the principle of progressive revelation — that is, a teaching which begins with elementary (or general) matters and proceeds to the more sophisticated (the particular). This is the normal way to teach. When the apostle Peter said that Christians ought to grow in grace and knowledge (II Pet.3:18), he expected all people to progress in the normal step-by-step fashion of doctrinal development that people throughout the ages have been used to. It should not seem odd that the books within the canon of the Bible were arranged in the same fashion. Proper teaching methods demand this approach.

A *seventh* and final principle in canonization involves the use of symbolic numbers. The number *seven* was of prime consequence. It had a special signification of which there was little ambiguity. Professor Muirhead had this to say on the meaning of *seven.*

> "Seven—Examples: 7 churches, spirits (Rev.1:4,11; 3:1), stars (1:16,20), candlesticks (1:13), lamps (4:5), seals (5:1; 8:1), horns and eyes (5:6), trumpets (8:2), angels (8:2), thunders (10:3f), heads (12:3; 17:3), angels with plagues (15:1), vials full of the wrath of God (15:7), kings (17:10), In view of this pervasiveness of 7, it is proof that 7 is pre-eminently the number of *perfection* or *completeness.* Seven represents the *perfect* of God in mercy and judgment in relation to men (as well as the total works of creation)" (*Dict. of the Apostolic Church,* vol.II,p.93, italics mine).

One could take a whole chapter to show the wonders found in the symbol of *seven* in the Bible and still not exhaust the subject. It provides an accent of *completion* and *perfection* to any theme.

One might wonder why we are mentioning this matter of symbolic numbers? This is because the subject is important in regard to the canonization of the Bible. The prime number associated with canonization is *seven*. The number is found in a variety of ways in the symmetrical design which exists within and between the books of the Old and New Testament. The recognition that numbers played an important symbolic part in the religious thinking of the writers of the Bible will go a long way in helping to show just what books represent the complete Scriptures.

In closing, the seven principles mentioned within this chapter, which motivated the actions of the men who wrote and canonized the Bible, are important ones to consider if one wishes to know just what books represent the Holy Bible in its earliest form. Throughout this book we will pay attention to all these principles (and others which are akin to them) in order to determine what the biblical writers themselves would say are the actual and authorized books of the Bible — and in what order they ought to appear in our modern versions.

3

The Original Number of Old Testament Books

The first century Jews believed there were 22 holy books that comprised the complete number of their divine scriptures. In almost all modern versions it is common to numerate the Old Testament as 39 books. This at first glance might give the impression that modern scholars have added extra books which the early Jews did not accept as divinely inspired. This, however, is not the case. We will show that our present versions have simply divided the official books of the Old Testament divergently than those who originated the canon. There can really be no doubt that we possess today the exact canon which Christ and the apostles accepted as the Holy Scriptures. But, true enough, the early Jews numbered the books differently, And the early numeration ought to be maintained today. When we do, some significant symbolic teachings emerge that can make us appreciate that we do indeed have the complete Old Testament scriptures. We must learn to accept the early Jewish viewpoint, *not* our modern way of looking at things. Thus, the original 22 numbering should be retained in all versions of the Bible today.

Throughout the New Testament we read that the Jews possessed *the* Scriptures. It was taken for granted, without argument or definition, that a commonly understood body of books was in existence which the Jews recognized as sacred. There is a good deal of contemporary testimony to substantiate this. Josephus, who was a priest and thoroughly conversant with Jewish affairs in the first century, referred to the standard copy of the Holy Scriptures which was deposited in the archives of the Temple and under the supervision of the priests (*War*, VII.150). Among the Jews this copy was known as "The Book of the Court" because all official synagogue scrolls were based on the text of this approved archetype (*Mishna Moed Katan* 3,4: *Pal.Tal. Sanhedrin* II, 200). The Book of Deuteronomy stated that such a standard copy should be retained by the priests in the Temple (Deut.17:18; 31:9-12).

In regard to the canonization of the Old Testament, these special Temple scrolls are important. They represented nothing less than the basic "constitution" governing all political affairs in Judaea, and the religious life of Jews everywhere. Though the Romans were in supreme command in Palestine, they nonetheless permitted native kings or rulers (for certain periods) to govern the people in a direct sense. Those administrators (even an autocrat like Herod the Great) found it necessary to heed the principles of the Mosaic legislation and the precedential laws that developed over the years. There was no way for any Jew to escape an expression of reverence for the lawbooks of Moses and the teachings of the Prophets. All Jews accredited the Temple scrolls as divinely inspired.

These sacred books were looked on as the "constitution" of the Jewish people. They not only recorded religious duties for Jews to perform (but more important to our discussion on the canonization), they were also the basis for *all* civil, financial, agricultural, and social activities. In a word, the Jewish state in Palestine (no matter who was governing it) was reckoned a theocracy and the heart and soul of its government had to rest, by popular demand, squarely upon the words in the sacred scriptures.

This point is vital in understanding matters concerning the canonization of the Old Testament because the Temple scriptures not only contained religious teachings but they provided laws and principles involving human politics — laws pertaining to the daily living of all Jews. Such basic "constitutional" documents would have been well known and of necessity must have been kept with a purity of contents. It is a foregone conclusion that people are keenly aware of laws which govern their *daily* affairs. Let us note how this fact can testify to the reliability of the Temple scrolls.

There were probably 8 to 10 million Jews in the world at the time, and about 3 million were in Judaea. Just like our own legislative or judicial systems, there were by the time of the first century countless codified laws based upon the "constitutional" laws of the Temple. With hundreds of professional lawyers in daily practice who were constantly involved in disputes and/or other matters of law, are we to imagine that it was possible for a single letter or syllable of the basic laws of Moses to be changed? Such a belief would be absurd. Indeed, there were also a battery of precedential laws which had developed over the years, supposedly based upon the scriptures, and even those could not be changed without due process. But in no way could "constitutional" laws be altered unless it were done in a legal manner. That would be like some American politicians trying to change the United States constitution. A revolution would develop if any of those laws were changed without proper legal procedures. It wouldn't make any difference if someone modified the original text of the constitution a hundred times over, there are literally thousands of copies in city and school libraries alone of what the original stated. If a single syllable of intended meaning in the constitution were tampered with, without due process of law, there would be a public outcry (even revolution). Surely the Jews in Judaea (and throughout the world) would have done the same thing if the standard copies of their "constitution" would have been corrupted. True, constitutional laws can be changed, but not without the knowledge and approbation of the people.

This is an important point in regard to the canonization of the standard texts of the Old Testament. The fact is, the Mosaic laws represented the *civil, governmental, societal,* and strict *religious regulators* which thoroughly dominated the lives of all Jews everywhere. Since matters of money, property and daily social activities were governed by those laws embodied in the Holy Scriptures (or the many precedential laws in existence), we can be certain that *all* copies of the "constitution" were the same throughout the country of Judaea, and even the Jewish world. No priest or king could (or would) have revised the basic words of the Temple scrolls. Even if this were possible, there were hundreds of copies of the scriptures in the synagogues located over the land. All these combined scriptural scrolls rendered some good checks and balances for the continued purity of the Temple and the synagogue scrolls.

Another point needs to be made. Ancient synagogues in Palestine were not simply places in which to worship on the sabbaths and holydays. They were nothing less than the Superior and Local courts of the nation. Are we to imagine that the synagogues (which were *courts.*) had basic constitutional laws (and even precedential laws) which differed from one another? Hardly. This fact has a great bearing on the matter of Old Testament canonization. This means that one should look to Palestinian Judaism as maintaining proper manuscripts of the Old Testament because in Judaea their writings were not simply religious documents, they were also a part of the civil and government codes of Jewish national life. This meant they were under the constant scrutiny of professional lawyers who would see to it that no word was changed. True, there might be a score of ways to interpret the words, but the words themselves could not be tampered with. For example, to give clients every advantage, lawyers could not pass the bar exam unless they could "prove" a hundred ways that pork was proper to eat (Lieberman, *Hellenism in Jewish Palestine,* pp. 62-64), yet no lawyer could change the words of Moses to say that swine was now permissible. Interpreting the law to one's advantage was one thing, but to change the actual words of the law was quite another—and this was impossible without due process.

This guarantee of purity would not extend to those texts of sectarians who wished to reside outside mainline Judaism, or if they lived under the jurisdiction of Gentile governments in Egypt, Rome, etc. Take for example the Dead Sea sects. Their documents show that they did not agree with many Temple regulations or its priesthood. And though some of their scrolls did match remarkably with later Masoretic texts which reflected the early (and official) synagogue versions of the Old Testament, they also allowed into their libraries a mixture of "non-mainline" books (some agreeing with Samaritan or Egyptian Versions). Those Jews who joined such private communal societies outside normative Judaism were prone to adopt their own rules and regulations. That's why they could use unauthorized texts to govern their activities.

The same could be said of the manuscripts of the Law maintained by the Samaritan communities. Those texts were indeed legal documents (as were those in Jerusalem) but they governed Samaritan society, not Jewish! It is said that Ezra the priest, back in the fifth century B.C., deliberately copied every Old Testament manuscript in his possession into the Babylonian script (rather than maintain the old Hebrew form of letters) in order for all people in Judaea to recognize the official Jewish texts from those of the Samaritans (who refused to accept the "Babylonian" letter styles).

Also, the early translations of the Hebrew Old Testament into Greek, (and intended only for the literary quests of King Ptolemy II of Egypt), were never used as legal documents for the functioning of a theocratic state. It is not to be expected that they would have the professional scrutiny applied to their accuracy as those retained by the Palestinian courts (synagogues.). And when later Hellenistic Jews who had lost much of their Hebrew language abilities wished to consult the scriptures in Greek, this was possible, but this was done only for curiosity or for private religious devotions. In no way could such unauthorized translations be used in matters of court. Imagine relying on a Greek text in law matters, when the Hebrew was available, and it was the original. No citizen of Judaea would think of placing his legal rights affecting his daily life on some Greek translation — especially an Egyptian one which was translated only for literary purposes. The only texts which those in Judaea would naturally accept were the original Hebrew ones deposited in the courts (synagogues) and the Temple. We must look to Jerusalem for the authorized Old Testament books.

The Canon of Josephus

The Old Testament books today are usually reckoned as being 39 in number. But the earliest records show the official numeration as 22 books. We will later see that the symbolic meaning to the number 22 affords a significant symmetrical balance to the Old Testament, and when those books are combined with those of the New Testament, the number 49 (7 times 7) is reached. This latter number figuratively means "completion" and "finality." We will see, however, that even the number 22 has a ring of "completion" to it when it comes to matters involving the Hebrew language. Note that Josephus said the divine scriptures of the Old Testament were 22 in number.

> "We have not a countless number of books, discordant and arranged against each other; but only two and twenty books, containing the history of every age, which are justly accredited as divine" (*Against Apion* 1.8).

To Josephus, who was an Aaronic priest, the Old Testament

scriptures contained only 22 books. These were the official books which were deposited in the Temple and represented the religious constitution of the Jewish people. In no way was Josephus speaking of a canon different from the normal Old Testament maintained by Protestants today (Ryle, *The Canon of the Old Testament*, p.178). The only difference centered on the manner in which the books were counted. For example, the early Hebrews reckoned the twelve Minor Prophets — from Hosea to Malachi — as *one book* in the canonical number of books, not twelve separate ones as most versions count them today! And also, the two books of Chronicles, and other historical books, were not divided as they are in most modern Bibles. There was anciently only one Book of Chronicles. But church leaders after the canon was established, and to please various Gentile peoples, divided many of the early books into two (or even four) divisions. This procedure resulted in the original numbering of 22 books being counted as 39.

The Original Twenty-Two Books

There were only 22 books to the standard Old Testament. This numbering can be traced back at least two hundred years before the time of Christ. It is found in the Book of Jubilees. Though Jubilees represents the theological opinions of Jewish sectarians of the Dead Sea community, the information in the books still reflects a great deal of normal Jewish sentiment. This is especially true when the author makes a simple statement that the Old Testament canon was reckoned as 22 books in number. Indeed, there was a special reason *why* the books had to be 22.

Annotated to the restored text of Jubilees 2:23 is the remark that God made 22 things on the six days of creation. These 22 events paralleled the 22 generations from Adam to Jacob, the 22 letters of the Hebrew alphabet, and the 22 books of the Holy Scripture. R.H. Charles maintained that this information concerning the 22 books should be retained in the text, even though it has fallen out of a few manuscripts. See Charles' note on Jubilees 2:23, *Apocrypha and Pseudepigrapha*, II.p.15. *Cf.*Kaufmann Kohler, "Book of Jubilees," *The Jewish Encyclopedia*, VII (New York: 1907), p.302. Thus, as early as the year 150 B.C. it was common for Jews to reckon the Old

Testament books as being 22 in number. Josephus must have been stating a well recognized numerical canon which was prevailing among the Jewish people of Palestine.

The 22 numbering is most interesting and fits in well with the literary and symbolic meaning of "completion" among early Jews. Recall that the Book of Jubilees insisted that the number represented the "final" and "complete" creations of God. Adam was the last creation of God (being the 22nd). Jacob, whose name was changed to Israel, was the 22nd generation from Adam — and Jacob was acknowledged as the father of the *spiritual* nation of the Lord. Also the Hebrew language became the means by which God communicated his divine will to mankind, it had as well an alphabet of 22 letters! And, finally, when God wished to give his complete Old Testament revelation to humanity, that divine canon was found in 22 authorized books. The medieval Jewish scholar Sixtus Senensis explained the significance of this matter.

> "As with the Hebrew there are twenty-two letters, in which all that can be said and written is comprehended, so there are twenty-two books in which are contained all that can be known and uttered of divine things" (William H. Green, *A General Introduction to the Old Testament*, vol.I,p.87).

Greeks, Syrians, Armenians, and Romans Acknowledge the Original 22 Numbering

While early Jews have stated that the original Old Testament was accounted to be 22 books in number, they were even outdone by Christian scholars. It will profit us to list the evidence for these well-known opinions.

1) *Melito* (170 A.D.), in agreement with the original Jewish reckoning, gave the number of Old Testament books as 22 (Eusebius, *Church History*, 4.26.14).

2) *Origen* (210 A.D.) also gave the same numbering: "It should be stated that the canonical books, as the Hebrews have handed them down, are twenty-two; corresponding with the number of their letters" (*ibid.* 6.25.1).

3) *Hilary of Poitiers* (360 A.D.): "The Law of the Old Testament is

considered as divided into twenty-two books, so as to correspond to the number of letters" (*Tractatus Super Psalmos*, prologue 15).

4) *Athanasius* (365 A.D.): "There are then of the Old Testament twenty-two books in number . . . this is the number of the letters among the Hebrews" (*Letter* 39.4).

5) The Council of Laodicea (343-391 A.D.): Twenty-two books (*Canon* 60).

6) *Cyril of Jerusalem* (386 A.D.): "Read the divine scriptures, the twenty-two books of the Old Testament" (*Catechetical Lectures* 2, 4.33).

7) *Gregory of Nazianzus* (390 A.D.): "I have exhibited twenty-two books, corresponding with the twenty-two letters of the Hebrews" (*Carmina*, 1.12).

8) *Epiphanius* (400 A.D.): Twenty-two books (*De Nensuris et Ponderibus*, 4).

9) *Rufinus* (410 A.D.): Twenty-two books (*Commentarius in Symbolum Apostolorum*, 37).

10) *Jerome* (410 A.D.): "That the Hebrews have twenty-two letters is testified . . . as there are twenty-two elementary characters by means of which we write in Hebrew all we say . . . so we reckon twenty-two books by which . . . a righteous man is instructed" (*Preface to the Books of Samuel and Kings*).

11) *Synopsis of Sacred Scripture* (c. 500 A.D.): "The canonical books of the Old Testament are twenty-two, equal in number to the Hebrew letters; for they have so many original letters."

12) *Isidore of Seville* (600 A.D.) said the Old Testament was settled by Ezra the priest into twenty-two books "that the books in the Law might correspond in number with the letters" (*Liber de Officiis*).

13) *Leontius* (610 A.D.): "Of the Old Testament there are twenty-two books" (*De Sectis*).

14) *John of Damascus* (730 A.D.): "Observe further that there are two and twenty books of the Old Testament, one for each letter of the Hebrew alphabet" (*An Exact Exposition of the Orthodox Faith*, 4.17).

15) *Nicephorus* (9th century A.D.): "There are two and twenty books of the Old Testament" (*Stichometry*).

16) *Jesudad, Bishop of Hadad, Syria* (852 A.D.) recognized a canon of twenty-two books (John E. Steinmueller, *A Companion to Scripture Studies*, vol.I, p.80).

17) *Hrabanus* (9th century A.D.) said the Old Testament was formed by Ezra into twenty-two books "that there might be as many books in the Law as there are letters" (Whitaker, *Disputation*).

18) *Moses of Chorene* the Armenian historian (c. A.D.1000 or early 6th century) "speaks of twenty-two books of the Old Testament. This was clearly the Jewish Canon" (Steinmueller, vol.I,p.81).

19) *Peter of Cluny* (1150 A.D.): Twenty-two books (Edward Reuss, *Canon of the Holy Scriptures*, p.257).

20) *John of Salisbury* (1180 A.D.): Twenty-two books (*ibid.*, p.258).

21) *Hugh of St. Victor* (12th century): "As there are twenty-two alphabetic letters, by means of which we write in Hebrew, and speak what we have to say . . . so twenty-two books are reckoned, by means of which . . . the yet tender infancy of our man is instructed, while it yet hath need of milk" (*Didascalicae Eruditionis*, 4.80).

22) *Richard of St. Victor* (13th century): Twenty-two books (*Tractatus Exceptionum*, 2.9).

These testimonies supply ample evidence that over the centuries (whether in Hebrew circles, or in Greek Orthodox, Syrian, Armenian, or Roman Catholic ones) the knowledge of the original number of Old Testament books was recognized as being 22. While the order of the books sometimes varied among the observations of these early Christians (due to their attachment to the Septuagint Version), they still persisted in retaining the proper numbering. On some occasions they would increase the number to 27. Epiphanius stated the Old Testament as having 22 books, but in two other places he increased the number to 27 (*ibid.* 22,23; *Adversus Octaginta Haereses*, 8.6). However, no extra books were added to the canon. Since five of the Hebrew letters, when used at the ends of words, take on different shapes, some early scholars divided the original 22 books into 27. This procedure can be dismissed as an oddity of a few writers which was really based on the original 22 letters. The significance of the number 22 (as we will soon see) was too ingrained in their consciousnesses to be lightly cast aside.

The Biblical Use of the Acrostic

There is a literary device found in the Old Testament which is both a poetic method for expressing a unified design in biblical composition as well as a technique of arrangement which emphasizes *completion* and *perfection*. It is called the acrostic.

The acrostic is a feature in which the first letter of a sentence begins with the first letter of the alphabet; the second sentence begins with the second alphabetic letter; the third sentence with the third letter, etc. In complete Hebrew acrostics, there are always 22 sentences, or multiples of 22, each beginning with the first letter *aleph* and successively going through the entire alphabet until *tau*, the last letter, is reached. If all the letters are utilized in a proper and consecutive fashion, then the psychological feeling that this literary device provides is one of accomplishment and fulfillment — a feeling of wholeness, flawlessness, and perfect order.

This is one of the reasons the early Hebrews saw that Adam, being the 22nd creation of God, represented God's prime and perfect physical creation, and that Jacob (whose name was changed to *Israel)* was the 22nd spiritual creation of God. The symbolic significance of the number 22, as found in the Old Testament acrostics, was recognized as emblematic of perfect attainment. Let us now notice some of the biblical acrostics which demonstrate this point.

The longest chapter in the Bible is Psalm 119. It is an excellent example of a biblical acrostic. Note that it is divided into 22 sections, each one having 8 verses. In its Hebrew original, the first 8 verses all commence with the first Hebrew letter *aleph*. The second set of 8 uses the second letter *bet*. And so it goes all the way through the Hebrew alphabet.

It should be apparent that there must be a purposeful design which the author is trying to accomplish by the use of such a literary arrangement. When all 22 letters are employed either with single verses or with verses in a series, it is obvious that the author intends to put an accent of perfection on the subject of his text. Psalm 119 is a discourse on all the faculties of God's law. The application of a perfect and complete acrostic is an emphasis upon the perfection and completeness of that law.

Another complete acrostic is found in Psalm 111 and also Psalm 112. These Psalms show that God will thoroughly and permanently redeem his people, and the acrostical sequence means to show this. Look also at the acrostic accent on the virtuous woman (Prov.31: 10-31). In this example every verse begins with each of the Hebrew letters in a perfectly consecutive manner. The author is stressing his portrayal of a complete and perfect woman. There is also an acrostic accentuation in the literary design occurring in the first three chapters of the Book of Lamentations. The prophet Jeremiah implemented this acrostical pattern to reinforce the completeness of God's destruction upon the kingdom of Judah.

In one way, it is to be regretted that these alphabetical refinements are not normally distinguished in English versions. Of course, it is nearly impossible to adhere to the alphabetic patterns and still give a faithful English translation. Nevertheless, the King James Version, though it does not retain the acrostics in translation, has shown its readers where they belong in Psalm 119.

An Incomplete Acrostic

There is in the Bible an acrostic which is deliberately deficient. This occurs when there are certain letters left out at particular intervals. When an acrostic is complete, the impression produces a feeling of perfection, but when one is employed with some letters missing in sequence it gives the feeling of frustration or let-down. When such incomplete acrostics are used, the image of discomfiture is intended.

Such an acrostic is found running through Psalms 9 and 10. Seven letters are purposely omitted. The author obviously determined it to be noticed by the reader as a broken acrostic. If the arrangement of the alphabetic letters is sequential in a perfect sense, the theme was meant to be that of precision and completeness, but if the acrostic style is broken and irregular, the subject which the composition is supposed to describe is also to be emphasized as *broken and irregular*. And look at Psalms 9 and 10. The Psalms are a connected pair which describe the same historical or prophetical theme. Both of them refer to a time of great tribulation on Israel (9:9; 10:1), and a time when a man of sin will be at work (10:18). It may well be that the author was meaning to emphasize the chaotic state of affairs which will prevail in such circumstances. So, with broken acrostics, the thrust of imperfection is given a decided stress, while with full and perfect acrostics the keynote is that of consummation and fault-lessness. The 22 books of the Old Testament, of course, are a *full* acrostic.

The Complete Old Testament

In regard to the Old Testament canon which was originally written in Hebrew characters, it can be seen why the ancients looked on the 22 books of the Hebrew Bible as corresponding to the 22 alphabetic Hebrew letters. When one realizes the significance of the acrostic style for emphasizing a completeness and perfection, it is an easy step to acknowledge that the 22 books of the Old Testament canon represent (in a symbolic sense) a complete and perfect canonical acrostic. Once the 22 books of the Hebrew canon were authorized and placed within the Temple archives as the ordained scriptures for Israel, no other books could be canonized in the Hebrew language. Figuratively, all the Hebrew letters have been used up. If any further revelation was to be forthcoming, it would have to be in another language.

A Further Recognition of Biblical Completion

It is remarkable that by the time of the apostles they were accustomed to refer to the Jewish scriptures (whether found in Palestine, Egypt, Asia Minor, Greece, or Rome) simply as "the Scriptures" or "the Holy Scriptures" (*e.g.* John 5:39; II Tim.3:15). And when the 27 books of the New Testament were canonized, it became even more evident that the original number of 22 books for the Old Testament was a divine and inspired number. Why is this the case? The answer is simple. When one adds the 27 New Testament books to the Old Testament 22, the number 49 is realized. What a significant number. This represents a figure of 7 times 7 — or, in the symbolic way the Jews looked on the number 7 in the first century, it expressed an emblematic sense of double completion. Notice how this would be seen by the Jews and Christians.

The number 49 was the sum of seven seven's or a multiple of seven times seven. Recall that the figurative meaning of the number 7 was that of completion. Prof. W. Taylor Smith said:

> "Seven often expressed the idea of *completeness*. So in 7 churches, 7 parables of the Kingdom, the 7 Beatitudes, etc. Even in Assyrian texts it denotes 'totality,' or 'whole' " (*Dict. of Christ and the Gospels,* Vol.II, p.248).

All students of the Bible have long realized the significance of the number *seven* in relation to the symbol of *completeness*. It should not appear strange that the same number (or its multiples — especially the sum of *seven seven's* or *seven* times *seven*, 49) would surround the sacredness of the divine canon of Scripture. It is because of this that I do not apologize for stressing the 49 books as being the full canon.

This biblical theme involving the number 49 strongly implies that the whole of the Bible is now complete when one combines the original 22 books of the Old Testament with the 27 books of the New Testament. We are thus given a numerical design which suggests (by the use of the symbolic numbers of scripture) a complete and final revelation from God.

The Present Number of 66 Books

When one counts the number of books in our present Protestant canon of the Bible (which normally excludes the extra apocryphal books) the number of books amounts to 66. This is an interesting number. It is arrived at by dividing various Old Testament books into a numerical pattern which corresponds to the early Greek Version of the Old Testament — which was placed in an arbitrary codex form in Egypt about the third century A.D. There is no Hebrew manuscript that follows this Greek Version. And look what happens when one pursues its enumeration of 66 books. The number of *man* is found all over the book. The Bible makes it clear that the number 6 is one squarely centered on fleshly man (or mankind). Note that the first man was created at the end of the *sixth* day (Gen.1:24-31). Throughout the Bible we have *six* associated with man (as distinct from God). The number 666 is found in the Book of Revelation as a number denoting *man* or a wicked person to appear at the end of the age (Rev.13:18). Not only that, when Daniel described the great image which began the "Babylonian phase" in ancient religion, its measure was 60 cubits high (6 times 10) and 6 cubits wide (Dan.3:1). Indeed, E.W. Bullinger said that all the letters in Daniel 3:1 describing the Babylonian image when added up (and all Hebrew letters had numerical values) come to 4662 — which is 7 times 666 (*Number in Scripture*, p.285).

From these indications alone, it does not seem proper to divide the

Holy Bible into 66 books. This even becomes clearer when we read what MacCormack said:

> "But has the number [66] no significance? Unquestionably it has, for six is man's number. . . . We find then, that the Bible, according to the Protestant Canon, and also that of the Orthodox Eastern Church, contains 49 books, if we take the reckoning current when the last portion of it was written, or 66 books if each one be counted separately. The latter number, in which 6 is plainly and emphatically seen, denotes that outwardly it is a human book and in human dress" (*Heptadic Structure,* p.145).

The number 66 does not look good from a biblical point of view. In order to arrive at a different (and more attractive number) the Roman Catholic Church at the Council of Trent in the sixteenth century officially accepted 11 of the 14 apocryphal works, and added them to the Protestant canon. Among other things one of the reasons this was done was to take away the odium attached to the number 66. The addition of 11 extra books made a much more appealing number, 77. However, this was still a modern refinement and did not reflect the significance of the original numbering. In fact, if one adds 11 apocryphal writings to the 49 books of the original, one arrives at 60 sections (a number that also smacks of a human symbol). What ought to be retained, as we will show throughout this book, are the original 49 books without the addition of any part of the Apocrypha.

The Present Jewish Numbering

Sometime in the last part of the first century or the beginning of the second, the Jewish authorities decided to re-divide the books of the Old Testament into 24 books rather than maintain 22. It appears that the Jews in Babylon were the first to devise this new number (Julius Fuerst, *Der Kanon des Alten Testaments*, Hamburg: 1850, p.4). This Babylonian influence in theological matters among the Jews is well known. In fact, it can be said that the Judaism that survived the first and second centuries is decidedly "Babylonian" in orientation. The reason for this is simple. Palestinian Judaism ceased to have major prominence because the Romans restricted Jerusalem from exercising its normal supremacy in religious matters. After all, the Temple was destroyed in A.D.70 and after A.D.135 no Jews were normally allowed within twenty miles of Jerusalem. This made the region of Mesopotamia an area of prominence among the Jewish community. And it was within that environment that the Jews began to re-number the books of the Old Testament to 24. It is not to be supposed that they added two extra books. They simply divided two of the original ones and arrived at a new 24 numbering. At some point in the second century, or perhaps as late as the third century, the Babylonian number of 24 began to obtain official status. The practice had certainly become current among the Jews by the time of Jerome (about A.D.400).

There may well have been political and religious reasons why the Jewish authorities made the change when they did. When the New Testament books were being accepted as divine literature by great numbers of people within the Roman world, all could see that the 27 New Testament books added to the original 22 of the Old Testament reached the significant number 49. This was a powerful indication that the world now had the complete revelation from God with the inclusion of the New Testament books. Since the Jewish officials were powerless to do anything with the New Testament, the only recourse they saw possible was to alter, in an authorized manner, the traditional numbering. The Babylonian schools simply divided two of the original books and made the total to number 24. Adding these to the 27 New Testament books gave a sum of 51 books — a wholly insignificant number.

The excuse given for re-numbering the books is amusing. Since it was recognized that the original 22 books equalled each of the letters of the Hebrew alphabet, it was felt that an alphabetic relevance had to be maintained. The medieval Jewish scholar Sixtus Senensis gave the normal explanation for the change. Since there was only one *yodh* among the 22 letters, and because the Jews started a peculiar habit of writing the unpronounceable name YHWH with three *yodhs, it was necessary,* so Sixtus tells us, *to re-number the Old Testament books* by the addition of two extra *yodhs.* Such a procedure is clearly an artificial literary device of late invention and could hardly have any relevance to the original numbering of the books of the Old Testament. One thing this contrivance does demonstrate is the longstanding respect that the Jewish people held for the concept that each book of the Old Testament equalled one of the Hebrew alphabetic letters.

The Tradition of Second Esdras

There is one book from the first century, however, which could be used as a witness that the change from 22 to 24 took place as early as about A.D.90. That book is Second Esdras. This work states that there were ninety-four books which were canonical: seventy were esoteric or mystery books and twenty-four were public ones. It has often been stated that this reference to 24 books refers to the official Jewish canon which was then reckoned as authoritative. On the surface this might appear to make sense, but there are major problems with the information. First, there is the direct testimony of Josephus (who also wrote about A.D.90 and was a Jewish priest of first rank) who said that official Judaism accepted only 22 books — the normal number of books going back all the way to the Book of Jubilees (c.150 B.C.). If an authorized change of the number had taken place by A.D.90, why didn't Josephus simply inform his readers about it? Indeed, Josephus was insisting in his reference that the Jews were stable and consistent with the appraisal of their Holy Scriptures (*Contra Apion*, I.8). If they had recently made the change, then the very thing Josephus was trying to prove would have been suspect. But there is another reason why Second Esdras is not all that reliable a witness. The section about the canon has been called into question by textual critics because of the variant readings of the numbers. Some texts instead of 24 have 94, some 204, others 84, and still others 974 (Ludwig Blau, *Jewish Encyclopedia* (1906), vol.III, p.142). The fact is, one can take 24, 84, 94, 204, or 974 as Second Esdras' witness to the number of canonical books. Do not all have equal authority? It seems much safer to take the testimony of Josephus as more authoritative than a book which has variant renderings of its numbers.

There can really be no serious doubt that the early numbering of 22 books for the Old Testament and the 27 books of the New Testament are indeed the correct numbers. This provides a divine canon of 49 books. When one looks at the symbolic significance of this number, one sees the theme of *completion* and *perfection*. We can also be assured that the external and internal historical evidence demonstrates that the Protestant canon of the Bible is the proper one which illustrates the complete and final biblical revelation. But we will also find that the books within the original canon were positioned very differently than is done today. In the next chapter we will see that the original Old Testament was divided into three distinct divisions, and that Christ recognized this tripartite arrangement.

4

The Tripartite Divisions

The Old Testament was originally divided into three parts called the Tripartite Divisions. The earliest documentary evidence that we have available (going back to 180 B.C.) tells us what the three sections were first called. This information is found in the Prologue to the apocryphal Book of Ecclesiasticus. While the man Sirach wrote the book about 180 B.C., his grandson composed the Prologue about 132 B.C. He mentioned the sacred books that his grandfather used in the writing of Ecclesiasticus. In three different statements he referred to the Tripartite Divisions of the Old Testament.

1) "The Law, the Prophets, and Others of like kind."
2) "The Law, the Prophets and the Other Books."
3) "The Law itself, and the Prophets, and the Remaining Books."

While the first two divisions are consistently called "The Law and the Prophets," the third division was given no technical name. But since the definite article "the" is used to describe the second and third occasions of usage, it shows that Sirach's grandson was no doubt referring to a definite set of books which then composed the final division. Beardslee, in the *Encyclopedia Americana* article "Bible," shows that the terminology imputes a recognized set of canonical books divided into three divisions.

"In the prologue to Sirach is a reference three times over to 'the Law,' 'the Prophets,' . . . and the 'Others' with suggestions of their unique value for culture and wisdom, and of their fulness and significance. This was written about 130 B.C. It seems to betoken a complete threefold canonical collection."

The Prologue is excellent documentary evidence that the Jewish people had in their midst an authoritative body of books in three divisions which was considered divine. The unanimous opinion of early Jewish scholars expressed conviction that the Old Testament scriptures were selected and placed in an official order by Ezra the priest (with the help of Nehemiah) in the fifth century B.C. For rabbinic assessment up to the seventeenth century of our era we can quote Humphrey Prideaux.

> "He [Ezra] collected together all the books of which the holy scriptures did then consist, and disposed them in their proper order, and settled the canon of scripture for his time. These books he divided into three parts: first, *the Law*; secondly, *the Prophets*; and thirdly, *the Ketubim* or *Hagiographa*, i.e. the Holy Writings; which division our Saviour himself takes notice of in Luke 24:44" (*Connection of the Old and New Testaments,* vol.I. (London:1858), pp.318,319).

What is important to the whole issue is the acknowledgment of the official tripartite arrangement by Christ himself. After his resurrection he rehearsed all the prophecies which were found in "the Scriptures" concerning himself and his mission. And, most significant to our present discussion, Christ then defined what *those* Scriptures were. His definition is the only one in the entirety of the New Testament which delineates the extent of the Old Testament. This affirmation is in the Gospel of Luke (a gospel intended especially for Gentiles). It was the Gentiles who needed the Old Testament canon spelled out. Such detail was not necessary for ordinary Jewish folk in the first century because they were aware of what books represented the scriptures. This must be the case because throughout the New Testament (at least 16 different times) the writers simply referred to the Old Testament as "the Scriptures" — *always* without enumeration. But for Gentiles it was a different story. The Gentiles, of course, would have needed to know what the proper books really were. Even the apostles themselves may have wanted an authoritative statement regarding the canon. The definition that Christ gave could hardly be more official, simply because he confirmed it to the apostles *after his resurrection from the dead.* — after he had once again assumed his glorified position with the Father. This is when Christ defined "the

Scriptures" as the Tripartite Divisions.

> "These are the words which I spake unto you, while I was yet with
> you, that all things must be fulfilled, which were written in the
> Law of Moses, and in the Prophets, and in the Psalms, concerning
> me. Then opened he their understanding, that they might
> understand *the Scriptures*" (Luke 24:44,45).

Notice that Christ referred to the Third Division as "the Psalms."
There is no doubt that he was alluding to the complete Third
Division. Since that section had no technical name in the first century
(it was either called "*the* Other Books," or "*the* Remaining Books," or
"*the* Writings," even "*the* Holy Writings"), it became common to
identify it by the name of the book which introduced it — the Book of
Psalms. There was nothing odd in using this procedure from the
Jewish point of view because they customarily named the Book of
Genesis by the first Hebrew word that introduced it. This was also
true of Exodus, Leviticus, Numbers, Deuteronomy, and even the
Book of Lamentations. There can be little doubt that Christ was
referring to the whole of the Third Division (all eleven books) when
he made his reference to the Psalms. There is a further proof of this.
In Christ's teaching about the martyrs of the Old Testament period
in Luke 11:49-51, we find him saying that the blood of all the
prophets from Abel (the first martyr) to Zacharias (the last martyr in
the canonical order of the Old Testament books) would be required
of that generation to whom he spoke (*cf.* Matt.23:35). Though in
point of time the last person mentioned in the Old Testament as
having been killed for his righteousness was Uriah (as recorded in
Jeremiah 26:20-23), in the canonical arrangement of the books, the
last was Zacharias mentioned in II Chronicles 24:20,21. It must
be understood that First and Second Chronicles in our present
Bibles were reckoned as only one book by the early Hebrews, and
that this book was the final one of the Third Division of the Old
Testament. This indication could very well mean that Christ was
referring to all the Old Testament martyrs from Genesis (book "A")
to Chronicles (book "Z"). This is just another biblical clue that Christ
recognized the books within the Tripartite Divisions (*the Law, the
Prophets, and the Psalms* — all eleven books of the Third Division) as

the official ones which comprised the Old Testament. That these books, and these books only, have been the authoritative Jewish ones from early times is a recognized fact. They are certainly the books that now make up their canon today.

The Witness of Second Maccabees

It was a well recognized belief near the end of the second century B.C. that the canon of the Old Testament was completed about three hundred years before the time of the Maccabees, in the time of Ezra and Nehemiah. Notice II Maccabees 2:12-15. Speaking about the Feast of Tabernacles, its author said:

> "Solomon also kept the eight days. The same thing was related also in the records and memoirs about Nehemiah, that he founded a library and collected the books about the kings, and the prophets, and the works of David, and royal letters about sacred gifts."

The author then related that the Holy Scriptures had been regathered after the Maccabean War (from 167 to 164 B.C.) and again could be read and followed. Notice that this reference has Nehemiah building a library and collecting the sacred books. This ties in well with the teaching of Josephus that the 22 books of the Old Testament were brought together and canonized in the time of Ezra and Nehemiah (*Contra Apion*, I.8). The library of Nehemiah (who was a high government official in the Persian Empire) could easily account for the mention of many ancient historical works in the Book of Chronicles [which we will refer to later]. Chronicles, the last book of the Old Testament, describes events which dovetail well with the historical environment during the time of Ezra and Nehemiah. There were, however, editorial remarks recorded in the book (genealogical records, etc.) until the time of Alexander the Great (c. 330 B.C.).

Let us now notice a point made in Second Maccabees about the canonization of the Old Testament. It said the literary works of "the kings and the prophets" were gathered together in the time of Ezra and Nehemiah! This indication could well be a reference to the Prophets' (the second) Division of the Tripartite arrangement of the

Old Testament. This is because the books about the "Kings" (our present books of Samuel and Kings) are immediately followed in the canonical order by the Major Prophets (Isaiah, Jeremiah, Ezekiel) then the twelve Minor Prophets. And it is exactly this order that we find recorded in Second Maccabees. But there is more. Second Maccabees then states that those "kings and prophets" were followed by "the works of David." Again, this is the precise order of the Jewish canon. The fact is, the Third Division of the Tripartite arrangement begins with "the Psalms of David," which even Christ himself recognized as the book which introduced the final division of the Old Testament (Luke 24:44,45). But the reference in Second Maccabees doesn't terminate with "the works of David" (the Psalms). It continues to state that the books to follow were "the royal letters." And in the biblical canon maintained by the official Jewish authorities, all the rest of the books in the Third Division were indeed "royal" or "government" documents just as the Book of Psalms itself was "royal" in origin. This fact has not been noticed by most people, but look at all the books in the Third Division — they have the theme of "royalty" running through them all just as Second Maccabees records.

The Book of Psalms (the first book) is a book authored by King David (Psalms 1 through 71), then a book *by* or *for* King Solomon (72), then those by the priests of David (73 to 88), the one for King Josiah (89), then the millennial or kingdom of God Psalms (90 to 106), followed by sundry Psalms of David (107 to 150) — including the Degree Psalms (120 to 134) which were composed for King Hezekiah (as we will also observe later). Thus, the Book of Psalms which introduces the Third Division is a book which has royal persons as authors or it presents themes which concern the kingdom of Judah, Israel, and the kingdom of God.

The *royal* Book of Psalms is followed by the Book of Proverbs. This book was authored primarily by King Solomon, with a section devised for King Hezekiah (chapters 25 to 29 inclusively), and Agur the King of Massa (30) and finally King Lemuel (31). The whole of Proverbs is a "royal document" as Second Maccabees describes the books positioned after those of the Prophets.

But it doesn't stop there. In the canonical order of the Old Testament books, the Book of Job follows Proverbs. Job was

described as a king and represented royalty (29:25). The Book of
Ruth comes next, and is manifestly a work about the early ancestry
of King David (it is a royal book which gives the genealogical history
of David). Then follows the Book of Lamentations. This was written
by the prophet Jeremiah for, as we will see later, King Josiah of
Judah. It also is a "royal book." Then we have Ecclesiastes which was
traditionally composed by King Solomon. After that, in the canonical
order, is the Book of Esther. She was Queen of Persia (again, a clear
royalty indication). Following Esther is Daniel. This book is one of
"royal" character. Not only does it discuss at length the history of
royal rulership from the time of King Nebuchadnezzar of Babylon
until the kingdom of God appears on earth, but it was written by
Daniel who was of royal Davidic stock — "of the king's seed, one of
the princes" (Dan.1:3). The next book in order was that of Ezra
(responsible for re-establishing the official government of God in
Jerusalem). With him was Nehemiah who may have been of Davidic
blood (*cf.* Nehemiah 6:6,7 where it states the Jews wanted to make
him king — and only those of Davidic ancestry could then legally
become king in the biblical sense). It should be understood that
in the original Jewish numbering of the Old Testament books, the
present two of Ezra and Nehemiah were always reckoned as one.
Thus, the predominant person who put into action the affairs of state
was Nehemiah. He was probably of royal ancestry and responsible,
so said Second Maccabees, of collecting the books for his library and
selecting a divine body of books for posterity. The last book of
the Third Division was that of Chronicles. It takes little study to see
that this book focuses on the establishment of Jerusalem and the
family of David as the legitimate rulers for the divine government on
earth. It is indeed a royal book too.

Thus, all the books of the Third Division (which commenced with
the Psalms) were royal books, or, as Second Maccabees called them,
"the royal letters." With this information in mind, it can be seen that
by 100 B.C., when Second Maccabees was written, the Old Testament
was already canonized and in the exact order as maintained by the
Jews today and also by Christ in Luke 24:44,45. Christ called the
Third Division "the Psalms." The use of introductory books or even
words to describe biblical divisions or sections was common by the
Jews. See Mishnah, *Taanith* 4:3; *Meg.* 2:3; 3:4,5,6; 4:10.

This practice of using introductory words as titles of whole sections or even divisions of literary works was well known. When the Nag Hammadi Library of ancient books was discovered in 1945 it was soon found that the introductory words of a work gave the whole composition its title. Prof. Frederik Wisse made this comment: "It is not unusual for the opening words of a tractate to function as the title for the whole tractate" (*The Nag Hammadi Library,* p.394).

And so it was with the Third Division of the Old Testament. It was called "the Psalms" by Christ because that was the book which introduced the division. This designation was also followed by the Jewish scholar Philo Judaeus who lived in the time of Christ. He regarded the Jewish canon as "the laws, and oracles that have come through the prophets, also with *the hymns* (psalms) and the other books" (*Cont. Life*). This is a reference to the Tripartite Divisions.

The Apostolic Constitutions

The Apostolic Constitutions was written about A.D.200. It purports to give some of the original teachings of the apostles. And while the work was trying to bring in Old Testament authority for some of its claims, it inadvertently confirms the commonly understood order of the books and Tripartite Divisions of the canon. It states that the Old Testament was composed of the Law, the Kings and Prophets, and the hymns of David (*Constitutions of the Holy Apostles*, 1.2.5). It is important to note that the Third Division is again called "the Hymns," just as Second Maccabees and Philo do. Such a description was a common variant of the name "the Psalms" which Christ used in Luke 24:44,45. Ancient literary usage shows this to be correct.

The Targums of Onkelos and Jonathan

In regard to the Tripartite Divisions of the original Hebrew canon, attention ought to be made to these two Targums. In the first century before Christ, many of the common people of Judaea spoke an Aramaic dialect which had become popular among the Jews while they resided in Babylon. Aramaic was akin to the Hebrew in many ways, but it still represented a different language. Even Ezra had to interpret the intent of the original Hebrew of the early Old Testament because the Jews had forgotten the Hebrew while in Babylon (Neh.8:1-8). From the time of Ezra onwards, it became common to make Aramaic paraphrases of the Old Testament. These works are called *Targums*. Near the time of Christ there were two Targums which reached a type of official status among the Jews. These were the *Targum of the Law* by Onkelos, and the *Targum of the Prophets* by Jonathan. The Talmud reveals that these two Targums were even used in synagogue services. And while the first two sections of the Tripartite Divisions were recognized as proper books to be read in synagogue services, the Third Division (which existed at the time) was not permitted to be paraphrased (so the story goes) because of a divine message against it (*Megillah*, 3a, The Babylonian Talmud). Though the Third Division was not at first paraphrased, this is still a testimony that that particular section of the Scriptures was already recognized as inspired and a part of the canon by the time of Christ.

And as far as the Talmud itself is concerned, it clearly supports the Tripartite Divisions as representing the official canon. Since the fifth century, the Jews have had a special name for the Old Testament. They call it the *Tanak.* This word is a manufactured one derived from the first letters of the titles of the threefold divisions. The Law (the first five books) was known as the *Torah.* The Prophets' Division was called the *Nebi'um.* And the Psalms' (or Writings') Division was known as the *Ketuvim.* In referring to these three divisions, they simply took the initial letters of the three titles (i.e. T, N, K) and formed the word *Tanak.* The Jews use this word to refer to the Old Testament canon as commonly as Christians use the word "Bible."

This practice shows the Jewish steadfastness in maintaining the Tripartite Divisions of the Old Testament which tradition (and the early records) show was handed down from the time of Ezra and Nehemiah. And since we have the express testimony of Christ himself that "the Scriptures" represented "The Law of Moses, the Prophets, and the Psalms (the Third Division)" (Luke 24:44,45), it seems odd that any Christian today would question the legitimacy of its official character. Should not Christ's appraisal be sufficient?

It is my belief that these ancient divisions ought to be retained in all versions of the Bible today. When this is done we will be afforded a better understanding of the Bible.

5

The Proper Numbering of the Books

The original number of books comprising the Tripartite Divisions was 22 — to equal the number of Hebrew letters. This corresponded to the books in the Protestant canon today, yet the originals were arranged and numbered differently (not as the present 39). Our modern way of counting the books is easy to explain. Whereas the 12 Minor Prophets (from Hosea to Malachi) were formerly written on *one* scroll and counted as *one* book (as Luke does in the New Testament — Acts 7:42 *cf.* 13:40), each of the 12 is now counted separately. This makes the sum to be 33, not 22. But the re-counting did not end there. The *one* Book of Chronicles is presently divided into two, as is Ezra-Nehemiah. This brings the sum to 35. But more dividing has been done. The four books we call I & II Samuel and I & II Kings were once reckoned as only *one* book. A relic of this book is found in the King James Version. If one looks at the introductions to those four books, it will be noticed that the secondary titles (as they are presently reckoned) were First, Second, Third, and Fourth Kings. These designations are the remnant names of the *one* composition called "The Book of Kingdoms."

> "The Greek collection of Samuel-Kings as one book with its division into four volumes was followed by all the ancient versions. The Greek title 'The Kingdoms' appeared in early titles of the Latin Bible; the Arabic as well as the Ethiopic, followed the Hebrew with 'Kings;' the Syriac used both titles, varying with the books. In the Latin Bible 'Kings' came into current use" (Montgomery, *A Critical and Exegetical Commentary on the Book of Kings,* (ICC), p.2).

Melito about A.D.170 and *The Apostolic Constitutions* (c. A.D.200) also affirmed that our four books of Samuel and Kings were once acknowledged as *one* book (Rawlinson, *Truth of Scripture Records*, p.325). The literary evidence within those sections sustains the unity of them all. As Montgomery states, our present books of Kings are "a continuation of the books of Samuel, but without clearly marked literary distinction" and that the modern partitioning was "divided for arbitrary convenience" (*ibid.* p.1). The truth is, there is no need to divide the *one* Book of Kingdoms into 4 separate books. But when this is done, it increases the original 22 books to 38. The King James Version (and most other versions) divide one other ancient book (which was once a single entity) and raise the original 22 books to our present 39 for the Old Testament. What was the remaining book that was divided? It was what we now call Joshua/ Judges.

Originally, the historical account from the death of Moses until the rise of Samuel the prophet was accounted as a single book. Later people, however, severed it into the books of Joshua and Judges. These books introduced the "Prophets' Division" and recorded the singular time when Israel *had NO kings* in contrast to the next Book of Kingdoms which recorded the history of Israel when *they HAD kings.* Internally, Joshua/Judges are a single literary composition, and they both have the earmarks of one author (whom the Jews recognized as Samuel), and even the apostle Peter referred to Samuel as the one who commenced the "Prophets' Division" of the Old Testament (Acts 3:24).

Thus, the original 22 books of the Tripartite Divisions were numbered in the following fashion:

THE LAW
1. Genesis
2. Exodus
3. Leviticus
4. Numbers
5. Deuteronomy

THE PROPHETS
6. Joshua/Judges
7. The Book of Kingdoms

8. Isaiah
9. Jeremiah
10. Ezekiel
11. The Twelve

THE WRITINGS (PSALMS)
12. Psalms
13. Proverbs
14. Job
15. Song of Songs
16. Ruth
17. Lamentations
18. Ecclesiastes
19. Esther
20. Daniel
21. Ezra/Nehemiah
22. The Book of Chronicles

The Testimony of Josephus

Josephus does not mention the Tripartite Divisions of the Old Testament in his account concerning the divine scriptures. He does, however, refer to the canon as being reckoned as 22 books. Let us notice what he says on the matter.

> "We have not a countless number of books, discordant and arrayed against each other; but only *twenty-two* books, containing the history of every age, which are justly accredited as divine. Of these, five belong to Moses, which contain both the laws and the history of the generations of men until his death. This period lacks but little of 3000 years. From the death of Moses, moreover, until the time of Artaxerxes, king of the Persians after Xerxes [*i.e.* to the time of Ezra and Nehemiah], the prophets, who followed Moses, wrote down what was done during the age of each one respectively, in thirteen books. The remaining four contain hymns to God, and rules of life for men. From the time of Artaxerxes, moreover, until our present period, all occurrences have been written down but they are not regarded as entitled to the like credit with those which precede them, because there was no certain succession of prophets. Fact has shown what confi-

dence we place in our own writings. For although so many ages have passed away, no one has dared to add to them, nor to take anything from, nor to make alterations. In all Jews it is implanted, even from their birth, to regard them as being the instructions of God, and to abide steadfastly by them, and if it be necessary, to die gladly for them" (*Contra Apion* I.8).

Josephus here says that the Jewish people late in the first century believed the Old Testament had been put together and completed in the days of Ezra and Nehemiah. It might be said that Josephus is bringing to witness some 8 million or so Jewish people since he was writing in the capacity of a priestly spokesman for his people. Note also that of the works written *after* the time of Ezra (including all the books of the Apocrypha) none was reckoned as being inspired of God since no one with the prophetic spirit had come on the scene after Ezra. It was a cardinal belief at the time that no one could write inspired scriptures without the person having a prophetic commission to do so.

It is significant to note that the Jews had a high regard for the official canon. They would not think for one moment of adding to, of subtracting from, or altering in any way the sacred books. This shows the firm confidence the Jews had for the inviolability of the Old Testament canon. Yet with all this, there seems to be an apparent discrepancy between Josephus' order of the Old Testament books and the traditional one accepted by Jews today. Josephus supposedly supports a canon of 5 Mosaic books, 13 of the Prophets, and 4 of Hymns and Precepts. In giving this enumeration, is Josephus presenting an order of books in which he disregarded the Tripartite Divisions? Without doubt. For example, the Prophets' Division never had 13 books within it, nor has the Psalms' Division been limited to 4 books.

Josephus was not referring to the actual Tripartite Divisions at all. But why did Josephus mention this odd (and quite unique) arrangement of the canonical books? The matter can become clear when we recall to whom Josephus was writing in this section.

Josephus' Intention

There are several reasons why Josephus avoided a precise reference to the Tripartite Divisions and the proper order of the Old Testament books.

1) He was writing to Gentiles — people who knew little about, or were unable to appreciate, the significance of the true arrangement of the canonical books.

2) His main intention for writing this passage, as is evidenced from the context, was only to demonstrate the extreme antiquity of the Jewish nation. Notice his emphasis upon the age in which things occurred. His immediate subject was the demonstration of Jewish longevity, not to give the Gentiles a disquisition on the proper order of the books within the sacred canon.

3) Gentile scholars of the first century were great encyclopaedists in their manner of classifying literary documents. Much as we do today in our modern libraries, it was common to arrange books according to subject matter. There was nothing wrong in this, of course (because such classification has the advantage of facilitating the teaching process), but if a true Greek were to look at the arrangement of the Old Testament books in the Tripartite Divisions (particularly to that of the Third Division), it would have been looked at as showing little rhyme or reason. True enough, the Third Division is harmonious in every way, but the arrangement is not in the Greek manner — we will see that the books were positioned for liturgical purposes for readings in the Temple. To explain this factor would have taken Josephus away from his intended design of showing the antiquity of the Jewish race and into another subject which the Greeks would not have easily understood. It is precisely because of this that he was not prepared to risk bewildering his Gentile readers by discussing the canonical arrangement. Instead, he himself, went over to the common Greek manner of classifying documents according to the chronological time periods to which they referred. And indeed, this is exactly what he tells us about his 13 books which he said were written by prophets. They "wrote down what was done

during the age of each one respectfully." Josephus, then, reckoned the sacred scriptures according to chronological composition, not the official canonical arrangement! [As a matter of fact, when later Christians in the early third century placed the Septuagint Version of the Old Testament into a codex form, they did indeed subjectivize the books as most normal Greeks would have expected.]

Once it is realized that Josephus was not attempting to reproduce the actual canonical order of the Old Testament books for his Gentile readers, it is possible to deduce what were the actual books of which he was speaking. There is hardly any doubt that Josephus' last 4 books of Hymns and Precepts were 1) Psalms 2) Song of Songs (the two books of the hymns); followed by 3) Proverbs and 4) Ecclesiastes (the books of moral teaching) (Ryle, *The Canon of the Old Testament*, p.176). The 13 prophetical books, written "down what was done during the age of each one respectfully," were arranged chronologically by Josephus. They were 1) Job, 2) Joshua/Judges, 3) Ruth, 4) Book of Kingdoms, 5) Isaiah, 6) Jeremiah, 7) Lamentations, 8) Ezekiel, 9) The Twelve, 10) Daniel, 11) Esther, 12) Ezra/Nehemiah, 13) Book of Chronicles.

Thus we have Josephus telling us he subjectivized those 13 books into their chronological arrangement without reference to their actual canonical order.

One other point needs to be made. It is a common assumption among some biblical scholars that Josephus arrived at his 22 numbering of the complete Old Testament canon by attaching the Book of Ruth to Judges and the Book of Lamentations to Jeremiah. There is not the slightest proof that this was the case. Indeed, that particular method of re-counting the books was not used until the third century A.D. when the Septuagint (Egyptian/Greek) Version was finally placed by Christians into a codex form of book. Before that time, the various scrolls of the Old Testament books were apparently not arranged in any official order by Egyptian Jews or Christians (unless in the official Palestinian Tripartite manner). The finalized Septuagint arrangement is a result of codexing the books, rather than leaving them as scrolls. This positioning is thus late and is no proof that Josephus (a hundred or so years earlier) combined

Ruth with Judges and Lamentations with Jeremiah.

> "It seems unwarranted to suppose that Josephus attached Ruth
> to Judges and Lamentations to Jeremiah without counting them.
> It is a conjecture without sufficient evidence to sustain it"
> (Briggs, *Study of the Holy Scripture,* p. 128).

It certainly is unwarranted. For one thing, this *guessing* transfers two
books out of the Third Division of the Old Testament and places
them in the Second, thereby upsetting the story-flow in both
divisions (to be explained in the next chapter). This procedure
destroys the unique characteristics of the Tripartite Divisions and
should never be done. Even some 400 years after Christ when the
rabbis who compiled the Jewish Talmud spoke of the order of the
sacred books, the suggestion was made that Isaiah (perhaps for
liturgical purposes) could best be positioned after Ezekiel (*Baba
Bathra* 15a) — a suggestion which had no lasting effect on the canon
itself — but this reckoning only concerned a transfer *within* a
tripartite division, *not* a re-positioning from one division to another.

Isaiah certainly does not belong after Ezekiel. In 180 B.C., the
Book of Ecclesiasticus gave a chronological rundown from Genesis
to the close of the Old Testament. Significantly, Sirach discussed in
proper canonical order Isaiah (48:22), Jeremiah (49:7), Ezekiel
(49:8), and then "The Twelve" (the Minor Prophets) (49:10). Prof.
R.H. Charles called attention to this fact that "The Twelve" were in
the precise order as the present Hebrew canon (*The Apocrypha and
Pseudepigrapha,* vol.I,p.505). Sirach was referring to a *canonical
order* of "The Twelve." His reference was not for chronological
reasons because some of the prophets making up "The Twelve" lived
before Isaiah. This is a clear indication that Sirach had a canon of
divine scriptures in front of him that he was referring to. It should
also be pointed out that he did not place the Book of Daniel right
after Ezekiel as our modern Old Testaments have it.

This is powerful evidence that the Prophets' Division of the canon
was established in the present Jewish arrangement over 200 years
before Christ began to preach. Josephus would have been well aware
of this official order. In the next chapter we will see why this
arrangement must be maintained for the sake of orderly teaching.

6

The Design of the Old Testament •

The most important individual who was responsible for designing and finalizing the Old Testament was Ezra the priest, who had Nehemiah as his political helper. It was the universal testimony of Jews and later Christians that Ezra and Nehemiah in the fifth century B.C. were the ones commissioned to complete the Hebrew canon (*Seder Olam* R30; *Contra Apion* I.8; Irenaeus, *Against Heresies,* 3.21; Clement of Alexandria, *Stromata,* 1.22; Tertullian, *Apparel of Women,* 1.3). What Ezra did was to select the books which were to be accepted as canonical, arranged them in proper order, and then edited them from beginning to end to make them understandable for the readers of his time (cf. II Esdras 14). [Such edits as "unto Dan" in Genesis 14:14 and the concluding sections of Deuteronomy about Moses' death can best be attributed to Ezra when he finalized the text of the Old Testament.]

He also changed the style of the Hebrew letters within the Old Testament books from the old Phoenician script of the early prophets to the "square script" which had become common for international communication by the fifth century. This was not done simply to facilitate the reading of the Bible but, more importantly, Ezra was able to establish at one full swoop an official canon of scriptures which was now (by the use of the new letter configurations) able to be distinguished from heretical Samaritan manuscripts which were written in the old Hebrew script. It has been supposed that Christ referred to this *square script* used by Ezra when he said not a jot or tittle would pass from the law until all be fulfilled (Matt.5:18). These small horn-like projections were not used in the old Hebrew script before the time of Ezra. If this is the case, then we have Christ's approbation for Ezra's alteration of the Hebrew letters from the old to the new style.

Ezra also changed the names of the calendar months from the old names (i.e. Abib for the first Hebrew month) to the common ones then in use (i.e. Abib became Nisan, etc.). This further delineated the Jewish calendar and its official holyday system from that of the Samaritans which Ezra and those in Jerusalem considered false. Thus, the changing of the style of letters and technical details concerning the calendar were simple acts (ingeneously utilized) which settled the majority of canonical and calendar disputes between the Jews and the Samaritans. (NEHEMIAH 8:8)

Ezra's Canonization

Ezra arranged the authorized scrolls into a proper order for teaching the people and deposited them with the priests in the archives of the Temple (Deut.17:18; 31:9). A group of 120 priests were ordained to be the Supreme Court of the land (known as the Great Assembly) of whom Ezra was the chief (Hereford, *Talmud and Apocrypha*, p.56). These priests also assumed the name "Sopherim" (i.e. *counters of letters in manuscripts*) because they were responsible for reproducing the canonical books for use in the synagogues throughout the land. They *counted* the letters in each manuscript they reproduced for the synagogues to insure that the letters agreed with the exact number found in the authorized Temple scrolls.

The 22 books within the Tripartite Divisions had their origin with Ezra and the Sopherim. After Ezra's death there were some genealogical additions and certain textual amendations made by the authorized Sopherim. Their job came to an end with the advent of Antiochus Epiphanes in 167 B.C. and the subsequent establishment of the Maccabean realm in 164 B.C. From that period the canon of the Old Testament was settled and we find the Book of Jubilees (150 B.C.) speaking of the 22 books as though they were a set of standard scrolls, and the Prologue of Sirach (132 B.C.) mentioned the official Tripartite Divisions as already established.

Thus, it was recognized that the Hebrew canon of 22 books (which corresponded to the 22 letters of the Hebrew alphabet) was then complete. This was the Bible of Christ and the apostles.

The Design of the Books

The books of the Old Testament were not haphazardly arranged. Their positioning was to afford a teaching of overall spiritual principles to the readers — especially to the priests who cared for the divine library and to the secular rulers who were supposed to execute the biblical legislation among the society of the people.

The supreme position of importance was accorded the first five books called the Law (Torah). The two divisions that followed (the Prophets with 6 books and the Writings with 11 books) were arranged with the authority of each division in view. First rank after the Torah belonged to the Prophets, while second rank went to the Writings ("the Royal Books"). This principle of rank is demonstrated throughout the pages of both the Old and New Testaments. It is seen clearly in the examples of Nathan commanding King David with direct orders from God (II Samuel 12) and with Elijah and Elisha instructing both Israelite and Gentile kings what they must do. This is actually the case with *every* prophet of the Bible — and this even included Jonah telling the Assyrian king and his people what God expected them to perform.

Among the prophets themselves there were degrees of rank. The most notable was that of *eldership.* It will be recalled that a cardinal principle of social rank among biblical peoples of all eras was that of respect for *elders.* From the elders of Pharaoh and Egypt (Gen.50:7), the elders of Israel (Exo.3:16), the elders of each city (Deut.25:7), the elders of the priests (Isa.37:2), to the elders of the Christian church (Acts 14:23; 15:6; James 5:14) and the 24 elders around the throne of God (Rev.4:4,10), the esteem given to *eldership* was thorough and consistent. The only rank higher than being an elder of any class in society was that involving a direct commission from God (e.g. Gen.41:40-44; I Tim.4:12). But in all aspects of normal social rank the standard procedure for recognized distinction was: "Ye younger, submit yourselves unto the elder" (I Pet.5:5).

In Jewish practice this esteem for elder rank was never abated. As an example of this, Philo (in the time of Christ) described the actions of the independent sect of the Essenes. Though they had an equality among themselves in many respects, the matter of eldership in rank was consistent with that of normative Judaism. "On the seventh day they abstain from their works and come to their holy places called synagogues, *and sit in ranks according to their ages*, the young below the elder, and they listen attentively in orderly fashion" (*Quad. Omnis Prob.* 81). This recognition of eldership in teaching was also shown by the apostle Paul when he said he had been trained in Jerusalem "at the feet of Gamaliel" (Acts 22:3).

The principle of *eldership* is seen in the positioning of books within the three sections of the Prophets' Division: 1) the Former Prophets, 2) the Major Prophets, and 3) the Minor Prophets. Certainly, there is a chronological aspect to *eldership* (being *older* in time), so the Book of Joshua/Judges is placed before the Book of the Kingdoms (our Samuel and Kings) because its theme concerns an earlier period in Israel's history when they had no kings, while the latter book (as its name implies) gives their history when they had kings (from Saul to Zedekiah and Jehoiachin). This obvious chronological disposition makes perfectly good sense as anyone can see.

The second section (the Major Prophets) is arranged in the identical format. Isaiah gave his prophecies in the middle of the eighth century B.C. while Jeremiah began his prophetic ministry about 627 B.C. followed by Ezekiel in about 592 B.C.

The third section (the Minor Prophets) also has a chronological basis to it. Though not everyone of the twelve books gives a precise dating, enough of them reveal the *eldership* principle in action because even the non-dated ones often have a reasonable historical context to show their chronological arrangement. This can best be seen by reviewing the last book (Malachi) first, then working backwards to the first book (Hosea). The beginning chronological reference (or a reasonable historical context) will indicate that each of the books (from 12 back to 1) is *earlier* to each other.

These chronological factors are important because they reveal a deliberate design being put into play by the canonizers which anyone can see. Just what the interpretations behind *those* arrangements are supposed to signify is for investigators to determine, but the chronological (*eldership*) aspect is not difficult to see.

The Writings' Division

We should remember that the eleven books of this Third Division were made up of "Royal or Government Books" (for rulers and leaders), but they are placed in an inferior position to the Prophets and they are *not* chronological. This inferiority of station as to their canonical disposition does not signify that they are books of inferior worth. In no way. It simply means they were not as important in the eyes of Ezra (the canonizer) relative to the purpose behind his arrangement of the 22 books. What must be understood is that the canon of the Old Testament was designed for teaching purposes. The books of the Torah were so needful for *all* Israelites that a three year cycle of reading through the books was established for the synagogues of Ezra's time and this reading from the Law was buttressed by selections from the Prophets. The first two divisions were what might be called *public books*. They were intended for general consumption by all Israelites without distinction. But this was *not* so with the eleven books of the Writings' Division. Though these Third Division books were as holy as the others, they were not generally considered writings which were primarily for the public. An example of this is found with the custom about the first century B.C. of paraphrasing the biblical books into the vernacular of the people. When it came time to paraphrase the books of the Third Division a command from God (a *Bet Kol*) was supposedly given *not* to perform this task of putting the writings of these books in the language of the common people (*Megillah*, 3a). True, the books were not really "secret" since they made up the last of the Old Testament canon (and could be read in the synagogues), yet they were not liturgically fashioned for synagogue use. In a word, they were *not* canonized to provide a teaching apparatus within a synagogue environment. The intended readers of these books (and the ones required to *heed* them) were individuals in an entirely different environment than the one of the general assembly each Sabbath. They were arranged for a teaching apparatus with a *Temple* context at the headquarters of the nation at Jerusalem, and they were primarily designed for the guidance and instruction of important civil and religious authorities. These were *federal* books intended mainly for the executives among the people. This is why they were reserved for *Temple* teaching. This can be seen, for example, with the five central books of the Third Division called the *Megilloth* (explained fully on pages 72 and 73). The Song of Songs, Ruth, Lamentations, Ecclesiastes and Esther were read and discussed at the five main religious periods *in the Temple*. This was also true of the Book of the Psalms. The 150 psalms were apparently read successively over a three year period *in the Temple* ("Triennial Cycle," *Jewish Encyclopedia* (1912), vol.XII, pp.255,256). Even the Book of Chronicles was a *"Temple"* book.

The Book of Chronicles is materially different from the Book of Kingdoms though they cover about the same historical ground. Ezra in Chronicles had another emphasis in mind when he wrote *this* book and he needed a historical basis to sustain it. His history was to provide 1) a proper genealogical account of *royal* and *priestly* ancestors, 2) to show former "good" and "bad" actions of the Davidic kings and the priests, 3) the proof that Jerusalem was the legal seat of government, and 4) that the Temple was the only lawful sanctuary for true Israel. Not only that, the Book of Ezra/Nehemiah had the same subjects as its theme: maintaining proper genealogical connections while securing Jerusalem and the Temple as the proper center of civil and religious government. Even Daniel (a book of the Third Division) in its chronological prophecy about the arrival of the Messiah (the Seventy Weeks' Prophecy) has as its theme: Jerusalem, the Holy Place (the Temple), and the assurance of the arrival of a true leader called the Messiah (Davidic or Priestly). The Book of Psalms also has major sections by King David and King Hezekiah, as well as a whole series of psalms about the Temple and the priests at Jerusalem. [See Appendix I for details on these matters.]

As a matter of fact, there was a historical reason why Ezra felt it was necessary to canonize the books of the Old Testament when he did. Knowing what these historical circumstances were can help us understand why he placed the eleven books of the Writings' Division in the manner he did and why he centered the reading of them (and the instruction derived from them) among the religious and civil authorities *at Jerusalem*. They were not systematically to be read in the synagogue services of the nation. It is important to notice what the historical factors were that prompted Ezra and the Great Assembly to write Chronicles and to canonize the Old Testament.

The main difficulty that Ezra had with the Jews at Jerusalem was false religious beliefs and customs entering Judaic society because of the *intermarriages* of Jewish men with heathen women. It was a very upsetting situation as Ezra viewed it because the intermarriages involved the civil and religious leaders among the Jews. It was especially bad because *the priests* (even the high priests) had been polluting their "holy seed" (Ezra 9 & 10, Neh.13:23-31; Mal. 1 & 2).

This was a major deviation from proper religious practice in the view of Ezra and he was so horrified at it and the prospects of what it could lead to that he thought it prudent to write the Book of Chronicles as a history of what had happened in the past when such things had occurred. A stable and consistent *Jewish* family life was at stake and Ezra used every device he could muster to get the Jewish leaders to realize the consequences of such "unholy alliances." This is the main reason he canonized the 22 Old Testament books and wrote the Book of Chronicles. The latter book was to provide future leaders a special history of what had happened in the past when heathen or impure women entered into the mainstream of Judaic society. It always resulted in an apostasy from God and it brought on severe and catastrophic judgments from heaven. Let's look at this.

Note that the first nine chapters of Chronicles emphasize Israelite *genealogy* to show how important a *proper* pedigree was. While David and Solomon are both honored for their work on the Temple and for establishing true worship at Jerusalem, Nehemiah was quick to point out the well-known escapades of Solomon as a detriment to him (Neh.13:26) though he had enough divine wisdom to put Pharaoh's daughter away from the holy places at Jerusalem (II Chron.8:11). But Solomon's rebellious son Rehoboam was a product of "*the* Ammonitess" (II Chron.12:13). He went into early deviations and the fact that he had "many wives" is stressed (II Chron.11:21-23). From that time onward, Ezra records in Chronicles (for his Jewish leaders) an account of the "good" and "bad" kings of Judah, and in almost every case the "good" kings had proper *Jewish* mothers and the "bad" kings either had heathen or reprobate mothers. And it was *this* very thing that Ezra was scolding the Jewish leaders of his time for doing. Ezra wanted to put a stop to it, and he did.

Now look at the Third (or Writings') Division of the Old Testament once more. It was Ezra who put the books together and he had a reason for doing it in the manner he did. These books were selected to show leaders, among other things, that godly *women* were proper to marry and evil *women* were to be shunned. In one way or another the eleven books of the Third Division are designed to show this. For example, the Book of Psalms introduces the Division and the psalm that highlights David's life is Psalm 51 showing his sin with Bathsheba who may have been a Hittite woman. She was the mother of Solomon who had so much trouble with non-Jewish women. The next book is Proverbs. Note how the first nine chapters emphasize "Wisdom" (personified as a woman) as well as the evils of false women. The last chapter, though, shows the ideal woman to marry. The next book is Job. His story is one of faithfulness in trial in spite of a very *faithless* wife. Job's tenacity, however, brings him double possessions and three beautiful daughters (Job 42:13-15). The next five books are the *Megilloth* and they emphasize, in one way or another, various types of women — both good and bad. The Song of Songs is about a woman (and women) interested in Solomon. The Book of Ruth shows an example of the ideal woman and how a man can be blessed with a truly converted woman. Lamentations is about Jerusalem personified as a royal princess gone wrong. In the Book of Ecclesiates Solomon is reported to have said that the real joy for men is to have a good job *and a fine wife* (Eccl.9:9), but that the 1000 women he had were more bitter than death to him (Eccl.7:26-29). The Book of Esther shows the power of a righteous woman to save the whole nation of Judah. After these five *Megilloth* books comes Daniel. He was the wisest man of the age, of royal stock, and one who had excellent and proper upbringing (Dan.1:3,4). And finally, the books of Ezra/Nehemiah and Chronicles (which end the Third Division) have as central themes the need for the leaders at Jerusalem to have nothing to do with heathen or impure women (who produce "heathen and impure" children), but to cherish and hold the proper *Jewish* women who would rear to adulthood proper and holy children. In effect, the Third Division was devised, among other things, to establish and to secure a godly *Jewish* family life among the leaders of the nation. This would then insure that all the people would have the right examples to follow in their own endeavors to be holy in the sight of God. Indeed, the establishment of the Old Testament canon itself (as well as the arrangement of the Third Division) was prompted because of this pressing need which Ezra and Nehemiah reckoned as so essential for proper devotion to God.

When one realizes the historical factors which caused Ezra to devise the Old Testament canon, then it is possible to understand some definite reasons for the design of the Tripartite Divisions which Christ called *"the* Scriptures." The books were arranged in the various divisions to teach all facets of Old Testament life in a proper and harmonious fashion. The arrangement of books by Ezra made little sense to later Greeks or Romans who failed to understand what a true *Jewish* society was supposed to be. They failed to grasp such things. This is one of the main reasons that later Gentile Christians in Egypt could not begin to appreciate the Palestinian arrangement of the Old Testament books. It simply did not make sense to them. This is certainly the case because the codexing of the Greek Old Testament in the third or fourth century by Egyptian Christians re-arranged the books into a subjective or encyclopedic fashion so as to "improve" the Palestinian Jewish design which made no rhyme or reason to them. And in our modern Bible versions we have also abandoned the Palestinian order designed and canonized by Ezra and gone fully over to the Egyptian arrangement. No wonder that many of us (including me) have not understood some of the central and significant teachings which the overall design of the biblical books can give. It is important, however, that we moderns restore the Bible back to its original form — both the Old and the New Testaments. When this is done we will have some major *new* tools which can open up whole *new* avenues of investigation into what the Bible is all about. The information in this book is a mere introduction to the matter.

As a matter of fact, there is yet another theme running through the books of the Third Division which deserves to be studied. It can show why Ezra grouped these particular books into his final division.

More Information on the Writings' Division

There is an important factor connected with the interpretation of those 11 books which is not often realized. Everyone of the books was thought to possess mystical meanings. They had symbolic or allegorical themes. The poetic style of the Psalms, Proverbs, and Job (as a point in fact) was capable of double meanings and it was the "wise" who were considered able to interpret their subjects. One was not to take for granted that only one meaning was possible. In fact, sometimes the words could have opposite meanings. Notice this with the proverbs recorded in Proverbs 26:4 and 5.

> "Answer not a fool according to his folly, lest thou also be like unto him. [Now note the contrast.] Answer a fool according to his folly, lest he be wise in his own conceit."

The proverbs were not intended to be simple one line truisms that required no esoteric or spiritual interpretations. They were actually supposed to be lead-in's into a deeper secret or spiritual interpretation that those with *wisdom* would be able to apply correctly as each circumstance required.

The Psalms were to be understood in the same way. There was something far deeper in meaning than the surface teaching of a psalm (or a whole division of psalms). A prime reference that sums up this attitude of interpretation is found in Psalm 78:2. "I will open my mouth in a parable: I will utter dark sayings of old" (verse 2). The same principle is found in the introduction to the Book of Proverbs. Note: "To understand a parable (proverb), and the interpretation; the words of the wise men, and their dark sayings" (Prov.1:6). A major example of such "dark sayings" is found in the discourse on "Wisdom" (Prov.8:22 to 9:18). Clearly, this section is allegorical.

The Book of Job also was a "Wisdom" book. It concerned one of the wise men of the east (I Kings 4:30) and the story was a metaphorical explanation of how good will conquer evil — and how good finally triumphs with a *double* blessing extended to the righteous (Job 41:9-17).

The next 5 books of the Third Division were called the *Megilloth* (the Festival Scroll). They were the Song of Songs (read every year at Passover), Ruth (recited at Pentecost), Lamentations (sung on the 10th of Ab — the anniversary of the destruction of the Temple by the Babylonians), Ecclesiastes (recounted at Tabernacles), and Esther (at the Purim festival in the month before Passover). Each of these books was believed to possess a great deal of symbolic, spiritual teaching. Notice them.

It has long been noted that the Song of Songs was selected to be included in the Old Testament because of its *mystical* significance. It was supposed to be a love song of God's courtship of Israel in Egypt (since it was read at Passover) but, strangely, the name of God [or any of its derivatives] is not found once in the book. This, along with its sexual overtones, led the early rabbis to attach an allegorical type of teaching to it. Indeed, it was not thought proper in talmudic times for any man under 30 to read the book because of its "erotic" nature. The whole matter of its being in the canon was resolved, however, when one understood the meaning of the book in the figurative manner.

The account of Ruth had far more meaning than a simple historical record of King David's ancestry. It was read at the end of the barley and wheat harvest (at Pentecost) and Ruth's gleanings, etc. afforded many symbolic meanings.

The Book of Lamentations had deep spiritual significance to it. The whole book is about Jerusalem being a symbolic woman — in this case, a widow with all her virgins and young sons gone into captivity. This was read on the anniversary of the destruction of the Temple by the Babylonians, and it became typical of a prophesied destruction which would occur to a future Jerusalem. Remarkably, the Temple of Herod (in which Christ and the apostles taught) was also destroyed on the 10th of Ab — the exact anniversary date of its former destruction.

The Book of Ecclesiastes was also a "Wisdom Book." It was the writing which gave the mystical clue to the cyclical nature of prophecy (to be discussed in the ninth chapter) (Eccl.1:5-9; 3:15).

The Book of Esther is a story about the complete redemption of the Jewish people from the genocide planned upon them in the fifth century B.C. This was represented as typical of a future genocide (Zech.13:7-9) and a consequent national salvation which will occur in its wake. The real story behind the Book of Esther can be understood if "wise men which know the times" (Esth.1:13) are consulted. The proper "wise men" are not those of the Persian king, but those who are the authorities of God (Dan.12:10). Esther is like the story of Job, but this time the whole nation of Judah is involved in a spiritual salvation from all their enemies.

The allegorical characteristics of the Book of Esther can be seen in the fact that the name of God, or its derivatives (as the Song of Songs), is not found in the Book of Esther — except in a hidden and mystical way. It has been pointed out that God's name may be acrostically found (*Companion Bible*, Appendix on Esther).

The next book in the Third Division (the one positioned after the

Megilloth is the most mysterious book in the Old Testament (if not the whole Bible): the Book of Daniel. It is the book *par excellence* that requires great wisdom to understand. Ezekiel called Daniel a great "wise man" and that none was like him in that time (Ezek.28:3).

This book was not intended for public use in synagogue readings. It was a book with allegorical and symbolic meanings attached to its contents. Only kings had been given the mysterious visions and dreams, and only archangels and Daniel the Prince of Judah were allowed to interpret them. Daniel himself was also given visions and the right to understand the enigmatic "Scripture of Truth" (Dan.10: 21) which has been the most talked about and most puzzling of all prophecies within the Bible. Scholars are still arguing over the meaning of it. The reason for its obscurity is because (as Daniel was told himself) the main message of the "Scripture of Truth" will not be opened up until the end of the age (Dan.12:4). The fact that its meaning is of a "secret nature" is one of the reasons that Daniel's prophecies appear in the Third Division and not among the ordinary prophets. Everything about the Book of Daniel is symbolic and allegorical. Even to this day it has not been understood in a sufficient way.

There are other reasons why the Book of Daniel is positioned within the Third (Royal) Division and not in the Second (Prophets') Division. For one, his prophecies are utterly different from the other prophets. They never start with the usual "Thus saith the Lord." He also had the unusual responsibility of prophesying almost exclusively of Gentile nations and their fortunes until the Messianic kingdom of God would arrive. He hardly touched on Israel except when they came in contact with the main Gentile kingdoms. The other prophets did the reverse — they mentioned Gentile nations as they came within the history of Israel. This is an extraordinary difference. It seems that Daniel was the "Gentile" or "international" spokesman of God — a spokesman for the whole world. He was chiefly responsible for interpreting dreams and visions given to Gentile rulers, and even his own visions were more about specific actions of the Gentiles than about Israel or Israelites. Futhermore, much of Daniel (chapters 2 to 7) was written in the "international" Babylonian tongue — not in the sacred Hebrew language. Observe also that all his prophecies were revealed while he was resident in the captial cities of the Gentiles, either Babylon or Susa (and none of his prophecies was given in the land of Israel).

The Book of Daniel was placed near the end of the biblical canon. There was a reason for this. He gave a major chronological prophecy that began with the going forth of a command to rebuild Jerusalem (Dan.9:24-27). Daniel was immediately followed in the canon by Ezra/Nehemiah which gave the benchmark for that command (Ezra 1:1-3). The Book of Chronicles came last of all in order to present an authoritative history of Judah, the priesthood, the Temple, and Jerusalem showing the specific place for one to watch in order to witness the fulfillment of Daniel's prophecies at the end-time. The last words of the Old Testament, in the original canonical order, are: "let us go up [TO JERUSALEM]." The canonical emphasis is to watch Jerusalem. This is where Daniel's final kingdom will be set up.

As a matter of interest, the last editorial remarks that Ezra added to the Law of Moses was about a prophet like Moses to arise. In his concluding words he made it clear that the prophets before his time were NOT the "Mosaic" prophet (Deut.34:10-12). Thus, the final words of the Law have its readers looking to the future for that particular Prophet (whom Christians saw as Christ Jesus). Also, the last words of the Prophets' Division revealed a prophecy about a future "Elijah" who was to come to Israel to introduce the Day of the Lord (Mal.4:4-6). Later Christians referred this fulfillment to John the Baptist who preceded Jesus Christ. And by the way, the word "Malachi" meant "My Messenger," and it was thought at an early date that this was simply a title for Ezra the priest — the one who formulated the Holy Scripture. And, as shown before, the final words of the Third Division of the Old Testament informs a person "to go up to Jerusalem" to learn of future historical and prophetical events. This is where Daniel's prophecies were to be fulfilled.

We thus find that the 11 books of the Third Division concern government matters, but they also have a considerable amount of esoteric and technical material concerning Jerusalem, the Temple, the priesthood, and the government headed by the House of David. These were not read in the regular readings of the synagogue services under normal circumstances. Certainly, all of the separate books of the Third Division were well known, but there was not the feeling that substantial teachings (certainly in matters of law) could come from books within the Third Division. That is the reason they were not referred to very much by Jewish authorities. Indeed, some people have wondered if some of the books (e.g. Song of Songs and Esther, not having God's name in them) should even be reckoned among the biblical books. They should, of course. When it is recognized that the 11 books of the Third Division were writings intended primarily for priests, kings, and other rulers within a Temple (not synagogue) background — and having a great deal of allegorical meaning within them — it can be seen why their public reading was not thought as important as the Law and the Prophets' Divisions. The books, however, have an overall significance. They contain an abundance of information concerning the proper geographical location for the administration of divine government on this earth, and they identify the people whom God has placed in charge of that government.

When all is said and done, the positioning of all the 22 Old Testament books into the official Tripartite Divisions is an essential factor in teaching the true scope of the Law, the prophecies for the future, and all aspects of divine government as they relate to Israel and the nations of the world.

7

The Old Testament Periods of Canonization

There were five periods in the history of Israel in which the canonization of sacred scriptures took place. The final collection was established in the time of Ezra and Nehemiah and, of course, this latter one must be reckoned the most important of all. But when one surveys the biblical evidence for the other periods, a great deal of instruction in overall biblical teaching can be the result.

In this chapter we want to give the *biblical* evidence for these times of canonization. There are some plain statements within the Bible which mention these periods but they are often not considered important by some scholars today. Since our emphasis in this book, however, is to focus on what the Bible says about itself, we believe it is essential to mention these periods which the Bible takes a considerable amount of space to relate.

The First Canonization

It was universally believed, until modern times, that the five books of the Law were written by Moses. The internal indications certainly claim Moses as the author, and there are many New Testament assurances of this fact. Simple reference to these five books (called the Pentateuch) shows them to be compositions written within the 40 years of the Exodus period. It appears that Genesis, Exodus and Leviticus were composed the first year. There can be little doubt that Moses had access to scrolls about historical events. Some of the genealogical portions even had titles, e.g. "The Generations" (Gen.2: 4; 5:1; 10:1, etc.).

The Book of Numbers was the journal of Israel's trek through the wilderness. The last entry (chapter 36) was written by Moses at the conclusion of those forty years, along with Deuteronomy which was produced within the last 60 days. (Compare Deut.1:3 with Deut.34.) Deuteronomy was formulated for a special reason: it was intended to teach Israel further laws and statutes they would need to know when they settled in the Promised Land. Almost all the laws in Deuteronomy pertain to an agricultural economy, not one within a desert or wilderness environment. As evidence of this, notice the types of animals recorded in Deuteronomy 14. In comparing them with Leviticus 11, there are — in some instances — different animals mentioned. In Leviticus, the animals were generally those native to the wilderness, or animals which Israel encountered south and east of Palestine, while in Deuteronomy the creatures were located in more habitable and civilized areas of the Fertile Crescent.

These variations do not show evidences of different authorship. The Book of Deuteronomy was a re-phrasing or re-application of the basic laws given in the wilderness which made them more appropriate for a settled land economy.

Moses Canonized the Law

Shortly before he died, Moses authorized the first five books of our Bible to be the divine Law of Israel. He then delivered them into the custody of the priesthood for safe-keeping. Moses ordained the Levitical priesthood to be the official guardians of the Law.

> "And Moses wrote this law, and delivered it unto the priests, the sons of Levi, which bare the ark of the covenant of the Lord, and unto all the elders of Israel" (Deut.31:9).

The Ark of the Covenant was a wooden chest enclosing the tables of stone, the rod that budded, plus the pot of manna (Heb.9:4). It constituted the central part of Israel's physical worship and was located in the Holy of Holies of the Temple. The scrolls of the Law were stored in specially designated sleeve compartments attached to the sides of the Ark (Deut.31:26). By this provision, the High Priest could consult the standard copies left by Moses. These original scrolls were seldom used, consequently, they did not become ragged and torn as those read regularly in assembly. All scrolls for public reading, however, were required to be faithful copies of the standard ones kept in the side of the Ark.

In later times, when Israel had kings, each king was supposed to write out with his own hand personal copies of the original "Ark Scrolls" as a surety that he would understand all the separate laws written therein.

> "And it shall be, when he sitteth upon the throne of his kingdom,
> that he shall write him a copy of this law in a book out of that
> which is before the priests the Levites" (Deut.17:18).

Eventually many copies of the basic Law were made. This was perfectly proper as long as the Temple priests supervised or performed the copying. Of course, over the centuries, even the standard "Ark" copies themselves had to be replaced. But it was not uncommon for reference scrolls made of animal skins to last in good condition for 500 years or more. The less often the scrolls had to be used, the fewer times they needed replacing. The standard "Ark Scrolls" were used so infrequently that the recopying of them was rare.

In New Testament times, these standard scrolls were even referred to as the "Temple Scriptures." Paul may have been referring to them in II Timothy 3:15. The word "holy" often means "temple," and Newberry translated it as such in his version of II Timothy 3:15. He believed that Paul was referring to the official scriptures which had been deposited in the Temple by Ezra when he completed the Old Testament revelation. All scrolls found in official synagogues throughout the world in the first century were in agreement with these standard "Temple Scriptures." Newberry's suggestion may well have been right.

The first period for canonization of sacred scriptures was in the time of Moses. It would be almost 500 years later before another canonization took place. We will come to see that there is a remarkable similarity to all the periods when the various canonizations of the biblical writings occurred. Thankfully, the men of the New Testament had the example of Ezra as a guide to canonization.

The Canonization Periods

The Book of Chronicles is the Old Testament book giving us information of the canonizations prior to the final one by Ezra. Indeed, this is one of the primary reasons for its composition. There were three historical periods discussed at length by Ezra: the times of David and Solomon; the times of King Hezekiah; and the times of King Josiah. We shall see that these very time periods were those when extra literature was added to the Law of Moses for Temple use.

We are left in no doubt as to Ezra's reasons for writing the important Book of Chronicles. Not only was he recording the three periods after Moses when canonizations occurred, but he also concentrated on matters relative to true worship and the fixing of proper rituals to be observed in the Temple. Chronicles gives us a full genealogical listing of the priests, Levites, and the House of David, showing how Jerusalem was to be reckoned the center of all true worship. The whole emphasis in the Book of Chronicles (which makes it so different from the parallel Book of Kingdoms) is upon Jerusalem as the center of God's divine government on earth. It shows how the true authorities (the proper priests and secular rulers) were associated with the Temple at Jerusalem — and not in any other area of the world. It was at Jerusalem that the standard of all religious teaching was to be located.

This is why Chronicles gives a great amount of detail to the history of the Ark (I Chron.13-16), the preparations for building the Temple, and the assignments of the priests and Levites in the Temple. And as said before, Chronicles also shows *when* and especially *where* the canonizations of the Old Testament were accomplished. The making of the Jewish scriptures was at Jerusalem, and at times when it was necessary to revitalize Temple services. This was also the case with the final canonization. Ezra resided at Jerusalem and Temple services were once again being authorized. By writing Chronicles, he was demonstrating that Jerusalem was always the place to which Jews needed to look as the source of all truth.

David's Canonization

The next period for canonization after the time of Moses was that of

David. The Israelites had been in possession of Mosaic teachings some 400 years. Throughout this period, they had used the portable Tabernacle as the central place of worship. But in the time of David, the religious system was becoming inadequate for accommodating great masses of people. The Tabernacle had now become ineffectual in handling the religious requirements of all the Israelites.

The time had come to establish a permanent building in which a more appropriate worship and regulated services could be made. With this in mind, David planned a Temple to be erected as an honor to God as a non-portable sanctuary for Israel.

The building of the Temple entailed other elaborate arrangements in regard to the services which would be performed within its precincts. For one thing, priests were no longer a handful in number as they were when Aaron was High Priest. Their number was now so great that they could not possibly perform the Temple rituals at once. David thought it was time to reevaluate the duties of the priesthood.

Under directions from Samuel (I Chron.9:22) David subdivided the enlarged priestly family into 24 divisions or courses (I Chron.24). Instead of the priests performing their Temple services at random, each priestly course was assigned specified times to do their ministrations. Each course was responsible for appointing one of its leading priests as chief priest, and to authorize him to select certain members of that course to serve with him at the Temple. Only those particular priests became responsible for offering the evening and morning sacrifices at the designated times.

The service of each priestly course lasted for one week — from Sabbath noon to Sabbath noon. Thus, each of the 24 courses served one week within a six month period. They repeated the procedure for the second half of the year. Over the period of a year, each course served in the Temple for two weeks (each week separated by a six month span), and all 24 courses served together at the three annual festival periods (Passover, Pentecost, and Tabernacles).

David's organization did not stop with the priests. The Levites and singers in the Temple were divided into 24 courses as well (I Chron.25).

This meant that, for all practical purposes, a new religious system had come to Israel. Instead of a temporary dwelling for God, there was to be a permanent structure. Along with this magnificent and rich building, there were to be regular successions of authorized personnel performing needed rituals in the Temple. All these things required definite liturgies to be ordained and followed. David, under the direction of Samuel, set about arranging all these matters into a proper order before the Temple was constructed by Solomon. We will now see that David's work necessarily involved canonization.

Temple Services Required Liturgies

The Levitical singers were authorized to sing appropriate songs in the Temple. These various singers had been divided into 24 courses (I Chron.25). The times for their singing, and what they were ordained to sing, were arranged by David with the help of Gad, the king's seer, and Nathan the prophet (II Chron.29:25).

David, as is well-known, was the most famous psalmist in the Old Testament. People customarily refer to the Book of Psalms as being of David's authorship. While this is not quite accurate — for some psalms were written by others — David certainly composed the great majority of the ones found within the Old Testament canon. A notable section of psalms entirely from the hand of David is that from Psalm 1 to 72 in our present Book of Psalms. At the end of Psalm 72 there is a subscription to all of those 72 psalms. It informs us: "The prayers of David the son of Jesse are ended." This does not mean that no more of David's psalms were to be found in later portions of the Book of Psalms. The subscription simply means that the preceding Psalms represented a set of 72 Davidic songs which were to be sung in some kind of succession by the 24 priestly courses. (Note that 72 is 3 x 24 and this number must have carried some relationship to the priestly courses.) Notice also that some of these Davidic psalms are titled "Korah's" (e.g. Psalms 44-49), to Asaph (Psalm 50), and for Solomon (Psalm 72). These psalms were written by David in honor of, or for, Korah and Asaph who were the Levites responsible for using these assigned psalms in the regular Temple services.

Indeed, David wrote many psalms for various Levitical singing groups. An example is found in I Chronicles 16:7. He composed a psalm in commemoration of a special occasion. Of this, Ezra says in Chronicles: "On that day David delivered first this psalm to thank the Lord into the hand of Asaph and his brethren." It was a psalm for Asaph but written by David.

Many of the titles of the psalms indicate to whom the psalm was to be delivered, or they signified the Levitical families responsible for singing those particular psalms in the Temple services.

Thus, the first section of 72 psalms which are found in our present Book of Psalms (Psalms 1 to 72) was probably the original collection ordained at the time of David. Later on, in the days of Ezra, the totality of the Law of Moses began to be read in synagogue services in weekly portions (about 20 verses each week). This allowed the complete five books of Moses to be recited, and commented on, over a three year period. These were known as Triennial Cycle readings because they took three years to complete. To correspond to this, another set of 72 psalms was no doubt added by Ezra to the first group, making 144 — enough for singing one psalm each Sabbath in the Temples services over a three-year period. Six other psalms were added to the final collection, making 150 in all, probably to account for the extra month in the calendar which occurred about every third year (Joseph Jacobs, "Triennial Cycle," *Jewish Encyclopedia,* Vol. XII, pp.255,256).

The point to remember is that David was probably the first to appoint the initial 72 psalms of our present Book of Psalms to be sung by the Levites at the Temple services. The official singing of these psalms involved canonization, because they had become part of the sacred services. To Ezra, singing Temple songs in regular succession clearly entailed their official canonization. [For more information on the design and purpose of the Book of Psalms, see a further study in Appendix I.]

Other Works Canonized During This Period

With a permanent religious society established in Israel by Solomon's time, there was need for additional literary works to direct the people in their religious duties. The Bible says that Solomon searched the books of the wise men of old to find what their teachings were. Solomon "was wise, he still taught the people knowledge; yea, he gave good heed, and sought out, and set in order many proverbs" (Eccl.12:9).

This tells us that Solomon did not originate all the proverbs for which he became famous. Certain ones now found in the Bible were composed by several wise men preceding him. In some cases, Solomon merely catalogued the wisdom from the pens of ancient wise men. He openly stated that he collected many proverbial sayings so that people might "understand a proverb, and the interpretation; the words of the *wise ones* [the Hebrew is plural], and *their* dark sayings" (Prov.1:6).

In a superscription to one group of proverbs (Prov.22:17 to 24:22), Solomon advised: "Bow down thine ear, and hear the words of the *wise ones.*" Another batch of proverbs was also "set in order" by Solomon or his editors and given the title: "These things also belong to the *wise ones*" (Prov.24:23).

Admittedly Solomon wrote many proverbs of his own, especially those from Proverbs 10 to Proverbs 22:16. But lots of others came from older sources that he had sought out and put in order. It could be possible that the section from Proverbs 1:6 to the end of chapter 9 might have been written by the patriarch Joseph. [See Appendix II for more information concerning the Book of Proverbs.]

It should be understood that at the time of Solomon, there must have been scores of books circulating in Israel — written not only by Solomon but by other important men. Some of those other works may have been used temporarily for divine services in that period. On the other hand, some books of our Old Testament may not have received their canonical status until Ezra selected them to be among the scriptural works. We are speaking of books such as Ruth, the Song of Songs and Ecclesiastes. The fact is, it was finally up to Ezra and the Great Assembly of priests to establish which books would enter the Old Testament canon. Though there was a type of canonization when the Temple was inaugurated, the real canon came from Ezra.

The Canonization by King Hezekiah

Circumstances surrounding the canonizations in the time of Moses, and of David and Solomon were entirely different from the three periods to follow — those in the times of Hezekiah, Josiah, and Ezra. In the first instance, Moses had plenty of "leisure time" to authorize the first five books as divine literature and to present them as the basic Law to Israel. Near the end of his life, Moses simply put finishing touches to the Law and delivered it for safekeeping to the official priesthood. He told the Israelites which books were divine and then charged them to obey them. No one argued with him about the matter.

In the reigns of David and Solomon, the only reason for adding certain literature to the already existing books of the Law was the establishment of the permanent Temple, with its elaborate services, and the expanded type of religious society that accompanied it.

There were no national emergencies facing either Moses or David and Solomon, and the establishment of the Tabernacle and later Temple services were accomplished in times of leisure. But all the other canonizations were produced under entirely different circumstances. When Hezekiah ruled, for example, canonization was forced upon the authorities because a time of great stress was besetting the nation.

At the beginning of Hezekiah's reign the national existence of Judah was in jeopardy of being destroyed. Assyrian invasion and captivity were threatening utter ruin to the nation and to Mosaic religion. This emergency prompted Hezekiah and Isaiah to move swiftly in placing their seal of authority upon certain sacred books that were then found in Israel. They sought to preserve all Temple books because it appeared as though the Temple services and all physical components of Judah's religion might soon be extinguished. They later came to realize that their fears were unfounded, but we can be assured that their expectations produced a further set of authorized books for use by the Temple authorities.

The Historical Background

Let us consider the historical period from Solomon to Hezekiah. After the time of Solomon, the religious purity of the Temple services gradually deteriorated. Such corruption ultimately became so widespread that idols and images of foreign gods began to be set up all over Judah (II Chron.31:1). The 24 specific divisions of the priests, Levites, singers and others, established by David for the purpose of organized Temple services, fell into confusion and practically passed out of existence. Things got so bad by the time of Ahaz, the father of Hezekiah, that many Jews, particularly Ahaz himself, thoroughly abandoned their religious duties to the God of their fathers.

Ahaz, we are told, actually stripped the Temple of its decorations, giving them to the Assyrian king as a present (II Chron.28:21-24). The Temple furniture was destroyed — Ahaz "cut them in pieces" then he "shut up the doors of the house of the Lord" (v.24) and instituted Syrian paganism as the official religion of Judah. He "made him altars in every corner of Jerusalem, and in every several city of Judah he made high places to burn incense unto other gods, and provoked to anger the Lord God of his fathers" (vs.24,25). For all practical purposes Judah had reverted to a heathen state.

It was in this heathenized society that Hezekiah acceded to the throne. Right from the beginning of his reign, he made a concerted effort to reform Judaic society. He desired to purify and rebuild the ruined Temple and to re-establish the Temple services with the priests and singers performing their prescribed duties.

> "He in the first year of his reign, in the first month, opened the doors of the house of the Lord, and repaired them. [They had been defaced and nailed up. Also the Temple had to be cleansed of accumulated filth after its sixteen years of disuse.] And he brought in the priests and the Levites" (II Chron.29:3,4).
>
> "Hezekiah appointed the courses of the priests and the Levites after their courses, every man according to his services, the priests and the Levites for burnt offerings and for peace offerings, to minister, and to give thanks, and to praise in the gates of the tents of the Lord" (II Chron.31:2).
>
> "He set the Levites in the house of the Lord with cymbals, with psaltries, and with harps, according to the commandment of David, and of Gad the king's seer, and Nathan the prophet: for so was the commandment of the Lord by his prophets" (II Chron.29:35).
>
> "Moreover Hezekiah the king and the princes commanded the Levites to sing praise unto the Lord with the words of David, and of Asaph the seer. And they sang praises with gladness" (II Chron.29:30).

Hezekiah even exceeded David in assigning certain psalms to be sung in regular Temple services. He included not only the performing of David's psalms (i.e. the first 72 psalms), but also certain ones assigned to Asaph. These specific psalms were the 11 which followed immediately after David's first 72.

Because of Hezekiah's actions in re-vitalizing proper Temple worship, he was classified as a righteous king who followed in the footsteps of his father David. In some ways he was reckoned to be better than David ("that after him was none like him among all the kings of Judah, nor any that were before him" — II Kings 18:5).

Doubtless, when Hezekiah first commenced to reign he followed the admonitions of Moses (Deut.17:18), and copied with his hand a personal copy of the Law. Taking office at the age of 25, and supported by the prophet Isaiah, he continued to do his utmost to reform the people and to restructure the religion of the nation.

> "[Hezekiah] wrought that which was good and right and truth before the Lord his God. And in every work that he began in the service of the house of God, he did it with all his heart, and prospered" (II Chron.31:21).

Re-establishing True Worship Involved Canonization

Hezekiah and Isaiah saw the need to assign more authoritative literature to Israel's divine library. Proverbs 25 reveals some of the canonical activity of Hezekiah and his helpers. A new section of the Book of Proverbs begins with these words: "These are also the proverbs of Solomon, which the men of Hezekiah king of Judah copied out" (Prov.25:1).

Of the 3000 known proverbs composed by Solomon (I Kings 4:32), Hezekiah ordained that a new group of them be selected for his own use. Thus, chapters 25 to 29 were added to the Temple collection which had already been "set in order" by Solomon himself. The source from which the men of Hezekiah obtained these Solomonic proverbs was probably the "Book of Acts of Solomon," a non-canonical work which contained "the rest of the acts [words] of Solomon, and all he did, and his wisdom" (I Kings 11:41).

Significantly, most of the proverbs selected by Hezekiah's men were designed to help a king or a ruler guide his people towards righteous ends. Take, for example, the theme of the first proverb in the new series: "It is the glory of God to conceal a thing, but the honor of *kings* is to search out a matter." This proverb no doubt reveals Hezekiah's own character — what was foremost in his mind in his service to God. Notice, too, that in the next proverb in Hezekiah's selection, the subject is again "kings." Two following ones are also about a "king," another about a "prince," and so on.

These five chapters of proverbs, copied by Hezekiah's men, clearly represented an addition to the canonical literature. In fact, the early Jews maintained that the "Men of Hezekiah" were a group of authorized men just like the "Great Assembly" of priests convened by Ezra and Nehemiah for the exact purpose of canonization (Louis Ginzberg, *The Legends of the Jews*, vol.VI, p.368). In addition to some of the proverbs, the Talmud says that Isaiah, some of the Minor Prophets, Song of Songs and Ecclesiastes were canonized by the "Men of Hezekiah" (*Baba Bathra*, 15a).

Hezekiah's Sign-Manual

Hezekiah brought up-to-date the canonical literature for use in the restored Temple services. One of the most striking evidences of Hezekiah's own activity in this canonization is a sign-manual found in the Bible which is attributed to him. This sign-manual is a combination of three Hebrew letters which occur at the end of every Old Testament book — except the five books of the *Megilloth*. Curiously, the sign-manual (which is in the Hebrew manuscripts of the Old Testament) has not been translated in any of the English versions.

The sign-manual consisted of three Hebrew letters which were brought together to form the basic root name of Hezekiah. The letters are: *het, zain* and *koph*, and they spell the name Hezekiah without the terminal *yah*.

This tri-grammaton, located at the end of 17 Old Testament books, served a dual purpose. Not only did it indicate the person of Hezekiah, but its meaning in translation is most interesting and instructive. Brown, Driver & Briggs' *Hebrew Lexicon* shows it means "to bind firmly together," "to be made firm," "to be confirmed," or "to be bound fast" (pp.304,395). In simple terms, *HZK* denoted "bound" or "confirmed." This represented the sign-manual of

Hezekiah and it could well have been his imprimatur. It signified that any book terminated by it was *bound* by the authority of Hezekiah — or the Men of Hezekiah.

This sign-manual occurs on every Old Testament book, with the exception of the five Festival Scrolls — called in Hebrew the *Megilloth*. These five are: Song of Songs, Ruth, Lamentations, Ecclesiastes and Esther. It is interesting that these five books have been the ones that a number of Old Testament critics, even from ancient times, have tried to eliminate from the biblical canon. Remarkably, these are the very books without the sign-manual.

Take, for example, the Song of Songs. Some over-zealous religious leaders have tried to diminish its authority. It has been described as "too erotic" and "lustful." Even the name of God, or its derivatives, is not found once in its text.

Consider also Ecclesiastes. Many have found fault with the pessimistic nature of this book and its "worldly" approach to theological matters. It even teaches there is no immortality of the soul.

Then there is Esther. The name of God is not found in the book and the only indication of any religious activity is the single mention of fasting. The book appears almost as if it were a secular composition.

And there is Ruth and Lamentations. These books have been considered mere appendages to important books of the canon. They are usually, in modern English versions, taken out of the *Megilloth* arrangement and attached to Judges and Jeremiah, with little attention given to them.

These five books of the *Megilloth* are the only ones in the Old Testament which lack the imprimatur or sign-manual of Hezekiah. But do they belong in the canon of the Old Testament? They assuredly do. Ezra positioned them in one special section among the Temple liturgy. Each book was to be successively read and expounded to the people at the annual holy days.

Since the official priests were ordered to read these books to the people each year, no one suspected that they were anything but canonical. Indeed, most criticism concerning the canonicity of these five books came after the Temple services ceased in 70 A.D. when the books no longer were being read at regular intervals. Yet they formed a part of the original 22 books of the Old Testament. The importance of reading these five *Megilloth* books in order is discussed in Appendix I.

The Sign-Manual Appears on Books
After the Time of Hezekiah

Following the canonization affected by Hezekiah, the sign-manual seems to be a seal for the reading of divine writings outside the regular Temple services. When later writers, such as Jeremiah and Ezekiel, had their prophecies placed among the sacred writings of the Old Testament, this same sign-manual was also affixed to the end of their books. And Ezra, at the final canonization, carefully placed the sign-manual on all books which he and the Great Assembly recognized, omitting it only from the five Festival Scrolls (which were being regularly read by the priests in the Temple).

What is interesting is the fact that at the end of certain books, the sign-manual is positioned inside an extended comment and the tri-grammaton became part of the comment. Dr. E.W. Bullinger mentions the practice of using the sign-manual after the time of Hezekiah:

> "The use of this tri-grammaton is uniform and continuous at the end of each book, until we come to the death of Hezekiah. Not until after that, at the end of the Book of Kings, do we meet with any departure from the addition of these three letters. There, for the first time, we find a different formula. Instead of the simple sign (HZK), we find two words, making a sentence — instead of forming the initials.
>
> "At the end of Kings, we have 'Be bound, and we will bind.'
>
> "This looks as though the subsequent editors, whether Josiah, Ezra, or others, understood the tri-grammaton as a solemn injunction transmitted to them; and they took up the work and carried it out in the same spirit in which it had come down to them, and said, 'Be bound,' and they responded. 'We will bind.' The same form [of two words] is used after Ezekiel, at the end of the Minor Prophets, the Psalms, Proverbs and Job.
>
> "We do not find it after the Song of Solomon, Ruth, Lamentations, Ecclesiastes, or Esther.
>
> "We meet with it again after Daniel, and after Ezra-Nehemiah

[always as one book] (Bullinger, "The Songs of Degrees," *Things to Come*, XIII (1907), p.112).

Interestingly, after the Book of Chronicles — the last book of the Hebrew Old Testament — we encounter the final, and longer, form of the sign-manual. Being translated, it reads: "Be bound. So we will bind. The Lawgiver is not straitened (or powerless)."

This comment is most instructive. Here Ezra and the Great Assembly probably added the final sign-manual to Chronicles, the last book of the Old Testament. In their comment, they not only wrote, "Be bound," which was the customary usage, but they added for extra emphasis: "We will bind." This showed that the Great Lawgiver [God] had given the whole and complete Old Testament revelation to the world. Thus Ezra and the Great Assembly of priests, having concluded the writing of the Book of Chronicles, finalized their responsibility of canonizing the Old Testament for all future time. Only a few editorial remarks were added later.

Other Works Canonized by Hezekiah

We are informed in the Book of Isaiah that Hezekiah actually wrote new psalms which were included in the singing services of the Temple. There psalms were written at the time when he recovered from his sickness — when the prophet Isaiah "took a lump of figs, and laid it for a plaister upon the boil" (Isa.38:21).

Because Hezekiah placed his complete trust in God to deliver him from his severe sickness, the Bible says he was granted another 15 years of life. In commemoration of this deliverance, he composed a particular set of psalms. Notice Isaiah 38:9. This begins a song which occupies the next 12 verses. It says: "The writing of Hezekiah king of Judah, when he had been sick, and was recovered of his sickness."

After this superscription begins the regular song — a beautiful psalm of thanksgiving to God for his protection and deliverance. And at the very end, Hezekiah finally records:

"The Lord was ready to save me: therefore [i.e. because of God's salvation] we will sing my songs [plural] to the stringed instruments all the days of our life [Hebrew: lives] in the house of the Lord" (Isa.38:20).

Note several factors concerning the writing of these psalms by Hezekiah. He said he composed several "songs," not only the one song recorded in Isaiah. He directed that "we" sing his new "songs" all the days of "our lives." This indicates that the nation of Judah —in the persons of the official Temple singers — would carry on the singing of these psalms of Hezekiah in future times. And importantly, notice that Hezekiah left directions that all the singing of his songs should be done on "stringed instruments in the house of the Lord." This indicates that the special psalms of Hezekiah were to be sung in an official capacity in the regular Temple services. They were to take their place alongside the psalms of David, Asaph, and the other psalmists of Israel.

The reason Hezekiah wrote these particular psalms is given in verses 19 and 20:

> "The living, he shall praise Thee, as I [Hezekiah] do this day: the father to the children shall make known thy truth... therefore, we will sing my songs to the stringed instruments all the days of our lives in the house of the Lord" (Isa.38:19,20).

Hezekiah wrote psalms so that fathers could tell their children, from generation to generation, of the glorious salvation of God — if only God's people would trust him. Hezekiah intended his psalms to be of permanent value to the people of God. This is why he had them canonized, making them a part of the regular Temple services.

Which Psalms Were Hezekiah's?

A good number of untitled psalms are found within our present Book of Psalms. Any of these, if they would fit the context of Hezekiah's time might have been written by him. The Bible does not make it entirely clear which ones came from Hezekiah, but James W. Thirtle and others think they have discovered the true psalms of Hezekiah. These are the enigmatical 15 "Degree Psalms," which now comprise Psalms 120-134.

Biblical commentators have long speculated as to the authorship of these untitled "Degree Psalms." Why are they called psalms of "Degrees," and when were they used in the Temple services? These questions may be answered in the solution offered by Thirtle.

> "The Songs of the Degrees are 15 in number. They correspond in number with the 15 years added to Hezekiah's life. Ten are by Hezekiah (corresponding to the number of "the Degrees" by which the shadow of the sun went backward on the sun-dial of Ahaz, II Kings 20:8-11). Five are by others (four by David and one by Solomon)" (Thirtle, *The Titles of the Psalms*, p.827).

Some commentators maintain that these psalms were sung on the 15 steps (assumed by combining Ezekiel 40:22 with 40:31) leading up to the Holy Place of the Temple: the first degree psalm as the priest stood on the first step; the second psalm on the second step, and so forth. Thus the fifteenth psalm would have placed the priest at the threshold of the Holy Place. This may well be true.

Jewish scholars believe the degree psalms were read in the autumn near the Festival of Tabernacles, some suggesting that their reading started on the first of the seventh month (the Day of Trumpets) and continued for 14 more days until the 15th of Tishri (i.e. the first day of Tabernacles) was reached. Thus, the readings would have symbolically directed Israelites towards the opening of the Millennial Age (that the Feast of Tabernacles depicted) when all on earth would prepare to approach the "Holy Place," as did the priests in the Temple services.

The Bible, however, nowhere clearly gives confirmation of these suggestions. It does show, however, that Hezekiah wrote psalms which found a place in the regular Temple services. This indicates they probably became a part of the Bible. And of all the psalms in our present biblical collection, the 15 degree psalms seem the most likely to be the ones composed by Hezekiah.

Isaiah Helped in Canonization

Before concluding our discussion on the canonization in Hezekiah's time, let us notice something about Isaiah. In the middle of the last century an Englishman, Ferrar Fenton, was translating the Bible into English. He gave an interesting observation concerning the role of Isaiah the prophet in matters involving the canonization of biblical books. Here is what he wrote:

> "In my study of the Historical Books of the Bible I had frequently
> wished for some clue to their writer, or writers.... One day whilst
> reading the Second Book of Chronicles in the Hebrew, I met that
> solution in its 32nd chapter and the 32nd verse, like a sudden
> flash of electric light, in the following words: 'The remainder of
> the actions of Hezekiah and his beneficent rule, are recorded in
> the Visions of Isaiah-ben-Amotz, the Prophet, upon the History
> of the Kings of Judah and Israel.'
>
> "The flood of mental light from those three lines dispelled my
> perplexities, and enabled me to see the great object of the six-
> sectioned History, by discovering its writer. Wondering that
> none had previously seen this . . . I took down the Authorized
> Version, and found that its translators had entirely, by inserting
> the little word 'and' after the name 'Isaiah the son of Amoz,'
> altered the structure and purport of the sentence as it stands in
> the original Hebrew, and thus destroyed the key it gave to the
> moral object and lessons of the historian, and to the identity of
> the writer of the Six Books [Joshua/Judges and the Book of
> Kingdoms]. A renewed study of those six books confirmed in my
> mind the accuracy of my conclusion by enabling me more clearly
> to see the unity of style and aim of their writer, Isaiah, which
> undoubtedly was for them to serve as an introduction to Isaiah's
> prophecies" (Fenton, *Translation of the Bible*, p.217).

Fenton may be right in his evaluation. However, to be exact, the
statement in II Chronicles 32:32 does not say the Book of Joshua/
Judges was among these writings of Isaiah. It merely says Isaiah
wrote "the history of the Kings of Judah and Israel." If this is a
reference to our canonical book, then it can mean that Isaiah wrote
the Book of Kingdoms (our present Samuel and Kings).

Another reason that Joshua/Judges should not be included among
Isaiah's writings is the reference given by the apostle Peter (Acts
3:24), which indicates that the Prophets' Division of the Old
Testament (the one that had as its composers "the prophets")
specifically commenced with the writings of Samuel. This indication
agrees with Jewish tradition which makes Joshua/Judges a work of
Samuel, not Isaiah. In I Samuel 9:9 we read: "He that is now called a
prophet was beforetime called a seer." Samuel was the first to be

called a prophet in an official capacity since the time of Moses. Thus, with Joshua/Judges located within the Prophets' Division (and at the very start of it), it is highly probable that Samuel was the book's author. Recall that it was he who first established the schools of the prophets throughout Israel — at Ramah, Bethel, Jericho, and Gilgal (I Sam.10:5, 10; 19:20; II Kings 2:3,5; 4:38). This means that there were no men called "prophets" before Samuel.

On the other hand, Isaiah could very well have been the author of the book which followed Joshua/Judges — i.e. the Book of Kingdoms, as Fenton suggests. [Recall that the Book of Kingdoms is now divided into our two books of Samuel and two books of Kings.] Several commentators, among them the early Old Testament scholar Moses Stuart feel that this reference to Isaiah (II Chron.32:32) certainly relates to the writing of our present Book of Kingdoms (Stuart, p.170). Observe also that in the Book of Chronicles Ezra speaks of the fact that Isaiah had written "the rest of the acts of Uzziah" (II Chron.26:22). The only place, apart from Chronicles, in which the events of Uzziah's life are recorded is in the Book of Kingdoms. This implies that Isaiah was the author of that book. Also note that II Kings 18-20 is identical with Isaiah 36-39, which again shows common authorship.

But what about the part of the Book of Kingdoms that records events after the time of Isaiah? This should give little problem. It was perfectly possible for later canonizers to bring the book up to date. The Talmud says that Jeremiah wrote the Book of Kings (*Baba Bathra*, 15a), but this could mean that Jeremiah was the one who finished the book. The composition of the main body of the work, however, seems to be Isaiah's.

Why was the Book of Kingdoms written by Isaiah? There was a good reason for it. As Fenton said, the historical books preceding Isaiah are a perfectly good introduction to Isaiah's prophecies. In the original order of the Old Testament, the Book of Kingdoms immediately precedes that of the prophet Isaiah. Would it not be natural for Isaiah to present a running history of Israel's obedience and their later rebellions and punishments before relating his prophecies of what would happen to them should they continue following in the footsteps of their forefathers?

If this solution by Ferrar Fenton is the true one, as seems most likely, the position of the Book of Isaiah following the Book of Kingdoms, as in the canonical order of the Old Testament, makes good sense and gives a reason for the writing of the Book of Kingdoms. This would help confirm Isaiah, along with Hezekiah, as one of the great canonizers of Scripture.

The Period of King Josiah

The time of King Josiah in the history of canonization is almost as significant as that of Hezekiah. The ominous conditions which prevailed with Hezekiah were again extant in Josiah's day. Only the actors had changed. Instead of the Assyrians threatening the existence of Judah, this time it was the Babylonians. And instead of Ahaz's evil, which blanketed Judaic society prior to the reign of Hezekiah, this time it was that of Manasseh and Amon. In some ways, the latter apostasy of Manasseh exceeded that of Ahaz. "So Manasseh made Judah and Jerusalem to err, and to do worse than the heathen, whom the Lord had destroyed before the children of Israel" (II Chron.33:9).

The re-introduction of Gentile paganism during the long reign of Manasseh was accomplished at the expense of Mosaic religion. The Temple services, carefully reinstituted by Hezekiah and Isaiah, again were neglected — and finally ceased altogether. Manasseh (like Ahaz before him) stripped the Temple of its furniture. Even blocks of masonry and ceiling rafters were removed and used in other buildings until the Temple structure itself became practically an empty hulk (II Chron.34:8-11).

The Book of Chronicles shows that the religious condition of Judah during Manasseh's reign was near the low point, but with the two-year rule of his son, Amon, the situation even worsened. "Amon trespassed more and more" (II Chron.33:21-23). However, he was finally murdered by his own servants (II Chron.33:24-25). At this point, Josiah, a mere child, was thrust onto the stage of history.

Josiah was one of the most remarkable men of the Old Testament. In his short life, the Bible states he maintained extraordinary character, even though his father and grandfather had been two of the most evil kings that the house of David ever produced. Despite the religious depravity of the environment into which he was born,

Josiah displayed a righteousness rivalling that of David and Hezekiah. In fact, the Bible says he even excelled those kings.

> "And like unto him [Josiah] was there no king before him, that turned to the Lord with all his heart, and with all his soul, and with all his might, according to all the Law of Moses; neither after him arose there any like him" (II Kings 23:25).

Long previously, in the reign of Rehoboam, a prophecy had been uttered about a certain Josiah who would destroy the heathen altars in the land of Israel (I Kings 13:1-3). That Josiah had now arrived.

The Re-Establishment of Temple Services

Josiah acceded to the throne at eight years of age. When he was 20 he began to "purge Judah and Jerusalem from the high places, and the groves, and the carved images, and the molten images" (II Chron.34: 3). Six years later, having cleansed the land of idolatry, he ordered that the Temple — which lay practically in ruins — be completely repaired and restored to its former splendor. He also ordained that all the priestly functions be reinstated. The whole religious environment in the land of Judah was renovated by Josiah. It seemed to be a renewal like that of Hezekiah.

Then, a significant event took place. While the Holy Place of the Temple was being repaired, Hilkiah, the High Priest — and the father of Jeremiah — came upon the neglected scroll of the Law (the standard copy placed in the sleeves of the Ark). Recognizing the importance of his find, Hilkiah had this archetype copy taken to King Josiah.

After thoroughly reading it for several days and noticing especially the curse-warnings within the Law, Josiah rent his clothes in repentance for himself and for the people of Judah. He discovered that even in his reformation he had not been accomplishing things in the precise manner required by the Law (II Chron.34:19). Endeavoring to do his best was not good enough for Josiah. He wanted to perform all the religious duties as prescribed by Moses.

In the Law which he had been reading were statements that if the people forsook God and his Law, then God would forsake them and send them into captivity. Josiah was terror-stricken when the impact of these warnings became clear to him. He saw immediately that time was running out for Judah. With the new-found Law in his midst, he pursued his reforming policies with even greater diligence. His zeal gained for him a promise from God that there would be *peace* in Judah for the remainder of his life.

> "Because thine heart was tender, and thou didst humble thyself before God, when thou heardest his words against this place, and against the inhabitants thereof, and humblest thyself before me, and didst rend thy clothes, and weep before me: I have even heard thee also, saith the Lord. Behold, I will gather thee to thy fathers, and thou shalt be gathered to thy grave in peace, neither shall thine eyes see all the evil that I will bring upon this place, and upon the inhabitants of the same (II Chron.34:27,28).

These words constituted a promise of peace and safety for Judah during the lifetime of Josiah. Those who shared Josiah's enthusiasm for reform received these promises with great joy. With Josiah being only 26 years old, they fully expected the curses of Deuteronomy 28 to be delayed at least 40 or 50 years.

Josiah Dies in Battle

Even though the rumblings of Babylonian armies were already being heard in the north, the people of Jerusalem felt those armies would not approach them as long as King Josiah lived. But, the promise depended on Josiah being prudent about his own safety.

A few years later, Josiah ventured north to confront the Egyptians and the Babylonians at the place which later became known as Armageddon. Within days, shock seized the Jews — they received news from a messenger that Josiah had sustained a severe wound from a chance arrow. But they were paralyzed with horror when the next messenger reported that Josiah had died — at the youthful age of 39. The prospect for two or three decades of God's protection, in which the God-fearing Jews had taken comfort, vanished overnight. Since Josiah was dead, nothing lay ahead for the Jews but certain drought, plague, invasion and captivity.

Protection for Judah Ceases

All hopes for the peace of Jerusalem appeared lost. The evils of Deuteronomy 28 were then expected to occur. Not only had an excellent king been taken from them, but his death meant the prophesied captivity upon the Jewish nation could then occur. Thus, "all Judah and Jerusalem mourned for Josiah" (II Chron.35:24).

It is no coincidence that from this time forward Jeremiah began his series of prophecies about the imminent captivity of Judah. Even at the critical moment of Josiah's death, Jeremiah composed an important work about the significance of that event.

> "And Jeremiah lamented for Josiah: and all the singing men and the singing women spake of Josiah in their lamentations to this day, and made them an ordinance in Israel: and, behold [said the author of Chronicles], they are written in the lamentations" (II Chron.35:25).

This is a remarkable reference to the writing of an Old Testament book: the Book of Lamentations. It was a prohetical song, to be sung in the minor or mournful key. The composition was written to commemorate the slaying of Josiah, and it carried with it a prophecy of the destruction to come. Jeremiah even referred to the death of Josiah in the Book of Lamentations. "The breath of our nostrils, *the anointed of the Lord [Josiah]*, was taken in their pits, of whom we said, under his shadow we shall live among the heathen" (Lam.4:20).

Jewish history since the time of Ezra mentions that this Book of Lamentations was commissioned to be sung in the Temple as an "ordinance" (Josephus, *Antiq.*X.78; cf.*Baba Bathra* 15a). It was ordained that Lamentations was to be sung each year on the 10th day of the month Ab — the anniversary of the burning of the Temple by Nebuchadnezzar. Even now, Jews read this composition of Jeremiah annually in commemoration of that destruction.

There is also another writing of Jeremiah which was written in mindfulness of Josiah's death. This was Psalm 89. The latter part of the psalm speaks about a great calamity that had occurred to Judah. An anointed person had been cast off (Psa.89:38). His crown had been destroyed (vs.39,44) and the covenant of protection given to David and his descendants seemed to be broken (v.39). The king had recently been killed in battle (v.43) and while only a youth (v.45). The enemies of Judah were now in much rejoicing (vs.41,42,51) and the strongholds of the country were to be broken down (v. 40).

This lament is found at the end of Psalm 89 and it describes the historical situation that existed in Judah at the death of King Josiah. Indeed, the previous 18 psalms (comprising the "Asaph Division" — the third book — of the Psalms) had as their general theme the destruction of the land of Israel, Jerusalem, and the Temple. It appears that Jeremiah wrote Psalm 89 to conclude the "Asaph Division" to the Book of Psalms. This, again, shows an authorization of scripture by Jeremiah.

The final touches of the canonization which started in the time of King Josiah took place in Babylon *after* the Jews had been taken captive. Jeremiah had first gone to Egypt, but he returned to be with the Jews in Babylon (because he recorded events which happened in Babylon some 26 years after the final captivity — Jeremiah 52:31-34). Jeremiah was then able to hand over to Daniel (the Jewish prince in Babylon) any remaining prophecies which he had written (or other books which he had rescued from the Temple). Thus, the canonization which began in the time of King Josiah ended with the final activities of Jeremiah in Babylon.

Daniel and the Sacred Writings

After Jeremiah's departure from the scene, Jerusalem and Judah continued in a desolate state for many years while the Jews remained in Babylon. But the preservation of the various books was not, during this period of captivity, left to unauthorized members of the Jewish community. We read that Daniel (who was of royal stock — "of the king's seed, and of the princes" — Dan.1:3), had been given a high literary position in Babylon.

> "[Daniel] was well favoured, and skillful in all wisdom, and cunning in knowledge, and understanding science, and such as had ability in them to stand in the king's palace, and whom they might teach the learning and the tongue of the Chaldeans" (Dan.1:4).

Lange's *Commentary* amplifies the meaning of this verse. Daniel's "learning" was "all literary knowledge." The phrase "skillful [cunning] in knowledge" signifies that he was adept in "various fields of knowledge as contained in books." Daniel was one who had "acquaintance with literature" ("Daniel," pp.59,61).

In effect, Daniel was chosen to be one of the librarians — later the chief librarian — in the court of Nebuchadnezzar at Babylon. The nature of Daniel's work brought him into contact with all types of literature which existed at the time. This included works which had been rescued from the Temple at Jerusalem. He was familiar with "the Law of Moses" (Dan.9:11); the "prophecies of Jeremiah" (Dan.9:2); the "prophetic books of Israel" (Dan.9:2) and certain other prophetic "books" which contained judgments upon the nations (Dan.7:10). There was also a work called "The Scripture of Truth" (Dan.10:21) which became a part of Daniel's own book and is recorded for us from Daniel 11:2 to 12:4. This latter prophecy is the most detailed prediction found anywhere in the Bible and it contains considerable information about events even future to us.

The Prophet Daniel was a very important link to the story of biblical canonization because he was the responsible person through whom the divine books of the Temple were preserved at Babylon. This enabled them to be returned to Jerusalem by Ezra in later years.

Ezra's Final Canonization

We now come to the period of Ezra and the Great Assembly. Although we have previously mentioned some reasons for the final canonization during Ezra's time, there are other observations that should be mentioned which can give us a better understanding of the subject.

There is one point which should never be forgotten: all of the canonizations preceding that of Ezra are only of historical interest to us. But the question of exactly which books represent the complete Old Testament today, can only be answered by understanding the canonization of Ezra and those 120 priests who comprised the Great Assembly. It is Ezra's final work which is the most important.

The reason for this should be apparent. While we can know when and by whom many of the books or portions of books were written, there are others about which we are uncertain. What about the books by Hosea, Joel, Job, Amos, parts of the Psalms or Proverbs? Until the time of Ezra, we have no certain knowledge of how and when they were reckoned as canonical — or if they ever were in early times.

Furthermore, though various suggestions as to which books David, Solomon, Hezekiah, etc. saw fit to canonize have been made in previous pages of this book, this was mainly possible because of hints given in Ezra's Book of Chronicles. It was Ezra (the "Second Moses") who gave to the Jewish world the official (and final) Old Testament to be read in the Temple and synagogues. This makes the canonization by Ezra the most important of all.

Ezra Edits the Whole Old Testament

There is a most important aspect of the Old Testament's final canonization. This concerns certain editing in the Bible for which Ezra was responsible.

At first it might seem almost irreverent to suggest that editing the Bible could be permissible to anyone — regardless of how important his office. Some might say: "Leave the Bible alone; don't touch a single letter of it." This may appear proper to us today, but Ezra felt that the Old Testament needed editing to allow the Jewish nation of his time to have the *complete* and *full* revelation of God in the Hebrew language.

Ezra's additions were not vast changes in the text of the Old Testament. These were small edits, mostly in earlier portions of the Law. His editorial comments were mainly restricted to simple parenthetical expressions explaining to the Jews of his time the contemporary geographical names of ancient places and towns that had been changed over the years.

Reference to a good biblical handbook will give the majority of these editorial remarks. One can be found in Genesis 36:31-39 which records the names of Edomite kings down to the time of King Saul. This section could not have been written by Moses because he would hardly have known the names of Edomite kings living 300 years after his death. Such indications as Judges 18:30 which records events 700 years *after* the period of the Judges is a further example of editing.

Ezra simply went through the early books of the Old Testament and brought them, in some important sections, to relevance with accurate "modern" geographical or historical facts. Moses did the same thing when he originally wrote the Law. He adopted the principle of bringing earlier historical documents of his time up-to-date. Even Moses introduced into the ancient records geographical terms familiar to Israelites of his time (Gen.2:14). This procedure adopted by Moses also gave Ezra the authority to do the same.

The prophet Samuel did a similar type of editing in his day. This occurred when the people demanded a king. "Then Samuel told the people the manner of the Kingdom, and wrote it in *the* book and laid it up before the Lord" (I Samuel 10:25). Samuel wrote "in *the* book" the manner of how a king was to govern, and what the rules of his kingdom were to be. Samuel wrote it not just in any book, but in "the book" which was "laid up before the Lord."

The only writing in existence with Samuel which was placed before the Lord was the Law of Moses. Thus the section about a king in Deuteronomy 17:18 was *not* written by Moses. This was the addition to the Laws that Samuel the prophet put in. "And it shall be, when he sitteth upon the throne of his kingdom, that he shall write him a copy of this law in a book out of that which is before the priests the Levites." Prof. Kirkpatrick remarks pertinently that Samuel:

> "wrote it in a book, and laid it up before the Lord. Literally, in *the* book. Possibly this important chapter [concerning the kingdom] was added to 'the book of the law' kept by the side of the ark 'before the Lord' " (*The First Book of Samuel*, vol.IX, Cambridge Bible for Schools and Colleges, p.112).

This seems certain. Samuel inserted the rules concerning kingship into the Law of Moses — the books which were preserved in the sleeves of the Ark (see also Deut.31:26). It is evident that the Law did not contain the rules of the kingdom prior to Samuel. Note that when the people clamored for a king in Samuel's day, they presented no appeal to the Law of Moses for support. Samuel himself was upset by the mere suggestion of having a king. Had the rules concerning the kingdom been already within the Book of Deuteronomy, there would have been no need for Samuel to express displeasure.

"This narrative [in the book of Samuel] . . . shows no indication of the law in Deuteronomy [concerning the kingdom] having been known in fact, either to Samuel, or to the people who demanded of him a king: had such been the case, it is incredible either that Samuel would have resisted the application of the people as he is represented as doing, or . . that the people should not have appealed to the law, as a sufficient justification for their request" (Samuel R. Driver, *A Critical and Exegetical Commentary on Deuteronomy,* 3rd ed. *ICC,* p.213).

Samuel took authority to write out the rules concerning the kingdom and he placed them in "the book which was laid up before the Lord." This example of Samuel gave Ezra even further historical precedent for adding a few editorial remarks to the Law of God in his time.

Ezra Adds Final Touches

One more example will show Ezra to be the most important editor of the Old Testament. At the end of Deuteronomy, we find some remarks concerning the death of Moses. "So Moses the servant of the Lord died there in the land of Moab . . . but no man knoweth of his sepulchre unto this day" (Deut.34:5,6).

It is hardly possible for Moses to have recorded his own death and then, in some curious prophecy, tell later people that his burial place was unknown "unto this day." These are editorial remarks added by Ezra at the final canonization.

Proof that the editor could be none other than Ezra is found in Deuteronomy 34:10. "And there arose not a prophet since in Israel like unto Moses, whom the Lord knew face to face."

It was promised (Deut.18:15-19) that there would arise one more major prophet like unto Moses in power and authority. That prophet was to be so great that his words would be like those of Moses. But of all the prophets who preceded Ezra, not one of them was the lawgiver (like Moses) or the maker of the New Covenant with Israel as a new Moses. So Ezra was informing his readers in his time through this editorial comment that none of the earlier prophets (such as Isaiah, Jeremiah or Ezekiel) was the prophet ordained to be like Moses. The Jewish people in the fifth century B.C. were being directed by Ezra, the compiler of the Hebrew Bible, to look forward to a future time for the coming of the great prophet. The Jews in the time of Christ were doing just that (John 6:14 and 7:40), and Christians came to believe that the prophet was Christ.

It should be mentioned that even after Ezra's death, some later members of the Great Assembly (the authorized supreme religious court of the nation) carried the genealogical tables of important priestly families down to the time of Alexander the Great (Neh.12:11, 22; Josephus, *Antiq.* XI.302).

Lost Books of the Old Testament

In conclusion, let us notice some books which are mentioned in the Old Testament but are not found in the pages of our Bible:

"The Book of the Wars of the Lord" (Num.21:14).
"The Book of Jasher" (Josh.10:13; II Sam.1:18).
"The Book of the Acts of Solomon" (I Kings 11:14).
"The Book of Nathan the Prophet" (I Chron.29:29).
"The Book of Gad the Seer" (I Chron.29:29)
"The Prophecy of Ahijah the Shiloite" (II Chron.9:29).
"The Visions of Iddo the Seer" (II Chron.9:29).
"The Book of Shemiah the Prophet" (II Chron.12:15).
"The Book of Jehu the Son of Hanani" (II Chron.20:34).
"The Sayings of Hosai" (II Chron.33:19).

Do these "lost books" belong in the sacred canon of the Old Testament? They do not. The last seven of these ten books were referred to by Ezra in the Book of Chronicles, and it was he who was responsible for canonizing the complete Old Testament. He mentioned these historical documents to support the truth of what he wrote in the Book of Chronicles, but he did not include any of them as a part of divine scripture. These were simple books of history which contained truthful records of the past (much like First Maccabees in the Apocrypha), but Ezra did not accord them divine status. This is significant. If Ezra did not reckon them as canonical, neither should anyone else. This is the case with all other books mentioned in the Bible but not found within the present biblical canon.

8

The Need for a New Testament

There can be no proper understanding of the New Testament canon (its development and formation) unless one factor is kept plainly in mind. It is this: The apostles never thought that a New Testament was necessary to leave for people of future ages until they finally realized that Christ was not returning to earth in their generation. Indeed, there is not the slightest hint in the Book of Acts (which closed its account in early A.D.61) that any of the books written by the apostles in the first 30 years of Christianity was destined to be placed into a canon of scripture. Why formulate a New Testament for posterity when Christ was expected to be on earth in a few short years? Such action would have seemed thoroughly unnecessary. However, when the apostles finally understood that Christ was not returning in the first century, it then became their major task to select and to write several books which could secure the truths of Christianity until Christ would actually return.

The close of the Book of Acts marks an important point in the history of the New Testament canon. During the historical period covered by that book the apostles were expecting Christ's second advent, and the closer they got to A.D.61 the more intense was their anticipation. As a matter of fact, when the Book of Hebrews was written in the early part of A.D.61, the expectancy was at its apex. In Hebrews 10:37 the Greek actually indicates that Christ's advent would occur in "a very little while" (Heb.10:37).

But the epistles written after A.D.61 make a sudden shift of emphasis. From then on, Paul abandons the theme of Christ's imminent advent and concentrates on matters which show a long period of time awaiting the Christian Church before that glorious event would occur. The year A.D.62/63 seems to have been the year of decision for the apostles (at least for the apostle Paul) in finally deciding that Christ would not return in the first century. This change of opinion may have come with the martyrdom of James during the Passover of A.D.62. James, the leader of the Jerusalem church, was thrown over the precipitous east wall of the Temple into the Kidron valley. The fall itself failed to kill him and he was finally stoned to death (Eusebius, *Eccl.Hist.*II.23). Just before his execution, he told the Jewish authorities at Jerusalem that Christ "is about to come in the clouds of heaven" (*ibid.*). There can be little doubt that that glorious event was expected very shortly.

The martyrdom of James must have had a profound effect on Jewish Christians because he was even a recognized figure among the Jewish community for his justice and righteous behavior. His contemporaries gave him the title: "the Sadec" (the righteous one). So respected was he by almost all parties in Jerusalem that it is said he was like a righteous high priest and able to enter the Holy of Holies (Eusebius, *ibid.*). Whether one wishes to believe all the traditions about James is not important in our present discussion, but it appears very probable that his violent death may have represented a major epochal event to the early Christian church.

The autumn of A.D.62 (six months after the death of James) was also significant regarding the return of Christ for another reason. This period commenced the sabbatical year for all Palestinian Jews (Wacholder, *Hebrew Union College Annual,* 1973, pp.153-196). To Jews the sabbatical years were important prophetic indicators. Daniel predicted that there were to be exactly 70 sabbatical cycles of 7 years until the kingdom of God would arrive on earth. He divided those 490 years into one period of 49 years (7 times 7 sabbatical cycles), another of 434 years (62 times 7 sabbatical cycles), and a final 7 year period which was divided into two sections of 3½ years each. These last 7 years of Daniel were thought by people of the first century to embrace a period of great trouble on Israel, the city of Jerusalem, and the Temple. The conclusion to that final 7 years was expected to witness the advent of the Messianic kingdom of God which was destined to take control over all Gentile forces in the world.

Since the Book of Hebrews and James (the Christian bishop of

Jerusalem) were expressing an imminence to Christ's return from heaven, the sabbatical cycle of 7 years which commenced in the autumn of A.D.63 and ended in A.D.70 must have been reckoned by the Jews as significant. We know this to be the case because Josephus said the Jews went to war with the Romans in A.D.66 (not long before the middle of that sabbatical period), and the people persisted in that war against all odds because they were trusting in the fulfillment of a divine oracle in their holy scriptures (*War*,VI.312). There can hardly be a doubt that Josephus was referring to the chronological prophecies found in the Book of Daniel. This may have been the reason that at the beginning of the sabbatical year of A.D.62/63 Josephus said that a man by the name of Joshua ben Ananias began a 7 years and 5 months verbal prophecy against the inhabitants of Jerusalem which ended with the destruction of the city and the Temple in A.D.70 (*War*,VI.300-309). Josephus reckoned the start of this man's prophecy as so important that he said it represented the commencement of God's warnings to the Jews that Jerusalem and the Temple would soon be destroyed.

Even though a great deal of significance must have been attached by the Jews to the start of the sabbatical cycle in the autumn of A.D.63 (it looks like they considered that particular cycle to have been the last 7 years of Daniel), there was, however, a problem with the prophetic statements of Daniel. Josephus himself admitted that the chronological statements in Daniel were very obscure and capable of a host of interpretations. For example, the Seventy Weeks' prophecy began its 490 years from a command to rebuild Jerusalem. But which "command" was this? Was it the one that was given in the first year of Cyrus as king over Babylon (539/8 B.C.), or was it the one commanded in Nehemiah's time (the twentieth year of Artaxerxes — 444 B.C.)? Or maybe the prophecy was intended to begin with the second year of Darius when the Temple was allowed to be built (515 B.C.) or perhaps the seventh year of Artaxerxes when Ezra went to Jerusalem to decorate the Temple (457 B.C.)?

There were other unknown factors associated with the prophecy. People wondered if there were any chronological gaps existing between the three main divisions of the Seventy Weeks' Prophecy? In the prophecy itself the wording of the Hebrew shows that its three sections were to be "cut out" of the historical time frame between the going forth of the command to rebuild Jerusalem and the arrival of the Messiah (Dan.9:24). This could indicate that some gaps of time might be expected between the three sections. Such a gap may have been imagined as existing for the years of the Maccabean (Hasmonean) rulers at Jerusalem (when Jews had their own sovereignty over Judaea), or there may have been other "gaps."

And besides that, how many days did the particular years of Daniel's prophecy consist? Were they to be reckoned as normal year lengths of 365¼ days? Maybe Daniel intended a 354 day lunar year, or perhaps an ideal 360 day prophetic year? No one in the first century knew for sure just what Daniel meant, and the various interpretations could cause several differences in the accumulative number of days, weeks, months, and even years for the fulfillment of the prophecy.

There were even more obscurities to the prediction than those mentioned above. When Daniel mentioned that the prophecy would see the emergence of "the Messiah," did he mean the anointed son of David, an ordained priest, or was it some prophet? Even if the proper "Messiah" could be correctly picked, there were other ambiguities that gave problems. Did Daniel mean that the first 483 years of the prophecy (the 69 sabbatical cycles) ended with his birth? Maybe the reference was to the Messiah's *bar mitzvah* when he reached the age of 12? Perhaps Daniel meant the year the Messiah became old enough to enter an army of Israel at 20? It is possible the prophecy could have referred to the Messiah becoming 30, the age when priests were ordained. Or maybe it indicated the time of the Messiah's coronation (either an official or *de facto* crowning) — which could happen at any time during his life? The truth is, there was not any proven method of prophetic interpretation in the first century which could give anyone a certain conviction regarding the meaning of Daniel. Because of these variables, the prophecy (and all others of the Old Testament) remained enigmatic both to Christians and Jews. And this is why Josephus called it, "an obscure prophecy."

In spite of this, it was commonly believed in the first century that the prophetical/chronological factors of Daniel were on the verge of fulfillment sometime within the latter half of that century. And the sabbatical period which began in the autumn of A.D.63 and lasted until the autumn of A.D.70 was a time when a great deal of Messianic expectation began to be rife in Jerusalem and throughout Judaism. It appeared to the Jews that the "Babylonian (Gentile)" system of government was about to terminate. It is interesting that A.D.63 (when the sabbatical cycle began) was exactly 666 years from 604 B.C. (the first year of King Nebuchadnezzar of the Neo-Babylonian Empire, mentioned as the head of gold in the second chapter of Daniel).

Symbolic Numbers and Prophecy

It must be remembered that the use of numbers (and the symbols behind them) played an important part in the interpretation of prophecy in the first century. The number 666 is associated, in the Book of Revelation, with the reign of the world ruler who will have ten nations under his power in the last generation before the kingdom of God appears on earth (Rev.13:18). The Babylonian writer Berosus believed that world history itself was governed by cycles of 60, 600, and 3600 years (*Frag.* 4). And the Bible shows that the number 6 (or its multiples) has symbolic teaching in it. When Nebuchadnezzar (the head of gold) set up a large idol in Babylon, its dimensions were 60 cubits high and 6 broad (Dan.3:1). This, of itself, may appear insignificant, but if one figures the numerical value of the Hebrew letters that make up the description of that idol, it comes to 4662 (which is exactly 7 times 666) (Bullinger, *Number in Scripture,* p.285). Conversely, Daniel and his three friends who refused to bow down before that idol found their names adding up to 888: Daniel (95), Hananiah (120), Mishael (381), Azariah 292) (Dan.2:17). In the Greek the name *Jesus* also added up to 888. The numbers 7 and 8 had to do with completion and righteousness, but 6 was almost always connected with man and his evil ways (note that Adam, the first man, was created at the end of the *sixth* day), and the man of sin who will be the antichrist at the end of the age has the number 666.

It no doubt appeared significant to the apostles and most Jews who lived in the first century that Nebuchadnezzar (the head of gold in Daniel's prophecy) began his first year of rule in 604 B.C. When one adds 666 years to that date, the start of the sabbatical cycle in A.D.63 is reached. Had this been the only prophetic indication concerning A.D.63, scant attention would have been given to the outcome. But when one adds 66 years to 604 B.C., the year 538 B.C. became evident. This happened to be the first year of Cyrus over Babylon who began the "silver portion" of Nebuchadnezzar's image. And remarkably, when one adds 600 years to 538 B.C., again the year A.D.63 is reached. This fact may have given the Jews even more interest in A.D.63 as a cardinal date in the interpretation of prophetic history, because Josephus made the definite statement that 600 years was looked on by the Jews (and others in the world) as an astronomical and historical cycle of time called "The Great Year" (*Antiq.*I.106). There is little question that Josephus obtained his information from Berosus, the Babylonian astronomer who lived in the fifth century B.C. It was probably held that the 600 year period from the start of the "silver portion" of the Babylonian image was important, and this worked out to A.D.63 as a concluding date.

That didn't end the prophetic symbolism of Nebuchadnezzar's image. There was prophesied to be a third world empire and it was represented by the "brass portion." This was to commence with a he-goat from the west pushing at the "silver portion" in the east. It was recognized by all prophetic interpreters in the first century that this represented Alexander the Great who started to conquer the Persian Empire with his victory at the Battle of Granicus in 334 B.C. And lo and behold, 396 years forward from that date again reaches to A.D.63. But what is important with the span of 396 years? This period happens to occupy a space of 6 times 66 years. This fact no doubt appeared too significant to be coincidental. It thus meant that the very years which commenced the gold, silver, and brass portions of Nebuchadnezzar's image (which gave a history of world empires from Babylon to the arrival of the kingdom of God), all had the numbers 6, 60, 66, 600, and 666 focusing on the year A.D.63. (Josephus refused to give any prophetic details regarding the arrival of the "iron portion" of the image — which he no doubt equated with Rome, *Antiquities* X.276. There must have been a host of chronological interpretations on this matter simply because there were several important periods of time when Rome interfered with the Jews in Judaea from the time of the Maccabees onward.)

The Christians, however, had an even more profound reason for expecting that a change in world history was about to occur in A.D.63. This was because of the "Immanuel Prophecy" found in Isaiah chapter 7 through chapter 12. The apostles identified the virgin birth of *Immanuel* (as translated by the Septuagint Version) with the virgin birth of Jesus (Isa.7:14). But what is often overlooked by commentators is the fact that a 65 year period was destined to be associated with *Immanuel* in order for him to overthrow the Syrians and the people of Ephraim and to bring in the Messianic kingdom described in Isaiah 11 and 12. Since Jesus was born in 3 B.C. (see my book *The Birth of Christ Recalculated* for proof), that period of 65 years would also have terminated in A.D.63.

Let us pay attention to this year A.D.63 for a moment. We will then be able to observe an important point regarding the end-time as conceived by the early Christians — and especially by the apostle Paul. If one will survey Paul's letters written *BEFORE* A.D.63, they present a prophetic anticipation for the soon occurrence of all the Old Testament prophecies leading up to the second advent of Christ, but as soon as A.D.63 passes (and the expected prophecies did not materialize as Paul thought), he thoroughly abandoned the concept of Christ's soon appearance and he put the second advent into the future. The key year even for Paul was the sabbatical year which ended in A.D.63. There are important indications to show this.

The End-Time Expectancy

When the apostle Peter delivered his first sermon to the Jews after Christ's resurrection he quoted a prophecy from Joel and said "the last days" were then upon the people of Israel (Acts 2:17). From that time forward the apostles continued to teach that they were at the end of an age. In the Book of Hebrews the mid-first century was being called "the last days" (Heb.1:2), "the end of the ages" (Heb.9:26), the day of reckoning was "drawing near" (Heb.10:25), it was only "a very little while away" (Heb.10:37). And in his early epistles Paul indicated he (and many of his readers) would still be alive at Christ's second advent (I Cor.15:50-52; I Thess.4:15).

It was felt in the middle of the first century that the conclusion of the world system was very near. The majority of Jews (and even the Gentiles) were of this conviction. As early as A.D.49 Jews in Rome were expelled from the capital because of tumults caused by Chrestus (a Messianic pretender) (Suetonius, *Claud.* 25). In A.D.54, the first year of Nero (who was the sixth emperor of the Romans as counted by the Jews because they considered Julius Caesar as the first prophetic ruler of the "iron kingdom"), Josephus said that so MAT.24:24 many false Christs began to appear among the Jews in Judaea that hardly a day went by that the Roman procurator did not put some of them to death (*Antiq.* XX.160,161). The start of Nero's reign over Rome was looked on auspiciously by many Jews. He was the "sixth emperor" and even in the Book of Revelation the apostle John was inspired to write that "there are seven kings: five are fallen, and one is [the sixth was then existing], and the other is not yet come; and when he cometh, he must continue a short space" (Rev.17:10). The Messianic kingdom was expected to arrive not long after the "sixth king" whom many interpreted as Nero. This is why at the beginning of his reign there was a great deal of prophetic expectation in Palestine. Lots of political upstarts claiming to be the Messiah came on the scene. Christ had prophesied that such imposters would arise who would lead people into the desert where their new "Moses" (the Christ) would show himself to lead the Jews to victory over the Romans. Christ told his disciples: "Wherefore if they shall say unto you, Behold *he is in the desert* . . . believe it not" (Matt.24:26). This very thing began to occur in A.D.54, during the first year of Nero. Josephus said:

> "Imposters and deceivers called upon the mob to follow them *into the desert.* For they said that they would show them unmistakable wonders and signs that would be conducted in precise agreement with God's will. Many people were in fact persuaded to follow them and they paid for their folly" (*Antiq.* XX.168).

At this very time arose the Egyptian false Christ. He led some 30,000 people to the Mount of Olives and the desert, proclaiming that he would cause the walls of Jerusalem to be destroyed. Though Felix the Roman procurator was able to rout the people under him, the Egyptian himself escaped, and about two years later the Roman authorities thought the apostle Paul to be that Egyptian renegade (Acts 21:38; *Antiq.* XX.169-172).

These disturbances broke out because of the Messianic expectations of the Jews at the time. But after the sabbatical year of A.D.62-

63 past, the anticipation grew even stronger. They were so intense by A.D.64 that when Rome was destroyed by fire on July 19th, the blame was placed on those expecting the arrival of the "New Age" of the Messiah (Christians were especially singled out for censure). Indeed, Nero near this very time was even advised by his astrologers to move his capital from Rome to Jerusalem because they said that sovereignty over the world was destined to arise in Judaea at that period (Suetonius, *Nero* 40). Both the Roman historians Tacitus (*Hist.* V.13) and Suetonius (*Vesp.* 4) mentioned the general feeling of people throughout the Roman Empire that the expected world empire would soon emerge.

All Christians shared this expectation because Christ himself seemed to indicate he would return *within one generation* from his crucifixion in A.D.30. We will see in a moment that most people of the time considered a "generation" to be 40 years in length. This meant that Christ would definitely set up his world government within 40 years after his crucifixion, that is, before the year A.D.70. This is why the apostle Paul expected that all the prophecies of the Old Testament would be fulfilled upon *that* generation — "upon whom the ends of the age are come"(I Cor.10:11). Christ had even made the statement that judgments upon evil people from the time of Abel (at the very start of Genesis) to the close of the Old Testament period, would have their accumulated force unleashed on *that* generation which existed in the first century. "Verily I say unto you, *all these things* shall come upon THIS GENERATION" (Matt.23:35,36).

Assertions such as these prompted the apostles to accept the conclusion that all the Old Testament prophecies uttered over the last 1500 years which pertained to the "end-time" (whether against Egypt, Assyria, Edom, Tyre, Babylon, Israel, etc.) would find their fulfillment *in their time.* The Book of Revelation adopted this style of interpretation. It assembled numerous prophecies from all parts of the Old Testament (disregarding the different time periods or peoples to whom the prophecies were first given) and it typically focused their combined fulfillment into a single generation. Revelation simply placed them altogether into a seven years' period (divided into halves) — which the Book of Daniel had done earlier — and placed their fulfillment in "the Lord's day" at the end of the age (Rev.1:10). The author thought this collection of prophecies, with new ones revealed to him, were "things which must shortly come to pass" (Rev.1:1). So quickly were they expected (apparently) that it appeared as though the ones who crucified Christ would be alive to witness the second advent (Rev.1:7; Matt.26:64).

The apostle Paul in all his epistles written before A.D.63 certainly spoke about the imminence of all end-time prophetic events and that many of his readers would be alive to observe the second advent (I Cor.15:51,52; I Thess.4:15-17). His early beliefs were solidly anchored in the conviction that "the time is short . . . the fashion of this world passeth away" (I Cor.7:29,31). At that time (A.D.55) Paul even discouraged people from getting married. It was not that he was against marriage of itself, but the present distress which was then on the Corinthian church plus the anticipated great trouble that was soon to occur on the whole world because of end-time events made him suggest the single state for people (I Cor.7:1-32). In the Book of Romans, written about a year later, he said: "Now is it high time to awake out of sleep: for now is our salvation *nearer* than when we first believed, the night is far spent, and the day is at hand" (Rom.13:11, 12). So certain was Paul of the soon arrival of God's kingdom that he told the Romans that "Satan would be crushed under their feet *very soon*" (Rom.16:20). To the Philippians he said: "The Lord is at hand" (Phil.4:5). The apostle James also told his readers it was "the last days" and that they should be patient "unto the coming of the Lord . . . for the coming of the Lord draweth nigh" (Jam.5:3,7,8). The apostle John was no less urgent in his appeal that the end of the age was near: "Little children, it is the last time: and as ye have heard that antichrist shall come, even now are there many antichrists; whereby we know that *it is the last time*" (I John 2:18).

The return of Christ in *that* generation which succeeded the resurrection of Christ seemed an assured thing because even Christ himself was thought to teach it. "Verily I say unto you, *this generation* shall not pass, till all these things be fulfilled" (Matt.24:34). Christ had told his apostles that they (back at that time) should watch for these prophesied events "for *ye* know not what hour your Lord doth come" (verse 42). All the contexts in which Christ instructed his apostles about prophetic matters suggest that many of the apostles would certainly be alive to behold them. Christ had also stated to some of them that they would not die before they would view the revelation of the kingdom of God as coming to earth (Matt.16:27,28).

Though the apostles knew that an exact knowledge of the prophetic chronology was not to be given to them (Acts 1:6,7), they were at first certain that the second advent would occur in their lifetimes. They even had some good clues as to its occurrence. The apostle Peter had been told that he would die an old man before Christ's return (John 21:18,19), but that John would "tarry until I come." It became the belief of many disciples that Christ would return before John would reach extreme old age (but after Peter's death). This made people feel that John would continue to live until Christ's advent (John 21:21-23).

These teachings gave a confidence that Christ's second advent would occur within *that* generation, but not before Peter would reach old age. It was easy to figure that a generation of time represented a 40 year period or thereabouts. This belief was supported by the fact that Peter at his baptism must have been about the same age as Christ (30 years of age). If one added 40 years to Peter's 30 years (so that he might reach "old age") then the ideal 70 years mentioned in Psalm 90:10 would be accomplished. This would indicate that Peter would be martyred a little before A.D.70, but that John would still be alive (awhile after Peter's death) to witness the second advent in person. So, they came to believe that a generation of time for all end-time prophecies to be fulfilled would have been within 40 years of Christ's resurrection.

There was even scriptural authority that a generation represented a span of 40 years. The Book of Hebrews recorded: "Your fathers tempted me, proved me, and saw my works *forty years*. Wherefore I was grieved with *that generation*" (Heb.3:9,10).

The fact that 40 years was "one generation" in prophetic interpretation was a well established belief. The number 40 itself was normally attached to the symbol of *trial, punishment, or special human experiences.* There are numerous examples to show this. Christ's temptation with Satan continued 40 days (Matt.4:2). The time between Christ's resurrection and ascension was 40 days (Acts 1:3). Moses spent 40 days on Mount Sinai receiving God's law (Exo.24:18; 34:18), and there was the 40 days' trip to the same area by the prophet Elijah (I Kings 19:8). There were 40 days and nights of the Flood (Gen.7:4,17) and Nineveh was granted 40 days to repent

(Jonah 3:4). We even have 40 days becoming 40 years in the judgment upon the rebellious Israelites for not entering the Promised Land when they were told (Num.14:34). Later, the Philistine servitude lasted 40 years (Jud.13:1), and the punishment on Egypt was prophesied to last 40 years (Ezek.29:11).

Even important periods associated with human life had the number 40 associated with them. The human gestation period, for example, is normally 40 weeks — and in biblical parlance this was considered 40 weeks of *trial* on women. A boy baby was purified 40 days after his birth (Lev.12:3,4) and 80 days (2 times 40) for a female (verse 5). While a human became of spiritual age at 30 years (Num.4:3; Luke 3:23), the person was ideally given a further 40 years of trial (or experience) in adult life (30 plus 40 years equalling the ideal 70 years of Psalm 90:10). Joseph, however, being reckoned the firstborn of Jacob was given a double blessing, and this included among other things a *double* period of full, adult life. He lived to be 110 years of age (30 plus two 40 year periods). Joshua also attained to the same 110 years of life (Gen.50:22; Josh.24:29). Moses, on the other hand, lived 120 years (3 times 40). The ancients considered it no accident that Moses was not only selected for his historic role at 40 years of age, but he also led the children of Israel out of Egypt at 80 (2 times 40) and died at 120 (3 times 40).

In fact, the 40 years' period of the Exodus became the standard number of years for reckoning a generation. This is found in important historical time periods mentioned in the Bible. The time from the Exodus to the building of the Temple in Solomon's reign was believed to be 480 years (12 times 40) (I Kings 6:1). David and Solomon were considered having ruled for 40 years each (II Sam.5:4; I Kings 11:42). Even King Saul was given 40 years (Acts 13:21) though his exact period of reign is difficult to determine in the Old Testament. And recall, the Exodus period itself was exactly 40 years, which the Book of Hebrews called "*that* generation" (Heb.3:9, 10). In short, it became common to acknowledge any generation, ideally, as being 40 years in length.

"Forty years represented a generation, and thus the number 40 became a round number for a *full period, a complete epoch.*" (Hastings, *Dict. of Christ and the Gospels*, vol.II.p.250).

It is easy to see a preoccupation that the apostles (and other Christians) must have had regarding the 40 years' period after Christ's resurrection. When Christ delivered the Olivet Prophecy in A.D.30 about the destruction of Jerusalem, he said it would occur in *"that generation."* And remarkably, the catastrophe did in fact happen in A.D.70 — exactly 40 years later.

The recognition of that 40 years' period as playing a significant part in the thinking of the apostles is most essential in understanding the background to the New Testament canonization. Those 40 years were partitioned prophetically into several distinct and critical periods. The main two periods were represented by a single 33 year span to accomplish the preaching of the Gospel to the whole world (in accordance with the command in Matthew 28:19). This evangelization of the world was to be fulfilled *before* the Abomination of Desolation would be set up in the Temple at Jerusalem. The second period was that of 7 years, which dovetailed with Daniel's last sabbatical cycle of 7 years' duration which was to occur just *before* the kingdom of God would come to earth.

And note this. With the generation of 40 years from Christ's resurrection ending in A.D.70, then 7 years before that date brings us once again to the crucial year of A.D.63 for the beginning countdown to the end. By A.D.63 the world should have been evangelized.

It should be realized by moderns that the apostles by A.D.63 believed that they had completely given the Gospel message "to the world" as commanded by Christ in Matthew 28:19. The meaning of the word "world" has to be interpreted in the manner the apostles perceived it in the first century. That "world" only included the parts of the globe to which they had been commissioned to preach. It should be noted that Paul in the Book of Colossians confidently stated that "all creation that is under heaven" had now received the Gospel —and this was accomplished in the sixth decade of the first century (Col.1:23). He also told the Romans that the Gospel message had been manifested "to *all* the nations according to the command of the everlasting God" (Rom.16:26). In the concluding years of Paul's ministry he acknowledged that the nations of the world had received the Gospel of Christ (I Tim.3:16).

To the apostle Paul, this preaching to all the nations assigned to the apostles back in the first century signified that Christ's prophecy that "this Gospel of the kingdom shall be preached in all the world for a witness unto all nations; and then shall the end come" (Matt.24:14) had been fulfilled by A.D.63. The apostles also thought that immediately on the heels of their final preaching assignments to people in the world, then the Abomination of Desolation would be set up in the Temple at Jerusalem to satisfy the teaching of Christ in Matthew 24:14 and 15.

Thus the single generation of 40 years which succeeded the crucifixion and resurrection of Christ was looked on by the apostles as the last generation before the second advent. It represented a span of 33 years for evangelizing the world, then followed by 7 years for the last sabbatical cycle of Daniel's Seventy Weeks (Dan.9:24ff). This last 7 years was prophesied to be divided into two sections of 3 and ½ years each ("a time, times, and half a time; 42 months, or 1260 days"). During the middle of that period the Abomination of Desolation would be set up (Dan.9:27) and at the end of it Michael, the archangel, would stand up to defend Israel at the time of their greatest peril (Dan.12:1). So it looked very possible that the year A.D.63 (in the autumn of the year) would start the final scenario of prophetic events leading up to the second advent of Christ.

Thus, the year A.D.63 became crucial to the apostles and early Christians in the interpretation of prophecy. Indeed, it looks like the Book of Revelation (as we will show later) was first written (its first draft) around A.D.56 or shortly thereafter. That book centered around a seven year period which was divided into two divisions that those who read it thought would no doubt commence with the Autumn of A.D.63. and Christ would be back on earth by A.D.70.

The Great Disappointment!

The only problem was: the prophecies they expected to be fulfilled *did not happen* at the time they thought. Indeed, here we are in the twentieth century and they still have not occurred. The fact is, they are reserved for "the generation" *that sees* the essential prophecies begin to take place. "When ye *shall see* all these things, know that it is near, even at the doors. Verily I say unto you, *This generation* [that is, the one that *sees* the prophecies begin to take place] shall not pass, till all these things be fulfilled" (Matt.24:33,34). Even Christ had told them that the apostles of that time were not to know the times or the seasons which the Father had put in his own power (Acts 1:6,7).

Once the year A.D.63 passed without the expected events starting to happen, the apostle Paul began to adjust his thinking on prophetic chronology. This fact can be clearly shown if one will pay attention to the teaching in the books of Paul which were written *after* A.D.63. While as late as A.D.61 we can read in the Book of Hebrews the superlative statement that the second advent was to occur in "a very little while" (Heb.10:37), in Paul's first letter to Timothy (written about A.D.64) he had changed his tune completely!

The Later Books of the Apostles

With the writing of First Timothy some prime alterations took place in the apostle Paul's approach to the second advent. We then find that he abandoned all hopes that Christ would return in that generation. In First Timothy he even began to encourage widows to get married and bear children (I Tim.5:14). This is quite the reverse of what he recommended in I Corinthians 7:25-35 when he was expecting the soon appearing of the prophesied events to precede the second advent. In no way was he recommending marriage back at that time. But when he wrote his first letter to Timothy, times had changed. He was now informing Timothy *that in later periods* many people would depart from the faith and begin to prohibit marriage (I Tim.4:1-4). His former attitude to marriage was revoked after A.D.63 because he was now encouraging it for younger widows.

He also instructed Timothy in a non-crisis way about the manner of selecting elders and deacons for future periods (I Tim.3:1). He commanded him to ordain no one suddenly (I Tim.5:22) but to take time to test any person wishing to be an elder (I Tim.3:10). He also gave specific commands regarding the method for the caring of widows in the church. All of these instructions clearly show that there was no longer any urgency concerning the second advent in Paul's mind. Timothy was now expected to build up the church organization by performing pastoral functions and instructing others in them. Paul also commanded that prayers be made for kings and rulers so that Christians might continue to lead a quiet and peaceable life (I Tim.2:1,2). And though Paul seemed to hint that Timothy in the future might possibly live to witness Christ's return (I Tim.6:14), he hastily pointed out that Christ would actually appear "in his own appointed times" (I Tim.6:15) — not at a date expected by individual Christians.

Paul continued this theme in his second letter to Timothy (about A.D.66/67). "This know also, that in the last days perilous times shall come" (II Tim.3:1) and in the future evil men and seducers shall wax worse and worse (II Tim.3:13). "For the time will come when they will not endure sound doctrine" (II Tim.4:3). Paul was also assured that he would not be alive at the second advent. "Henceforth there is laid up for me a crown of righteousness, which the Lord, the righteous, will give me *at that day*" (II Tim.4:8).

Much the same is found in Paul's letter to Titus (written near A.D.63). He instructed Titus to ordain elders in the cities of Crete so that the church might continue to grow and receive the true doctrines of Christ (Tit.1:5-9). There was no appeal to Titus, or the people of Crete, to prepare for the immediate end, as was evident in most of the epistles of Paul up to A.D.63.

We should also look at the epistles to the Ephesians and Colossians. These letters were written at a time when Paul was in prison (Eph.4:20; Col.4:3,18). But they were not composed during Paul's first Roman imprisonment, as was Philippians, because in Philippians he was expecting the soon return of Christ (Phil.4:5). This was not so in Ephesians or Colossians. In fact, Paul plainly taught the Ephesians that the young Christian men of that time should plan to get married (Eph.5:31). This advice, of course, entailed the having of children and rearing them to adulthood. Paul even promised that if the children obeyed their parents they would then enjoy a long and natural life on earth (Eph.6:1-3). (We will see later that the books of Ephesians and Colossians were written after A.D.63.)

It also ought to be mentioned that the information in the first and second epistles of Peter display the same dichotomy of belief. In his first epistle he informs his readers that these are "the last times" (I Pet.1:20) and that "the end of all things is at hand" (I Pet.4:7). He spoke of "the fiery trial which is to try you" (I Pet.4:12) and that "the time is come that judgment must begin at the house of God" (verse 17). These latter two verses seem to indicate strongly that the great persecution which Christ prophesied to occur on Christians just before the second advent is what Peter had in mind.

But then notice the drastic change in Peter's second epistle. As a matter of fact, the theme is so different that many scholars cannot believe the same man wrote both epistles. There is, however, no difficulty in accepting the letters as coming from the apostle Peter. After all, they record that both came from "Simon Peter" and he even mentioned he wrote the first epistle (II Pet.3:1).

What had happened was a change in prophetic understanding regarding the time when the second advent would actually come to pass. Peter then referred to "the last days" as being in the future and that there would be people complaining that Christ has delayed his coming. "Where is the promise of his coming," they will be saying (II Pet.3:4).

Peter even had to explain why the expected second advent in the first century did not materialize. "Beloved, be not ignorant of this one thing, that one day is with the Lord as a thousand years, and a thousand years as one day. *The Lord* GOD *is not slack concerning his* PROMISE *coming*" (II Pet.3:8,9).

In the non-biblical book of First Clement, written in the last decade of the first century, the author makes a reference to this portion of Second Peter. "Let not the scripture refer to us which mentions how wretched are the double-minded, those who harbor doubts in their souls and say: 'We have heard these things even in our father's time, and yet *we have grown old, and none of these things has happened to us*' " (I Clement 23:3). This attitude was reminiscent of Christ's own teaching that there would be people who will say: "My lord delayeth his coming" (Matt.24:48). He followed up this statement with the parable of the Ten Virgins which taught that no one would know the precise time of Christ's return (Matt.25:1-13).

There is an important point to make in this teaching about the "delay." It shows that many people were setting particular dates (even a year, a month, or a day) for the second advent. After all, no one could ever claim that Christ "delayeth his coming" unless he was persuaded that a certain time must have been selected by some authorities for the event, and that time passed without incident. Without doubt, even the apostles themselves were setting dates in the middle of the first century. The crucial year for the apostle Paul was at or near A.D.63. The other apostles may have selected this year (or perhaps by A.D.67 when the middle of Daniel's seventh sabbatical cycle would be reached). Of course, none of us can be absolutely sure of the exact date for their expectancy, but it can be known that up to A.D.61 the apostle Paul was anticipating the soon coming of Christ, and after A.D.63 he had abandoned the hope.

What did this do with the teachings of the first draft of the Book of Revelation if it were written just a few years before A.D.63? It would have brought the authority of John into question (and even that of Christianity itself because the Book of Revelation was purported to have been given by Christ Jesus himself). We will have more to say on this in future chapters.

But what did Peter do once the year A.D.63 passed without the expected end-time events occurring? He made an about-face in his teaching concerning the time of the end and Christ's return. This is when he began to talk about a day with Lord is as a thousand years. He may then have realized that at least another 2000 years lay in front of him and that generation before the Second Advent could occur. The knowledge of this fact would have prompted him (as well as John and Paul) to begin a selection of important apostolic writings to comprise a canon of the New Testament. These official books were to be the standard guide for Christian teaching "until the day dawn, and the day star arise in your hearts" (II Pet.1:19).

We now need to ask ourselves what happened in A.D.63 (and thereabouts) which caused the apostles to abandon their hope in the return of Christ in their generation? This question will be considered in the next chapter. Suffice it to say now that none of the apostles thought of producing a New Testament canon as a supplement to the Old while they were expecting the soon return of Christ. Why form a book of instruction for the future, when Christ would be back on earth in all his glory in a few years, or even months?

Once it was recognized that a considerable lapse of time was going to intervene before the actual end-time could begin, there then began to be a stepped-up activity among the apostle to develop an author- ized collection of books and letters which could officially maintain a standard text of Christian doctrine for all future generations.

9

The Prophetic Environment of the First Century

There is an important principle that must be borne in mind if one wishes to understand the actions of people who think they are living at the end-time. This especially applies to those who are convinced the Bible and its prophecies are true and will in no way fail. It simply means that *every prophecy* that the Bible says is destined to be fulfilled during that end-time will indeed take place. And if one expects that a generation of 40 years will witness the completion of *all* prophecies, then one must look at the historical events happening within that period to see how people living at the time would interpret their relevance in bringing the age to a close.

Since it can be shown that the apostles (along with Jewish and even Gentile people) were anticipating the dawn of a new age within the first century, it will pay us (who wish to understand what prompted the apostles to believe the things they did) to study the historical events which were then occurring and try to find out how those occasions were appraised. Obviously, the apostles were keenly aware of what was happening in the historical environment around them and they were carefully observing the political situations. They were even told by Christ to "watch" for prophetic signs (Mark 13:37).

What were some of the historical events which inspired them to imagine that the end-time prophecies were being fulfilled in the first century? What made the apostle Paul believe that A.D.63 was a cardinal year for the expectation of prophecy? We have discussed some of the reasons in the last chapter, but we now need to look at the matter even closer. It will help us get a firm grasp of apostolic thinking on the matter of prophecy, and it will aid us in determining *when* the New Testament canon came into existence and *why* it was necessary to formulate a standard text for Christian belief.

The main prophecy was Christ's teaching which seemed to say that he would return from heaven within *one generation* from his resurrection from the dead. This made the period of 40 years an important benchmark for prophetic fulfillment. Such a period had excellent credentials from the Old Testament as being a significant span of time, especially in prophetic and allegorical teachings. It was commonly accepted that the Exodus experience in the time of Moses was a type of that which was to occur just prior to the arrival of the Messianic kingdom. Since it took Moses 40 years to get the Israelites from their "baptism" at the Red Sea to the borders of the Promised Land, so it was thought in the first century that it would take 40 years from the "baptism" of the Christian Church at Pentecost in A.D.30 (Acts 2) until Christians would see the real Promised Land of Christ by A.D.70.

In actual fact, the 40 years' period of the Israelite Exodus from Egypt was a favorite theme for allegorical application in interpreting events among the Jews (and consequently Christians) who lived in the first century. It was felt that the events which Moses and the Israelites encountered were destined to have a repetition in the generation prior to the emergence of the kingdom of God on earth. The New Testament writers certainly maintained this belief.

The writer of the Book of Hebrews devoted two chapters to explain how the period of the Exodus was being reflected in *that* generation. He taught that Christ had succeeded Moses and that he was the one responsible for leading God's people into the true *rest* of the kingdom of God (Heb.3:5,6 and following verses). The fact that Christ possessed the name of "Joshua" (Jesus) was a reminder of his prophesied role. Just as Joshua once led the children of Israel into the Promised Land, so the true "Joshua" (Jesus) was typically leading Christians across the Jordan River into a "sabbatical period" of a thousand years (Heb.4:8-10). This belief in a millennial existence for Christians is further explained in II Peter 3:8-10 and Rev.20:1-4 with the early Book of Barnabas (15:4) and Justin (*Dial.*81.1*f*).

The apostle Paul was active in presenting this "Exodus theme" in his allegorical teachings. The passage through the Red Sea repre-sented baptism (I Cor.10:2), and the temptations that the Israelites endured for those 40 years were examples of Christian experiences in Paul's day (verse 6). Indeed, the apostle Paul made an exact association between what happened under Moses in the Exodus period and what would befall Christians under the leadership of Christ. He said the Exodus events were *types* of occurrences then under way at "the end of the age."

> "Now all these things [of the Exodus] happened unto them for *types*; and they are written *for our admonition*, upon whom the ends of the age are come" (I Cor.10:11).

Thus, the events of the Exodus (with the wanderings in the wilderness and how Israel reached the Promised Land) became types of Christian experiences which would result in a salvation in Christ. Even today it is common to make the analogy. We are all familiar with the music of black folklore which tells of leaving oppression and "goin' into Canaan's Land," or "Michael, row the boat ashore . . . across the muddy Jordan." Crossing the River Jordan at the end of the 40 years' Exodus period became a type of entering the true Christian rewards which Christ has prepared for his people. And it was looked upon as something more than simple allegory. Christ himself seemed to say that only one generation would elapse for all things in the Old Testament to find fulfillment.

The apostles at first believed that the generation of 40 years after the resurrection of Christ (in repetition of the Exodus period) was to witness the final age just before the Millennium. The Old Testament seemed to support this prospect by its insistence that history and prophecy were to be interpreted in a circular fashion. Many modern commentators of the Scripture have not understood this principle for prophetic fulfillment, but the apostles were very much aware of it and attested to those cyclical events in history and prophecy. It was also common among the Gentiles to believe that historical events happened in cycles (Berosus, *Frag.* 4). The gist of the biblical belief was this: Significant historical events of the past were ordained by God to be repeated at special times in the future. There were several scriptures which sustained this concept of the historical cycles. It was believed that history was ordained to repeat itself.

> "The sun rises and the sun goes down; back it returns to its place

and rises there again. The wind blows south, the wind blows north, round and round it goes and returns full circle. All streams run into the sea, yet the sea never overflows; back to the place from which the streams ran they return again. . . . What has happened *will happen again,* and what has been done *will be done again,* and there is nothing new under the sun. Is there anything of which one can say, 'Look, this is new'? No, it has already existed, long before our time" (Eccl.1:5-10 NEB, italics mine).

"Whatever is has been already, and whatever is to come has been already, and *God summons each event back in its turn"* (Eccl.3:15 NEB).

"Produce your cause, saith the Lord, bring forth your strong reasons, saith the King of Jacob. Let them bring them forth and show us *what will happen:* let them show *the former things,* what they be, that we may consider them, and know the latter end of them; or declare us *things to come"* (Isa.41:22).

The apostles applied these Old Testament teachings concerning the reoccurrence of important historical events to their own time.

"For whatsoever things *were written aforetime* were written for our [first century] learning, that we through patience and comfort of the scriptures might have hope" (Rom.15:4).

"But there were false prophets also among the people, *even as* there shall be false teachers among you" (II Pet.2:1).

And again:

"Now all these things [of the Exodus] happened unto them for *types:* and they are written for our admonition, upon whom the ends of the age are come" (I Cor.10:11).

An encouragement for the cyclical interpretation of prophecy was found in the Book of Daniel concerning the renewal of the three world kingdoms (or empires) out of the four world empires which were mentioned in the prophecies of Daniel Seven. It states in verse 12 that their kingdoms would be prolonged, but in verse 17 it shows that those kingdoms which once were in existence in the sixth, fifth and fourth centuries before Christ will be renewed together at the end of the age. This is the cyclical manner of prophecy being placed in action. Out of the fourth empire of Daniel Seven would emerge a ruler who would be like Nebuchadnezzar of old who would become a symbolic *type* of a future man of evil called the son of perdition, the man of sin (II Thess.2:1-8), or the Beast (Rev.13). Thus we see a duality principle in action. A man of the past would symbolically come forth at the end of the age to pursue the same kind of evil as his predecessor. And though people of the twentieth century may feel that such beliefs are absurd, our modern opinions have no bearing on the issue. It is what the people of the first century thought that can best explain their opinions, not what we might believe today.

This cyclical view of history (and how the fulfillment of prophecy was often believed to be a repetition of events or the re-appearance of personalities from the past) applied not only to evil people, but there are examples of righteous counterparts in the Christian period.

The Duality of Personalities

Not only were prime historical events of the past expected to be repeated, but (like King Nebuchadnezzar) there were to be a renaissance of historical personalities. These people were thought to come in the spirit of the former person. A major doctrinal teaching of the apostle Paul was based on this belief. Paul taught that Adam was a physical type of the spiritual Christ (Rom.5:12-19) and that Christ was considered as being "the last Adam" (I Cor.15:45). The identification did not stop with Adam. The New Testament writers thought of Christ as "the second David." Whole sections of Old Testament references to King David, particularly in the Psalms, were applied in the duality sense to Christ (Psa.2; 22, etc.). The birth of Isaac and his intended sacrifice in the area which later became Jerusalem were also reckoned as types of the birth and crucifixion of Christ (Gal.3:16; Rom.4:19; Hebrews 11:11 and verses 17-19). Reference was even made to a young woman in Isaiah's time who, by the cyclical principle of interpretation, became identified with the virgin Mary who lived over 700 years later (Isa.7:14; Matt.1:23). And let us not forget the identification of John the Baptist who came in the spirit of Elijah. The real Elijah appeared to Israel some 900 years before John (Matt.11:14).

Prophets destined to appear in the future were connected with personalities who lived centuries before. The High Priest Joshua, living some 500 years before Christ, was told that he and his companions were to be *signs* (translated "wondered at" in the King James Version) to signal important future events. Two of those contemporaries of the High Priest were called the "olive trees" of the Temple. These personalities were later identified in the Book of Revelation (in a dual sense) with two future witnesses prophesied to appear on earth just shortly before the advent of the kingdom of God (Rev.11:1-12). These prophets were ordained to repeat the miracles that Moses and Elijah performed while they were on earth (Rev. 11:6). This was like Moses and Elijah re-appearing in person — but this time together, and in a prophetic unity at the end of the age.

Christ, however, became the apex of all typical achievement. The apostles thought Christ to be the composite fulfillment of all the righteous accomplishments of the patriarchs, prophets, and kings of the Old Testament. Even the whole nation of Israel at the Exodus became likened to the infant Christ when he was brought out of Egypt by his parents (Hos.11:1; Matt.2:5). Christ was also reckoned as the Rock who followed Israel out of Egypt (I Cor.10:4) now making his re-appearance on earth at the proper ordained time. He typically became the "second Moses" and the "second Joshua" to lead true Israel (the Christian Church) out of spiritual bondage (Heb.3 & 4).

One of the main reasons the apostles saw Old Testament personalities and events as having a dual significance in Christ and other New Testament individuals is because they believed that the kingdom of God was to be established on earth in their generation. In a word, the apostles felt "the ends of the age" were upon them (I Cor.7:29; Phil.4:5; Heb.10:25,37; I John 2:18). This meant, to them, that all prophecies throughout the Old Testament (no matter where they were found or in what time they were given) were to be applied to the generation which succeeded the resurrection of Christ. And even though the interpretation of these prophecies was allegorical, this did not dissuade them from making practical applications regarding them. And while it is not usual for us of the present day to think in this fashion, the historian must relate how those of the first century thought in order to understand their motives for doing what they did.

Recall that the Book of Revelation drew prophecies from all over the Old Testament and combined them into a single prophetic framework which was destined to occur within one generation. This resulted in ancient prophecies referring to Babylon, Tyre, Assyria, Egypt, Edom, etc. being culled together into one prophetic scenario to occur in a single generation just prior to Christ's second advent. Indeed, this type of prophetic interpretation was not limited to Christians alone. When one surveys the apocalyptic literature that was being written around the time of Christ, one sees much evidence of this type of explanation being in vogue. People were identifying all types of ancient nations with political entities existing in the first century. There were the Dead Sea sectarians who lived just before and during the time of Christ who interpreted the prophecies of Habakkuk about early Chaldeans as now being the people of Chittim (which they acknowledged as the Romans of their day). After all, it was evident that many of the ancient prophecies had not yet found fulfillment but it was firmly expected that all of them would occur. The generation of fulfillment was anticipated to last for 40 years (or thereabouts). And to the apostles that crucial end-time period was presumed to occupy a 40 years' interlude after Christ's resurrection. Clearly, they thought the prophetic cycles of history would find an accomplishment in their lifetimes.

Thus, when the last sabbatical cycle of Daniel's Seventy Weeks' Prophecy was expected to commence (A.D.63 to A.D.70), it was believed that a new and re-born Nebuchadnezzar (or a man coming in the spirit of the earlier Nebuchadnezzar) would set up an Abomination of Desolation in the Temple at Jerusalem (Dan.11:21-35). Once that would happen, it was naturally believed that the rest of Daniel's prophecy from 11:36 on through to 12:4 (the part that all prophetic interpreters knew had never happened) would occur.

The Expectation of A.D.63

The one main event that had to take place before the last sabbatical cycle of Daniel could transpire was the destruction of the city of Jerusalem and the Temple. It was made clear in Daniel 9:26 that those structures had to be destroyed before a covenant involving one sabbatical cycle could commence (verse 27). The latest this could happen and still have the last 7 years of Daniel's prophecy remain within the 40 years' generation from Christ's resurrection *was in A.D.63*. Even this crowded a lot of events into the last 7 years' period. For one, the ruined Temple and City had to be hurriedly rebuilt for the Abomination of Desolation was expected to be placed in the Holy of Holies after 3½ years of the final 7 years had elapsed. If the Book of Revelation were written about A.D.56 (we will discuss this later) then this would have been an acceptable interpretation because the first 3½ years saw a measuring reed (for construction) associated with the prophecy of the Two Witnesses (Rev.11:1). So, since Daniel said the last 7 years could not start until the Temple was in ruins (Dan.9:26), some power had to arrive on the scene to cause that destruction. This major event was expected to occur. At all odds, for the final sabbatical cycle to commence and still be within the 40 years' generation from Christ's resurrection, the end-time events had to start by A.D.63. And true enough, this year seemed to have some good credentials [see previous chapter] to buttress one's confidence.

But note this. There was another event which had to take place *before* the last 7 years of Daniel could begin. The Roman Empire had to be overthrown. This is a little known fact among biblical interpreters regarding the prophetic anticipation of those in the first century, but it is one of the expectations that would have allowed Daniel's last sabbatical cycle to start. The reason for this is plain.

There was hardly a prophetic interpreter in the first century who did not consider the Roman Empire as being the "iron legs" of the Babylonian image (Dan.2). And in A.D.63 those "iron legs" were as strong as ever (and we know from later history that they were to remain strong for the next 300 years). But Daniel's interpretation of the image made it clear that the "iron legs" would break up into ten divisions, some strong as iron and others weak as miry clay. Since these ten kingdoms were to be associated with the "little horn" (the new "Nebuchadnezzar"), Rome had to disintegrate into the ten kingdoms. There were also other prophecies showing this. In Daniel. "the ships of Chittim" mentioned in 11:30 were identified in history as being Roman, and in the first century it was common for most Jews prophetically to consider Chittim as the Romans. In the prophecy of Balaam, it was mentioned that in "the latter days" the ships of Chittim would attack Assyria (the Parthian Empire) and the Hebrews (who in the first century were represented by the Jews) (Num.24:14 with 24). And though the Assyrians and Hebrews would be afflicted, it was the Chittim who would "perish for ever" (verse 24). Thus, a major world war was expected which would overthrow the "iron legs" of the Roman Empire. The outcome would witness ten kings taking over the Roman territory with the aid of the "little horn" who would come out of the area north and east of Palestine (from the same region as the empire of the Assyrians). These ten kings appeared to be identified in Psalm 83 (a psalm that had never been fulfilled -- nor has it been to this day). These were the people of Edom (the very people who then had control of Judaea in the persons of Herod's descendants), the Ishmaelites (the Arabs of the eastern deserts), the Moabites (located east of Jordan), the Hagarenes (Arabs of the south), the Gebalites (the people around Mount Hermon), the Ammonites (east of Jordan), the Amalekites (commonly associated with the Macedonians), the Philistines (found in southwest Palestine), the Tyrians (the people of Lebanon), and Asshur (the ancient Assyrians then represented as the Parthian Empire?). These were the only identifiable "ten nations" mentioned in the Old Testament, and it was believed that they would quickly take over control in the Middle East after the demise of the "iron legs" of the Romans.

It appeared as though Jerusalem and the Temple might well be the focal point of this world war between the East and the West and that a partial destruction of Jerusalem would take place. The prophet Daniel had made it clear that Jerusalem was first to be "destroyed" before his last sabbatical cycle of seven years could commence (Dan.9:26,27). The key to everything, however, was the fall of the "iron legs" and the emergence of the "ten kings" made of iron and miry clay (Dan.2:41-43). It was to be in "the days of *these kings* that the God of heaven would set up a kingdom which shall never be destroyed" (Dan.2:44). It was at the end of Daniel's last period of seven years that Christ was expected from heaven. But not before the "iron legs" of Rome were first overturned. Even Christ seemed to prophesy about Rome's breakup into segments when he stated that nation would be rising up against nation, and kingdom against kingdom (Matt.24:6,7). This worldwide rebellion against Rome was to be the beginning of the end-time sorrows (verse 8), which were to occur *before* the final end-time events would happen (verse 6).

Indeed, when the "little horn" was destined to come on the scene, the nation of Egypt would have broken away from its political allegiance to Rome and then be a free and independent power, along with the Libyans and Ethiopians (Dan.11:43). Even the nations of Moab, Ammon and Edom would also be independent countries and no longer a part of the Roman Empire (Dan.11:41). The nation of Edom was especially to become a prime force among the ten kings, with armies from all the nations of the world gathered within it for a major showdown with the Messiah at the time of his arrival (Isaiah 34 with Isaiah 63:1-4). [There were several interpretations about who this "Edom" represented in the first century. The word "Edom" can mean *man* or *mankind* (and James, as head of the Jerusalem church, interpreted it this way by quoting Amos 9:11 in Acts 15:17). Some even considered "Edom" to mean the final "Kingdom of Man" (the 666 kingdom of Revelation) and head of the other nine kings of the end-time confederation. Others thought of Edom as Judaea itself under the rulership of the Herod's. Still others imagined it to be Rome and not the literal "Edom" southeast of Judaea. It was this interpretation that finally prevailed in later Judaism.]

The point that must be understood is that *all* the prophecies connected to end-time events (no matter where they were found within the Old Testament revelation) were expected by first century Jews and Christians to have a complete fulfillment within that very generation. Thus, Daniel's last sabbatical period of seven years was to start with the Roman Empire being destroyed and ten kings arising from its ashes. This is what the apostles and most Jews were looking for in the middle of the first century.

The apostle Paul was no doubt referring to the collapse of the Roman Empire when he told the Thessalonians as early as A.D.50 that the advent of Christ was not then imminent since the prophesied apostasy had not yet occurred (II Thess.2:3). This was because a powerful personality was "holding down" or "hindering" the arrival of the Man of Sin and the great apostasy (verses 6 and 7). Since it is clear in Paul's comments that he had been giving the Thessalonians a commentary on the prophecies of Daniel, the only "hinderers" mentioned in those prophecies were angelic powers who had control over the nations (especially those directing affairs within the world empires mentioned in Daniel). It should be recalled that the angel

Gabriel informed Daniel that "the Prince of Persia *withstood me* (hindered me) one and twenty days" (Dan.10:13). There was also the angelic prince over the empire of Alexander who was also a "hinderer" to Gabriel (Dan.10:20). In fact, it was believed in early times that all the nations had angelic powers ruling over them and that all of them were ultimately under the control of Satan (Matt.4:8-11; Eph.6:12). On the other hand, the nation of Israel had the archangel Michael in charge of its affairs (Dan.10:21). Michael is the only angelic authority recorded in the Bible who had the power to overcome these "hinderers" over the various nations on earth.

These angelic powers were believed to battle with one another in heavenly spheres and the outcome of those wars was reflected in the history of nations on earth (Rev.12:7-17). Whatever people today may think of such beliefs is not at issue in our discussion. It is what the ancients thought that can help us understand the history of the first century. And certainly, the apostle Paul believed that there were angelic powers in charge of the various nations of the world. And in Daniel, those over the Gentile nations were often the "hinderers" of righteous angels. Only Michael the archangel had superior powers, as far as information in the Bible is concerned. And the apostle Paul could see in A.D.50 that the angelic powers in charge of the Roman Empire were still very much in command of the Roman government. There was then no evidence to Paul that the angelic powers of the prophesied ten nations to arise from the ruins of the "iron legs" were winning any celestial battles which would have ramifications on earth. This is why the apostle Paul told the Thessalonians that the angel in charge of the Roman Empire was still "hindering" the arrival of the ten nations and the "little horn" of Daniel. Paul told them about the thing *hindering* the emergence of the Man of Sin. This "thing" was no doubt the Roman Empire. But it was a personality actually doing the *hindering*. This must have been the angel over that Empire (II Thess.2:6-9). As stated before, the only kind of "hinderers" in the Book of Daniel were the angelic powers ruling over the various nations, so Paul must have been referring to those hinderers (or more specifically to the *one hinderer* over the Romans) who still prevented the arrival of the "little horn." It was Roman power, the empire of the "iron legs," which stood in the way of the emergence of the false messianic figure who would control ten kings after the collapse of the Roman Empire. This meant that as long as the Romans were strong and in solid control of Palestine, there could be no Antichrist coming forth from the eastern areas of the Empire.

There was also one other important point of prophecy that had to be fulfilled. It was plain in the long prediction found in Zechariah chapters 12 to 14 that for a short time before the introduction of the kingdom of God on earth (and no doubt because of the collapse of the Roman Empire), the people of Judah would once again become a powerful, independent nation among other peoples of the Middle East. It was felt that a restoration of Israel to independent nationhood and the revival of the Davidic kingdom would occur just before the coming of the "Day of the Lord." This restitution was a part of the task that a future "Elijah" would accomplish (Mal.4:5,6) — a person who would finish what John the Baptist had begun (Mark 9:11,12). This restoration was mentioned by Peter as something that must occur just before the return of Christ — indeed, it would be *that* very event which would signal the revelation of the Messiah from heaven (Acts 3:19-21). This is what Zechariah no doubt referred to when he said that Judah would once again become a powerful and independent nation (with the Davidic dynasty restored) just prior to the establishment of the Messianic kingdom (Zech.12,13, and 14). The first six verses of Zechariah 12 spoke particularly of this restored condition of Judah to a renewed prominence in the land of Palestine.

> "In that day will I make the governors of Judah like an hearth of fire among the wood, and like a torch of fire in a sheaf; and they shall devour all the people round about, on the right hand and on the left; and Jerusalem [which the prophecy shows was lately destroyed] shall be inhabited again in her own place, even in Jerusalem" (Zech.12:6).

Of course, people in our own time usually see this as pointing to the nation of Israel today, because it seems to fit so well (and it may be true), but we have to remember that back in the first century, when the apostles thought that the end of the age was upon them, those prophecies in Zechariah (and all the other end-time prophecies found throughout the Old Testament) were expected to have their fulfillment in that generation. With this belief firmly held in their minds, the apostles had no alternative but to imagine that the breakup of the Roman Empire was inevitable (with ten kingdoms emerging from its ruins), then there would be Judah, for a short time, overthrowing the Herodian rulers to bring about a restoration of the Davidic dynasty (Zech.12:8-14). This would be followed, so they thought, by a Great Tribulation upon Judaea which would witness the destruction of 2/3rds of the population (Zech.13:7-9). Soon after that holocaust the prophecy of Zechariah said that the Lord would arrive on the scene at the Mount of Olives to deliver Judah from their troubles and that they would then be blessed (Zech.14:1-21).

Since these prophetic events had never occurred to the Jews before, the apostles believed that Christ would be the one to place his feet on the Mount of Olives at his second advent. It must have been clear to them that *all the events* mentioned in Zechariah (and in other prophecies) had to take place *before* Christ could come back to earth. And the last possible year for the sequence of events to begin and have their fulfillment by the end of the 40 years' generation from Christ's resurrection was the year A.D.63. That year, however, came and went without any clue that the Romans would invade the Parthians and the Jews, let alone lose the war. In fact, just the reverse happened. The off and on wars of the Romans and Parthians which lasted through the first nine years of Nero's reign came to an end in the Spring of A.D.63 with Parthian envoys appearing in Rome with a proposal that offered terms of capitulation to the Romans (*Cambridge Ancient History,* X,pp.770-773).

Instead of a world war starting between the East and the West in A.D.63, followed by a revolt of the various kingdoms within the Roman dominion, to fulfill Christ's prophecies (Matt.24:6,7), just the opposite occurred. Rome had now become stronger than ever. With the passing of A.D.63 (the last possible year for the start of Daniel's last sabbatical cycle of seven years to occur within the 40 years' generation from Christ's resurrection), Paul came to the conclusion that the "iron legs" were going to continue in power for much time to come. The prophesied ten kings or the "little horn" were not now going to appear.

The apostle Peter not long after also became convinced that a great deal of time was still left in world history before the second advent. That's when he wrote his second epistle and said that a day with the Lord is as a thousand years. This was Peter's acknowledgement that Christ had not really delayed his coming. The apostles simply came to realize that Christ taught that the actual end-time would arrive upon a particular generation which would "see" the events of Matthew 24 and Zechariah 12 to 14. But with the year A.D.63 over, it became obvious that the generation which succeeded Christ's resurrection was *not* the prophesied one. This was the signal to Paul (and shortly afterwards to Peter and John) that it had become necessary to formulate a standard body of Christian documents which would last the *ekklesia* (the church) until those end-time events would actually occur.

Indeed, it took apostolic authority to canonize some of the books that were already circulating among Christians because some of them were speaking about the *soon coming* of Christ back to this earth and this would have meant that the books themselves were suspect of giving false teachings by some people. One of the reasons we can be assured that the writings of the New Testament are reliable is because several of the books do not try to hide the fact that the beliefs contained in them showed the *soon coming* of Christ yet they were still placed within the canon to give this misunderstanding of the early apostles. Respect for the Book of Revelation in particular went down considerably (along with the reputation of the apostle John who wrote it) in the eyes of some people when A.D.63 came and went without the detailed events prophesied in that recorded vision having occurred in that generation. It took the apostle John a long time to regain his standing even among the Christian congregations (as well as among the ordinary Jews and Gentiles who were not Christians). Only after Jerusalem was destroyed just as Christ said it would be (and about 35 years later) were the main points of the Book of Revelation revealed once again to John and the book finally became recognized as referring to the end-time generation and not that one back in the first century.

In the next chapter we will show the historical events that *did* develop from A.D.63 onwards which were highly significant in the creation of the final doctrines of the apostle Paul and Peter, and why the New Testament canon had to be established to direct the Christian *ekklesia* (church) with a standard body of documents that would remain authoritative until the actual second advent of Christ would take place.

10

The Completion of the Book of Acts

The official canonical history of the Christian church concludes with the two years' imprisonment of Paul in Rome (Acts 28). This was in A.D.61. Still, there were many important and highly significant events which occurred after that year. Why these occurrences were not recorded in the Book of Acts is a subject we will cover later, yet it is essential to fill in the historical environment in order to find the reasons for the canonization of the New Testament. This is what will be done in this chapter.

We now know there was no thought of forming a New Testament canon before A.D.63. After that date, however, the apostle Paul realized that the time of the end would not occur in that generation. But as late as A.D.61 Paul was still of the opinion that it was possible for Christ to appear very soon from heaven. That is what prompted him, at his release from his first Roman imprisonment, to proceed forward in finalizing his preaching of the Gospel to the world. He had been assigned all of the Gentile areas from Asia Minor to Spain in the west. And in A.D.61 he went to Spain in order to complete his mission. This was the last thing Paul had to accomplish in order for Christ to return to earth. Christ had made it clear that "this gospel of the kingdom shall be preached in all the world for a witness unto all nations; and then shall the end come" (Matt.24:14). To the people living in the first century "all the world" normally meant the government system under which they lived, and to the Jewish people in particular it signified all areas of the world in which the Jews resided. People back in that period did not construe the phrase "all the world" to mean the totality of the globe. When Luke said that Joseph and Mary had to appear at Bethlehem for the birth of Christ because "all the world should be enrolled" (Luke 2:1), he was only referring to the world which was under the sway of the Roman government. And in the case of the apostle Paul, "all the world" to him only indicated the specific areas of our planet that were assigned to him by the early apostles. Paul's "world," however, did embrace the region of Spain. This is why, after his release from his first Roman imprisonment in A.D.61, he made his journey to the final area allotted to him for preaching the Gospel.

There is really no doubt that Paul went to Spain because Clement of Rome, in the last decade of the first century, stated that Paul "taught righteousness *to the whole world*, having travelled to the limits of the west" (I Clement 5:7). Clement was well aware what the phrase "the whole world" meant to first century people and he stated that Paul completely fulfilled that responsibility by finally preaching "west of Rome" — in the region of Spain (Rom.15:24-28).

The finality of Paul's preaching in the geographical districts designated to him presents us with an important piece of knowledge regarding the time of composition for some New Testament books. Look first at First Timothy. In speaking about the mystery of Christ, Paul told Timothy (in A.D.64) that Christ "was preached among the nations and was believed on in the world" (I Tim.3:16). This indication gives evidence that Paul had already gone to Spain and that he had, by A.D.63, returned to the East. The fact that Paul had travelled to Spain (the extremity of his "world" assignment) is also a helpful clue to the time the Book of Colossians was written. There are two statements in that epistle which clearly date its writing to a period *after* Paul's journey to Spain (which took place from A.D.61 to 62). Notice Colossians 1:23.

> "Do not be shifted away from the hope of the Gospel which you heard, *and which was preached IN ALL CREATION under the heaven,* of which Gospel I Paul became a minister."

This means that Paul had already accomplished his trip to Spain by the time he wrote Colossians, and this resulted in "the whole world" having been evangelized as far as Paul was concerned. This is emphasized a few verses earlier in Colossians 1:6.

> "You heard the word of truth of the Gospel which has presented

itself to you, even as it is bearing fruit and increasing *in all the world."*

These references showing that Paul's "world" had been evangelized when he wrote Colossians help us to date several epistles. One of them is what we presently call "Ephesians." When one compares the subject matter of Colossians with Ephesians it becomes obvious that the two letters were composed at the same time. Indeed, the letter titled to "the Ephesians" was really the one which Paul called "to the Laodiceans" in Colossians 4:16. The cities of Colossae and Laodicea were located very near one another in the eastern section of the province of Asia. And in some early manuscripts, the title "Ephesus" in the first verse of the epistle to "the Ephesians" is left blank and a space provided for the insertion of an unknown destination. There is even internal proof in the "Ephesian" epistle itself that it could not have been written solely to the Christians at Ephesus because Paul said in Colossians that he had never seen any of the people of Colossae or Laodicea face to face (Col.2:1). And he said virtually the same thing in this so-called "Ephesian" letter. In Ephesians 1:15 Paul stated that he had only *heard* of the faith of those to whom he was writing in "Ephesians" and that he had never seen them face to face. But this was not the case with the actual Ephesians. This is because Paul had been to Ephesus on several occasions, even staying for two years at one time (Acts 19:10). Paul certainly was well acquainted with many Ephesians. This is evidence that the so-called letter of Paul to the Ephesians which we presently find in our New Testament was not intended to go to the people of Ephesus (though it is probable that the letter finally wound up at Ephesus at a later time). Actually, the "Ephesian" letter is the one which Paul called "to the Laodiceans" (Col.4:16). And, there is ancient testimony that suggests this. Prof. Alan MacNeile points out that "the most important authorities [among them the Sinaiticus manuscript and ancient codices known to Origen] omit 'at Ephesus;' Marcion (and, according to Tertullian, other heretics) styled the epistle 'to the Laodiceans' " (*Intro. to Study of the New Testament.,* p.176). This ancient appraisal was probably correct.

We now come to an important point regarding the letters to the Colossians and the "Ephesians" (that is, to the Laodiceans). We find that Paul wrote them while he was in prison (Eph.4:1; 6:20; Col.4:3,10,18). The letter to Philemon which we presently have in our New Testament canon was also written by Paul while in bondage (Philemon 10). And in his letter to Philemon, Paul mentioned that he was about to be released from that particular imprisonment (verse 22) and he wanted Philemon (who must also have lived near Colossae) to prepare a lodging for him (verse 22). Paul was about to be freed and he wanted to stay awhile with Philemon. This soon release from prison is also mentioned in Colossians and "Ephesians." Paul asked the Colossians to pray "that God may open to us a door for the word, to declare the mystery of Christ, on account of which I am in prison, that I may make it clear, as I ought to speak" (Col.4:3,4). There is a similar request in Ephesians 6:18-20. "That utterance may be given me in opening my mouth boldly to proclaim the mystery of the gospel, for which I am an ambassador in chains; that I may declare it boldly, as I ought to speak." Paul felt that a new opportunity was opening to him to further spread the teaching of "the Mystery" of God. His imminent release from that imprisonment was no doubt viewed by him as the door beginning to open.

We now need to ask an important question. In what area of the world was Paul's imprisonment when he wrote the epistles of Colossians, Ephesians, and Philemon? We have a good clue to the location when we read Paul's second letter to Timothy which he wrote from Rome. He mentioned that Onesiphorus had proved to be of great service to him while in Ephesus and that Timothy had been well aware of the help given by Onesiphorus (II Tim.1:16,17). Indeed, if one reads II Timothy 1:15 through 18 carefully, it will be seen that those four verses speak about Paul's experiences while he was in Asia (v.15), particularly in the city of Ephesus (v.18). And in the midst of speaking about the events that happened to him at Ephesus, Paul said that Onesiphorus helped him *while he was in his chains* (v.16). Paul also put into the same context a parenthetical reference that Onesiphorus *had ALSO* sought him out in Rome (v.17). Paul, however, was informing Timothy about Onesiphorus' help *when he was in an Ephesian imprisonment,* not his current one at Rome. When this is realized, a flood of light comes on the scene with more details of what happened to Paul in Asia, particularly at Ephesus. This information makes it almost certain that Paul wrote "Ephesians,"

Colossians, and Philemon during an imprisonment at Ephesus, *not* from either of his two at Rome or the one in Caesarea. An Ephesian confinement has been recognized by scholars (Guthrie, *NTI*, p.474).

Clement, the Roman elder of the late first century, said that Paul underwent *seven* major imprisonments (I Clement 5:6). These may well be identified in the New Testament: the first was recorded in Acts 16:23, then there were at least two at Corinth (II Cor.11:23 with Rom.16:7), a fourth when he spent two years at Caesarea (Acts 26:29), a fifth at his first Roman imprisonment, the sixth was the one at Ephesus when he wrote the letters of Colossians, Philemon, and "Ephesians" (II Tim.1:18), and his seventh (and final imprisonment) was at Rome during which he was executed (II Tim.1:8; 2:8,9; 4:16).

Regarding the development of the New Testament canon, we need to look closely at that sixth imprisonment at Ephesus. It is an important one in an historical sense because it gives a chronological benchmark for the writing of several epistles of Paul. Since this incarceration occurred *after* his visit to Spain, we can now determine when certain important letters were composed. Let us look at the matter.

The first epistle that Paul wrote after having visited Spain was Titus. In that letter he mentioned that he had left Titus in Crete to evangelize the island and to raise up churches in its various regions. This entailed the ordination of ministers to pastor each church. Obviously, Paul was well aware by this time that Christ was not going to return from heaven in that generation. Everything in the context of the epistle to Titus suggests that Paul thought a long period would elapse before that glorious event. If we allow Paul to have preached about a year or so in Spain, this would indicate he returned to the East about A.D.63—probably going first to Crete with Titus, and then on to Nicopolis in Western Greece where he decided to winter (Titus 3:12). The Sabbatical Year of A.D.62 to 63 was in full swing.

The following Spring Paul journeyed north to Macedonia (perhaps with a brief stop in Ephesus to see Timothy — I Tim.1:3). After spending some time in the area of Macedonia, he wrote his first letter to Timothy which we have in our New Testament (I Tim.1:3). This was probably in the Summer of A.D.64. In that letter he mentioned a specific doctrine which he called "the Mystery" (I Tim.3:16). This new doctrine which he explained in detail in the epistles to the Colossians and "Ephesians," had never been revealed in previous ages (Eph.3:1-11; Col.1:26). When one reads the accounts carefully it can be seen that this teaching was a brand new revelation only given to him and others when it was recognized by Paul that the prophesied end-time events leading up to Christ's second advent had not occurred in A.D.63. The revelation of that new doctrinal teaching must have been given to Paul around this same year because he told the Colossians and "Ephesians" that "the Mystery" had *NOW* been revealed to the apostles and prophets by the Spirit (Col.1:26; Eph.3:5). This majestic teaching may well have been revealed after the A.D.63 disappointment to help explain why Christ was not returning in that generation. (There is evidence, however, that the apostles Peter and John thought there might still be a chance for the Abomination of Desolation to be set up in the "midst of the week" — the "midst of the week" would, of course, have been 3½ years within the sabbatical cycle from Autumn A.D.63 to Autumn A.D.70, which works out to near Passover in A.D.67. Something happened in the Spring of A.D.66, however, that caused all the apostles to accept the fact that Christ was not returning back at that time. This occurrence will be explained shortly.)

But by the year A.D.63, the apostle Paul was able to see that the Roman Empire (the "iron legs" of Daniel's image) was not going to collapse to allow the prophesied ten kings to emerge on the scene. He then became confident that the time of the end was far into the future. The final revelation of "the Mystery" appears to have been a substitute of encouragement for the disappointment of A.D.63. That doctrine was related in detail in Paul's letters to the Colossians and "Ephesians," and it was revealed to him most likely between his letter to Titus (A.D.63) and that of First Timothy (A.D.64).

After writing First Timothy in Macedonia, Paul returned to Ephesus in A.D.64. He then preached in the area and was finally cast into prison (his sixth major imprisonment). This is when he wrote Colossians, Philemon, and "Ephesians." It is noteworthy that Paul described himself as "an old man" when he wrote Philemon, so the time period must have been very late in Paul's ministry. It fits in perfectly with this late imprisonment in Ephesus.

He was then released from bonds early in A.D.65 and went to Laodicea and Colossae (Philemon 22). From there he continued his journey into Galatia (specifically to Antioch, Iconium, and Lystra) (II Tim.3:11). He encountered stiff opposition and persecution in this area (we will explain *why* a little later). After his stay in Galatia he began his last trip to Rome, to his final imprisonment and death. Whether Paul was placed in custody in Galatia and escorted back to Rome, or whether he went on his own accord, is not stated. He may have returned through Troas, at the northwestern part of Asia Minor, but instead of going the land route through Macedonia and Illyricum to the Adriatic Sea, he journeyed to Corinth then Malta (II Tim.4:20) finally arriving in Rome. He must have reached Rome in the Autumn of A.D.65. After awhile, probably in middle Autumn, he wrote his second letter to Timothy asking him to come to Rome with John Mark before the Winter of A.D.65/66 set in (II Tim.4:21). It was sometime around the Autumn or Winter of A.D.66 that he met his death by execution.

The Historical Environment

We now need to retrace our tracks and look at the political and religious events which were occurring in Judaea and the Roman empire from A.D.62 to the time of Paul and Peter's deaths (A.D.66 to A.D.67). As far as the New Testament historical record is concerned, the evangelist Luke in the Book of Acts stopped his narrative near the Summer of A.D.61. The book ends so abruptly and without an "Amen" to close it that many people have thought the book was never finished, or that the later parts of it were for some reason taken away. Whatever the case, it can be stated without controversy that some of the most profound historical events involving the Christian church (and certainly the canonization of the New Testament) transpired *after* the close of the Book of Acts. What we need to do is to look carefully at those few years that succeeded the New Testament historical record because they contain information of developments which greatly affected the writing of the last letters of the apostles and the reasons for the formation of the New Testament canon.

The first major occurrence was the martyrdom of James, the brother of Christ and head of the Jerusalem church. This happened at Passover in A.D.62 (Eusebius, *Eccl. Hist.* II.23). This was followed by the sabbatical year of A.D.62 to A.D.63 and the commencement of a prophetic dirge against Jerusalem and the Temple by a man named Joshua ben Ananias (*War*, VI.300-309). Josephus, who was an eyewitness to all affairs from that time to the destruction of Jerusalem and the Temple, said that the inauguration of this prophetic dirge by Joshua ben Ananias was the start of the ruin of the Jews in Palestine. It was then that "sickness fell upon our city, and everything went from bad to worse" (*Antiq.* XX.214). The malady started with the Feast of Tabernacles of A.D.62 (and shortly thereafter). "From this date were sown in the city the seeds of its impending doom" (*War*, II.276). From the Autumn of A.D.62, and for seven years and five months, Joshua ben Ananias continued to cry out "Woe to Jerusalem." Since Christ himself had said that Jerusalem and the Temple were to be destroyed (Matt.24:1,2; Luke 21:20) this may have been a reason why many Christians retreated from Palestine at that time. Eusebius, the Church historian of the fourth century, said this very period was when the apostles and disciples who were in Judaea began to be scattered around the world (*Eccl.Hist.* III.1). Thomas was supposed to have gone to Parthia, Andrew to Scythia, and the apostle John went to the western parts of Asia Minor (around Ephesus) where he stayed until his death (*ibid.*). In fact, Eusebius said (and there is little doubt to disbelieve him) that the apostles not long after the death of James in A.D.62 "were driven out of Judaea" (III.5). With chaos beginning in Palestine, and knowing that the prophesied destruction of the country and Jerusalem was imminent, there is historical evidence showing many Jewish people leaving the country for other areas of the Roman Empire. Indeed, the emigration became so intense that by the year A.D.64 (when the Roman procurator Florus took over rule in Judaea) Josephus said that people from all over Judaea, even whole cities and regions of the country, sought refuge in other provinces of the Roman Empire (*War*, II.278,279). A great influx of Jewish people from Palestine began to swell the eastern provinces, and this especially involved the provinces of Asia Minor (modern Turkey). Among the refugees was John the apostle who went to Ephesus. Phillip and his virgin daughters went to Hieriopolis near Laodicea. This vast movement of Jewish people (Christian and non-Christian alike) provided some social and political problems to arise in the areas to which they immigrated.

It was at this time that Peter wrote his first epistle from Jerusalem (which he cryptically called "Babylon" like that of the Book of Revelation 17:5 with a further reference in Revelation 11:8). Peter was one of the chief apostles to the Jewish people (Gal.2:7-9). It is interesting that Peter called his readers, who were scattered through the areas of northern and western Asia Minor "alien residents" (ones who were living temporarily in those northern areas) (I Pet.1:1,17; 2:11,12). They were not long time residents of the provinces in Asia Minor. And since there was a mass exodus of Jewish people out of Palestine in the Spring and Summer of A.D.64 into other provinces of the Roman Empire, it is conceivable that Peter wrote his first epistle primarily to those Jewish/Christians who left Palestine en masse (with other Jews) from A.D.62 up to A.D.64.

This large exodus of Christian people from Palestine may account for one of the reasons why only very few were left in Judaea by A.D.66 when the last remnants of Christians retreated to the city of Pella some 60 miles northeast of Jerusalem (Eusebius, *Eccl.Hist.* III.5). This final retreat was in the Summer of A.D.66 (after an oracle given in the Temple at Pentecost that even the Deity was leaving the Temple).

The city of Pella was a Gentile city of modest size. For these remnant Christians to find a temporary residence there shows that their number must have been relatively small. While the Book of Acts records that there had been *tens of thousands of Jews* who believed in Christ in A.D.56 (and they were all ardent law-keepers), within ten years (by A.D.66) only hundreds (or at best a thousand or so) fled from Jerusalem and the countryside of Judaea to the Gentile city of Pella. The fact that they made their way to Pella, instead of the mountain and wilderness areas around Palestine, shows they were aware that the second advent of Christ was no longer an impending prospect. It was clear in the teachings of Christ that the actual end-time generation of Christians in Palestine should flee to the mountains and wilderness — a perfect description of the region of Edom in which the city of Petra was located (Isa.16:1-4; Matt.24:16; Rev.12:14). But Pella was *not* a mountainous or wilderness area. The fact that the few Christians left in Jerusalem and Judaea went to Pella is sufficient evidence they were convinced that the prophesied events associated with the second advent were not then happening.

We will later see in this chapter that a major diminution of the Christian population in Judaea was not only because of a mass exodus of people from Palestine from A.D.62 to A.D.64, but there were vast numbers who abandoned the Christian faith after the great disappointment of A.D.63. Many of them joined the revolutionary forces in the Roman/Jewish War of A.D.66 to 70. The New Testament records this lapse from their previous convictions. When the crucial year A.D.63 passed, and no significant end-time prophecies which Jesus said would occur were then happening, thousands of Jewish Christians began to deny the new faith and the sovereignty of Christ, along with the authority of the apostles. We will later see that the apostle Peter in his second epistle was speaking about this great apostasy which began to occur just before the Roman/Jewish War got into full swing.

We now need to look at the historical environment of the period around the year A.D.64. The events of that year played a significant part in the history of Christianity.

First of all, there was the great fire of Rome which started on the 19th of July. Much of the magnificent city of Rome was ruined in the flames and this proved to be a profound historical occurrence. The repercussions of it were echoed around the whole of the Empire.

There was speculation that Nero himself had ordered Rome's destruction so that a new city (with "modern" facilities throughout) could emerge from the ashes of old Rome. Indeed, a new city was begun with the prospect that Nero's name would identify it. There were also suggestions made by some of Nero's astrologers that he ought to move his capital to Jerusalem because it was then a popular belief that a new world empire was on the verge of fulfillment, and that it would be established in Palestine (Suetonius, *Nero* 40).

There was an air of Messianic expectation that a "Christ" would then take control of the entire world. This belief was widespread even at Rome. This is one of the main reasons that the fire of Rome was blamed on a "Chrestus" (a Messiah figure) who was attempting to establish a world government by the overthrow of the Roman Empire. Recall that in Jewish circles it was normally believed that the kingdom of the "iron legs" (the Roman Empire) was to be destroyed in order for ten kings to have dominion just prior to the establishment of the world order. The fire of Rome was seen as a beginning to the fall of the Empire. (The apostle Paul, however, had been preaching since A.D.63 that the real fall of Rome and the emergence of the kingdom of God on earth, were to be far into the future.) Nonetheless, people calling themselves "Christians," even true Christians, were blamed for the fire of Rome. This resulted in a major affliction throughout the Roman Empire against all people who claimed to be Christians. The first epistle of Peter, speaking about a fiery trial which was then occurring upon many Christians throughout the world (I Pet.5:9), appears to have been written in the late Summer or Autumn of A.D.64, at the exact time when the persecutions of Christians for the fire of Rome began to reach their apex. Peter's description of the great fiery trial then upon the Christians of Asia Minor and his emphasis that in spite of the circumstances people should still obey the government of the emperor and his assistants seem to reflect the political environment of this period of persecution (I Pet.2:17 with 2:23; 3:14; 4:12).

The second major event of A.D.64 which affected Christians was the completing of the Temple (begun about 80 years before by King Herod) (*Antiq.*XX.219). This was especially important to the Jews because it now meant that their Messiah could arrive. The Temple was fully restored and it was ready for a proper national worship to accommodate the rule of the Messiah.

It is interesting that at the very time the finishing touches were being made to the Temple, the apostle Paul was then teaching the revelation called "the Mystery" in which he said that "the middle wall of partition" in the Temple at Jerusalem was now abolished and destroyed in the eyes of God (Eph.2:14). What a paradox. Paul was speaking about the destruction of the physical Temple as a means to reach God at the very time it was completed and put into final operation. Paul was even teaching that the type of Temple that God now desired was made up of "new men" (not physical Jews or others who depended upon the Temple at Jerusalem) (Eph.2:14-22). This teaching no doubt aroused a great amount of hostility to Paul among the Jews (even Christian Jews since they were all zealous for the Law of Moses).

The apostle Paul had a long history of teaching against the need for the physical ceremonies of Moses concerning circumcision, the

Temple, holy days, the exclusion of Gentiles, etc. (Gal.2:11-14; II Cor.11:4 to II Cor.12:11; I Tim.1:6,7; Tit.1:10-14). But now it was almost more than those who were zealous of the Law could take. Paul was now saying (about A.D.64) that the Temple itself was no longer the spiritual dwelling place of God and that its "middle wall of partition" was now (in a symbolic sense) leveled to the ground.

This revelation of "the Mystery" got Paul in difficulty especially with the Jewish people of Asia Minor. The large influx of Palestinian Jews into the area (and many Jewish/Christians were among them) from A.D.62 to A.D.64 made the region quite hostile to Paul and his "new-fangled" teachings which abrogated (from their point of view) the Law of Moses to which they held tenaciously. Many Jewish Christians simply did not know what to make of the teachings of the apostle Paul. He had had a long history of irritating them with his doctrines which they thought were contrary to the Law, and now he was making it even more difficult for them to accept him when he was tearing down the significance of the Temple at the very time the structure was completed. This was almost too much for many Jewish Christians to take. As a result, when he went to Galatia in A.D.65 (among the vast numbers of new resident aliens from Palestine, and ardent law-keepers), Paul encountered intense hostility to his message and he mentioned this in his last letter to Timothy (II Tim.3:11). Indeed, after the revelation of "the Mystery" the situation went from bad to worse. Paul's teaching, even among professing Christians, was looked on as so revolutionary and counter to all traditional teaching among the Jews that people turned against him almost wholesale. So replete was this rejection of Paul's teaching that Paul told Timothy that "all the men in Asia have turned away from me" (II Tim.1:15). Most of the Jewish Christians simply gave up on Paul. His teaching that the physical Temple at Jerusalem was irrelevant and of no spiritual value in the doctrine of "the Mystery" was too much for many of them to swallow. Even some of Paul's dearest co-workers turned away from him when he began to teach his widesweeping anti-traditional doctrines that he recorded in Colossians and "Ephesians." Even Demas, his close associate and friend, found it impossible to side with Paul in these matters (II Tim.4:10). Demas preferred the Christianity "of this age" (in whatever way he interpreted it) than the spiritual system of belief the apostle Paul was talking about.

What irritated the Jewish Christians so much was Paul's insistence that the sabbaths, holy days, the new moons, and the food laws of the Mosaic Law *were no longer essential to keep EVEN FOR JEWS*. While Jewish Christians could barely tolerate Paul as long as he said that Gentiles did not have to be circumcised and keep the external ceremonies of the Law, they went totally against him when he said that Jewish Christians could discontinue the use of them as well (Eph.2:14-22).

What provoked the Jews more than anything, however, was Paul's appraisal that the Mosaic Law was altogether inferior to the new revelations of Christianity. Paul was teaching that the Law was given to Moses by the hand of a mediator, and that that particular mediator *was not God* (Gal.3:19,20). It was "the angel of the Lord" who spoke to Moses at the burning bush, and coming in the name and authority of God, who actually gave Moses the Law (Acts 7:30,31). This chief angel had other angels to help him when he gave Moses the Ten Commandments and the other laws. Stephen said that Israel "received the law by the disposition of angels, and have not kept it" (Acts 7:53). In the Book of Hebrews it was stated that the Mosaic Law had been "spoken by angels" (Heb.2:2). Even the Jewish historian Josephus was aware of the general belief among Jewish people that the Law had been given through the agency of angels. He said: "We have learned the noblest of our doctrines and the holiest of our laws through angels sent from God" (*Antiq.* XV.136).

While it was normally accepted that God used angels (and particularly "the angel of the Lord") to give the Law in his name, Paul even went further and called them the "elemental spirits" (the principalities and powers) which Christ had triumphed over at his crucifixion (Col.2:8,14,20 — see the RSV or Moffatt for the proper translation of these important verses). Indeed, Paul even referred to the Law of Moses as "a religious system derived from the angels" (Col.2:18, note the original Greek which makes this clear). And this "religion of the angels" was no longer in force for Christians, whether they be Jews or Gentiles.

> "Blotting out the handwriting of ordinances that was against us, which was contrary to us, and took it out of the way, nailing it to his cross, and having spoiled principalities and powers [the ones

who gave the ordinances], he made a show of them openly, triumphing over them in it. Because of this, let no man judge you in matters of eating or drinking, or in respect of an holyday, or of the new moon, or of the sabbath days, which things are a shadow of things to come. The body [the actual *body*, not the shadow] belongs to Christ" (Col.2:14-16).

Paul was beginning to teach with the new revelation of "the Mystery" that Christians were dead to the ordinances of the "elemental spirits" which gave the Law to Moses. Something better had come and it was the teaching of God's Son himself. The Law of Moses had been completely superseded and made irrelevant as a means to salvation.

While this may make perfectly good sense to Christians today who have long respected Paul's teachings on these matters, it was not so with the early Jewish Christians. Many of them considered these revolutionary doctrines as blatantly heretical and a complete apostasy from the original teachings of the early apostles. It must be recalled that most Jewish Christians were "zealous of the law" and were very careful in keeping all the Mosaic customs (Acts 21:20,21). There can be no doubt that vast numbers of Jewish Christians disowned Paul and his doctrines which he boldly asserted in the books of "Ephesians" and Colossians. This could easily account for the reason that *all Asia* repudiated Paul in early A.D.65.

Since Paul said that those in the province of Asia turned away from him, we need to ask about the apostle John's reaction to Paul's teachings. There is little reason to doubt that John was living in this very region of Asia Minor when the great rejection of Paul took place.

John was quite conservative in his understanding of the Gospel. In his writings of the middle 60's A.D., he insisted his readers should recapture the teachings which were given "from the beginning" (I John 2:7,13; 3:8,11; II John 5). The wording in his three epistles seems to decry any type of "new-fangled" teachings that were then emerging on the scene. To John, his emphasis was back to "the beginning." But near A.D.64 we find Paul advocating the new revelation of "the Mystery" right in the area where the apostle John was living and preaching. On the surface it seems strange that Paul said not one word about meeting with John or having a combined preaching effort with him. Were they at odds with one another at this time? Paul stated about a year later that "all the men of Asia have turned away from me" (I Tim.1:15). It is true that Paul did not say that John himself had turned from him, but John was almost certainly in Asia at the time and it seems definite that John was not at first like-minded with Paul in his renouncement of the Mosaic requirements even for the Jewish Christians.

It should be recalled that there is not one bit of evidence in the New Testament that John and Paul ever associated with each other in their separate ministries. At an early conference in Jerusalem it was agreed that James, Peter and John were to concentrate their efforts on preaching to the Jews while Paul and Barnabas were to go to the Gentiles (Gal.2:7-9). But a short time later, when the subject of cirumcision regarding the Gentiles was discussed in Jerusalem, there is no mention that John even attended the conference (Acts 15).

The truth is, the original apostles who were first ordained by Christ before the crucifixion were zealous for the retention of the Mosaic Law within the doctrinal teachings of Christianity. This was not the case with Paul. He came to see the matter through completely different eyeglasses and the apostles at Jerusalem became well aware that Paul was not in the camp of the law-keepers. This resulted in a continuous and deep-seated suspicion of the apostle Paul among the authorities at Jerusalem (cf. Acts 21:18-25). This mistrust of Paul certainly included the apostle John who made a point of advocating a retention of early teachings. So, it appears that John was not at first fond of Paul's doctrines. Not only was Paul espousing that the food laws of Moses were defunct, but also the sabbaths, the holy days, the new moons, and even the ordained regulations governing the holy Temple were now abolished. Did the apostle John and the other Jewish Christians of Asia Minor (and there must have been thousands in the area by A.D.64) completely abandon Paul and his "new-fangled" and "heretical" teachings?

And what about Peter? When he wrote his first epistle to the "aliens and temporary residents" of the various provinces of Asia, he was instructing people who were directly within the areas that Paul had long ago evangelized. Indeed, the apostle Paul made it clear that he in no way would teach in regions not assigned to him (II Cor.10:13-16), and even Peter and John had commissioned him some 15 years earlier to the Gentile regions of Galatia and Asia. But now, here was Peter writing to Paul's regions of responsibility and probably at the very time Paul was there. He says not one word to or about Paul. This seems strange if they were both in a harmonious relationship at the time. Paul's teachings that the very fabric of Mosaic requirements was now irrelevant in matters of attaining a righteousness in Christ was considered a heretical teaching to most Jewish Christians. The apostle Peter was certainly aware of their attitude to such revolutionary and anti-traditional teachings. Perhaps he was trying to conciliate matters by not referring to Paul and what he was then advocating. Peter emphasized that all of them have "compassion for one another, to love the brethren, to be pitiful and courteous to all" (I Pet.3:8). Paul had long irritated most Jewish Christians with his abandonment of Moses even for the Gentiles. But now he was instructing Jews that the Mosaic sabbaths, holydays, new moons, food laws, and even the Temple itself were no longer efficacious in showing a righteousness in Christ. This no doubt was the straw that broke the camel's back.

And what was the apostle John's attitude to Paul's doctrines? There can hardly be a doubt that John was in the region of Asia Minor when Paul made his final tour of preaching in the area. And the people in the regions where Paul had so long labored were so upset with him that the vast majority simply gave him up for lost (II Tim.1:15). Indeed, even shortly later when Paul was once again in prison in Rome he told Timothy that even his close associates in Rome had deserted him and that "only Luke is with me" (II Tim.4:11).

The progressive teaching that Paul finally arrived at appeared too reactionary to most early Christians, especially Jewish Christians. Even Peter and John may have lifted their eyebrows when Paul went as far as he did in his statements that the Old Testament ritualistic requirements were now abandoned as a means of reaching a righteousness in Christ.

Thankfully, however, this repudiation of Paul was not to last long as far as Peter and John were concerned (and the other Christians who followed them). Within two years of the Christians of Asia Minor renouncing Paul, Peter and John came to be solidly within the camp of Paul. Something happened to make them change their minds.

The Acceptance of Paul's Teachings

The Christians who rejected Paul about A.D.65 did not have long to wait to see that he was correct about the Temple and the physical requirements of Moses. There were some major events concerning the Temple which happened in the Spring of A.D.66 that changed the minds of conservative Jewish Christians who continued to trust in its value. Those events were so striking and profound in the interpretation of Christian doctrine that it will pay us to look at them.

Josephus records three major miraculous occurrences dealing directly with the Temple which happened over a two month period in the Spring of A.D.66, just a few months before the major Roman/Jewish War broke out that saw the destruction of the Temple and the city of Jerusalem. The first incident took place on the eighth day of Nisan just before the festival of Passover. We should let Josephus tell us in his own words what happened.

> "Before the revolt and the disturbances which led to the war, at the time when the people were gathering for the feast of unleavened bread, on the eighth of the month Nisan, at the ninth hour of the night [at 3 o'clock in the morning], so brilliant a light shone around the altar and the inner temple that it seemed to be broad daylight; and this continued for the space of half an hour. By the novices this was regarded as a good omen, but by the sacred scribes it was at once interpreted in accord with the events which happened afterwards" (*War*,VI.290).

This was an interesting phenomenon. How would the wise among the scribes have interpreted this visitation and departure of the great light — the shekinah glory of God? For those who used the illustrations of the Old Testament as a guide, it would not have been difficult to figure out. It was recorded in the Holy Scriptures that when Israel came out of Egypt under the leadership of Moses, they were led by a cloud during daylight and a pillar of light at night (Psa.78:14). Throughout the whole period of the wilderness journeys of Israel the cloud and the light remained over the Tabernacle (Num.9:15-23). As a signal to move from place to place, the cloud and the light would be "taken up" and lead them to a different location (Num.9:17). Thus, the portable Tabernacle (which was considered the residence of God) was to be moved from its former place to another site when the cloud and the light were "taken up." There was no doubt that the removal of the shekinah glory from its former position meant that God himself was moving away from that location. So, the great light of God appeared directly over the altar and sanctuary on Mount Moriah at Jerusalem. It did not stay there, however. After thirty minutes of light which had the brillance of mid-day, the light then removed itself from the site of the Temple. If the holy sanctuary would have been a tent (like the Tabernacle in the wilderness), this would have been sure evidence that God was moving his sanctuary to a different area on earth. But there was one problem with the situation of the Temple in A.D.66. It was no longer a portable Tabernacle. Josephus said that those who were wise among the scribes interpreted this as a signal that God was moving away from Mount Moriah. This would have proved to be a dire predicament for the physical Temple (which had just been completed about two years before) because it was not possible to transfer the Temple (stones and all) to another location. With the shekinah glory departing from the precincts of the Temple this meant that God himself was preparing to move from Mount Moriah, to leave it behind as an "empty dwelling place." Indeed, when the next two signs about the Sanctuary are considered, it shows that God was truly deserting the Temple itself and that the building would be no more sacred than Herod's palace. Let us now note the second of these miraculous signs. Josephus said it was equally spectacular:

> "At that same feast, the eastern gate of the inner court at the sixth hour of the night [at midnight] opened of its own accord. This gate was of brass and very large and heavy, seeing that when it was closed each evening it took twenty men to shut it. It had bolts sunk to a great depth into a threshold made of a solid block of stone. The guards of the temple ran and reported the matter to the captain, and he came forward and with great difficulty managed to close it. This again to the uninitiated seemed like the best of signs, since they thought that God had opened to them the gate of blessings; but the wise understood that the security of the temple was leaving of its own accord and that the opening of the gate meant it was a gift to the enemy, interpreting the sign in their own minds as showing its impending desolation" (*War*, VI. 293-295).

Within a week after the great light of the shekinah glory was illuminated and "taken up," here was the massive Nicanor Gate of the Temple being opened up of its own accord. Josephus said the wise among the Jews were able to interpret this as a sign that God was getting ready to leave the Temple and to hand it over to the Romans for destruction. Indeed, Jewish records speak of the "gates" of the *Hekel* (the Holy Place) opening of themselves forty years *before* the destruction of the Temple in 70 A.D. "Forty years before the Temple was destroyed . . . the gates of the *Hekel* opened of their own accord, until R. Yohanan b. Zakkai rebuked them [the priests] saying: '*Hekel, Hekel*, why alarmist thou us? We know that thou art destined to be destroyed. For of thee hath prophesied Zechariah ben Iddo [Zech. 11:1]: Open thy doors, O Lebanon, and the fire shall eat thy cedars'" (*Yoma* 39b). The doors of the *Hekel* in Herod's Temple were eight stories high and in front of them was the veil that tore in two at Christ's crucifixion. Those doors had to open as well to gain entrance to the Holy Place. *That also happened in 30 A.D.* But back to 66 A.D.

There was a third miraculous sign even more to the point. This occurred about 50 days later on the Day of Pentecost and it clearly confirmed that the Deity was abandoning the Temple. The sign was not given in a corner (where no witnesses could see it) but it was shown to the combined body of 24 priests who represented the 24 orders of the Aaronic priesthood. There could have been no higher authorities in Judaism to receive such a manifestation of divine intentions. It was often thought that when momentous changes in religious or political systems were taking place, it required some clear sign from God. The witness of all 24 chief priests was powerful evidence to people of the first century that the supernatural event did in fact occur. Notice Josephus' description:

> "Moreover, at the festival which is called Pentecost, the priests on entering the inner court of the temple at nightfall, as their custom was in the accomplishment of their ministrations, stated that they first became aware of a commotion and a roar, and after that the voice of a great multitude saying 'We are departing hence'" (*War*, VI.299).

This was interpreted at the time that the Deity himself was then leaving the Temple as the two previous signs had shown he would.

(The fact that the supernatural voice said "We" rather than the singular "I" was no problem to first century Jews. They were well aware that the Deity went by the name of *Elohim* which was a unified plural designation, and even in Genesis the plural pronoun "Our" was associated with the personality of God. See Genesis 1:26 and 3:22.)

This departure of the Deity from the Temple at Pentecost of A.D.66 was exactly 36 years (to the very day) after the Holy Spirit was first given in power to the apostles and the others at the first Christian Pentecost recorded in Acts 2. And now, on the same Pentecost day, the witness was given that God himself was abandoning the Temple at Jerusalem. This meant that the Temple was no longer a holy sanctuary and that the building was no more sacred than any other secular building. Remarkably, even Jewish records show that the Jews had come to recognize that the shekinah glory of God left the Temple at this time and remained over the Mount of Olives for 3½ years. During this period a voice was heard to come from the region of the Mount of Olives asking the Jews to repent of their doings (*Midrash* Lam.2:11). This has an interesting bearing on the history of Christianity because we now know that Jesus Christ was crucified and resurrected from the dead on the Mount of Olives — the exact region the Jewish records say the shekinah glory of God remained for the 3½ years after its departure from the Temple on Pentecost, A.D.66. This would have signified to the apostles that a new site of interest became the exact spot where Christ was crucified, resurrected, and ascended back to heaven. The Jewish reference states that the Jews failed to heed this warning from the shekinah glory (which they called a *Bet Kol* — the voice of God), and that it left the earth and retreated back to heaven just before the final siege of Jerusalem by the Romans in A.D.70.

What did these supernatural signs connected with the Temple mean to the apostles who lived at the time? They must have been a certain signal that the revelation of "the Mystery" given to the apostle Paul and others about the irrelevance of the Temple was indeed correct. From Pentecost A.D.66, no thinking person among the Christians, who respected these obvious miraculous signs associated with the Temple, could believe that that structure was any longer a holy sanctuary of God. Josephus himself summed up the conviction of many people who came to believe that God "had turned away even from his sanctuary" (*War*, II.539), that the Temple was "no more the dwelling place of God" (*War*, V.19), because "the Deity has fled from the holy places" (*War*, V.412).

If the apostles Peter and John, and other Christians who held steadfastly to the teachings of Christ, had any doubts about Paul's teaching in "the Mystery" about the irrelevance of the physical Temple at Jerusalem and the elements of the Law that made up Judaism, they would certainly have had none after the wonderous events that took place at Jerusalem in the Spring of A.D.66. In fact, there was another major sign which occurred within that same period that seemed to be an exact fulfillment of Christ's own prophecies concerning the destruction of Jerusalem, the Temple, and the country of Judaea. Christ had said that there would be "fearful sights and great signs shall there be from heaven" (Luke 21:11). And Josephus reports that things very similar to Christ's predictions happened just before sunset on the 21st day of the Hebrew second month — the last day of the Second Passover season (Num.9:11).

> "On the twenty-first of the month Iyar, there appeared a miraculous occurrence, beyond belief. Indeed, what I am about to relate would, I think, have been reckoned a fable, were it not for the statements of eyewitnesses and for the calamities that happened afterward which deserved to be foretold. For before sunset throughout all areas of the country, there were seen in the air many chariots and armed battalions coursing through the clouds and encircling the cities" (*War*, VI.297-299).

Christ had told his disciples that "when ye shall see Jerusalem compassed with armies, then know that the desolation thereof is nigh" (Luke 21:20). And here is Josephus saying that there were many witnesses throughout Judaea who saw such wonderful and awesome sights in the heavens concerning Jerusalem and the other cities of the country being encompassed with armies.

When one considers this marvelous display of heavenly signs along with the other three portents of God abandoning the Temple at Jerusalem, it has to be concluded that Peter, John and the other Christians of the time must have been impressed with the phenomena. We are told by Eusebius that it was immediately after the conclusion of these signs that the few remaining Christians in Jerusalem and

Judaea packed up their belongings and left for Pella some 60 miles northeast of Jerusalem. They clearly recognized by this time that the main events associated with the prophesied second advent of Christ would not take place in that generation. There could be no Abomination of Desolation stand in the holy place of the Temple (Matt.24: 15), when there was no "holy place" remaining in the Temple in the eyes of God. Many Jews felt the Temple had been, by Pentecost A.D.66, consigned by God to destruction. Christians realized that there would have to be another Temple built in the restoration prior to the second advent (Acts 3:19-21) in order for a future Antichrist to place an Abomination of Desolation within it.

The abandonment of the Temple by God at Pentecost of A.D.66 made Peter and John realize that Paul's teaching was indeed correct — no matter how hard it was for them to acknowledge. And it was immediately after the miraculous events at Jerusalem that Peter and John began to think it was necessary to leave future Christians (who would live in the ages ahead of them) with a divine library of authorized books which could keep them informed of what the actual truths of Christianity really were. And with the apostle Paul still alive in Rome in the early Summer of A.D.66 and without any hope of release from Roman custody, the apostle Peter decided to journey to Rome to discuss with Paul what to do about the future. By mid-A.D.66 it was evident to Peter and John that Paul had been given special revelations concerning the fulness of the Gospel and these needed to be collated with other books to make a standard textbook of proper Christian doctrine which would last until Christ's second advent from heaven.

In this chapter we have shown the events which occurred after A.D.61 (after Luke closed the Book of Acts). But why didn't Luke record these matters which were so important in the reckoning of Christian history? Is it because the events indicated a complete reversal of love and respect for Paul by the very apostles of Christ? Luke was Paul's right hand man, and Luke loved Paul and his teachings which he believed to come from God. Maybe this is the answer. Whatever the case, we can know for sure that Peter and John changed their minds in favor of Paul. The miraculous occurrences which happened at the Temple in Jerusalem (which no one could deny had come to pass) were enough to vindicate Paul in the eyes of other apostles. The abandonment of God from the Temple itself in the Pentecost incident of A.D.66 (when all the 24 priests heard the voice say: "We are leaving here") was enough to convince most ordinary Christians that Paul's teaching was right after all.

In the next chapter we will see that Peter prophesied of the Jewish/Roman War that was, by mid-A.D.66, immediately on the horizon, and that Jude records what happened at the beginning of that conflict. The fact that the outbreak of that war was foreseen by Peter and that it would result in the destruction of Jerusalem, the Temple, and the national existence of the Jews, made it even more imperative for Peter to formulate a New Testament canon in order to preserve the true Christian doctrine for those who would survive the prophesied holocaust.

11

The Jewish/Roman War and Canonization

The death of James, the Lord's brother, at Passover A.D.62 was a major turning point in the history of Christianity. As long as James was alive he headed the government of the Christian church from Jerusalem with practically a monarchial type of rule. The New Testament states that it was James to whom reports were given (Acts 12:17), to whom most apostles submitted (Gal.2:11-14), from whom executive doctrinal decisions were once rendered for the church (Acts 15:13-19), and also to whom the apostle Paul reported and complied regarding doctrinal issues (Acts 21:18-26). Paul even stated that his preaching among the Gentiles would have been in vain had he not gained the approbation of James and the other Jerusalem apostles (Gal.2:1,2,9,10). James was the most powerful man in the Christian church, and he was also held in high esteem by many of the rulers and laity within mainline Judaism. The second century writer Hegesippus said that many of the ruling class of the Jews believed in Christ and that some of the Scribes and Pharisees thought that the popularity of James was so vast that there was "a danger that the entire people would accept Jesus as the Christ" (Eusebius, *Eccl.Hist.* 23). Even in the Book of Acts James stated that there were "many tens of thousands of Jews who believed, and they are all zealots for the Law" (Acts 21:20) including a great crowd of priests (Acts 6:7). James even demanded of Paul that he offer animal sacrifices in the Temple with four other Jewish Christians to prove that "you are walking orderly and also keeping the Law" (Acts 21:24).

As long as James was alive there was a general unanimity of belief among Christians throughout the world. There was a strong emphasis on keeping the Law among the Jews and even the Gentiles were subjected to a less restricted version of it. With the death of James at the Passover A.D.62, it became a different story — and very quickly. It appears that a crisis in leadership developed. When a strong monarchial type of leader dies, and without another powerful ruler ordained to follow, it is common for the basis of power to be dispersed among the most prominent of leaders who remain. And this appears to be what happened within the Christian church. We find the apostle John within three or four years of James' martyrdom stating that *many* rebels (not just a few) were now emerging on the scene and they were coming from within the Christian church itself (I John 2:18,19). Many of them who had formerly accepted and believed in Jesus were then beginning to deny his name (I John 4:1,2), and these former Christians were no longer listening to or submitting to the original apostles (I John 4:6). And even with some of those who remained within the bosom of the external church, John recorded that some elders were rejecting his authority (III John 9,10).

It wasn't only the apostle John after the death of James who was unable to control the rebels, but the apostle Peter said that destructive sects would soon rise within the pale of Christianity (even feasting among Christians themselves), committing abominable acts and denying that Christ would return to earth (II Pet.2:1,2,13; 3:3,4). And Jude (the brother of James) said that what Peter was given "advanced knowledge" about (II Pet.3:17) was then beginning to happen (Jude 3). This breakdown in a centralized government which was once headed by James is also seen in people's attitudes to the apostle Paul — "all men in Asia have turned away from me" (II Tim.1:15).

It was the unexpected death of James in A.D.62 that put the matter of Christian leadership into disarray. While up to that time the Book of Acts shows a consistent and orderly government that was effectively administered from Jerusalem (albeit with strains here and there), with James' death, it seems like insurrection, dissension, and many doctrinal doubts began to surface within the portals of Christendom. Remarkably, this is the very time that the Book of Acts comes to an abrupt halt in its historical narrative. It is almost as if Luke (though full well knowing, and perhaps even recording, the later history from James' death onward to Paul's) could not bear to place within the canon of the New Testament the unfortunate events which happened within Christendom just prior to the Jewish/Roman War of A.D.66 to 70. However, John, Peter, Jude, and Paul gave hints of it in their letters written after James' martyrdom.

Thus, the death of James and the failure of the end-time events which they thought would lead up to the second advent of Christ in that generation were epochal in the history of Christianity. This is what led to the breakdown of a once powerful Jewish Christianity in Palestine. Eusebius tells us, and there is no reason to doubt his account, that at this time "the holy apostles and disciples of our Savior were scattered over the whole world. Thomas, tradition tells us, was chosen for Parthia, Andrew for Scythia, John for Asia [western Turkey], where he remained until his death at Ephesus" (*ibid.* III.1). This exodus from Palestine was not simply because they planned to take the Gospel to the world as peaceful missionaries. In no way. Things had now changed and most Christian authorities, and along with them much of the laity who remained in the teachings of the apostles, "were driven out of Judaea" (*ibid.* III.5). Indeed, by A.D.64 vast numbers of Jews of all political and sectarian persuasions left Judaea for other areas in the Roman Empire, and this involved the populations of whole cities and inter-city regions of Palestine (*War*, II.277-279). Thus, the central church government of Christendom was greatly disturbed with the death of James. The tens of thousands of Jewish believers in Christ (when James was alive) either renounced Christianity, moved out of Palestine, or accepted numerous doctrinal beliefs with new and often rebellious leaders who rejected even the administration and teaching of the original apostles. Matters went from bad to worse in Palestine and Eusebius said the reason the Jewish/Roman War took place soon after, according to Josephus, is because God was judging the nation for the martyrdom of James (*ibid.* II.23). Whatever the case, the year A.D.62 (and the sabbatical year from Autumn A.D.62 to A.D.63) was the turning point in the history of early Christendom. It led to a most devastating war in Palestine and, for all practical purposes, the end of Jewish Christianity.

Peter Prophesied the Jewish/Roman War

It is hardly realized today but the New Testament tells us that the apostle Peter gave a prophetic warning of the Jewish/Roman War before it occurred, and that Jude (the brother of James) mentioned how the fulfillment of Peter's prophecy was happening in his day. The New Testament also records how the arrival of that war also helped the apostles to finally canonize the New Testament.

We should recall that the miraculous events which occurred in the Spring of A.D.66 caused all remaining Christians in Jerusalem to abandon the city to the destruction that Christ said would happen. It appears that Peter himself remained in Jerusalem until the Pentecost sign of A.D.66. When he wrote his first epistle about A.D.64 he was then in "Babylon" (I Pet.5:13). This was a cipher for Jerusalem, not Rome. The "Mystery Babylon" which John wrote about in the Book of Revelation was the city of Jerusalem. After all, it was recognized by the apostles that the "iron legs" of Daniel (which most considered to be the Roman Empire) were to give way to ten toes (ten nations) which would have as their head a "little horn." This person was called by a variety of names: the Man of Sin, the Son of Perdition, the Beast, and the Antichrist. This evil man was not to establish his capital at Rome, but he would sit in the inner Temple at Jerusalem (II Thess.2:4). Most people who lived in the first century had the conviction that at that very time world dominion would come forth from Jerusalem — not from Rome or any other city. This expectation was one of the reasons that prompted Nero to burn down the city of Rome. He had been told that it was now time to move his capital to Jerusalem because it was destined for world empire to emerge from there (Suetonius, *Nero* 40).

At Pentecost in A.D.66, however, the sign of God's abandonment of the Temple at Jerusalem was given to the 24 chief priests who ministered in the inner sanctuary: "We are leaving from here." This was a signal to Peter (and to the remaining Christians in Jerusalem) to flee the city. And they did. Most retired to Pella about 60 miles northeast of Jerusalem, from where they probably were quickly transported by their Greek neighbors into safer areas. In some regions east of the Jordan the Gentiles "escorted to the frontiers any who chose to emigrate" of those Jews "who showed no revolutionary designs" (*War*, II.480).

The apostle Peter may have been with these last remnants of Christians to leave Judaea. But he did not remain in Pella, or any area of the Middle East. He had an important mission to perform before he died. The apostle Paul was at that time in prison at Rome. And since it was then apparent that Christ was not returning in that generation it became imperative to bring together a set of standard books (like those of the Old Testament) which would have the authority of the apostles behind them. The maintenance of purity within Christian doctrine required a diligent effort of the leading apostles to provide a canon of New Testament scriptures which would last "until the day dawn" (II Pet.1:19). Thus, it appears that Peter in the Summer of A.D.66 journeyed, via Ephesus, to Rome to see the apostle Paul about this very matter. Indeed, there would have been no other reason for Peter to have gone to the capital city of the Empire, other than to consult with Paul before his death concerning the canonization of the New Testament — the most important endeavor that the apostles could leave for future generations.

There can really be no doubt that Peter finally went to Rome and that he and Paul conversed together shortly before their deaths. About A.D.170 Dionysius, who was the minister in charge of the Corinthian church, mentioned that both apostles "taught together in Italy and were martyred about the same time" (Eusebius, *Eccl.Hist.* II.25.8). Irenaeus also said that the church of Rome was established and founded "by the two most glorious apostles Peter and Paul" (*Against Heresies,* III,3. 1-3). Then there was Gaius, a Roman elder who lived near the end of the second century. He said that it was possible to point to the very tombs of the apostles Peter and Paul in the vicinity of Rome. These were the tombs "of those who founded this church [the church at Rome]" (Eusebius, *ibid.* IV.22.3). Really, there is hardly a scholar today who would not say that the historical evidence for both Peter and Paul to have been in Rome in the last years of Nero's reign is very strong indeed. True enough, when Paul wrote his last epistle to Timothy, Peter was not yet in Rome (nor is there any solid evidence that he had ever been there before), but there is every reason to believe that Peter finally went to Rome just before Paul's execution, and that he met the same sentence a short time later. The fact that Peter went to Rome is important because *he must have gone there FOR A PURPOSE.* What was the reason that he went so far away from his Palestinian home to go to Italy?

The historical evidence suggests that Peter went to Rome in

A.D.66. Since there was no longer any need for him (or other Christians) to remain in Jerusalem after the final Pentecost sign in A.D.66, the Summer of that year would have been the most logical time for his trip. Jerusalem and Judaea were thus deserted by the Christians in the early Summer of A.D.66. Then by late Summer, Peter found himself in Rome in conference with the apostle Paul. They had only one reason to be together, and both of them were intent on performing the responsibility that lay before them.

After being in Rome a few weeks before the martyrdom of Paul (and recognizing that his own execution was near), Peter wrote his second epistle to those in Asia Minor — the former area assigned to Paul and where the apostle John was then in residence. It was in that epistle that he spoke about the canonization of the New Testament, but he also prophesied of the coming war between the Jews and the Romans. The whole of Peter's second chapter describes an apostasy from the truth, and it was to be a widespread lapse of former Christians into a rebellion against God and against all constituted authorities no matter who they were. He even warned that the revolt would eventually occur among the readers of his second epistle and it would result in the many (not the few) turning away from the true teachings of Christ into a state of utter depravity and rebellion to God and their abandonment of human authority.

It should be noted, however, that Peter's prophecy of what was to happen, *had not yet occurred* when he wrote his second epistle. He told his readers that he was giving them "advanced knowledge" of the sedition so that those who were true to Christ would be on guard against the coming errors (II Pet.3:17). By early Autumn of A.D.66 the major problems had not yet surfaced, but they would. Peter said there "*will be* false teachers" (II Pet.2:1); who "*will bring in* destructive sects" (v.1); and that many (not the few, but *the many*) "*will follow* their acts of loose conduct" (v.3); and that "they *will make their way into* your midst" (v.3); and that people "*will be corrupted*" (v.12). Note that all of Peter's references were for the *future*.

Though Peter was aware that such depravity was forthcoming, it was not yet a fullgrown reality when he wrote his second epistle in the Autumn of A.D.66. But the case was different when Jude, the brother of James (and also of Jesus), wrote his letter to those who had received Peter's second epistle. If one will read Jude's short letter carefully, it reveals that he was starting to write his readers about the common salvation which all people had in Christ, when *all of a sudden* a disaster had begun to happen which caused him to postpone that particular instruction. Something just erupted which rendered it urgent to communicate with them about the immediate situation. What had happened? The answer is simple. Jude followed closely what Peter had predicted. Here was Peter saying *what will* occur, but Jude was now saying it *is presently erupting!* It was nothing less than the outbreak of the Jewish war against the Romans. He was making a hurried appeal that his readers not be caught up in the error.

> "Beloved one, though I was making every effort to write you about our common salvation, *I found it of urgent necessity* to write you encouraging you to put up a hard fight for the faith which was once delivered to the saints" (Jude 3).

While Peter was fully aware that such a condition of insurrection and debauchery would develop among many of the Christians to whom he wrote, Jude put the actions into the present tense. Note how he said they had now begun to occur. People were now *"denying Jesus Christ"* (v.4); they *"are defiling the flesh,"* they *"are disregarding* high offices,"* and they *"are blaspheming the ones of glory"* (v.8); they *"are blaspheming* things that they know not"* (v.10); they *"are unreasoning animals"* (v.10) and *"are corrupting themselves"* (v.10). They are also the ones who *"are in your love feasts"* and are shepherds who *"are feeding themselves* without fear"* (v.12). They *"are murmerers, complainers about their lot in life"* and they *"are admiring people for their own gain"* (v.16).

How could such evil be connected with God-fearing Christians? It almost seems like a contradiction. Why were so many of Peter's and Jude's readers involved? How could these filthy dreamers, corrupters of human rights, despisers of people in authority, and denying Christ and even counteracting the heavenly powers themselves find a lodging *within* the Christian community? And worse yet, these reprobates were even participating with Christians in their love feasts (II Pet.2:13; Jude 12). This rank and file rebellion seems so counter to the first principles of belonging to the Christian faith that hardly anyone imagines that such a thing could happen in a regular

Christian environment. And this is true. In no way could such a widespread upheaval of insubordination take place in a Christian church today, and especially for the church members to allow such reprobates to continue feasting with them in their religious ceremonies.

What in the world was happening? Why did the revolt occur so suddenly (yet it was prophesied by Peter that it would develop)? The answer is clear if Bible students today will only realize what Peter and Jude were talking about. It was nothing less than the revolt against the Romans in Palestine, and the potential for insurrection was beginning to spread, at first, even among the Jews in other provinces. It was Peter and Jude warning the true Christians not to take part in the national revolt against the Roman Empire. But Peter prophesied that such warning would fall on deaf ears as far as the majority were concerned. Peter said that it would be the *many* (not the few) who would relinquish their faith in Christ and begin to participate in the war against Rome (II Pet.2:1). And Jude was now saying that the defiance had started.

The very things that Jude said were beginning to occur were what Josephus said that many of the Jews in Palestine adopted in their rebellion to Rome (*War*,IV.238-365). The reason the revolutionaries had denied Christ is because they felt the prophecies given to John earlier recorded in the Book of Revelation had completely failed.

> "Where is the promise of his coming? for since the fathers fell asleep, all things continue as they were from the beginning of creation" (II Pet.3:4).

When it is realized that Peter was foretelling the revolt against Rome and that *many* (again, it should be noted, *NOT THE FEW*, but the *many*) would abandon their faith in Christ and participate in the war effort against Rome, the description of Peter makes sense. This is the only reasonable explanation which can account for true Christians having to put up with reprobates sharing a part in their festivals without being excommunicated from their midst. Such feasts were the national festivals ordained by Moses which all Jews everywhere participated in. There would have been no way for a few Jewish Christians to prevent a great number of people within any predominantely Jewish community from observing the national feasts.

No one can rationally explain how true Christians could let rebels of the nature mentioned by Peter engage in a celebration of their festivals unless they were the national feasts of Moses that were being discussed. All Jews shared in such festivities, and these would have been celebrated by all even in times of civil or national wars. Observe that in the American Civil War it was common for soldiers of both the Union and the Confederacy to keep the same Christmas and the same Easter. And even if some of the soldiers had no personal religious convictions of their own, it would still have been common for all of them to share in any Christmas dinners (if they were able to have them). In times of war it is even normal for the participants to forget temporarily their sectarian differences and to join hands to overcome the common enemy. The Jewish people who fought the Romans (though they were in various political camps) shared one Temple, singular religious festivities, and were (so they thought) defending the common traditions of them all. It is interesting that Josephus said that throughout most of the war, and even among the different political divisions, the various groups in Jerusalem allowed worshippers of all camps to have free passage into the Temple to offer their religious devotions to God (*War.* V.15,98,99).

Certainly, the whole nation kept the feasts ordained by Moses in Jerusalem and throughout all Judaism. Jewish Christians observed these days as well, and Peter along with Jude told true Christians to beware of those denying Christ who were participating in the ceremonies of the holydays and yet advocating war against the Romans. The cry of the revolutionaries was "come over to the cause of *liberty*" (*War,* IV.282); fight for the "defense of *liberty*" (IV.273); become "the champions of *liberty*" (IV.272). This is exactly what Peter said the rebels described in his epistle would tell the people. They were also "promising them *liberty*" (II Pet.2:19).

While the quest for *liberty* may have seemed a noble gesture in itself, the men who were saying such things were anything but noble. The very things that Peter said would take place, and that Jude said were then occurring, were what Josephus said happened in Jerusalem once the war got under full sway. Jude said that the rebels "are setting at nought dominions, and rail at dignitaries" (Jude 8). Josephus records: "Every law of man was trampled underfoot, every requirement of religion was ridiculed by those who scoffed at the oracles of the prophets as rogue's stories" (*War*,IV.386). They thought nothing of the sanctity of the Temple or the priests who conducted the services therein. They "railed dignitaries." Josephus: "These men converted the Temple of God into their stronghold and refuge from popular upheavals, and made the Holy Place the center for their tyranny. To these horrors was added a vein of ironic pretense more galling than the actions themselves. For, to test the complete subservience of the people, and to show their own power, they dared to appoint high priests by lot. . . . to them this sacrilege was a subject for jests and ribald mirth, but the other priests watching this mockery of their law from a distance burst into tears and bemoaned the degradation of their ceremonies" (*War*,IV.151-153,157). "These dregs and the scum of the whole country have squandered their own property and perpetrated their lunacy first upon the towns and villages around, and finally have poured in a stealthy stream into the holy city; these scoundrels are so utterly impious that they have desecrated even holy ground. They can be seen, shamelessly getting drunk in the Temple and spending what they have stolen from their victims to satisfy their insatiable appetite" (*War*,IV.241-242).

Jude said they "are murmers, complainers, walking after their own lusts and their mouths speaking great swelling words" (Jude 16). Josephus echoed the same things as occurring in Jerusalem during the war. "Here are native born Jews, brought up according to our customs and called Jews, *strut* where they like over the inner sanctuary itself, with hands still reeking with the blood of their countrymen" (*War*,IV.183). "Setting aside the families from which the high priests had always been drawn, they appointed to that office base persons of no family, in order to gain partners in crime" (*War*,IV.148).

Peter was well aware that many Jewish Christians would be tempted to join these "fighters for liberty." There were tens of thousands of believing Jews in Judaea in A.D.56 (Acts 21:20) and many of these did not migrate out of Palestine with the others from A.D.62 to A.D.64. And only very few went to Pella after the Pentecost sign of A.D.66. The majority gave up the type of Christianity that the apostles were teaching and stayed behind in Palestine to war with the

Romans. There were also many Palestinian Jews who were among the Jews (and Christians) of the Dispersion. It was these people that Peter and Jude were writing about. They were warning the Jewish Christians in Asia Minor, and elsewhere, not to follow in the rebellious ways of most of the nation because they were going to come to a "swift destruction" (II Pet.2:1) and a "judgment of desolation" (v.3). He said their cities would be turned into ashes just like the ruin of Sodom and Gomorrah (II Pet.2:6). And this is exactly what happened. When the prophecies given by John contained in the earlier version of the Book of Revelation failed to materialize, there was a widespread defection from Christian belief by vast numbers of Jewish Christians. They then went to war with the Romans, and lost.

When it is realized that Peter and Jude were describing the ravages of the Jewish/Roman War of A.D.66 to A.D.70, we can then date those epistles pretty closely. Since Peter was giving "advance knowledge" of what would happen to the Jews, we can date his epistle to about Autumn A.D.66, and since Jude said the conflict Peter talked about had now begun, then sometime after the period of Tabernacles (when the Roman General Cestius retreated from besieging Jerusalem which caused the war effort to begin in earnest) must be the time Jude wrote. Both epistles were mainly designed to warn true Christians not to take part in a war with Rome because it would lead to utter destruction. And, it did.

The apostles came to see that Christ was not going to return in that generation and establish his kingdom on earth. The signs that preceded the war and the start of the rebellion itself had a profound effect upon Peter, John, Jude and the other Jewish apostles. They came to believe that God had deserted the city of Jerusalem and the Temple. And the Jews who put up a physical defense to maintain their traditional system of religion, brought nothing but utter disaster to those in Palestine. All the apostles were finally able to understand that the teaching which Christ had granted to the apostle Paul was indeed the correct one and that no longer was the outward physical worship of the Temple the Christian way to righteousness.

In the next chapter we will see that the destruction of a physical government centered at Jerusalem required that a canonical edition of Christian doctrine be developed (like the Old Testament scriptures) in order that Christians would have a proper standard for reference which would last them "until day dawn" -- until the time that Christ would actually return from heaven. To that task Peter, Paul and finally John placed their efforts and it resulted in a set of 27 books being bound together to form what we call the New Testament.

Indeed, canonization meant the rescue of some books which many people deeply held in suspicion because of their remarks about the *soon coming* of Christ back to earth sometime during the seventh decade of the first century. The canonization process meant that the early version of the Book of Revelation was resurrected from the disdain that many people showed for it (because of its supposed failed prophecies) and it was placed in the New Testament canon. The restoration of the Book of Revelation was an essential need. It finally became clear to John and his helpers (when he found himself in a renewed visionary experience on the Isle of Patmos) that the prophetic teaching of those visions had to do with the end-time generation, and not with that one in the seventh decade of the first century. Interestingly, even after the Book of Revelation was canonized by John himself, it was still held suspect in some quarters for several centuries afterward.

The important thing that must be realized is the fact that what we call the New Testament today records information about the formation of the Holy Scriptures for the Christians *ekklesia* (church). The New Testament itself speaks about its own canonization. Hardly anyone today pays attention to what the apostles said about canonization, but we feel it is time to put the matter into proper perspective. It was the apostles themselves who put together the New Testament books -- not some unknown church group or groups of the second and/or third or fourth centuries. The next chapter will explain.

12

The Canonization by Peter

The apostle Paul could survey the historical environment within the Christian community of late A.D.66 and what he saw disturbed him very much. It was nothing like the relatively stable condition that existed up to the time of James' death in A.D.62. Not only was it apparent that Christ was not returning to earth in that generation, but the Christian church was now being bombarded from within by many people teaching a variety of false doctrines. These ranged the gamut from being actively rebellious against all constituted authority (both religious and secular) that Peter prophesied about in II Peter 2, to the statements of the apostle John that *many* antichrists had arisen among Christians who were changing the fabric of Christian teachings about the nature and mission of Christ. The apostle Paul appraised the chaotic situation that had come on the scene since the death of James in A.D.62. "All the men of Asia have turned away from me" (II Tim.1:15). The prospects for the future were no brighter.

> "Now the Spirit speaketh expressly, that in the latter times some shall depart from the faith, giving heed to seducing spirits, and doctrines of devils. Speaking lies in hypocrisy; having their conscience seared with a hot iron" (I Tim.4:1,2).

> "For the time will come when they will not endure sound doctrine; but after their own lusts shall they heap to themselves teachers, having itching ears; and they shall turn away their ears from the truth, and shall be turned unto fables" (II Tim.4:3,4).

There was by A.D.66 a corruption of the Christian faith occurring on all sides and the immediate and future outlook was even more dismal. At least, this is what the apostles thought. And worse yet, Peter knew by the time he wrote his second epistle that he was soon to die, that Paul's fate was already set, and that an insurrection against apostolic authority was underway on a large scale, and still there were many years (even centuries) ahead for the Christian church.

With such a prospect in front of him, it became essential to provide that future church with the purity of the truth of Jesus Christ as Peter and the rest of the original apostles understood it. It would seem a dereliction of duty for the apostles to abandon any attempt to secure the true teaching which they had the responsibility to preach. Some standard reference document or book (or a canon of Scripture) was needed that could be reckoned by all as an official statement of the real truth of Christianity. This was especially important for the future, for if the original apostles themselves could not stem the tide of false doctrine and rebellion to Christ while they were yet alive, what would happen in the generations ahead *without them?* Would it not seem reasonable to any rational person that some document of an official character be produced by the apostles before their deaths so that later people could have in their midst the basic (and pure) truth of Christ if they wanted it? The apostles were well aware by A.D.66 at the latest that Christ was not returning to earth in their generation. Does it seem sensible that the apostles would simply die and let others (whom they knew nothing about) formulate an official set of standard scriptures? If they couldn't trust the doctrines of many (probably *most*) in their midst, how could they depend on those of later times whom they didn't know at all — and with the prophecies informing them that heretical teachings were going to get more out of hand? "But evil men and seducers shall wax worse and worse, deceiving, and being deceived" (II Tim.3:13). Clearly, the apostles were aware of the situation and they were not going to be negligent in answering the need. Indeed, the last few months of Peter and Paul's lives were devoted *to the very project* of leaving to those of the future (which includes you and me) an official standard of written works which would secure, for all who wanted it, the true Gospel of Jesus Christ. In short, it was the apostles themselves who saw the need for a New Testament canon of scriptures, and it was they who produced it.

When Christians finally came to the realization that Christ was not returning to earth in the first century, they began to write accounts of Christ's life and his teachings for posterity, and they were doing it in the manner they thought best. Luke referred to this and said that "many" were composing such Gospels (Luke 1:1). While this might appear a good thing at first sight, it must be remembered that these written Gospels were being produced within an environment of religious and political insurrection. How could one be certain they were presenting an accurate account? This is when Peter and John began to show concern about the matter. If any was fully aware of what Christ did and taught, and if anyone was able to sanction the accuracy of any written history of Christ's life, it was the apostles. Something had to be done to provide a shining light of truth to those of the future. It was within this background that Peter wrote what we call today his second epistle. Let us see what Peter did to secure for those of the succeeding centuries the purity of Christian teaching.

The principal subject of Peter's second epistle was "the precious and exceeding great promises" of Christ (II Pet. 1:12). To preserve these for posterity he explained what he was about to do.

"Wherefore, I shall be ready, always, to remind you of these things [the promises of Christ], though you know and are firmly fixed in the present truth [the truth that Peter was presently giving them]. And I think it right, as long as I am in this tabernacle [this mortal body], to stir you up by reminder, knowing that the putting off of my tabernacle cometh swiftly, even as our Lord Jesus Christ showed me. But I will also give diligence that at each time [notice this phrase '*at each time*'] you may be able after my death to recall these things to remembrance. For not by following cunningly devised fables, made we known to you the power and presence of our Lord Jesus Christ, but we were eyewitnesses of his majesty. For he received from God the Father honor and glory, when such a voice was borne to him by the Majestic Glory, 'This is my beloved Son, in whom I am well pleased.' And this voice we heard borne out of heaven, when we were together with him in the Holy Mount. And we [who were with him on the Mount of Transfiguration] have the prophetic word more confirmed [than these fablers]; whereunto you do well to take heed [to our sayings], as to a lamp shining in a murky place, until which time the day dawn, and the day-star arise in your hearts. Knowing this first that no prophecy of scripture is of its own evolvement. For

no prophecy was ever borne by man's will; but men spake from
God, being borne on by the Holy Spirit" (II Pet.1:12-21).

It is important to realize that Peter was aware of his impending death
(John 21:18,19). But even though death was imminent he assured his
readers that "I shall be ready, *always*, to remind you of these great
and precious promises." How was it possible for such ready
reminders to always be in their midst if he was going to die in a matter
of days or weeks? Any verbal type of admonition that he might give
them would perish with him at death. But Peter said he would make
sure that Christians would *always* have the truth with them. The only
way this could rationally be accomplished is for Peter to leave them
with some authorized written record. "But I will also give diligence
that *at each time* you may be able after my death to recall these things
to remembrance."

The phrase *"at each time"* gives us an interesting bit of information.
It means that his readers could return again and again to consult the
document after his death in order to be assured of what those great
and precious promises of Christ really were. Clearly, he is speaking
about a written document. The *Expositor's Greek Testament* says that
Peter is about to leave "some systematic body of instruction"
(vol.V.p.129). The *International Critical Commentary* is even more
specific in its realization that written records were being left.

> "It seems clear that what is promised is a document, to which his
> disciples would be able to turn and confirm their belief . . . . The
> apostle does not say that the document of which he is speaking
> should be written after his death, but that it should be written so
> as to be of use after his death" (vol. "Peter" p.265).

> "The whole clause signifies that there shall be left behind, when
> Peter is dead, some record to which at each occasion, when the
> need arises, they may appeal for a reminder of his lessons, which
> they would probably not have always in remembrance" (*The
> Speaker's Commentary*, NT vol.IV.pp.244,245).

We have in this account of Peter a record of his task in canonizing
some part (or parts) of the New Testament. The *Speaker's Commentary* continues: "I will not be wanting on my part says Peter, to supply
you with the means for your guidance and encouragement when I am

taken from you" (p.245).

Peter, moreover, was not the only one involved in this canonization. When one reads Peter's account carefully, it says "we" (plural) will not be leaving you "fables" (plural) but the truth inspired by God's Holy Spirit. The description of this document as given by Peter shows that it would contain not just *one account*, but that "we" would not be giving the church cunningly devised "fables" (plural). It is important to recognize that it was not only Peter who was leaving these documents to serve as a standard for Christian teaching. Someone else was behind the effort. The person was the apostle John. Peter makes this clear in the context of Second Peter. "For not by following cunningly devised fables, made *WE* known to you the power and presence of our Lord Jesus Christ, but *WE* were eyewitnesses of his majesty.... And the voice *WE* heard borne out of heaven, when *WE* were together with him in the Holy Mount. And *WE* have the prophetic word *more confirmed.*"

There were three human beings with Christ on the Mount of Transfiguration. They were Peter and the two sons of Zebedee (John and his brother James). James, however, was the first of the apostles to be killed (Acts 12:1,2). When Peter wrote his second epistle, only John and he were the remaining apostles who had been given the opportunity of being in the Mount of Transfiguration and to hear the voice of God himself. To Peter, this unique and majestic experience was proof positive that he and John had been given the word of prophecy in a *"more confirmed"* way. While many persons might have taken it in hand to write several accounts of Christ's life and teachings, Peter was making it clear that *only he and John* had the proper authority to do so in an inspired way. This is why he reminded his readers that *"we* [Peter and John] have the prophetic word more confirmed" — more than any others who might write Gospels in the future or who had written them in the past. Indeed, they were the ones who had been graced with the power of the Holy Spirit to do such things: "no prophecy was ever borne by man's will; but men spake from God, being borne on by the Holy Spirit." Peter did not believe that this kind of prophetic responsibility originated within the mind of man. "Knowing this first that no *prophecy of scripture* is of its own evolvement [or, private origination]."

Notice the phrase "prophecy of scripture." Peter had just said that both John and he were commissioned with a more confirmed "word of prophecy." He then interpreted what this signified by equating it with the "prophecy of *SCRIPTURE*" which was not of man's origination. In a word, Peter is saying that the documents that he and John were leaving to the church were to be considered like any "prophecy of scripture." The use of the word "Scripture" brings the matter of inspired writings into the picture. In simple language, Peter was saying that the two remaining apostles to the Transfiguration were collecting a set of official works which would have their apostolic approbation and that these documents were to be considered by Christians as "more confirmed" than any others in circulation. And besides that, they were to remain in their presence to be consulted "at each time" they had occasion in order to learn the truth of "the great and precious promises" of Christ. These were to last until the second advent of Christ and esteemed as being on an equal basis with the Old Testament Scriptures.

> "I stir up your sincere mind by reminder; that you remember the words spoken before by the Holy Prophets, AND the commandment of the Lord and Savior *through your apostles*" (II Pet.3:1,2).

Peter Canonized Paul's Writings

Peter was aware that there were many people during his time (especially conservative Jewish Christians) who were highly suspect of Paul and his teachings. It seems that even Peter himself may have raised his eyebrows on occasion. But by A.D.66, things had changed. In the Spring of that year the miraculous signs associated with the Temple at Jerusalem had taken place (with sure evidence that God had abandoned the Temple) so the teachings of Paul began to be understood by the other apostles in a better light. This is one of the main reasons, if not the only one, why Peter journeyed to Rome in the Summer of A.D.66 to see the apostle Paul before he met his death as a martyr. The discussions between the two apostles were no doubt very productive because we have Peter informing his readers that Paul had also provided some basic spiritual information on what the Gospel of Jesus Christ really was. Peter and John finally sanctioned the insertion of Paul's letters into a body of divine literature to last until the second advent of Christ. Peter felt it was necessary to mention that Paul's epistles were also inspired.

Peter knew that some people of his time were doubting the inspiration of Paul's teachings, and that in the future some might even moreso question their legitimate standing. For one thing, he was not an original apostle of Christ. This prompted Peter, who knew when he wrote Second Peter that he was soon to be executed, and that many years of history yet remained before the return of Christ, to be reminding his readers that Paul's letters were also reckoned as divine Scripture. Peter informed them:

> "And account that the longsuffering of our Lord is salvation; even as our beloved brother Paul also, according to the wisdom given him, wrote you, as also in all his letters, speaking in them of things hard to understand, which the unlearned and unsteadfast wrest, as also *the other scriptures,* unto their own destruction" (II Pet.3:15,16).

This reference of Peter is a clear indication that he recognized the letters of Paul (no doubt a particular set of letters) as being as inspired as the Scriptures of the Old Testament. The *Expositor's Greek Testament* was assured that an equal rank was being accorded: "The examination of the whole passage [of Peter] . . . leads to the conclusion that the Epistles of St. Paul are regarded as in the same rank with the Old Testament Scriptures" (vol.V,p.101).

It seems as if the apostle Paul was then dead when Peter wrote his second epistle. Note that Peter referred to Paul's activity as being in the past. "Paul . . . wrote you, as in all his letters" (II Pet.3:15). Furthermore, the fact that Paul's letters were being twisted out of context indicates that Paul was no longer alive to counter the charges or to write additional letters clarifying the difficulties that Peter and the others found hard to understand.

> "The reference to Paul, to be found in the Second Epistle of Peter, is favourable to the supposition that the apostle of the Gentiles was now dead; as, had he been still living to correct such mis-interpretations, it would scarcely have been said that in all his epistles were things 'hard to be understood' which 'the unlearned and unstable' wrested 'unto their own destruction' " (Killen, *The Ancient Church*, p.159).

The second epistle of Peter is actually the key to the first canonization of the New Testament. It is an official statement to show how he and John (not long before Peter's death) gathered together some written records which the apostles themselves either wrote, had authorized to be written, or sanctioned already existing works into a position of canonicity. If one would simply believe what Peter said about this matter, it would have to be reckoned that Peter's second epistle was written, among other things, for the express purpose of showing that the apostle John and himself were the ones ordained of God to leave Christians with the canon of the New Testament. This means that it is not the later church who, in some unknown and haphazard way, collected the 27 books of the New Testament to be attached to the 22 of the Old and formed what we call the Holy Bible. In no way. The biblical evidence points solidly to the apostles themselves as the ones who canonized the New Testament books. It was they who saw in their own generation the urgency, just before their deaths, of securing such a canon. With false doctrines and rebellion (even to apostolic authority) on all sides, and with future prospects looking even worse, they completed their task of preaching the Gospel to the world by starting and finishing the canonization of the New Testament. I have not the slightest doubt that this is the case. The next chapters of this book will help to show the rationality of this belief.

13

The Authority to Canonize the New Testament

The apostles of the first century had in their midst the complete and final Old Testament scriptures. This canon, with its various books and divisions, served as a model for any further canonization involving New Testament books. The environmental background inherently governing the outlook of the Jewish people of the first century was created on account of the social and religious standards which were established at the time the Old Testament was canonized. Though there were some differences, of course, the basic framework of society was retained from this earlier time. This common religious heritage allowed the New Testament to develop along similar lines to the Old. Prof. Souter said:

> "The idea of a canon, or exclusive selection of sacred books for use in public worship, is ultimately derived by the Church from Judaism, and some account of the formation of the Jewish Canon of the Old Testament seems necessary as a model on which, consciously or unconsciously, the later New Testament Canon was formed" (*The Text and Canon of the New Testament*, p.149).

This belief was also shared by the eminent textual critic Prof. Gregory (*Canon and Text of the New Testament*, p.13). If this is the case, then we should look for some high-ranking priests or a prophet with the rank of Moses having a hand in the creation of the New Testament, because this is certainly the manner in which the Old Testament came into existence.

Some historians would have people believe that the church of the early second century probably formulated the final New Testament. There has always been a problem with this appraisal because there is not a sliver of evidence that such a thing took place. The truth is, when the early church fathers began to talk about the canon of the New Testament near the end of the second century, it is assumed that it was already in their midst. The first recorded discussion among Catholic scholars about the books of the New Testament only concerned whether certain books in the canon were of lesser rank, not which books were needed to form the official canon (Eusebius, *Eccl.Hist.*, III.25).

> "What is particularly important to notice is that the New Testament canon was not demarcated by the arbitrary of any Church Council. When at last a Council — the Synod of Carthage in A.D.397 — listed the twenty-seven books of the New Testament, it did not confer upon them any authority which they did not already possess, but simply recorded their previously established canonicity. As Dr. Foakes-Jackson puts it: 'The Church assuredly did not make the New Testament' " (Bruce, *The Books and the Parchments*, p.111).

Actually, if one will read Second Peter carefully and analyze it for what it says (as we did in the last chapter), it shows that it was the apostles Peter and John who officially canonized the New Testament books. And those two apostles possessed the authority of Christ himself as well as the testimony of the Old Testament to accomplish this important task. Christ even informed his disciples that he was going to complete the revealed word of God to mankind. Look at Matthew 5:17:

> "Think not that I am come to destroy the Law or the Prophets: I am not come to destroy, but to fulfill."

This verse should be noticed carefully. Though Christ assured the disciples that the Old Testament would remain steadfast in its sanctity, he did say he would *fulfill* the Law and the Prophets. What does the world "fulfill" actually mean? Charles B. Williams, in his translation of the New Testament, provides a footnote to this verse which reflects its intention. He said that the word signified "the picture of Old Testament teaching as an unfilled cup, but filled by Jesus" (footnote *g*).

Williams provides the accurate meaning of this word. "To fulfill" signified to bring things to the brim — to the very top. It is like having a glass half-full of wine. By adding more wine, one could fill the glass to the top. Thomas Newberry, the editor of the *Englishman's Bible*, shows Matthew 5:17 as meaning: "think not that I am come to unbind the Law, or the Prophets: I am not come to unbind, but to fill up" (*Footsteps of Truth*, New Series, XI.p.281). It simply means that Christ thought of himself as responsible for bringing the revelation of God to its complete fulfillment — to the very brim. In effect, his adding to the Law and the Prophets was an authority for attaching his written messages to those of the Old Testament. Jewish scholars have long understood this to be the meaning of Christ. In the *Talmud* they regarded Matthew 5:17 as reading: "I came not to destroy the Law of Moses, but to add to the Law of Moses" (*Shabbath* 116b; cf. A.Edersheim, *Life and Times,*, p.537,n.2).

Christ did not mean that he would personally add to the Law and the Prophets by composing books of his own. A reading in the Old Testament itself revealed to the apostles that it was *they* who were to be responsible for the writing and selecting of documents which would comprise the New Testament. In a section of Isaiah which the apostles understood as applying directly to the life of Christ on earth, they found a prophetic responsibility also given to them. It was written in the long prophecy of Isaiah chapter 7 to chapter 12, and the section pertaining to the apostles themselves was in 8:13-17.

> "Sanctify the Lord of hosts himself; and let him be your fear, and let him be your dread. And he shall be to you for a sanctuary; but for a stone of stumbling and for a rock of offence to both houses of Israel, for a gin and for a snare to the inhabitants of Jerusalem. And many among them shall stumble, and fall, and be broken, and be snared, and be taken. *Bind up the testimony, seal the Law AMONG MY DISCIPLES.* And I will wait upon the Lord, that hideth his face from the house of Jacob, and I will look for him" (Isaiah 8:13-17).

Though the above message was written in the eighth century before Christ, the apostles interpreted it as having a contemporary reference to them. There can be no doubt of this because both Peter and Paul referred to Isaiah 8:14 as having an application to their times. Peter taught that Christ had become the chief corner stone, but to the disobedient of Peter's day, he had become "a stone of stumbling, and a rock of offence" (I Pet.2:6-8). Paul, speaking of the Jews' rejection of Christ, wrote: "As it is written, behold, I lay in Sion a stumbling stone and a rock of offence" (Rom.9:33).

Understanding that the apostles thought that Christ fulfilled Isaiah 8:13-17 in *their* time, they were able to learn a great deal about their own responsibilities. Isaiah told his readers that this "stone" and "rock" would "bind the testimony and seal the Law *among my disciples*" (Isa.8:16). The actual "binding" and "sealing" which could once have been accomplished by Isaiah's disciples in that time was no doubt interpreted by the apostles as typical of what the Rock of Israel (Christ) was to do through his own disciples (verse 18).

What do the words "bind" and "seal" signify? The Hebrew for the word "bind" means "to close, to seal up." The word "seal" means practically the same — "to cap off, to enclose." This is exactly what the apostles did with the message which the "Stone" and "Rock" gave them. They were to complete it. Bind it up. Close it shut. The authority to perform such an important job may have been reflected in Christ's teaching that the apostles had power "to bind on earth" (Matt.16:19). The word "to bind" has the significance of authorization or giving judgment, just as the word "to unbind" means "not to receive or accept." Recall again the intention of Matthew 5:17: "I am not come *to unbind* the Law or the Prophets." Christ did not wish to undo the Old Testament, but his disciples were commissioned to add to and complete the Bible. In a word, they were to bind, seal, authorize and canonize the Law and Testimony of Christ.

More Evidence

When one reads through the New Testament, it is possible to observe a number of important statements which indicate that further scriptures beyond the Old Testament were destined to emerge. Just before his crucifixion, Christ gave his disciples some instructions regarding their role in receiving new and significant messages from God.

"I have yet many things to say unto you, but ye cannot bear them now. Howbeit when he, the Spirit of truth is come, *he will guide you into all truth:* for he shall not speak of himself; but whatsoever he shall hear, that shall he speak: and *he will show you things to come.* He shall glorify me: for he shall receive of mine, and shall show it unto you. All things that the Father hath are mine: therefore said I, that he shall take of mine, and shall show it unto you" (John 16:12-15).

The above scripture has Christ telling the disciples that the Spirit would "show you things to come" (verse 13). This indicates that the understanding of prophecy would be afforded them. Was this a reference to the Book of Revelation? That book is wholly devoted to prophecy — to "things to come" (Rev.1:1). In the next chapter we will show information that will demonstrate that Revelation was prophesied by Christ to be written by the apostle John.

There is another point about the section of scripture transcribed above. Christ said that *all* the truth was going to be given to the apostles back in the first century. In John 16:13 the text actually says that the Holy Spirit "will guide you into *all THE truth.*" The definite article indicates that the truth, the whole truth, and nothing but the truth would be dispatched to them. This is an important point because it shows that the Christian church did not have to wait until the third or fourth centuries before all the truth could be given. This is quite different than is usually taught today. It is normally assumed that the canon of the New Testament came into existence sometime in the early or middle second century, and was finalized in the fourth century. This is patently not true. Augustine, one of the most ardent supporters of the organized church of the fourth and fifth centuries believed that the New Testament canon came into existence in the time of the apostles themselves. He stated:

> "Distinguished from the books of later authors is the excellence of the canonical authority of the Old and New Testaments; which, *having been established in the time of the apostles,* hath through the succession of overseers and propagators of churches been set as it were in a lofty tribunal, demanding the obedience of every faithful and pious understanding" (*Contra Faustum Man.* 11.5).

How different from what is generally accepted today. In our present age, it is common to hear that the second, third, or fourth century church canonized the New Testament in some of its church councils. This is in no way true.

> "The striking fact that the early councils had nothing whatever to do with forming the Canon of the New Testament, has been so emphasized by a number of writers that one is astonished that it is not more widely known" (Urquhart, *The Bible*, p.37).

Christ, however, made it clear that the disciples would receive "all the truth" back in the first century. This truth was then written down and finally canonized by Peter and John.

> "We have not followed cunningly devised fables, when we made known unto you the power and coming of our Lord Jesus Christ, but were eyewitnesses of his majesty. . . . We also have a more confirmed word of prophecy" (II Pet.1:16,19).

The apostles had the word of prophecy *more confirmed*. What does the word "prophecy" mean in the context in which Peter used it? Most people would automatically assume that it means they could foretell the future. But in the way Peter meant it, it did not have that meaning in the above reference.

All Jews of the first century understood the word "prophecy" in a much broader sense. There were three different ways of looking at it. It certainly signified the classical meaning of being able to tell the future, and the person able to do this was customarily called "a prophet." But the apostle Paul also used the word as meaning one who *spoke forth* the word of God no matter if the message was about the future, the present, or the past (I Cor.14:5,24,25). This latter usage simply signified one who preaches the Gospel. Yet there was a third meaning, and this is what Peter had in mind when he said that he and John had "the word of prophecy more confirmed." This usage meant that the people who could be called such "prophets" were those under the prophetic spirit and able to write inspired scripture. Josephus, the Jewish historian, was well acquainted with this type of usage for the word "prophet" or "prophecy." He said that no succession of prophets had come on the scene within Judaism from the time of the Persian king Artaxerxes (the fifth century B.C.) — at the close of the Old Testament canon — until and including the first century (*Contra Apion*, I.8). In a word, Josephus thought that "the spirit of prophecy" had ceased with Ezra, Nehemiah, and the Great Assembly who canonized the Old Testament.

The fact is, all the writers of Holy Scripture were called *prophets* even if they did not possess the prophetic office as did Elijah, Isaiah, Malachi, etc. For example, David, Solomon and Asaph the psalmist were called *prophets* though their writings were not in the Prophets' Division of the Old Testament (Matt.27:35; Acts 2:30; 7:48; Matt. 13:35). Indeed, the use of *prophecy* by holy men of God reached back to the very beginning of history. Abel, the son of Adam, was called a *prophet* (Luke 11:50). And in Acts 3:21 and Hebrews 1:1 we are told that the practice of *prophecy* extended back to all past time, to the very beginning of the world.

The Jews in Christ's time simply believed that all holy men of God were *prophets* and that all their writings were *prophecies*. This, of course, did not mean that they all foretold future events (*cf.* John 4:19; Acts 11:27; 13:1; 15:32; I Cor.12:28,29,37; Eph.2:20; 4:11; Tit.1:12). And, most significantly to our present study, any holy man of God who wrote any part of Holy Scripture was called a *prophet*. Prof. Lee remarks that it was an "invariable rule that all witnesses of the Old Testament should be prophets" (*Inspiration of the Holy Scripture*,p.60). Whitaker also recognized that *any* writer of Scripture was thought to be a *prophet* and to possess the prophetic spirit (*Disputation*, pp.49,50). This indication was followed throughout the New Testament. When Christ said: "Abraham saith unto him, they have Moses and the Prophets" (Luke 16:29), he was not referring to the Prophets' (i.e. the Second) Division of the Old Testament. He meant *all* the writers of Scripture who followed Moses. Luke noted this: "Having begun from Moses and *all the prophets*, he [Christ] expounded unto them *in all the Scriptures* the things concerning himself" (Luke 24:37). When Paul reasoned with the Jews out of the Law and the Prophets (Acts 28:23) he was teaching from the *whole* Old Testament. And these *prophets* of the Old Testament ceased their activities when the canon was completed. Like Josephus, Jews were well aware that "prophecy ceased" when the canon was finally established (*cf.* Ecclesiasticus 36:15; I Macc.4:44-46; 9:27).

Peter, however, said the *prophetic word* was restored with him and John. This clearly shows that he and John were informing their

188

readers that they were going to present them with a new batch of inspired scriptures to accompany the books of the Old Testament. (For a further demonstration of this use of the words "prophet" and "prophecy" in the first century, see Lee pages 53-60 and Whitaker pages 49-52.)

The Prophetic Spirit Restored With the Apostles

When one reads Second Peter in the proper way, it shows that he was telling his readers that the prophetic spirit had been revived and that the apostles had the authority to use it for the production of inspired scriptures. That is what he and John were going to leave to the Christian church before they died. The reason for writing Second Peter was to tell Christians of this fact. Their writings (and the other documents which they sanctioned) were not going to be like the fables of others because Peter and John had "the word of prophecy more confirmed." The books they were selecting were God-ordained and as inspired as the Old Testament. "Knowing this first, that no prophecy of the scripture is of any private interpretation" (II Pet.1:20). The word *interpretation* in the King James' Version actually means "origination" or "evolvement." Peter was indicating that the prophetic scriptures which he and John were giving to the church were not their own private ideas and words. They were nothing less than the direct teachings of God. This dogmatism of Peter is reflected also in his evaluation of the apostle Paul's epistles which he mentioned as being on an equal par with "the other Scriptures" of the Old Testament (II Pet.3:15,16). Certainly, if Paul's letters were in A.D.66 being reckoned as Scripture, the letters of James, Jude, Peter, and John were as well. The apostles were assured by A.D.66 that "the prophetic spirit" had returned to earth in the persons of Peter, John, and Paul. This was a signal that more Holy Scriptures would be written to present the final messages of God to the world.

As anyone can see, I have emphasized (and re-emphasized almost to *ad nauseam*) the matter that Second Peter records the power of Peter and John to canonize the New Testament, but I do not apologize for it. This is simply because most people, even scholars, have failed to see the point of what Peter was saying that the matter has to be accentuated. Peter was plainly trying to show that he and John were given "the word of prophecy more confirmed" in order to canonize more writings into the sacred library of books, as had Ezra and Nehemiah in their day. Peter was simply exercising his authority to write, collect, assemble, and design a New Testament canon. This official group of books was expected to remain in an authoritative way "until the day dawn" — until the second advent of Christ back to this earth. That is exactly what the epistle of Second Peter states and I see no reason why Christians today should not accept it.

Paul Recognized His Part in Canonization

At the end of the Book of Romans is an interesting section of scripture which relates to the matter of canonization. Not only did Peter consider that he and John were endowed with the word of prophecy in a confirmed and official way, the apostle Paul also admitted that he was graced with the same authority. Paul said that his writings concerning the message of Christ were to be acknowledged as "the Prophetic Scriptures." This meant that Paul thought he was writing *sacred* Scriptures. Note the context of Paul's belief.

> "Now to him that is of power to establish you *according to my Gospel,* and the preaching of Jesus Christ according to the revelation of the mystery, which was kept secret since the world began, but now is made manifest, *and by the Prophetic Scriptures,* according to the commandment of the everlasting God, made known unto all nations for the obedience of faith" (Rom.16:25,26 see original Greek for "the Prophetic Scriptures," italics mine).

Paul did not mean in the above statement that the knowledge of the mystery was to be found in the earlier prophets of the Old Testament, as the King James' Version would lead one to believe. He expressly stated that the teaching given to him had remained a secret until Christ came, and that it was now being divulged to the world through Paul and the other apostles. This fulness of the teaching of Christ was what Paul called "my Gospel" (verse 25). The spiritual information came to Paul through a torrent of revelations. Paul explains:

> "And lest I should be exalted above measure through the

abundance of revelations, there was given to me a thorn in the flesh, the messenger of Satan to buffet me, lest I should be exalted above measure" (II Cor.12:7).

Paul was referring to the operation of the Holy Spirit in leading him, as it did the other apostles, into what Christ called "all the truth." Christ said that the apostles would finally receive the complete truth from him (John 16:13).

Paul made mention of this fulness of the Gospel in his Ephesian epistle.

"How that by revelation was made known unto me the mystery; which in other ages was not made known unto the sons of men, as it is now revealed unto his holy apostles and prophets by the Spirit" (Eph.3:3,5).

This is pretty plain. The mature teaching of the mystery was that part of the Gospel which Christ knew his disciples could not bear before they received the Holy Spirit after the resurrection of Christ. And Paul was now given his apostolic commission to present new prophetic scriptures to people in the world. Paul even realized that he was the one responsible for preaching the full and final teachings of God.

"Wherefore I am made a minister, according to the dispensation of God which is given to me for you, to fulfill [that is, the same word used by Christ in Matthew 5:17 — "to fill to the top"] the word of God. Even the mystery which hath been hid from ages and from generations, but now [in the middle 60's A.D.] is made manifest to his saints" (Col.1:25,26).

This is an important statement relative to the canonization of the New Testament. It tells us in no uncertain terms that Paul knew he had been given a special commission to help fulfill (that is, to "fill to the top") the word of God. This is why Paul had little reluctance in telling people about the high calling that he had. The teachings he recorded represented the very commandments of God. "If any man think himself to be a prophet, or spiritual, let him acknowledge that the things I write unto you *are the commandments of God*" (I

Cor.14:37). These are strong and authoritative words. No man could make such assertions unless he was convinced in his own mind that he had the prophetic office to write inspired scripture. Notice also:

> "Now we have received, not the spirit of the world, but the Spirit which is of God; that we might know the things that are freely given to us of God. Which things also we speak, not in the words which man's wisdom teacheth, *but which the Holy Spirit teacheth*" (I Cor.2:12,13).

> "We thank God without ceasing, because, when ye received the Word of God which ye heard from us, ye received it not as the word of men, but as it is in truth, *the Word of God*" (I Thess.2:13).

When one comprehends that Paul himself was aware of his role in completing the full message of God to this world, then the statements of Peter in his second epistle can begin to make sense. Peter readily acknowledged that the apostle Paul was given an equal commission along with himself and John, to write "prophetic scriptures." This is exactly what Paul called his own writings in Romans 16:25,26 and the apostle Peter boldly ranked those writings of the apostle Paul alongside the writings of the prophets in the Old Testament (II Pet.3:15,16).

It is no wonder that Peter, after the miraculous signs concerning the Temple in Jerusalem which happened in the Spring of A.D.66, made his way to Rome. His journey would have been for only one purpose: to see Paul before the martyrdom of them both. It was to discuss and to formulate a number of letters and writings which would comprise a sacred canon of New Testament books.

The meeting was successful. Peter then wrote his second epistle to those throughout the region of Asia Minor about this canonization. This last letter of Peter was written especially to inform Christians about the conclusion of this important task. Peter, Paul, and John were giving to the world the final revelation of God in written form. It was new sacred scripture, written under the prophetic spirit, which would last the Christian church until the return of Christ to this earth. Just when, and by whom, the finishing touches of the New Testament came into final form will be discussed in the next chapter.

14

The Apostle John and Canonization

The apostle Peter was in Rome when he wrote his second (and last) epistle. Paul was then dead, and Peter himself had only a short time to live. This is why he told his readers in Asia Minor that he was leaving them some official documents (which included the epistles of Paul) that would keep them informed of the truth until the return of Christ to the earth. The authority to perform such a task was essentially in the hands of the three apostles who had been with Christ on the Mount of Transfiguration: Peter and the Sons of Zebedee (James and John). And since Peter said that "*we* have the word of prophecy more confirmed" (II Pet.1:19) it strongly implies that the apostle John was still alive and some way involved with Peter in this canonization. And indeed he was alive. Christ had given John the promise that he would live beyond the martyrdom of Peter, even to remain alive "until I come," or as Christ expressed it in the Greek, "until *I am coming*" (John 21:22,23).

The beliefs of the early church were just as strong that John was in Asia Minor (notably in Ephesus) from the middle 60's A.D. until his death, as they were that Peter died in Rome about A.D.66 or A.D.67. There is little reason to doubt the truth of these beliefs. This would mean that the apostle John was among the people in Asia Minor to whom the apostle Peter wrote in his second epistle. In effect, the epistle was telling John what he and Paul had done in Rome concerning the canonization of the New Testament scriptures. It informed people that Peter was putting in the hands of the apostle John the final job of sanctioning and completing an ordained body of inspired scriptures for the Christian church. To Peter, John was the only other person who had the prophetic spirit to accomplish such a task, since he was the only person left alive who had been given that commission on the Mount of Transfiguration.

This special authority of John can be seen in a number of verses within the New Testament revelation. For one, it should be noted that the three men who witnessed the Transfiguration were the only men of the original apostles who were given specific titles by Christ. There was Simon (whom he titled *Peter*, a stone) and James and John (whom he called *The Sons of Thunder*). See Mark 3:16,17. These are the original apostles who were given distinctive titles by Christ in order to convey some special assignments that they were expected to complete. Peter was to be associated with Christ (the Rock *himself*) in the creation of the Christian church. This was accomplished in its initiation phases with Peter on the Day of Pentecost some 50 days after the resurrection of Christ (Acts 2). Peter was also given the "keys of the kingdom of heaven" (Matt.16:19). These were to allow him the power to open "the doors of the kingdom" to those who would hear the Gospel. It even entailed an authority to bind or to loose people regarding their entrance into that kingdom. (This power was later extended to all the apostles, John 20:23.) And it appears certain that one of the main methods by which Peter would be able to exercise the power of the "keys" was to be in charge of the canonization of the New Testament. The information in the canon would "open the doors" to all people who would read and heed the written messages therein.

The other two apostles who received specific titles were the sons of Zebedee — James and John. They were reckoned by Christ as being *The Sons of Thunder*. This title has proved a little mysterious to many interpreters of the Bible because it gives one the impression that the two brothers were headstrong, impetuous, intolerant and authoritarian. And, this is true. But when it comes to analyzing the letters of John he appears to sanction a conciliation among peoples (especially those who claim the common Christian faith) and that love and harmony ought to exist in Christian relationships (I John 2:9-11). John was also the one that Christ had a natural fondness for than the other apostles (John 13:23; 19:26; 20:2; 21:7,20). But when one looks at the biblical account about the actions of these two brothers, they do appear to be stern and uncompromising in their attitudes to evil. They were the ones who asked Christ if fire should come down on the heads of the Samaritans (Luke 9:54), and (with their mother) their ambitions were so high that they asked Christ for positions of supreme leadership alongside him (Matt.20:20-24). They were certainly *not* mild-tempered. They were to be men of *"Thunder."* In Hebrew "thunder" (*kol*) meant the *Voice of God* (Exo.9:23; Psa.29:3; Jer.10:13; etc.). The title could signify that they were to speak like God himself—as personal spokesmen for God.

This title gave them a special rank of authority and, along with Peter, they were the only apostles to witness the Transfiguration and to hear *the voice* of God the Father himself (and in vision to see Moses and Elijah) (Matt.17:1-9). This experience rendered the jurisdiction of those three men as superior to the other apostles and it singled them out for a special purpose. Peter was to be in charge of church affairs (Matt.16:17-19), but James and John were to have the distinction of being "The Sons of Thunder" — to *thunder* forth his words to the people *as did Moses.* And though James died early without being able to show that authority in a lasting way, his brother John was responsible for writing every word of the Book of Revelation. This was Jesus Christ using John to be his spokesman — to be the Voice of God to the people of the world. He was "the Thunderer" to the world of God's message of judgment.

> "And I saw another strong angel . . . his face as the sun, and his feet as pillars of fire . . . and when he cried, *the seven thunders spake their VOICES.* And when the seven thunders spoke, I was about to write, and I heard a voice from heaven saying, Seal what things *the seven thunders SPOKE*" (Rev.10:1-5).

The apostle John was specifically commissioned to write what the Voice of God (like the Thunder) would relate to him. This is why he wrote his Gospel and the Book of Revelation to be included in the canon of the New Testament. Such a task shows that John was more specially selected to produce a canon of scriptures which would proclaim the official Voice of God than even Peter or Paul. This is no doubt the reason that Peter sent his second epistle (with the canonization that he and Paul had accomplished in Rome) directly to John in Ephesus. It was recognized that he was the actual one in charge of authorizing the final scriptural books. This is why Peter emphasized the experience that he and John had witnessed on the Mount of Transfiguration with Christ (II Pet.1:16-19). The fact that this display of Christ's authority was given only to Peter and the Sons of Thunder showed their high rank among the apostles and the Christian church. It even got them into trouble, temporarily, with Christ when their mother (who understood the special relationship of her two sons to Christ) asked that both of them sit on either side of him when he came into his kingdom (Matt.20:20-23). Christ could not give them that authority since that was only within the power of the Father, but John did sit by him and recline in his bosom at the Last Supper (John 13:23). This may indicate the special relationship after all.

There may be more concerning the rank of John than meets the eye. It is usually not understood, but the mother of James and John was none other than Salome (Matt.27:56 with Mark 15:40) who was the sister of Mary, the mother of Christ (Hastings, *Dict. of Christ and the Gospels,* vol.I.p.846). This means that Christ and John were *first cousins.* James, the head of the church at Jerusalem, and Jude (the writer of the short epistle) were also his *first cousins.* Unlike Peter or Paul, the apostle John would have been acquainted with Christ from childhood. No wonder he had been close to Christ. It seems that a "family tie" to Christ was important in an authority sense. The first cousin status of John to Christ may account, in one way, why he and his brother were afforded such a high position of rank. Along with Peter, the two Sons of Thunder were prominent in the history of the Christian church both before and after the resurrection of Christ. Note some indications which show this.

Besides having been specially selected to witness the Transfiguration and hear the voice of the Father himself, Peter, James and John were with Christ when he raised Jairus' daughter (Mark 5:37). They were a part of the limited group who heard the Olivet Prophecy of Christ (Mark 13:3). Peter and John (note that Peter's name is placed *first*) were the two apostles who were sent to make ready the Passover (Luke 22:8). In the Garden of Gethsemane it was Peter, James, and John who were especially near Christ (note, again, the positioning of their names, Peter first and John last) (Mark 14:33; Matt.26:37). In the record about the appearance of Christ after his resurrection at the Sea of Galilee, Peter and the Sons of Thunder have special mention (John 21:2-7). And when it came time to be sent on assignments by Christ note that John is the prominent one with Peter doing most of the executive work. Indeed, when the two are mentioned together, it is always "Peter and John" (Acts 3:1,11; 4:13; 8:14). And in the last discourse that we have in the Gospel of John, it is Christ first talking to Peter to tell him that he would die a martyr's death for his faith, but that John would continue to live "until I am coming" (John 21:15-23).

The association of Peter and John together in crucial times for preaching the Gospel, or in receiving important doctrinal teachings from Christ was no accident. And even the fact that Peter's name appears *before* that of John's (when they are mentioned together) shows a rank of authority. It is significant that in the manuscript order of the New Testament books, Peter's two epistles among the seven General Epistles are positioned *before* the three of John. This arrangement of names is according to the rank of authority of the men.

One more thing about John should be mentioned. Not only were his mother and Christ's mother both sisters (and this gave John some preeminence) but we find that Mary (and obviously her sister, Salome) were in some way connected with priestly ancestry. Polycrates in the late second century said that "John, who leaned back on the Lord's breast, became a sacrificing priest wearing the mitre, a martyr and a teacher; he too sleeps in Ephesus" (Eusebius, *Eccl.Hist.*III.31; V.24). If John was indeed of priestly ancestry, then it follows that his father Zebedee was a priest. As for his mother (Salome, who was sister to Mary), both Salome and Mary could have Aaronic (priestly) ancestry as well. One should recall that Mary was a kinswoman to Elizabeth (the wife of Zacharias who was an Aaronic priest and the father of John the Baptist) and Elizabeth herself was recognized as "a daughter of Aaron" (Luke 1:6). This means that both Mary and Salome could be reckoned as being of priestly descent. A great error of some is to imagine that the genealogy of Christ as given in Luke is Mary's genealogy. In no way is this true. Mary's ancestry is not even discussed in the two genealogies.

The Bible would allow that Zebedee and Salome (the father and mother of the apostle John and his brother James) were both of priestly ancestry, thus John himself would have been a priest. At the last supper, John sat directly on one side of Christ. He was close enough to hear Christ whisper to Judas (who also was a priest, as I have shown in my book *Secrets of Golgotha*, pp.266-269). Such a position of eminence would have been natural in such a social setting. Besides that, when Christ was taken to Caiaphus the High Priest in Caiaphus' Temple house on the morning of his crucifixion, John was able to walk into the quarters of the priests (and was known intimately by Caiaphus) (John 18:15,16). For proof that Christ's trial was in the Temple, see my *Secrets of Golgotha*, pp.221-235.

These biblical indications alone are enough to show that the apostle John was of priestly ancestry, but there is also the teaching in the Book of Revelation that John was able to go into the innermost sanctuary of the Temple and to count those who did service there (Rev.11:1,2). This shows that John (and his brother James) were indeed priests. These two cousins of Christ being priests made them authorized to canonize books for the Bible. Also, these "Sons of Thunder" would have grown up with Christ in Nazareth. They would have *known him* very well. This is why John (with Peter) had "the word of prophecy more confirmed." This special rank is no doubt the reason Peter handed the material that he had collected and arranged in Rome to John in Ephesus for the final canonization of the New Testament. He was a "Son of God's Voice" and eminently qualified to do the job. The title that Christ gave him points to that authority, and the fact that he witnessed the Transfiguration was another proof. John, then, became the final *"Thunder* (Voice) of God"* to the Christian church. He became the official spokesman for the truth. This role seems reflected in the introduction of his first epistle. He represented many of the original apostles when he wrote First John. Note how clear this fact is in John's prologue.

> "What was from the beginning, what *we* have heard, what *we* have seen with *our* eyes, what *we* beheld, and *our* hands handled, concerning the word of the life (and the life was manifested, and *we* have seen and witness, and declare to you the life, the eternal, which was with the Father, and was manifested to *us*); what *we* have seen and heard declare *we* to you also, that you also may have fellowship with *us*, yes and *our* fellowship is with the Father, and with his Son Jesus Christ, and these things *WE WRITE* that our joy may be full. And this message which *we* have heard from

him and announce to you, that God is light and in him is no darkness at all" (I John 1:1-6).

John makes it plain that when he wrote his first epistle, many of the original apostles and others must have still been alive. They were now associated with him as witnesses to the truth of what John was saying. But then, beginning with chapter two, John ceases to mention the "WE" and starts a singular pronoun: "My little children, *I write unto you*" (I John 2:1). His reference to the first person singular continues throughout the rest of the first epistle, and is only abandoned in one verse (I John 4:14) where he reverts to the "WE." The point is, the role of John in the writing of that epistle shows him being a Spokesman for a body of witnesses who saw Christ in the flesh! This is John exercising his commission as being a Spokesman for others which was given to him by Christ.

John's Final Canonization

The Gospel of John must have been written for the generality of the Christian church as a final summing-up of the teachings of Christ. It has seemed reasonable to most people that John had the other three Gospels in front of him when he wrote his account, and that his Gospel was an attempt to round-off and complete the message which Christ had given in the flesh. Everything points to it as being the latest of the Gospels to be written. Not only is it squeezed into a position between the Gospel of Luke and the Book of Acts (which normally should be in tandem to one another), but it records events which people of a later time would find relevance. For example, the raising of Lazarus from the dead is one of the most outstanding miracles in the Bible, but it has been a headscratcher why the other three Gospels said not one word about it. But if the other Gospels were written sometime earlier (when Lazarus was still alive) and they recorded the occurrence of that miracle, it stands to reason that such publicity would have made it impossible for Lazarus to carry on any kind of normal life. He would have been deluged with questions from his admirers, and his enemies would have wanted to silence his testimony to the extraordinary power which was manifested by Christ. But by the time John wrote his Gospel, Lazarus could have been dead and the account of his miraculous resurrection could be given without personal injury to Lazarus. This explanation is as good as any as to why that glorious miracle was not recorded in the earlier Gospels. It can also show that John's Gospel was not written early.

The Gospel appears to be a late composition because there is a fully developed theological position presented on every major event in the life and teachings of Christ. In fact, John's account is a thorough-going interpretation of Christ's life rather than a simple historical narrative. It is decidedly contrary to the materialistic concepts that were often associated with the Messianic beliefs in ordinary Jewish theology. John gives a "spiritual" twist to almost all the various teachings of Christ. His concepts show that a good deal of long and well-thought-out principles had been determined as representing Christianity, and they were very distinct from Judaism.

The general feeling that one gets in reading John's Gospel is that it was written to supplement and to round-out the information supplied by the first three Synoptic Gospels. John emphasized the fact that *"all the truth"* was then in one's grasp through the agency of the Holy Spirit, and that all future events which were important for the Christian church to know were then completely available. Note once again the teachings of Christ in John 16:12,13.

> "I have yet many things to say to you, but you cannot bear them now. But when he, the Spirit of truth, comes, he shall guide you *into ALL the truth,* for he shall not speak from himself; but whatsoever things he heareth, these shall he speak, and he will declare unto you *the things to come."*

It is significant that John insists that the Holy Spirit will deliver "all the truth," that it will come through divine inspiration, and that it would involve the understanding of future (prophetic) events. These two verses given by John are powerful vindications that the Christian message was *complete* when John wrote his Gospel. John's final comments in his Gospel reflect this same conclusion.

> "And many other things did Jesus also do, the which *if they be written every one,* I suppose that not even the world itself would in the future find a place to contain the books written" (John 21:25, Greek expanded).

These concluding remarks by John make one feel that John thought any further Gospels were redundant. In paraphrase, John was saying "Thousands of Gospels could be written in the future about Christ, but these four are enough. So be content and don't be desirous of obtaining more information about Christ and his teachings other than that which I have given you."

When Was the Book of Revelation Written?

It is important to date the times of composition of the various New Testament books because this is the first step in providing a benchmark to help determine when the final canonization took place. The Book of Revelation is cardinal to the whole issue. Since there is strong tradition that the apostle John lived till the end of the first century and that Revelation was written by him near his death, this would seem to date the completion of the canon to about A.D.96 to 98. There have been, however, a good number of scholars over the past hundred and fifty years who have leaned heavily toward the late 50's or early 60's A.D. for its composition simply because the historical indications within the book point directly to that time. And true enough, if John was recording historical events contemporary with the writing of the book, then the composition must be dated to about A.D.60. Let us look at some of the reasons for this.

It will be recalled in previous chapters that the apostles, and many Jews and Gentiles, were expecting the soon appearing of the Messianic kingdom on earth. The critical date for the apostles appears to have been the sabbatical year of A.D.62 to A.D.63. Up to that time the apostle Paul was emphasizing the nearness of the second advent, but by A.D.63 or A.D.64 he had adopted a completely different attitude to the matter. The apostles Peter and John may have waited until after the miraculous events in the Spring of A.D.66 concerning the Temple before they decided for certain that Christ was not returning in that generation, but whatever the case, the period before A.D.62 was alive with expectation.

This fact brings us to the first reason why the Book of Revelation could have been written around A.D.60 (if there is a historical basis to its contents). This is because the book presents, in a profound way, the nearness of the second advent.

> "The Revelation of Jesus Christ, which God gave unto him, to
> show unto his servants things that must *shortly* come to pass . . .
> for the time *is at hand*" (Rev.1:1,3).
> "The Lord God of the holy prophets sent his angel to show unto
> his servants the things which must *shortly* be done. Behold, I
> come *quickly*. . . . for the time *is at hand*. . . . And, behold, I come
> *quickly*. . . . Surely, I come *quickly*. Amen. Even so come, Lord
> Jesus" (Rev.22:6,7,10,12,20).

This appeal to the soon advent of Christ is also found in the messages
to the Seven Churches of chapters two and three.

> "I will come unto thee *quickly*. . . . Repent; or else I will come unto
> thee *quickly*. . . . hold fast *till I come*. . . . thou shalt not know what
> hour I will *come upon thee*. . . . Behold, I come *quickly*. . . . Behold, I
> *stand at the door and knock*" (Rev.2:5,16,25; 3:3,11,20).

Coupled with these verses about the imminence of the second
advent, there was John's reference that some of the people who
actually pierced Christ at his crucifixion would seemingly be alive at
his return (Rev.1:7). Further, John describes the Temple at Jerusalem
as being very much in existence in Revelation 11:1,2 and this would
demand a pre-A.D.70 period before the Temple was destroyed.
John's indication that Jerusalem had a population of about 70,000
persons (Rev.11:13) could only apply to the time before the war. In
fact, the Tenth Legion occupied the central area of Jerusalem after
A.D.70 and in no way could the population be then about 70,000.

Another point that shows an early date of composition are two
statements made by John in which he indicated that to be reckoned
as Jewish was, in that time, an honorable and desirable thing. The
two references concern the desire of some people in the church to be
Jewish, though in actual fact they were not Jews (Rev.2:9; 3:9). These
two statements indicate an early writing of Revelation because after
the Jewish/Roman War of A.D.66 to 73 there was hardly a heretical
Christian (or any Gentile Christian) who wanted to be identified with
the Jewish people. During and after the war the Jewish people were
held in disdain throughout the Roman Empire because of the war
and (what Gentiles considered) their anti-social behavior. But *before*
A.D.66 it was quite popular among Christians to be "Jewish." The

biggest problem that Paul had to cope with among his Gentile converts was their persistent hankering to become Jews or to adopt Jewish ways. Paul even found them wishing to be supervised by Jewish/Christian authorities (II Cor.11 & 12). But this desire of Christians to identify with the Jews stopped forthwithly by the end of the Jewish/Roman War. Indeed, the Book of Barnabas which was written near the end of the first century by a Jewish/Christian was decidedly anti-Jewish in its themes. It is well recognized that even the Gospel of John, from beginning to end, is never flattering to the Jews. So the references in Revelation that people were still desiring to be identified with Jews is evidence against a post-A.D.70 period for its composition.

Another reason for suggesting an early writing is the mention that some heretics were calling themselves "apostles" (Rev.2:2). To imagine that one could be an apostle like the original ones selected by Christ was seldom, if ever, imposed upon the Christian church after A.D.70. This is because there were special New Testament requirements to become an apostle that later people had no hope of meeting. For one, it was essential that each apostle had to have "seen" Christ (I Cor.9:1) and there had to be many miraculous signs associated with their ministries (II Cor.12:12). It is noteworthy that the later church, after A.D.70, had no quarrel over who was or was not an apostle. But in pre-A.D.70 times, this was a major problem (II Cor.11:13-15). So, the reference to false apostles of Revelation 2:2 would tend to place the writing of the book before the fall of Jerusalem if a historical basis is what John intended.

There are other reasons to suspect a pre-A.D.70 date for the writing of the Book of Revelation. If one will observe closely the historical features that seem to be found in the book, one has to look within the emperorship of Nero or the rule of Agrippa the Second to find such occurrences. For example, when John wrote the book he mentioned that five rulers had already ceased to have power and that a sixth was then having the sovereignty (Rev.17:10). All realize that at the time John wrote the Book of Revelation the principal world empire was Rome. If John had in mind the Roman emperors when he spoke of the sixth ruler, then the composition of Revelation was in the time of Nero (A.D.54 to A.D.68). Though Nero was actually the fifth emperor, but in a prophetical sense the Jews reckoned Julius Caesar as the first emperor (*cf. Antiq.*XVIII.33,225). The second was Augustus; the third, Tiberius; fourth, Gaius; fifth, Claudius; and the sixth was Nero.

Or, if one thinks John was talking about the rulers of Jerusalem rather than Rome (since it is clear that John's "Mystery Babylon" was Jerusalem), it could reasonably be suggested that Herod the Great was the first king of the prophecy and that Agrippa the Second was the "sixth." [Eusebius quoted an early prophetic belief that once the Jews ceased having native kings, the Messiah would then be able to arrive on earth (*Eccl.Hist.*I.6). The prophecy was interpreted as starting with Herod.]

So, if Herod, the non-Jew, were reckoned as being the first king, the second would have been his son Archelaus, the third the Roman government which controlled Judaea until the rule of Agrippa the First (who would have been the fourth)(A.D.37-45). The fifth was again the Roman government (A.D.45-56), and the sixth king (if Jerusalem, not Rome, is made the center of John's prophecy) would have been Agrippa the Second (A.D.56 to 70).

Whether one looks at Rome or Jerusalem as the political power being discussed, we find the historical indications are almost parallel to the years of Nero's rule. Thus (if a contemporary historical basis is found in the Book of Revelation), the date for its writing was somewhere in the period A.D.54 to A.D.68. But there is a further factor that could help pinpoint the time even closer.

In Revelation there is given a clear reference to the city of Laodicea as being rich and prosperous (Rev.3:17,18). But in A.D.60/61 Laodicea suffered a devastating earthquake (Tacitus, *Ann.* 14.27). It is hardly possible that Laodicea could have been rebuilt and once more rich and prosperous by the beginning of the Jewish/Roman War in A.D.66 -- or even before the death of Nero (A.D.68). Thus a date just before A.D.60 for the composition of the book could make good sense. And, as stated earlier, A.D.56 to 60 is just before the critical sabbatical year of A.D.62 to A.D.63 which was expected to usher in the major events leading up to the second advent of Christ. The Book of Revelation was certainly emphasizing the soon appearing of Christ's return from heaven. From all of this, it seems reasonable that Revelation could have been written from about A.D.56 to 60, just before the end-time events were expected to occur.

This, however, is just the problem with the early date for its composition. Since the information within the Book of Revelation is reported to have come from Jesus Christ himself, and not John (Rev.1:1), this seems to indicate that even Christ, some 30 years after his resurrection and ascension to heaven, was confident of his return to earth very quickly. He was persistent in the book that "I come quickly." But Christ, of course, did not come back as depicted in the Book of Revelation or the other New Testament books. It would be daft indeed to imagine that Christ actually did come back to earth between A.D.63 and A.D.70. Yet, strange as it may seem, there appears to have been a few people who insisted that he did. By the year A.D.65 Paul was reporting the errors of some people who believed that a resurrection from the dead had already occurred (II Tim.2:18). Since the apostles taught that Christ's second advent would be accompanied by the resurrection from the dead, there must have been some who taught that Christ had somehow "returned" — perhaps in a mystic or secret manner. Paul, however, assured Timothy that this in no way had happened.

The fact is, Christ did not return "quickly" in the decade of the 60's A.D. Indeed, the very teaching of the Book of Revelation stated quite dogmatically that the end-time events would occur "quickly," may have been the precise reason why so many Jewish people in Palestine turned against the teachings of Christianity just after A.D.63 and prepared to go to war with the Romans as Peter and Jude reported. They no doubt began to believe that the whole prophecy had failed, and that the teachings in the Book of Revelation were false.

As for me, the answer seems clear. The Book of Revelation has no chronological or historical relevance in its message as far as the first century is concerned. It is describing a special time in the future called the Day of the Lord in which all end-time events will take place. The text simply says that John "came to be in the Spirit in the Lord's Day" (Rev.1:10), that is, he was transported in vision into the Day of the Lord. Even his "seeing" the visions in the Isle of Patmos had a visionary aspect to them because, again, the text says: "I came to be in the isle called Patmos." It was a spiritual, or visionary, experience that took him to Patmos, not something literal. Indeed, the whole book is made up of symbolic and allegorical teachings which must be carefully interpreted to understand their literal applications.

The allegorical illustrations throughout the book were intended to describe events at the end of the age, not those of the first century. We find that John was witnessing in vision the crucial events leading up to the Day of the Lord, those that incorporated it, and those concerning the outcome of the "Day" (Rev.1:19). Thus, when Christ said throughout the book that his return from heaven was to occur very quickly, those statements have to be interpreted within the time period near the Day of the Lord. If this is the way Revelation is to be understood, then the events must be reckoned as allegorical and prophetic without reference to any past historical events or chronological time periods.

When was Revelation written? If one looks at the traditional evidence that comes to us from the middle second century and shortly afterward, one has to date the composition of the Book of Revelation to the last decade of the first century (Irenaeus, *Adv.haer.* 5.30.3). There is little doubt in my mind that this period is the time that the Book of Revelation was canonized. Indeed, because so many people felt the prophecy was a dismal failure, it had to be given again to John (or at least re-verified), and this was done about A.D.96. John even stated in Revelation that a further prophecy was to be given concerning the end-times (Rev.10:8-11). Christ told Peter he would die an old man by martyrdom (John 21:18,19) but that John would remain "until I am coming" (John 21:22,23).

This statement by Christ has been seen as an enigma to many for generations. Just what did he mean that John would live beyond the death of Peter "until I am coming"? Even in the first century there was confusion over the prophecy. Some people thought it meant that John would continue to live until the second advent (verse 23). John, however, assured his readers that Christ did not mean that. Indeed, he couldn't have intended that meaning because Christ had earlier prophesied that John and his brother James would both undergo martyrdom (Matt.20:23). The New Testament said that his brother James was killed by Agrippa the First (Acts 12:2), and other early records relate that John was also martyred for his faith in his later years of life (Eusebius, *Eccl.Hist.* III.31).

What then, did Christ mean when he said John would live to an old age beyond Peter's death "until I am coming"? The answer is simple if one will let examples within the biblical revelation be the guide. A similar statement was made by Christ in Matthew 16:27,28. Let us quote it in full.

> "For the Son of man shall come in the glory of his Father with his angels; and then he shall reward every man according to his works. Verily I say unto you, *There be some standing here, which shall not taste of death, till they see the Son of man coming in his kingdom.*"

In Luke's Gospel the parallel account says that the fulfillment of that very prophecy happened just eight days later (Luke 9:28). And true enough, some of those apostles (namely Peter, James and John) *did see* or *observe* Christ "coming" in the glory of his Father. That occurred when they were taken to the Mount of the Transfiguration and Christ was glorified in their presence. It was like a "second advent" because Moses and Elijah were also seen with him, and that type of experience would only be actually seen at the resurrection of the dead which was to happen at the exact time of his second advent (I Cor.15:50-55; I Thess.4:13-18). And most importantly, it should be noted that the glorious event of the Transfiguration was *not* an actual "second advent." The whole affair was a *vision* (Matt.17:9). This prophecy of Christ, that some would not die before they would *see* him coming in his kingdom, did in fact take place 6 days later (or 8 days later inclusively). That is when the *vision* of Christ's second advent took place.

With this example in mind, look once again at what Christ told Peter in John 21:22,23. Peter was to be martyred in old age (which happened to the apostle about A.D.67), but John would remain on earth "until I am coming." This is what transpired. Christ had told the disciples that the Holy Spirit would inspire the apostles into a knowledge of "all the truth" and also "declare to you *the coming things*" (John 16:13). They were to be given an understanding of prophecy, of future events. And in John 21:22,23 Christ was informing Peter who it would be who would remain "until I am coming," to see "those things." It was to be the apostle John.

Christ's statement in John 21:22,23 was nothing more than a prophecy that the apostle John would remain on earth beyond Peter's death to *see* Christ's coming in vision — like the vision on the Mount of Transfiguration. In short, he was giving him a prophecy about the message in the Book of Revelation which would again be shown (and revitalized as a proper prophecy of the end-time) after the death of Peter. And remarkably, we are told four different times in Revelation that John was taken in spirit (which means in "vision") into a period of time or locations to see the prophesied end-time events (Rev.1:10; 4:1,2; 17:3; 21:10). All of this concerned the "coming" of the Lord back to earth. But more than that, the exact Greek word which described the time unto which John would live was erchomai, "I am coming" (John 21:22,23). And note what is found in the Book of Revelation itself. In Revelation 2:5 we find the same word erchomai -- and it occurs throughout the book (Rev.2:16;3:31; 16:15; 22:7,12,20). These occurrences of the same word as found in John 21:22,23 represent a link-up of John's Gospel with Revelation.

And while the main prophecies of the Book of Revelation were no doubt given to the apostle John somewhere around A.D.56 to 60, and most people felt the prophecy met with an utter failure within a few years before the destruction of Jerusalem, John remembered that he was told by Christ that he would live long after the death of Peter to witness the Second Advent and the prophetic occasions associated with it. The prophecies were again reiterated to him. This was indicated in the Book of Revelation itself. "And he [Christ] said to me, 'Thou must prophesy again before many peoples, and nations, and tongues, and kings'" (Rev.10:11 KJV).

The upshot of this matter means that the final canonization by John must have taken place long after Peter and Paul were dead. Things will make far better overall sense when this is accepted as nearest to the truth. In a later chapter we will show why this understanding becomes important in evaluating the proper manuscript order of the New Testament books. It means that the complete number of 27 books was sanctioned by the apostle John (and his helpers). Those writings were placed in their various divisions and in a particular order so that the Christian congregations, from the close of the first century, would have a divinely inspired set of books which would dovetail with the 22 Old Testament books to form the canon.

It is now time to look at the divisions and order of those New Testament books which were canonized by John. The next chapter begins with a survey of the Gospels and the Book of Acts.

15

The New Testament Pentateuch

There are five books in the New Testament which represent the basic teachings of Christ within a historical framework. They are called (to identify them in a literary sense) the four Gospels and the Book of Acts. The first four books account for the period when Christ taught in the flesh (both before and after his resurrection) and the fifth occupies the period from the conclusion of his earthly teaching (Acts 1:4-11) and continues with the progression of that teaching (now directed from heaven) until it reached the city of Rome.

There is a unity of purpose and design within these five historical books! Indeed, the Book of Acts is as much a "Gospel" as the first four, though it is common to designate only Matthew, Mark, Luke and John by the literary term "Gospels." This is because the fifth book is simply a continuation of Luke's Gospel. It would be perfectly proper to designate Luke's first composition "The First Gospel of Luke," and the Book of Acts "The Second Gospel of Luke." The internal evidence shows that both are truly "Gospels" in the strict sense of the word. This means there are really *five* Gospels in the New Testament, not four.

This fact has been recognized by scholars. While Luke's first Gospel deals with the teachings of Christ while he was in the flesh, the second is the Gospel of the Holy Spirit directed by Christ from heaven. Note the appraisal of Ehrhardt. "The whole purpose of the Book of Acts...is no less than to be the Gospel of the Holy Spirit" (The Construction and Purpose of the Acts of the Apostles, *StTh*, XII, 1958, p.55). Professor Guthrie also agrees with this conclusion. "Since Luke-Acts must be considered as a whole, and since the first part possesses the character of a Gospel, *the second part must be viewed in the light of this fact"* (*New Testament Introduction,* p.350, italics mine). Indeed, Luke himself links the two books together in a literary and structural manner. He said his first work was written to describe what Jesus *began* to do and teach (Acts 1:1) and that he was simply continuing the narrative in his second work.

Professor van Unnik also expressed the view that Acts was a confirmation and continuation of the Gospel message of Luke for those who had no personal acquaintance with Christ while he was in the flesh (*Nov. Test.,* IV. 1960, pp.26-59). In simple terms, the Book of Acts must also be acknowledged as a "Gospel." This means, again, there are *five* Gospels in the New Testament: Matthew, Mark, First Luke, John, and Second Luke. It is important that these *five* books be reckoned as a unit — which could be called the Pentateuch of the New Testament.

These books were placed in a first rank position within the New Testament canon for a purpose. They were not intended to be biographies of Christ's life. Their main emphasis was to show the progression of the teaching of the Gospel from its beginning in Galilee (Acts 10:37) to Jerusalem, then from Jerusalem (the capital of the Jewish world) to Rome (the capital of the Gentile world). All five books when reckoned together provide people with the historical proof that the Gospel was indeed preached to "all the world" as a fulfillment of Christ's commission to the apostles (Rom.16:26; Çol.1:23; I Tim.3:16; II Tim.4:17). With this as one of the bases for their inclusion in the canon, it can be seen that the 22 books following the "New Testament Pentateuch" present the rest of the doctrinal teachings which make the Christian message complete and universal. That message was designed to reach out and embrace *all nations of the world,* not just the Jews. Thus, this Christian Pentateuch was written and placed in first position within the New Testament canon to represent the Christian "Torah" (the central "Law") of the whole Bible.

Why a New Testament Pentateuch?

The Jews of the first century acknowledged the profound authority of the Law of Moses above all other writings. There was nothing that could remotely compare with that Law in matters of importance or prestige. That Law was found in the first five books of the Old Testament: Genesis, Exodus, Leviticus, Numbers and Deuteronomy.

When it came time to canonize the New Testament, it must have occurred to the apostles that the New Testament "Law" would most naturally be composed of five books. There would have been nothing odd about this because many parts of the Old Testament were constructed around the symbolic number *five*. It was the number of "Law." For example, the 150 psalms which made up the Book of Psalms were arranged by the Old Testament canonizers into *five divisions,* and they paralleled the five books of the Law. (See Appendix I for proof.) Even the basic law itself, the Ten Commandments, was reckoned in the Jewish manner as being five laws relating to God (the first five, including the fifth dealing with parents) and the remaining five having to do with human affairs.

The number *five* in relation to Law is found in another way. It should be remembered that the Old Testament laws were symbolically required to be inscribed on the hand and in the forehead (Exo.19:9, 16). The "head" represented the intellect (with its *five* senses) and the hand symbolized work (with its *five* digits) which indicated the performance of the Law in an active and physical way.

The number "five" was also associated with Old Testament canonization in another way. The Festival Scroll (known as the *Megilloth*) was made up of five books (Song of Solomon, Ruth, Lamentations, Ecclesiastes, Esther) which were ordained to be read at the five Jewish festivals (Passover, Pentecost, 10th of Ab, Tabernacles, Purim). As a further significance to the number, the middle book of the *Megilloth* (Lamentations) was also divided into five distinct sections. Even in the New Testament itself, scholars have found that the Gospel of Matthew has a fivefold arrangement. "It has been suggested that Matthew's fivefold scheme was patterned on the fivefold character of the books of the Law, the idea being that the author was attempting to provide a 'Pentateuch', as the new law for the community of the new Israel, that is, the Christian Church" (Guthrie, *New Testament Introduction,* p.31).

Whatever the case, the fivefold symbolic characteristic associated with matters of Old Testament Law is well known by biblical scholars, and the apostles could not have been unaware of its unique numerical significance. And with the "historical" books of the New

Testament (that is, the Gospels and the Book of Acts) being five in number, and that they provide a logical and consecutive narration on the progress of Christian teaching from Nazareth, to Jerusalem, and then to Rome, the arrangement of these books into a fivefold unit by the canonizers must be reckoned as not a matter of chance. There was a deliberate design intended by using this procedure.

Why the Gospel Arrangement?

While the orthodox Christians recognized the first four Gospels as canonical, there were some of the third and fourth centuries who proposed a change in the manuscript order. Because John and Matthew were original apostles of Christ (while Mark and Luke were not), a minority were prone to place the Gospel of John right after Matthew because of apostolic rank. This was, however, only an academic suggestion which found no permanent approval. There was no reason for such a change because it can be shown that Mark and Luke were simply the secretaries for two apostles: Peter and Paul. It was common in the first century for men of authority to have amanuenses (official secretaries) to write their letters or books for them. Paul used such people on many occasions. His writing of the Book of Romans is an example. "I Tertius, who wrote this epistle, salute you in the Lord" (Rom.16:22). Most, if not all, of Paul's epistles were actually written by amanuenses whom he maintained on his staff of transcribers. Since Luke was a companion of Paul, it is perfectly proper to assume that Luke's Gospel and the Book of Acts were actually the historical record which Paul called "my Gospel" in Second Timothy 2:8.

As for the Gospel of Mark, it has long been known that John Mark was recognized as the secretary, or amanuensis, of the apostle Peter. Indeed, in the Gospel of Mark the great humility of Peter is conspicuous in all parts of it. Where anything is related which might show Peter's weakness, we find it recorded in detail whereas the other Gospels often show Peter's strengths. In Mark there is scarcely an action by Christ in which Peter is not mentioned as being a close observer or communicant. All of this affords a reasonable deduction that the writer of the Gospel of Mark was an eyewitness and close observer of the events recorded about Christ's life from the baptism of John to his crucifixion in Jerusalem. The ancient testimony of Papias, in the early second century, that Mark was the secretary of the apostle Peter (and not the actual eyewitness himself) has such good credentials, and the internal evidence of the Gospel itself is so compatible to this view, that it seems evident the Gospel of Mark is really the Gospel of Peter.

The Order of the Four Gospels

The first Gospel in the canonical order is that of Matthew. Why should his Gospel come first in order? Though Matthew was certainly of lesser rank within the Christian authority dispensed by Christ than Peter and John, there is another side of the story. The actual name of Matthew was Levi (Luke 5:27-29). This shows that he was of Levitical descent, and in an Old Testament order of priority this would have accorded him a first position among ordinary Jews! Besides that, it can be easily seen that his Gospel was oriented to Jewish people, not to the Gentile world. His reference to the "kingdom of heaven" rather than the "kingdom of God" is a sure sign of this. In the Jewish world of the first century, it was illegal to utter the divine name of Yahweh in public. Only the High Priest was able to say it on the Day of Atonement (or in private when no one would hear the sound of the august name). Matthew abides with this belief by adhering to the custom. There is even traditional evidence that the Gospel was first written in Hebrew (or Aramaic) which the Jews of Palestine found more suitable to use in their holy writings. Matthew was also the ideal person to bridge the gap from the Old to the New Testament because the preservation of the earlier revelation had been committed to the priests (Deut.31:9) and Matthew was both a Levite and an apostle.

The Gospel of Matthew is a perfectly good account of the life and works of Jesus which was designed to satisfy the queries of those with strong Jewish persuasions. It may be that Matthew (Levi) was the amanuensis of James, the brother of Christ, and leader of all Jewish Christians when the Christian church was established in Jerusalem. If this is the case, it was important that Matthew was a Levite. To Jews this gave him a precedence in rank over Peter (responsible for the Gospel of Mark) who was only a Galilean Jew of ordinary stock.

But there is one other point why Matthew's Gospel must be accorded a position of first rank among the Gospels. The apostle Paul made it abundantly clear that Christ's teachings were designed to go to the Jewish people *first* (Rom.2:9,10). Paul, when speaking to the Jews in Galatia, said: "It *was necessary* that the Word of God should *first* have been spoken to you" (Acts 13:46). This principle is consistently followed by Paul and the other apostles in their preaching of the Gospel to those throughout the world. Paul was keenly aware of this need. This is just another reason why the "Jewish" Gospel of Matthew had to appear first in the divine library of the New Testament. And, of course, that is exactly where we find it in the manuscripts.

It should be easy to understand why the next Gospel should be that of Peter (Mark) followed by that of Paul (Luke). Peter was the apostle to the Jews (though with Gentile connections), while Paul was the one to go primarily to the Gentiles.

What then, about the Gospel of John? Why is it last, and intervening between the Gospel of Luke and the Book of Acts which were written by Luke (for Paul) and are clearly two books that should normally be placed in parallel to each other? The fact is, John was the last to write his Gospel. His work is more of a summing-up of events that the others skimmed over or did not feel important to relate. And even the fact that John's Gospel separates Luke's Gospel from the Book of Acts is a sure sign that his Gospel was written last. It also helps to show that the final canonization of the New Testament was accomplished by the apostle John. It will be later shown that John's Gospel and the Book of Revelation (and perhaps his three epistles) were written and put into final form at the close of the first century. This late date could help explain why John's Gospel seems to be "wedged" between Luke's Gospel (First Luke) and the Book of Acts (Second Luke).

In summation, let us look once again at the New Testament "Pentateuch." First priority of position is accorded to the Gospel of Matthew who wrote primarily to the Jewish people. He was a Levite whom the Jews would respect as one with Old Testament authority to write the truth of God to Israel. Second comes the Gospel of Mark, which is actually Peter's Gospel. It has both a Jewish and Gentile emphasis. Recall that Peter started out in his Christian experience

214

by preaching only to Jews and other circumcised peoples closely akin to the Jews, but it was he whom Christ directed to go first to the Gentiles. At the end of his life, Peter was finally in Rome (with the apostle Paul) and the Gentile emphasis to the preaching of the Gospel was also recognized. Thirdly comes the Gospel of Luke. It was by a Gentile (the physician Luke) on behalf of the Gentile apostle, Paul. This is the reason it is in third rank in the official positioning of the Gospels. In fact, in the first canonization made by Peter and Paul in Rome somewhere near the end of A.D.66, it may well be the case that the Gospel of Luke and the Book of Acts were positioned in tandem to one another. But this was not the end of the story. The apostle Peter sent the canonical books which he and Paul had arranged to the apostle John in Ephesus. That is when John wrote his Gospel. Then John, at a later date, simply moved aside the Gospel of Luke and the Book of Acts (which normally should be placed directly next to each other) and wedged his Gospel between them. Since it was the last official Gospel written, it was also accorded last place.

There is another reason for this placement. John's Gospel is thoroughly Gentile (or Samaritan) in its environment. Though the Jews are often mentioned, the descriptions of them are always unflattering. Whereas the Gospel of Matthew is so careful not to offend Jewish sensitivities in matters of religion, the other Gospels progressively become less Jewish in their orientation and the Gospel of John abandons any desire to please a Jewish audience. Nevertheless, it is plain to see that the principle "to the Jew *first*" is adhered to in the arrangement of the first four Gospels. It went from the *thoroughly Jewish* emphasis (Matthew) in a progressive way to the *thoroughly non-Jewish* (John).

With John's Gospel added to the other three Gospels, plus Luke's Book of Acts, there became a fivefold canon of books which amounted to a New Testament Pentateuch — just like Moses had given his fivefold Pentateuch in the Old Testament. This allowed 22 Old Testament books to be flanked on one side of the New Testament Pentateuch and 22 New Testament books to be flanked on the other. This made a perfect balance of books on either side. Thus, the fivefold books of the New Testament Pentateuch became the *center* section — the divine fulcrum for all the books of the Bible.

Those five historical books present to mankind a divine account of how the Gospel started from a town in Galilee called Nazareth. How it finally went to Jerusalem. And from Jerusalem, it reached out to the center of the Gentile world — to Rome itself. From there, Peter and Paul sent the divine books which they canonized back to the apostle John in Ephesus where he added his own works. John continued living some 30 years longer within the region of Ephesus awaiting the final visionary experience he was promised about end-time events (the second and up-to-date viewing of the Book of Revelation). All of this occurred about A.D.96, and not long afterward he died a martyr as predicted by Christ (Matt.20:22,23). But before his death, John finalized the writing, arranging and editing of the New Testament canon and presented it to the Christian elders who lived in the area of Ephesus. It was thus at Ephesus near the end of the first century (not Jerusalem or Rome) where the canonization was completed. Since that time the world has had the 49 sacred books (7 times 7) which make up the Holy Bible. And the divine focal point of that revelation is the New Testament Pentateuch.

There is a most important principle which must constantly be remembered relative to the canonization of the Christian Pentateuch and the other New Testament books (and I do not apologize for repeating it): The Gospel must always go *first* to the Jews and *lastly* to the Gentiles. This factor of preeminence is found in the positioning of the books of the Christian Pentateuch and in all contexts of the New Testament. Everywhere the apostles Peter and Paul preached, they went to the Jewish people first (Acts 11:19; 13:14, 14:1; 17:1,10; 18:4; 19:8; 28:17). "It was necessary that the Word of God should *first* have been spoken to you" (Acts 13:46). This is why, as we will see in the next chapter, the seven General "Jewish" Epistles (James, I & II Peter, I, II & III John, and Jude) must precede the fourteen of the apostle Paul in the New Testament canon. This is the exact arrangement maintained in the early manuscript order of the New Testament books, and the one that should be followed today.

16

The Seven General Epistles

In the earliest and best manuscripts the seven epistles of James, I &
II Peter, I, II & III John, and Jude are placed before the fourteen
epistles of the apostle Paul. And this is where they belong! Prof.
Scrivener, after examining over 4000 manuscripts of the New
Testament, said:

> "Whether copies contain the whole or a part of the sacred
> volume, the general order of the books is the following: Gospels,
> Acts, *Catholic Epistles,* Pauline Epistles, Apocalypse" (*Intro. to
> Criticism of the New Testament,* 4th Ed., vol.I, p.72).

The term "Catholic" in the above quote is not a reference to a church
denomination. It meant in earlier times "universal" or "non-
localized." It signified a group of letters which went to no specific
church, but they were intended to go to the generality of people, and
in the case of these seven epistles, it meant the "Jewish" people.
Thus, the term that most people today use to refer to this division of
the New Testament is "General Epistles." This is the designation
that we will use to avoid a wrong conclusion that they were intended
to go to the Roman or Greek *Catholic Churches.* Just the opposite
was the case because for the most part their readers were Jews, not
Gentiles as were the Romans and Greeks.

In our present discussion, we are only interested in the position of
these seven epistles within the New Testament canon. There is no
doubt that the evidence supplied by the manuscripts places them
right after the Christian Pentateuch (Gospels and Acts) and before
those of Paul. Salmon shows the judgment of every one of the textual

critics of the last century:

> "This is the position [the General Epistles before Paul's]
> assigned them in the critical editions of Lachmann, Tischendorf,
> Tregelles, Westcott and Hort" ("Catholic Epistles," *Dict. of the
> Bible,* Hastings, vol.I,p.360).

More scholarly evidence to support the propriety of these conclusions
was given in the first chapter of this book. As Professor Gregory
pointed out, scholars and laity should not view this matter with
indifference. He felt it was important that the manuscript order
should be retained in modern versions and translations (*Canon and
Text of the New Testament,* pp.467-469). As one of the giants in the
field of New Testament textual criticism, we feel that his admonition
should be heeded and that our present versions should be corrected
to accord with the manuscripts. But there is more evidence for this
even outside the manuscripts. It comes from the Bible itself. There
are seven biblical reasons which indicate why the General Epistles
must precede those of Paul in the order of the New Testament books.
Let us look at them.

The Biblical Evidence

One of the cardinal rules of logic is that discussions on any subject
should proceed from the general to the particular. And these seven
epistles are called "General" for several reasons.

(1) Each of the books was written to general areas where Jews
were and not to a specific church like those of the apostle Paul.
James, for example, directed his epistle to the "twelve tribes
scattered abroad" — in all areas where Israelites were. Peter, on the
other hand, became a little more specialized regarding the geographical areas in which his readers lived, but still, his two epistles
were directed in a general way to those "scattered throughout
Pontus, Galatia, Cappadocia, Asia and Bithynia" (I Pet. 1:1; II
Pet.3:1). John and Jude were so "general" regarding the geographical
locations of their readers that they gave no territorial identifications
at all. The decided impression that one gets when reading these
seven epistles is that they were intended to be read by a large body of
people, notably people of Jewish extraction in various regions of the

218

world. Paul's letters, on the other hand (with the exception of one) were written to specific churches or individuals. And it is normal that the "general" should precede the "particular."

(2) These epistles contain only general teachings. Notice that there are no discourses on what baptism means, how to observe the Lord's Supper, how to conduct oneself in the liturgies of the church, etc. Really, the only instructions that we find in these seven epistles are quite general and basic. James even spoke of his readers as going to war with one another: "Whence come wars among you" (James 4:1). He also wrote of the rich among them as severely oppressing the poor (5:1). These statements have led some to wonder if he was speaking to converted people at all. The theme of the epistle of James seems to be giving an overview (or an introduction) to the basic concepts of Christianity. Indeed, there are only two short references to Christ (1:1 and 2:1) and if they were dropped from the text, the whole epistle could easily have been called a simple Jewish exposition on Old Testament values and theology (cf.Guthrie, *New Testament Introduction,* p.756).

This Old Testament theme presents no problem if one understands that the work was intended simply to be a Christian introduction of a general nature to people representing the twelve tribes of Israel. It would have been quite ridiculous to tell "the twelve tribes" in an introductory letter how they were to act in the Christian church, and in what order the Christian ministers should preach, etc. In fact, the people to whom James wrote were not attending any Christian church — they were still members of various synagogues (Jam.2:2, Greek). James was speaking to Jews who were just beginning to learn what the first principles of Christianity really were. This is why his book is positioned directly after the Book of Acts. It was intended to provide some preliminary teachings of Christianity without involving the readers in major doctrinal issues. The epistles following James were meant to set forth more completely the Gospel of Christ (and positioned so as to present in a progressive manner the maturer doctrines of Christianity).

We find the same thing in Peter's epistles, though the geographical destination is more defined than James and his doctrinal matters are a little stronger. Yet Peter is still giving general teaching. "As newborn babes, desire the sincere milk of the word, that ye may grow thereby" (I Pet.2:2). Peter was followed by the three letters of John. They focus on the general need for love to be expressed among brethren and that people should pay attention to the first principles of Christian teaching — adhering to the primitive and basic doctrines which were given "from the beginning" (I John 2:7,13; 3:8,11; II John 5). And though Jude homes in on a specific problem that was facing the Christian community when he wrote, his emphasis is still "that ye should earnestly contend for the faith *once delivered* to the saints" (Jude 3). Jude then described a condition happening within the Christian church that some people have thought incompatible with the strict moral and doctrinal disciplines in the churches which Paul supervised. True enough. But the seven General Epistles were not designed to give theological or ecclesiastical information. These were general letters dealing with large groups of people (mostly Jewish) who were still adhering, in many cases, to the national concepts of Judaism. This is why these epistles were placed before those of Paul. They present teachings for an "infant" stage to the understanding of Christian doctrines and church discipline.

(3) These seven epistles were also written by men who were commissioned to preach the Gospel to the Jewish people, and the messages (as we have seen) show that they were primarily intended for Jews. The apostle Paul recognized this special commission, and how it differed from his.

> "And when James, Cephas, and John, who seemed to be pillars, perceived the grace that was given unto me, they gave to me and Barnabas the right hands of fellowship; that we [Paul and Barnabas] should go unto the Gentiles, and they [James, Peter and John] unto the circumcised" (Gal.2:9).

The role of these three "pillar" apostles was very prestigious in the Christian community, and they were given charge over the Jewish people in the church. This gave them a position of priority. Even Paul admitted it.

> "I am not ashamed of the Gospel of Christ: for it is the power of God unto salvation to everyone that believeth; *to the Jew first, and also to the Greek*" (Rom.1:16; 2:9,10).

As we have been showing throughout this book, it was essential that the Gospel be given to the Jewish people first. Christ was adamant that this be done and he set the example by refusing to preach to outright Gentiles (Matt.15:21-28). And even in the first period after Christ's resurrection, the apostles spoke only to Jews about Christ (Acts 11:19). When it finally became permissible to grant Gentiles an opportunity to hear the Gospel, Paul still gave the Jewish people the priority of hearing. "It *was necessary* that the Word of God should *first* have been spoken to you [to you Jews]" (Acts 13:46). Paul always went to the Jews *first* wherever he wished to preach (Acts 11:19; 13:14; 14:1; 17:1,10; 18:4; 19:8; 28:17).

This principle alone would make it necessary to place these seven "Jewish" epistles written by the prime "Jewish" apostles to front rank ahead of the fourteen epistles of Paul to the Gentiles.

(4) These seven epistles have first position because their authors had seniority over Paul. This is made clear by Paul himself. He referred to these "pillar" authorities at Jerusalem as being "apostles before me" (Gal.1:17). Philastrius, in the fourth century, observed that the seven General Epistles must have priority over Paul for this one reason alone (Moffatt, *Introduction,* p.13). And why not? Throughout the whole of the Bible the superiority of *eldership* is recognized. Even Christ pointed out the special position of seniority that the original Jewish apostles had: "And ye shall also bear witness, because ye have been with me from the beginning" (John 15:27). We should remember that when Matthias was elected to be numbered among the apostles in the place of Judas, it was acknowledged that a prime requirement for apostleship necessitated that men "companied with us all the time that the Lord Jesus went in and out among us, beginning with the baptism of John" (Acts 1:21,22). This recognition of eldership was accorded those apostles who preceded Paul. In Romans 16:7 he said: "Salute Andronicus and Junia, my kinsmen, and my fellowprisoners, who are of note among the apostles, *who were also in Christ before me.*" These examples are enough to show that a preeminence was given to the "pillar" apostles even by Paul and had he the opportunity to position the various books within a New Testament canon, there can be no doubt that Paul would have given a superior position to the "Jewish" apostles who wrote to the "Jewish" people. And significantly, this is exactly the disposition which the manuscripts maintain.

(5) Not only did the Jerusalem apostles have seniority over Paul, they also had greater administrative authority. Paul said that James, Peter and John (the main writers of the General Epistles) *were the pillars* of the church (Gal.2:9). It was to them that Paul had to go in order to settle the question of circumcision among the Gentiles. He went "to them of reputation [that is, to them of recognized authority], lest by any means I should run, or had run, in vain" (Gal.2:2).

This scripture tells us much. In no uncertain terms Paul said that had he not cleared his teaching concerning the non-need for Gentiles to be circumcised with the pillar apostles in Jerusalem, all his preaching would have *been in vain.* But when the three pillar apostles heard the whole story of what God was doing through Paul among the Gentiles, they "gave to me and Barnabas the right hands of fellowship; that we should go unto the heathen, and they unto the circumcision" (Gal.2:9). This rank of authority was demonstrated by James at the Jerusalem conference. It was James who gave the final decision on what the Gentiles could and could not do (Acts 15:19).

In matters of rank, Paul was well aware that he was the "least" of the apostles. Speaking of his later call to the apostleship, he said:

> "And last of all, he [Christ] was seen of me also, as one born out of due time. For I am *the least of the apostles*, that am not meet to be called an apostle, because I persecuted the church of God" (I Cor.15:8,9).

Throughout the Bible the principle of those in the greatest authority having supremacy over lesser ones is maintained. In the first portion of the Book of Acts, we find the name of Barnabas placed before that of Paul, but later (when Paul was given more administrative authority) the placement is reversed. Barnabas was a Christian prior to Paul and he was a Levite (Acts 4:36). This at first gave him a rank above Paul in the eyes of the Jews. This was finally changed (Acts 15:2) and only temporarily reversed when they were once again within a Jewish environment at Jerusalem (Acts 15:12).

All of this shows why, in the New Testament canon, the General Epistles of the "pillar" apostles are placed first to accord with the Jewish positioning of superiority. Modern scholars have recognized this. Prof. Ernest F. Scott of Columbia University says:

"In our English New Testament, the General Epistles are placed near the end of the volume, just before the Book of Revelation. The Greek manuscripts put them as a rule, immediately after the Gospels and Acts, and before the writings of Paul. This was no doubt in recognition of the fact that they bore the names of the Apostles who were directly associated with Jesus, and whose authority, therefore, might be considered superior to that of Paul. In keeping with this principle, the first place of all was accorded to the Epistle of James. Its author was assumed to be no other than James, the Lord's own brother" (*The Literature of the New Testament*, pp.209,210).

(6) The General Epistles must also precede Paul's because they give the proper approach to the understanding of Paul's doctrinal letters. It was Peter who told his readers that Paul's teachings were "hard to be understood" and that one should be careful in interpreting them (II Pet.3:16). Now, where would a person expect to find such a warning? In our present order of biblical books, Peter's caution has been placed *after* one would have already studied Paul's fourteen epistles! What an odd place for such an admonition. Would it not be better to find Peter's statement in a section of scripture which was intended, in the first place, to be an introduction to the doctrinal dissertations of Paul? That is where it is found if one leaves the books in the order sanctioned by the early manuscripts.

There are even more reasons for placing the "Jewish" apostles before Paul. Doctrinal matters can be given a better understanding if the books are left in the proper order. For example, Paul said that Abraham was justified by faith (Rom.4:2) while James said by works (James 2:21). There is really no contradiction. If one will first read the *practical* application of faith as rendered by James, before the more *philosophical* aspect as encountered in Paul, the two concepts can be harmonized very well. For James, a faith expressed without works is no faith at all, even though a faith based solidly on works, that Paul spoke of, was equally not proper.

Similarly, in trying to comprehend the full teaching of other doctrinal matters, if people would tackle Paul's epistles *after* having absorbed the introductory and basic instruction within the General Epistles, a much easier task would await them in comprehending the fulness of the Gospel. It seems odd that people would want to enter

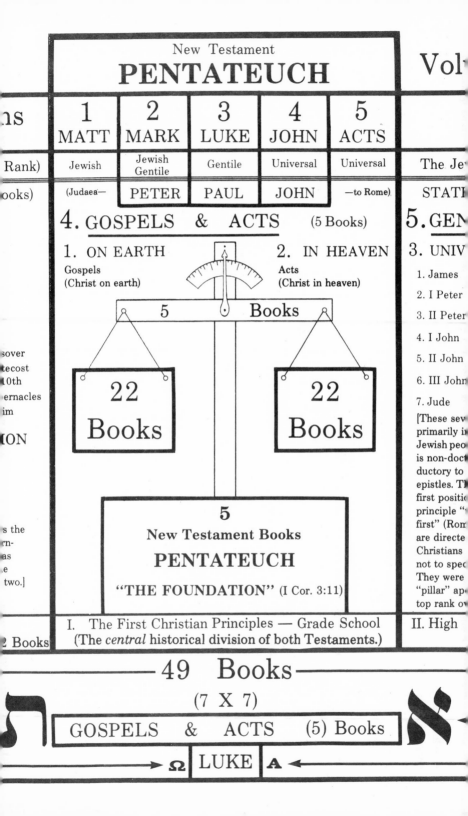

New Testament
PENTATEUCH

Vol

	1 MATT	2 MARK	3 LUKE	4 JOHN	5 ACTS	
ns (Rank)	Jewish	Jewish Gentile	Gentile	Universal	Universal	The Je
ooks)	(Judaea—	PETER	PAUL	JOHN	—to Rome)	STATI

4. GOSPELS & ACTS (5 Books)

1. ON EARTH
Gospels
(Christ on earth)

2. IN HEAVEN
Acts
(Christ in heaven)

5 Books

22 Books

22 Books

5
New Testament Books
PENTATEUCH
"THE FOUNDATION" (I Cor. 3:11)

5. GEN

3. UNIV

1. James

2. I Peter

3. II Peter

4. I John

5. II John

6. III John

7. Jude

[These sev
primarily i
Jewish peo
is non-doc
ductory to
epistles. T
first positi
principle "
first" (Rom
are directe
Christians
not to spec
They were
"pillar" ap
top rank o

sover
tecost
0th
ernacles
im

ON

s the
rn-
as
e
two.]

I. The First Christian Principles — Grade School
(The *central* historical division of both Testaments.)

II. High

2 Books

—— 49 Books ——
(7 X 7)

GOSPELS & ACTS (5) Books

→ Ω LUKE A ←

3	Grand	Divisions
v (1st Rank)	The Gentile (2nd Rank)	**World Holocaust**
(7 Books)	CHURCH (14 Books)	GOD (1 Book)
ERAL	**6. PAUL**	**7. REVELATION**
:RSAL	**4. 7 CHURCHES**	**7. PROPHETIC**

6. PAUL

4. 7 CHURCHES

1. Rom.	I.	The
2. I Cor.		ABC's of
3. II Cor.		Christian
4. Gal.		Doctrine

5. Eph.	II.	The
6. Phil.		XYZ's of
7. Col.		Doctrine

| 8. I Thes. | III. | The |
| 9. II Thes. | | End-Times |

5. MILLENNIAL

| 10. Hebrews | Temple |
| | Symbolism |

6. MINISTERIAL

11. I Tim.	The
12. II Tim.	Epistles for
13. Titus	Professional
14. Phile.	Leaders

7. REVELATION

7. PROPHETIC

Revelation

The
Book of Sevens

1. Seven Churches
2. Seven Golden Candlesticks
3. Seven Stars
4. Seven Spirits of God
5. Seven Lamps of Fire
6. Seven Seals
7. Seven Horns
8. Seven Eyes
9. Seven Angels
10. Seven Trumpets
11. Seven Thunders
12. Seven Thousand Men
13. Seven Heads
14. Seven Crowns
15. Seven Last Plagues
16. Seven Golden Vials
17. Seven Mountains
18. Seven Kings

[The Book of Revelation
has all the earmarks of
being the final book of both
Testaments.]

n epistles were
tended for the
le. Their theme
inal and intro-
'aul's doctrinal
ey are placed in
n to fulfil the
> the Jew
ins 2:10). They
to Jewish
n general and
fic churches.
vritten by the
stles with
er Paul.]

| School | III. College | IV. Post Graduate Studies |

←——— 22 Books ———→

←——— 24 Books ———→

Designed by Gary E. Arvidson.

THE GEOGRAPHICAL DESIGN OF THE HOLY SCRIPTURES

The Temples of Solomon and King Herod were designed to be permanent replicas of the Tabernacle that Moses constructed in the wilderness. There were some peripheral differences between the permanent Temples and the Tabernacle, but their central designs were always retained. The architectural necessity was the retention of the three distinct compartments known as the Holy of Holies, the Holy Place and the Court of Israel. That is, the western portion of the Sanctuary had the compartment called the Holy of Holies with an eastern entrance. Just to the east of that was another compartment called the Holy Place where the priests did their daily administrations. It also had an eastern entrance. Further east was the large compartment called the Court of Israel where ordinary Israelites were allowed to congregate. In the Tabernacle this large eastern Court also had a single entrance on its east side. Besides these three compartments, surrounding the Tabernacle was the Camp of the Israelites (its outer limits being 2000 cubits from the Holy of Holies where the Ark of the Covenant was housed). Just to the east of this outer limit of the Camp was the Altar of the Red Heifer which was positioned precisely east of the entrances to the Court of Israel, the Holy Place and the Holy of Holies.

The Temple Symbolized the Garden of Eden

These three compartments found in the Tabernacle and the permanent Temples were analogous to the three divisions of the Garden of Eden. The Holy of Holies was the spot in the Garden where God appeared to Adam and Eve "in the cool of the day." The Holy Place itself represented the whole of the Garden which was located in the Land of Eden. The Court of Israel represented the Land of Eden and in its western part (after the expulsion of our first parents from the Garden region) was an altar on which Cain and Abel offered their sacrifices. This altar was located at the east entrance to the Garden. But further east (and outside the limits of Eden) was the Land of Nod into which Cain was banished. A further altar was raised up in Nod on the east side of Eden on which the sin offering for Cain and his descendants would be offered to cleanse them of sins. This was analogous to the Altar of the Red Heifer which was also east of the Tabernacle and the permanent Temples. In the time of Christ, this Altar of the Red Heifer was situated directly east of the Temple entrances near the summit of the Mount of Olives. This was the region of Golgotha where Christ (the greatest sin offering of all time) was offered for the sins of Israel and the world. See my book "Secrets of Golgotha" which shows this.

The Jews Are the Legal Custodians of the Holy Scriptures

The 22 books of the Hebrew and Aramaic Scriptures along with the 27 books of the Greek Scriptures (representing 49 books in all, that is, 7 times 7 books) are found in seven precise divisions: 1) The Law of Moses, 2) The Prophets, 3) The Writings or Royal Section, 4) The Gospels with Acts, 5) The General Epistles, 6) The Epistles of Paul, and finally 7) The Book of Revelation. These books were

3	Grand	Divisi
The Law	The Church (1st Rank)	The State (:
GOD (5 Books)	CHURCH (6 Books)	STATE (1
1. LAW	**2. PROPHETS**	**3. PSALM**
1. LAW	2. FORMER	5. WISDOM
1. Genesis	1. Joshua - Judges	1. Psalms
2. Exodus	2. Book of the Kingdoms	2. Proverbs
3. Leviticus		3. Job
4. Numbers	3. LATTER	
5. Deuteronomy	3. Isaiah ⎫	**6. FESTIVA**
[The Old Testament Penta-	4. Jeremiah ⎬ MAJOR	4. Song =
teuch is the beginning	5. Ezekiel ⎭	5. Ruth =
division of the Holy		6. Lamen. =
Scripture. The following	4. MINOR	7. Eccl. =
two divisions of the O.T.	6. The Twelve	8. Esther =
are subsidiary to the Law.	1. Hosea ⎫	
The Prophets' division is	2. Joel ⎪	**7. RESTOR**
superior in rank to the	3. Amos ⎪	
Psalms' (or Royal)	4. Obediah ⎬ Assyrian	9. Daniel
division because the	5. Jonah ⎪ Period	10. Ezra-Nehemi
prophets were direct	6. Micah ⎪	11. Chronicles
emissaries of God and	7. Nahum ⎭	
were responsible for	8. Habakkuk ⎫ Chaldean	[This third divis
instructing and admonish-	9. Zephaniah ⎬ Period	Royal (state or
ing rulers and kings. The		ment) section a
positioning shows authority	10. Haggai ⎫ Restoration	inferior in rank
of rank and teaching.]	11. Zechariah ⎬ Period	prophets of divi
	12. Malachi ⎭	
Basic Law	Priests & Prophets	Kings & Rul
5 Books **+**	6 Books **=** 11 Books	**+** 11 Books **=**

א ←————— **22 Books** ————→

A ←——————— 2 4 Books ———————

"College" (Paul's Epistles) without first mastering "High School" (the General Epistles).

(7) The seventh reason why Paul's epistles belong after the seven General Epistles concerns the canonization of the New Testament itself. Since there had been a great deal of doubt among some first century people, especially Jewish Christians, regarding the validity of Paul's teaching and the inspiration of the letters he wrote, Peter thought it necessary to inform his readers that Paul's letters were indeed as inspired as the Old Testament (II Pet.3:15,16). Since Peter knew it was the responsibility of himself and John to perform the actual canonization of the New Testament according to the command of Chirst (II Pet.1:12-20), it was seen to be essential that they sanction the body of Paul's letters which had been selected to be included in that canon. Obviously, it would have been the normal thing to inform people that Paul's epistles were inspired *before* people would begin to study them!

Note that Peter (in his second epistle concerning canonization) referred to the inspiration of Paul's epistles at the last moment of his writing. This again indicates that the authority of Peter and of John superseded that of Paul. The apostle Paul was not only mentioned *last* by Peter, but his fourteen epistles were also placed in *last* position. And, indeed, they had to be. The teaching in them was of a highly sophisticated nature and represented the meat of the word of God. If the Christian Pentateuch (the Gospels and Acts) could be reckoned the basic "Elementary School" for Christian development, then the seven General Epistles would be the "High School," and the fourteen epistles of Paul would be the "College." And, to conclude the illustration, it would mean that the Book of Revelation, which occurs last of all in the manuscripts, would be the "Post-Graduate Studies."

The Order of the General Epistles

The principle of rank and subject matter is the reason that the epistle of James must precede that of Peter, and Peter those of John and Jude. Professor Scott, quoted above, shows this. "In keeping with this principle [of superior rank], the first place of all was accorded to the epistle of James." This is true enough. Even Paul recognized the rank of the pillar apostles in this fashion. "And when James, Cephas [Peter], and John, who seemed to be pillars . . ." (Gal.2:9). The order of mention is exactly in conformity to the principle of rank. It is no wonder that the General Epistles follow this exact order in the New Testament canon. This is a clear sign that the authority concept was being followed precisely.

The Concluding Evidence

There is a final point that should be mentioned which shows a major difference between the seven General Epistles and the fourteen of Paul, and it is significant enough to warrant the epistles of the "Jewish" apostles preceding those of Paul. Notice once again the authors of the seven General Epistles. James and Jude were legal brothers of Christ. This made James and Jude to be of royal Davidic stock. Since the Book of Acts ends with teaching the Jews in Rome about the Kingdom of God, the very next section of the New Testament is dominated by James with Jude (two royal scions of David) who carry on the theme of entering the Kingdom of God. Both Peter and John take inferior roles in this regard. Peter was actually from ordinary Jewish stock (perhaps from Simeon) while we will see that John was of priestly ancestry. Though Peter was clearly the top apostle in rank, James (the brother of Jesus) was of Davidic blood and he became head of the Jerusalem congregation. These men (James, Peter, John and Jude) were the top representatives of the Davidic dynasty, ordinary Jews, and the Aaronic priesthood.

With the apostle Paul, it was different! Though he was a Jew by religion and upbringing, Paul was a descendant of the Tribe of Benjamin. This may appear at first to be an insignificant distinction but to first century Jews, among whom genealogical matters were of utmost importance (I Tim.1:4; Titus 3:9), it had a bearing on authority and prestige. The fact is, Benjamin was the *last born* of Jacob's twelve sons. There was no tribe in Israel on a lower rung of authority by reason of birth. Even in the list of the twelve tribes recorded in the Book of Revelation, *Judah* is placed first (Rev.7:5) and *Benjamin* last (verse 8). As a matter of fact, because of the wickedness of the tribe in the period of the Judges, the other eleven tribes were on the verge of killing every descendant of Benjamin

(Judges 20 and 21). This was avoided at the last moment when the remaining 600 men of Benjamin were able to marry women of their brother tribe Manasseh. Some years later the first king of a united Israel was Saul, a Benjaminite. The Bible shows, however, that this ascendancy of the *least born* tribe was not to last. Judah finally took its prophesied lead (Gen.49:8-12) and David was installed as the first legitimate king of Israel.

Benjamin, moreover, was not totally rejected in this rise to power of Judah. When the Temple was built by Solomon, it was placed inside the Tribe of Benjamin right on its southern border with Judah, on Mount Moriah in the city of Jerusalem. It was predicted that God would "dwell" between the shoulders of Benjamin (Deut.33:12). It was thought that by placing the Temple within the precincts of the *least born* tribe, the other eleven tribes would not be squabbling over who was the most powerful with God. This stratagem worked, up to a point. But when the northern ten tribes of Israel revolted from the rule of the Davidic dynasty after the death of Solomon, Benjamin remained firmly devoted to Judah. After all, Jerusalem and God's true Temple were in their territory. From then on, the fortunes of Benjamin were connected with those of Judah. There was even a special relationship established, in a religious sense, between Benjamin and Judah, and the Bible recognized it. Unlike their early wickedness, the tribe seems to have become (as a whole) the "righteous" anchor that Judah needed to prevent it from being swallowed up by the Assyrians when northern Israel was taken captive. Though the Tribe of Judah is quite often rebuked for their ways, the Tribe of Benjamin after the time of Solomon is always spoken of by the Chronicler and the prophets in mild and often laudatory terms. Indeed, the prophet Jeremiah (who was a priest from the area of Benjamin) offered the Benjaminites safety from the Babylonian holocaust that was coming upon Jerusalem in his day (Jer.6:1), and so certain was Jeremiah that Benjamin would find shelter once again in their own land that he bought some property in Benjamin and sealed the deed in a jar to be evidence for possession after the Babylonian Captivity (Jer.32:8-44).

The descendants of Benjamin became especially important to Judah after the Babylonian Captivity. When Haman the Agagite maneuvered to have the whole of the Jewish race murdered by the edicts of the Persian emperor, Queen Esther, the wife of the emperor, managed to prevent this from happening. Esther was a Benjaminitess (Esther 2:5,6) and her uncle Mordecai (the prime minister of Persia) were instrumental in saving the whole of the Jewish people from destruction. It was "Benjamin" interceding the Gentile ruler to save "Judah."

This contact of Benjamin between Judah and the Gentiles was not to end with Esther and Mordecai. One of the most important Benjaminites of all time was the apostle Paul (Acts 13:21; Rom.11:1; Phil.3:5). Here was a member of the *least born* tribe of Israel playing a profound role as a mediator, once again, between Judah and the Gentile world. It was the Gentiles under Paul's supervision that sent the Jews of Palestine much material help in the time of famine (Acts 11:28-30; Rom.15:26). But more than that, the apostle Paul was responsible for preaching the Gospel of reconciliation between the Jews and all peoples of the Gentile world (Eph.2:11-22). Here was "Benjamin" coming to rescue Judah once again to make people in the world love and honor them, but it was also "Judah" coming to the rescue (through Christ) for the salvation of the whole world (II Cor.5:18,19). And Paul was a mediator between the two groups.

It is ironic that the Bible records the *least born* of Israel giving the most spiritual teaching to those with more birthright authority. And though Judah possessed the kingship of David and the seat of Moses, and because of this they should be accorded first rank, yet it was the least ranked tribe (Benjamin) that provided the most spiritual truth to Judah and the world. It seems that this is the way the Bible says God works. It is interesting that Abraham (the father of the faithful) was the *youngest* son of Terah (compare Genesis 11:26 and 12:1 with Acts 7:4). Jacob was the *youngest* son of Isaac yet he got the blessing and the birthright. Ephraim was the *youngest* son of Joseph yet he obtained birthright status. Moses was *younger* than Aaron yet he assumed supreme power over Aaron (God's High Priest) and over all Israel. David was the *youngest* of Jesse's children yet he became heir to the grandest royal dynasty ever afforded mankind. And it doesn't stop there. The first Gentile to receive the Gospel of Christ was an Ethiopian black man (far removed from the race of Israel) and a eunuch to boot — both conditions would render the man unable to enter the Temple of God. And the first uncircumcised Gentile to receive the Gospel was Cornelius, a Roman centurion of the hated occupation forces within Palestine. From this, it seems as though the *least born* or those most unfavored to receive customary honors and prestige are the very ones who are picked to bring the most spiritual blessings to the world. Christ taught that "many that are *first* shall be *last*; and the *last* shall be *first*" (Matt.19:30).

This is the way it was with the apostle Paul! Though he was in an inferior position from all the social and religious ranks within Judah which had to do with birth, he was the one whom God graced with fourteen epistles in the New Testament. This makes Paul the most prolific writer of books in the Bible, and yet he was *least born* in rank. Of course, this does not mean that we should exalt Paul's epistles to first position ahead of the kinsmen of Christ (who were of Judah and of royal Davidic ancestry and the ones taught by Christ himself), but it does mean the Bible can honor any person to a high position of esteem no matter if he or she is on the lowest pedestal of social, religious or political rank. As for Paul, his own estimation of his position of rank is well recorded: "And last of all he was seen of me also, as one born out of due time [without any birthright status]. *For I am the least of the apostles,* that am not fit to be called an apostle, because I persecuted the church of God. But by the grace of God I am what I am: and his grace which was bestowed on me was not in vain; but I labored more abundantly than they all: yet not I, but the grace of God which was with me" (I Cor.15:8-10). Though Paul was the *least* of all New Testament leaders, his abundant labor gained for him the right to have his name indelibly stamped on more books of the Bible than anyone else.

In conclusion, it should be recognized that the seven General Epistles truly belong in first rank position right after the New Testament Pentateuch (and ahead of Paul), but God has a way of making the "last" to be "first" — *first* in spiritual values. It was Paul's devotion and his abundance of work for the cause of the Gospel that allowed him to have first honor in the amount of books in the Bible (II Cor.11:18-28). In spite of this fact, the world has no authority to reposition Paul's epistles in advance of the General Epistles.

17

The Epistles of Paul

The proper manuscript order has the fourteen epistles of Paul following the seven General Epistles. There is, however, a major variation that differs from the present arrangement of the King James' Version (and maintained by virtually every other version since the invention of the printing press). Modern editions have placed the Book of Hebrews at the very end of the Pauline collection of books. This is what some church officials of the Western Church (Carthage and Rome) did in the late fourth century contrary to the best manuscripts and the opinions of most officials in the Eastern Church.

The proper positioning of the Book of Hebrews is right after Second Thessalonians — just before First Timothy. Nearly all the best manuscript evidence supports this. Scrivener writes:

> "In the Pauline epistles, that to the Hebrews immediately follows the second to the Thessalonians in the four great codices Vaticanus, Sinaiticus, Alexandrinus, and Ephraemi" (*Introduction*, Vol.I,p.74).

In the margin of his work, Prof. Scrivener lists some of the many manuscripts which position the Book of Hebrews in this fashion. The evidence for this arrangement is so strong that one wonders why Hebrews was moved out of its manuscript order and placed at the back of Paul's works? The reason is not difficult to discover. Scrivener mentions a major purpose why the Western Church relegated Hebrews to last position. It was —

"an arrangement which at first, no doubt, originated in the early
scruples prevailing in the Western Church, with respect to the
authorship and canonical authority of that divine epistle."

The Latin section of the church found it difficult to believe that the
epistle was even from the pen of Paul and because of this many
refused to accept it as belonging in the New Testament. Most
easterners had no major reservations about the book. Jerome, the
great western scholar and translator of the Latin Vulgate version (a
translation from the Hebrew and Greek into the Latin language),
shows the differences of opinions among the Eastern and Western
sections of the church regarding the Book of Hebrews. In his letter to
Dardanus, Jerome wrote:

"To our own people [Christians], we must say that this Epistle,
which is inscribed 'To the Hebrews,' is received as the Apostle
Paul's, not only in the churches of the East, but by all the
ecclesiastical writers of former times. But the Latins do not
receive it among the canonical scriptures" (Whytehead, *A
Handbook to the Canon and Inspiration to the Scriptures,* p.131).

There was a belief that Paul, the apostle to the Gentiles, had no
reason to be writing to the Jews. This, of course, is not a proper
evaluation. When the apostle Paul was commissioned by Christ on
the road to Damascus, he was told to preach to Israelites as well as
Gentiles (Acts 9:15), and throughout the history of Paul's ministry he
always went to the Jews first. Indeed, he understood that it was
absolutely essential to do this. Paul said: "It was necessary that the
word of God should *first* have been spoken to you [the Jews]" (Acts
13:46). Paul's motto was: "The Jew *first,* and also the Greek
(Gentile)" (Rom.1:9,10).

There was every reason for Paul, the finest Christian intellect of
the time who was thoroughly trained in Jewish law and customs (Acts
22:3), to have written a treatise to Jewish people (or those with strong
Judaistic tendencies) about the typical nature of the Temple services
ordained by Moses. The New Testament canon would have suffered
from a prime deficiency had not such a work been included. And the
Book of Hebrews fits this to a tee. Most Christians of the East simply
accepted it as Paul's (or written by a secretary of Paul). It certainly

had "Pauline" characteristics associated with it, especially since the majority of manuscripts placed it in the interior of Paul's collection of canonical letters. And another point. If Hebrews is not Paul's, then there are 13 epistles of Paul, whereas 14 (2 times 7) has a canonical symmetry to it, 7 (or its multiples) being the symbolic number of *completion* and *finality*. Prof. Bacon comments:

> "The anonymous epistle anciently superscribed 'To the Hebrews,' was connected in the East with the letters of Paul. Even in the West, where the statements of all the Fathers down to the fourth century are opposed to Pauline authorship, its position in the Canon, when admitted, was next to those of Paul" (*Introduction to the New Testament,* p.140).

Moffatt, the translator of the Bible, said, regarding the manuscript location of Hebrews: "The position of Hebrews within the Pauline body of letters is usually between the ecclesiastical and private epistles (Eastern Church) or after the latter (Western Church)" (*Introduction to the Literature of the New Testament,* p.17). The ecclesiastical letters to which Moffatt had reference are: Romans, Corinthians, Galatians, Ephesians, Philippians, Colossians and Thessalonians. The Easterners and the best manuscripts placed the Book of Hebrews immediately after his letters to those seven churches, and just before Paul's pastoral epistles: those to Timothy, Titus and Philemon.

The Design of Paul's Epistles

The fourteen epistles of Paul are arranged into three parts in the New Testament canon. The *First Section* consists of nine epistles to seven church congregations: (1) Romans, (2) Corinthians, (3) Galatians, (4) Ephesians, (5) Philippians, (6) Colossians, (7) Thessalonians. The *Second Section* is composed of one general letter, the Book of Hebrews. The *Third Section* is called in modern circles the Pastoral Epistles, the private letters to individual pastors: Timothy, Titus and Philemon.

Look at the first section, which, from ancient times, has been technically named "Paul's Letters to Seven Churches." In the

Muratorian Canon (written about A.D.180), there is a general reference to this first section:

> "The apostle Paul himself, following the example of John [in the Book of Revelation], wrote by name to Seven Churches. True, he wrote twice to the Corinthians and Thessalonians for their correction, but he shows thereby the unity of the Church; for John also in Revelation, though he writes to seven churches only, yet speaks to all" (cf. Bacon, p.52).

Victorinus, who wrote about A.D.290, also gave an interesting comment about Paul's seven churches. After observing that God rested from all his labors on the seventh day, Victorinus continued to mention the symbolic use of the number *seven* in biblical matters. In the course of his discussion, he stated:

> "That in the whole world there are Seven Churches; and that those churches called seven are one general church as Paul has taught; and that he might keep to it, he did not exceed the number of Seven Churches, but wrote to the Romans, to the Corinthians, to the Galatians, to the Ephesians, to the Philippians, to the Colossians, to the Thessalonians. Afterwards, he wrote to particular persons, that he might not exceed the measure of Seven Churches: and contracting his doctrine into a little compass, he says to Timothy: 'That thou mayest know how thou oughtest to behave thyself in the Church of the living God' " (Lardner, *Credibility*, vol.III,p.177).

Cyprian of Carthage (c. A.D.250) also recognized the symbolic teaching behind the fact that Paul wrote only to Seven Churches. In the first book of his *Testimonies*, having quoted the words of Hannah "the barren has born seven, and she that has many sons is waxed feeble," he continued by saying, "the seven sons represent Seven Churches; for which reason Paul wrote to Seven Churches; and the Revelation has Seven Churches, that the number seven may be preserved" (Lardner, vol.III.p.41). In another book, after having mentioned the seven golden lampstands in the Book of Revelation and the seven pillars in Solomon's Proverbs upon which Wisdom built her home, Cyprian added:

> "And the Apostle Paul, who was mindful of this authorized and well-known number, writes to Seven Churches; and in the Revelation our Lord sends his divine and heavenly instructions and commands to Seven Churches and their angels" (*ibid.*).

Many other ancients took note of the significant number of churches to which Paul wrote. Among them were Jerome (about A.D.400) (Horne, *Introduction*, vol.I,p.75) and Isidore of Seville (near A.D.600) (Lardner, vol.V,p.137). More recently, Dr. E.W.Bullinger made some pertinent remarks showing the symbolic reasons why Paul wrote to Seven Churches (*The Church Epistles,* p.85).

> "Seven Churches [by Paul] were addressed as such by the Holy Spirit. Seven being the number of spiritual and final perfection. Is it not remarkable that the Holy Spirit addressed Seven Churches and no more: exactly the same number as the Lord himself addressed later from glory [in the Book of Revelation]?"

This is a proper evaluation. In Paul's epistles to his Seven Churches there is to be found the main New Testament teaching concerning doctrinal matters to be taught in the Christian church. This is why the subjects of repentance, faith, baptisms, the Holy Spirit, etc. are discussed at length in the letters to these Seven Churches. It can be no accident that the number was *seven*, and no more. The number, as the ancients mentioned, was also followed by the apostle John when he wrote the Book of Revelation. Frank W. Beare, Professor of New Testament Studies at Trinity College, Toronto, goes so far as to say that John in Revelation followed the example of Paul.

> "The device of introducing an apocalypse by a sequence of letters to seven churches but issued together under cover of a general letter...can only be explained as indicating that the author [of Revelation] had before him a corpus of Pauline letters similarly constructed" ("Canon of the New Testament," *The Interpreter's Bible,,* vol.I,p.522).

This appraisal makes perfectly good sense. The number *seven* was universally acknowledged in the biblical world as signifying *completion* and *perfection,* and with many features of the Old and New

Testaments being typically dominated by this number, it would have been odd for Paul not to have used it in some capacity. There was a definite reason why the General Epistles were seven in number; why Paul's came to fourteen in number (but written to Seven Churches); and why the Old and New Testaments together amount to seven divisions with 49 (7 times 7) books in the original enumeration.

The Order of Paul's Epistles

It is well recognized by scholars that Paul's letters are not arranged in any chronological order. "It is notorious that the order of epistles in the book of the New Testament is not their real, or chronological order" (Davies, "Paul," *Dictionary of the Bible,*, p.744). Indeed, the earliest book was no doubt Galatians but it appears in third position after his epistles to the Romans and Corinthians which were written some 5 or 6 years afterwards. The seventh church of Paul was represented by the Thessalonians, but those two epistles were composed about 14 years before Ephesians and Colossians which were positioned before Thessalonians. This shows that they could not have been arranged with any chronological factors in mind.

Some have thought they were placed to indicate the authority of the various churches since the Book of Romans appears first in the Pauline corpus of books. But there are problems with this theory. While it would be easy to infer that the first two areas of Rome and Corinth might fit this reason, it is not quite the same with the next epistle, that to the Galatians (unless it could be maintained that it appears next because Paul was writing to a number of cities, and not just one). Ephesians however is a definite difficulty. It wouldn't be a problem *if* it could be shown that the epistle was indeed written to the church at Ephesus. But biblical (and other) evidence makes it almost certain that another city was in Paul's mind, and the one with the best credentials is Laodicea. In no way could that city have any preeminence over Philippi (a colony city) or Thessalonica which was the most populous city in Macedonia and the most significant in the province (which included Philippi). But Thessalonica is in seventh position (after Philippi) though it was the provincial capital and a *free city* which gave it a high independent rank among Roman cities.

It is a lame theory that Paul's Seven Churches were arranged according to a "rank-of-the-cities" order.

The real reason for Paul's allocation of the letters to his Seven Churches is based on the principle of progressive teaching. In any book for teaching a subject, one starts with the simple and general instruction first and then proceeds in a step-by-step manner until the advanced and sophisticated teachings are reached. As stated in the last chapter, the five books of the Christian Pentateuch give the "Elementary School" of divine instruction, the seven General Epistles proceed to "High School," and the Epistles of Paul present the "College." But even here, Paul starts out with the "Freshman Year" first, the "Sophomore" second, etc. All books of instruction even in our modern world arrange their material in this fashion. It would be absurd to do otherwise. How could one perceive how to perform calculus without first knowing simple arithmetic, then algebra, etc.? And so it is with the various divisions and books of the New Testament. The elementary teachings are given first and the more advanced come later. This is the manner in which the epistles of Paul are arranged.

Early Christians were quite aware that this was the reason for the disposition of the New Testament books. Euthalius (c.A.D.450) mentioned Paul's epistles in the proper manuscript order and then proceeded to explain why they were positioned that way. He said the order was according to the Christian growth that the readers had to whom they were sent, beginning with the least mature and proceeding to the more advanced. To Euthalius, in his comments from the epistle to the Ephesians, he said this was evident from several points. For one, the epistle to the Romans was placed first because it contained instructions for those who had just learned the first principles of the Gospel. But after Ephesians came Philippians. That epistle was written to the faithful who had made progress and had brought forth much fruit. And at the end of his enumeration of Paul's fourteen epistles, Euthalius expressly said that they were arranged according to the maturity of the readers (Lardner, vol.V.p.71). This same opinion was stated by another Church Father, Theodoret. "The Epistle to the Romans has been placed first, as containing the most full and exact representation of Christian doctrine in all its branches" (*ibid.*). It comprised the ABC's of Christian doctrinal discussion, especially to show the basic teachings of repentance, faith, etc.

The Book of Hebrews Illustrates
the First Principles

The best appraisal showing why the books of the New Testament canon are arranged the way they are comes from the apostles themselves. Since they wrote the books, they ought to be better equipped to explain why they placed them in the order they did. The Book of Hebrews contains information on what the apostles considered were the step-by-step doctrinal subjects for Christian growth and understanding. They are found in Hebrews 6:1,2. Paul gave *seven* steps that lead to a full maturity in the knowledge of Christ. He called them the principles of the doctrines of Christ. They are: (1) repentance from dead works, (2) faith toward God, (3) the doctrine of baptisms, (4) the laying on of hands for the reception of the Holy Spirit and its gifts, (5) the resurrection of the dead, (6) the judgment of the future, and then (7) perfection. Paul began his discourse in the Book of Hebrews on these steps by mentioning *perfection* first, and then he gave the six progressive factors which would lead a Christian to the attainment of that seventh and final phase.

Remarkably, this is the exact order of doctrinal teaching which people must master and perform in order to be mature Christians in Christ (at least, this was the method utilized in the early history of the church). People were first required to repent, then express faith, be baptized, obtain the Holy Spirit. This made it possible for them to share in the resurrection at Christ's return, be able to receive their rewards in judgment, and finally reach a perfection in Christ. The apostle Paul called those seven doctrines the first principles of the Christian faith.

The Book of Romans
and the First Principles

The teaching of those seven doctrinal principles as found in Hebrews 6:1,2 are progressively followed in Paul's writings and in the order of his epistles. Notice Paul's instructions in the Book of Romans. In the first two chapters Paul talked of turning from sin. He was instructing people to repent of their ways, and he concluded his first doctrinal

236

discourse by saying: "The goodness of God leadeth thee to *repentance*" (Rom.2:4).

The next three chapters (3,4 and 5) concern the doctrine of *faith* just as the Book of Hebrews mentioned the second principle as also being faith. Paul summed up this doctrinal teaching in Romans with his classic statement: "Therefore being justified by faith, we have peace with God through our Lord Jesus Christ: by whom also we have access by faith unto his grace wherein we stand" (Rom.5:1,2).

The third principle of the Christian doctrines in Hebrews was *baptism*. In Romans chapter 6 Paul follows his subject of *faith* with a discussion on baptism. "Know ye not, that so many of us as were baptized into Jesus Christ were baptized into his death" (Rom.6:3). Paul was being guided by the step-by-step principles which he later wrote in the Book of Hebrews.

The next topic in Hebrews was the laying on of hands to receive the Holy Spirit. And, true to form, chapters 7 and 8 of Romans follow the progressive pattern with Paul's discussion on the need and the work of the *Holy Spirit*.

> "But ye are not in the flesh, but in the Spirit, if so be that the Spirit of God dwell in you. Now if any man have not the Spirit of Christ, he is none of his.... But if the Spirit of him that raised up Jesus from the dead dwell in you, he that raised up Christ from the dead shall also quicken your mortal bodies by his Spirit that dwelleth in you" (Rom.8:9,10).

The fifth and sixth principles mentioned in the Book of Hebrews were the *resurrection* and the *judgment*. And chapters 9, 10 and 11 of Romans give a discussion on how God will bless all Israel and the Gentiles with a resurrection and a righteous judgment. [The biblical judgment is not always a punishment for sin. It can mean, and often does, a judgment to receive righteous rewards. See Psalm 98.]

The seventh principle in the Book of Hebrews was *perfection*. And the doctrinal portion of Romans ends with Paul's teachings that a full redemption will come to all Israel and mankind. Man will become just like God in perfection. "For of him, and through him, and to him are all things: to whom be glory forever" (Rom.11:36). The Book of Romans, then, provides the Christian with an introduction to the essential doctrines of Christianity. And Paul gave them in the perfect order of the first principles that he recorded in Hebrews 6:1,2.

First Corinthians

The same formula of progressive doctrinal teaching is found in First Corinthians. While the first three principles of Christian doctrines (repentance, faith and baptism) were discussed more extensively in the Book of Romans in a technical sense, the practical side of those subjects is found in the first eleven chapters of First Corinthians. But more sophisticated matters dealing with the Holy Spirit and the resurrection are more fully discussed in First Corinthians. Three chapters (12 to 14) are devoted to the gifts and operations of the Holy Spirit, and a whole chapter (15) is given to the subject of the resurrection from the dead.

That First Corinthians is also a basic doctrinal book (like Romans) illustrating the "first principles," is made clear by Paul himself. He told those in Corinth because of their newness in Christ that they were only able to receive the "milk of the word."

> "And I, brethren, could not speak unto you as unto spiritual, but as unto carnal, even as unto babes in Christ. *I have fed you with milk, and not meat:* for hitherto you were not able to bear it, *neither yet now are ye able*" (I Cor.3:1,2).

The above assessment of Paul shows that he, himself, considered his teachings to the Corinthians to be for spiritual infants. While the Book of Romans was written to people he had never met before (and those who needed the ABC's of his essential doctrinal teachings), the Corinthians received more personal attention (and correction) yet his instructions to them were still intended for children in the faith. The Corinthians received teachings which were slightly more advanced than those to the Romans. Recall that he had never met the Romans face to face when he wrote them (Rom.1:11; 15:16,20), but he had already spent some 18 months among the Corinthians before he composed his two letters to them (Acts 18:11). In spite of that length of time in personally ministering to them, they still needed the firstfruit teachings of Christ. He appealed to them not to be children any longer (I Cor.14:20), but they still were. In his second epistle, written just a few months later, he was still reminding them: "I speak unto you as children" (II Cor.6:13).

The next book of Paul in the canonical order is that to the Galatians. The Galatian churches had been graced with much more personal teachings of Paul (than those in Rome or Corinth) when he wrote them — perhaps as much as four or five years. But they had become so far removed from the true Christian faith that Paul reprimanded them for returning to the "schoolmaster" (the Law of Moses) (Gal.3:24); they had reverted to being a child once again (Gal.4:1-6).

Notice the progression of teaching within the epistles of these first three churches of Paul. He had never seen the Romans and presented them with the ABC's of Christian doctrines. The Corinthians had learned a little more having had Paul in their midst for 18 months, and the Galatians had been given even more teaching with four or five years of instruction — but all three churches were still children in the faith. Hardly any of them was spiritually mature. But it became a far different story with the next three churches.

Ephesians, Philippians and Colossians

When one reaches these three epistles in the canonical order of the New Testament books the childhood phase of Christian teaching has finished. The people receiving these teachings were those who progressed into a mature stage of Christian development. In those epistles the apostle Paul no longer instructed them in the basic principles. Nowhere does he discuss in detail anything about repentance, faith, baptisms, the Holy Spirit, the resurrection or judgment. His main interest now is *perfection*. In the highest sense Paul tells these readers that they are now "joint heirs, joint bodied, and joint partakers of Christ in glory." The mature phase had arrived for those who had advanced to the "Ephesian message" and such people were expected to act like children no more. Paul stated that God's spiritual gifts had been given

> "for the perfecting [maturing] of the saints, for the work of the ministry, for the edifying of the body of Christ: till we all come in the unity of the faith, and of the knowledge of the Son of God,

unto a perfect [mature] man, unto the measure of the stature of the fulness of Christ: that we *henceforth be no more children* tossed to and fro, and carried about with every wind of doctrine" (Eph. 4:12-14).

The doctrines being discussed in these later epistles represent the fulness of the Gospel of Christ. Paul even said that such teachings were the full Gospel message.

"Wherefore I am made a minister, according to the dispensation of God which is given me to fulfill [that is, *to fill to the top*] the word of God; even the mystery which hath been hid from ages and from generations, but now [with the writing of Colossians] is made manifest to his saints" (Col.1:25,26).

The three epistles of Ephesians, Philippians and Colossians provide mature teachings. If people satisfactorily reach the capabilities of mastering the information in these epistles, then they have gone beyond the "milk stage" and into the "meat." Romans, Corinthians and Galatians could be reckoned the "Freshman and Sophomore" stage of "College," while Ephesians, Philippians and Colossians are the "Junior and Senior" phase.

The Epistles to the Thessalonians

The Seven Churches of the apostle Paul end with the two to the Thessalonians. As the number *seven* symbolically means *completion* and *finality,* so there were two books of instruction written to this seventh church which deal, primarily, with end-time events. In both, the theme is the coming of the Man of Sin (also called the Wicked One or the Son of Perdition), the Second Advent of Christ, and the resurrection from the dead for the righteous saints. In a word, the *seventh* church speaks of the *conclusion* of the age. And what a fitting place to discuss such issues. If Christians would progress in their development through the milk (or children) phase of their spiritual growth (shown in the First, Second and Third churches) and then succeed in their advancement through their meat (or mature) phase (shown in the Fourth, Fifth and Sixth churches), then they would be expected to obtain their rewards which are described in the two epistles to the Seventh Church. The reason the epistles to the Thessalonians are positioned in seventh place (though they are two of the earliest epistles written) is that no one can procure the rewards of the first resurrection associated with Christ's return unless the person has mastered the teachings recorded in the previous six churches.

It is interesting that the Mosaic holyday which typified the arrival of the kingdom of God on earth and the resurrection from the dead, was the Day of Trumpets. This was a festival which ushered in the *seventh* Hebrew month in which the final Mosaic holydays occurred. There were *seven* such holydays, and the last four were ordained to happen in the seventh month (Lev.23).

The Day of Trumpets which commenced this final, seventh month of the festival year was introduced by the blowing of trumpets, hence the name "The Day of Trumpets." Indeed, each month was proclaimed with the blowing of a trumpet (Num.10:10). Since the Mosaic festival year was seven months long, the blowing of the trumpet at the beginning of the seventh month was, in calendar and prophetic significance, "the last trump." And when the seventh trumpet sounds in the Book of Revelation, the kingdoms of this world become the kingdoms of Christ and he then begins to reign (Rev.11:15). And what do we find in Paul's teaching to his *seventh* church (Thessalonians)? We find that its central theme concerns this end-time event.

> "For the Lord himself shall descend from heaven with a shout,
> with the voice of the archangel, and with *the trump of God:* and the
> dead in Christ shall rise first" (I Thess.4:16).

There could be no better position to place the two epistles which focus on the time of Christ's advent than in the *seventh* station of Paul's letters to the churches. And in the manuscripts this is precisely where they are found. It was no happenchance affair that this was the case.

The Book of Hebrews

In the proper manuscript order of the New Testament books, Hebrews comes immediately on the heels of the Seventh Church!

This treatise gives very advanced teaching. In fact, Paul made the explicit statement in Hebrews 6:1-3 that he would not speak of the first principles in the Book of Hebrews. He devoted the entire book to mature doctrinal matters on the typical meanings behind the Temple services. It was essential for such subjects to be covered, and who better to do it than the apostle Paul (who was trained at the feet of the great rabbi Gamaliel)?

Though the Book of Hebrews, by Paul's own definition, is very mature instruction, why does it follow the Seventh Church (Thessalonians)? Why couldn't it, after all, be allotted its modern position at the very end of Paul's epistles? An analysis of the contents can show why it should be retained in its proper order as found in the early manuscripts. Let us look at the matter closely.

It is important to note that the first two chapters are devoted to showing the superiority of Christ *over all angels*. This was important for Paul to demonstrate because it was well recognized in the first century by the Jewish authorities that the Mosaic law had been given to Israel through the agency of angels — and Paul mentions this fact in Hebrews 2:2. Indeed, *this present age* (until the second advent of Christ) was reckoned as being in the charge of angels, both good and bad (Dan.10:13-21; Matt.4:8-10). But Paul, in the Book of Hebrews, was not going to discuss the kingdoms of this world during the time angels are in a limited control. He was going to give some advanced spiritual teaching about the role of the Temple, the priesthood, the festivals, and the ceremonies in the future millennial kingdom of God once Christ Jesus would be back on earth. Paul, then, introduces the reason for writing the Book of Hebrews in chapter 2, verse 5.

"For it is not to angels that he has subjected *the world to come, ABOUT WHICH WE ARE SPEAKING."*

This is the real title to the book. Paul's theme of which he was speaking was *the world to come* — the "Sabbath-rest to the people of God" (4:9). Paul's subject was about the "Millennial rest," and the whole section from 3:7 to 4:12 is about that "rest." Paul shows the meaning of the Day of Atonement rituals which are symbolic introductions to a Millennium theme. Chapter 8 concerns the marriage of the Lamb *after* Christ's return. In 9:11 and 10:1 he states

242

that Christ is the High Priest "of good things to come." And there is the eleventh chapter. This is about the promises which will finally (at the "better resurrection") be given to the Old Testament saints. He mentions that the New Jerusalem will be a reality during this future time (11:16). Thus, the whole Book of Hebrews is symbolic teaching about rewards to the millennial saints *after* Christ returns. This is why the book must be positioned *after* Paul's two epistles to the Seventh Church (Thessalonians) which speak about the events associated with Christ's second advent. And this is exactly where the best manuscripts position Hebrews. That is where it should remain.

The apostle Peter may have referred to this epistle of Paul in his last letter (II Pet.3:15,16). He mentioned that the people of Asia Minor had received a technical letter from Paul. Peter said the writing of Paul concerned matters relating to the time of the end and the Day of the Lord (as Peter himself was discussing in his third chapter). It could well be that it was the Book of Hebrews that Peter had in mind. Recall that Paul had been commissioned to preach to Israelites as well as Gentiles (Acts 9:15) and this treatise about the real meaning behind the Temple services (both those of the past and that one to occur in the future) is probably the book Peter was referring to.

From all this, there is a logic to the manuscript order in which we find the Book of Hebrews. Its major subjects pertain to the fulfillment of the promises which Christ said he would perform once he returns to earth as depicted in Paul's Seventh Church.

The Pastoral Epistles of Paul

The remainder of Paul's letters were personal communications which he wrote to ministers of churches. The four epistles of Timothy, Titus and Philemon contain matters on church government and discipline. They were written from one professional minister to other ministers. It should be self-evident that instructions intended solely for practicing ministers would concern very mature matters. This is why they appear in last position among Paul's writings. These were letters to those who had already gone through "College" and had "graduated from a Theological Seminary". Within their contexts there is not a shred of instruction on what the first principles of Christian doctrine represent. The reason for this is because those doctrinal principles had adequately been covered in the previous books positioned in the canonical order of Paul's writings. On the other hand, the Pastoral Epistles have information on how to maintain a proper government, a pure doctrine, and a correct discipline in established church congregations. It would have been daft indeed to position such books at the beginning of (or distribute them among) the former epistles of Paul. This is why they must be left in their position (following the Book of Hebrews) as shown in the early manuscripts.

But there is more. Why do we find the four Pastoral Epistles in the order that we do? There can be little question here. Just as James, Peter, John and Jude were positioned in their order of rank within the seven General Epistles, so it is with these three men. Timothy had the superior distinction (and given two epistles) because he was the minister in charge of the churches under Paul in Western Asia Minor. Titus was in the lesser responsibility of managing the churches in the island of Crete, a smaller and less significant area. As to Philemon, we are not told in what region he ministered (or even if he was a full-fledged minister), though it seems that he was a resident of the eastern part of the province of Asia. Surely, the greater responibility of Timothy gave him first position, and it must be the same of Titus over Philemon. We might even recognize a degree of prominence among these three men by the length of Paul's letters to them. Timothy was given two epistles in ten chapters. Titus one epistle in three chapters. And Philemon received only a very short letter from Paul. On this point, the scholar Lardner, who spent considerable time surveying the literature of early Christian writers in the first centuries of Christianity, came to this conclusion:

> "Among these epistles to particular persons those to Timothy have the precedence, as he was the favorite disciple of Paul, and those epistles are the largest and the fullest. The epistle to Titus comes next, as he was an evangelist. And that to Philemon is last, as he was supposed by many to be only a private Christian. Undoubtedly Titus was a person of greater eminence, and in a higher station than Philemon. Moreover, by many, the design of that epistle was thought to be of no importance" (*Credibility,* vol. VI, pp. 338, 339).

There may even be a nationality order maintained in the four Pastoral Epistles. Paul always held to the concept that the Gospel should go to the Jew first, and then to the Gentiles. It is well known that Timothy was half Jewish (Acts 16:1), which rendered him a "full Jew" in the eyes of the Jewish people because his mother was Jewish! We know that Titus was a Greek (Gal.2:3) and since Philemon follows him, this no doubt indicates he was also a Gentile.

From the foregoing discussion, we have seen some clear internal evidence from Paul's epistles why the early manuscript order of his books must be retained in all versions of the New Testament. The theological and social teachings found in the New Testament which dominated the pyschological thinking patterns of the apostles demand that the manuscript arrangement of the books be maintained. And though we later find a few manuscripts which show some differences of arrangement, these can be recognized as exceptions to the rule. And indeed, these exceptions (which can normally be explained as sectarian variations) help to prove the rule rather than the establishment of another. Thus, even the Sinaiticus manuscript which places Paul's letters between the Gospels and Acts (an oddity if there ever was one) would not encourage anyone to believe that its order of books should be preferred over the vast majority of other manuscripts.

There are other variations in a few isolated manuscripts. The order of the Gospels or that of the General Epistles are on rare occasions different from the normal manuscripts, and the Book of Hebrews has been rarely found next to Galatians (no doubt because Hebrews was thought in some circles to have been written to the people in the Galatian area). Again, these are clear exceptions to the rule and could never be seriously considered as having apostolic approbation.

The prime difference in the arrangement of the biblical books (which has dominated all modern versions of the Bible) is that which Jerome established in the fifth century when he produced his Latin Vulgate version. The influence of Jerome (the theological dispositions and opinions of *one man*) has been the main reason that *all* modern versions of the Bible have been so topsy-turvy in their order of books. But Prof. Gregory (the great textual scholar) has made it clear that the Greek manuscript order should be retained in all Bibles. It *"is the order to which we should hold"* (*CTNT*, p.469).

18

The Canonization of Paul's Epistles

There was a common goal which dominated the last few months of the lives of Peter, John and Paul. If one will read their final works, when each was well aware that his death was on the immediate horizon, it can be seen what their desires were. It was most essential that a canon of divine New Testament scriptures be created which would last the world as a standard for Christian teaching until the Second Advent of Christ. The apostles came to realize that Christ was not returning in their generation, and that a day in prophetic interpretation was a thousand years (II Pet.3:3-13). This meant that many hundreds of years remained in human history before the symbolic "Sabbath" called the Millennium (Heb.4:11) could arrive. 7000 YRS. And with the great apostasies mentioned by Peter and John in full swing (II Peter 2 and I John 2:18,19; 4:1); with vast numbers having rejected Paul (II Tim.1:15); and with ministers abandoning the authority of John (III John 9,10), and especially with future prospects for retaining the purity of the Christian Gospel being more ominous (II Tim.3:1-7; 4:2-4; II Pet.3:3), *the apostles had to take matters in hand to preserve the truths of Christianity*. They would have been remiss in their duties had they simply died and left the world without a standard of righteousness to rely on. This is why Peter came to the conclusion that he and John must leave the Christian church with writings inspired by the Holy Spirit to last them "until the day dawn" (II Pet.1:19). Thus, the two prime apostles, who were eyewitnesses to the Transfiguration of Christ and who heard the very voice of the Father himself, set about their task. In doing so, Peter mentioned that not only did he and John possess the word of prophecy in a more confirmed way than others (II Pet.1:19), but that Paul's epistles (the ones being left with the church) were also as inspired as the Old Testament scriptures (II Pet.3:15,16).

Since it is clear that the apostles Peter and John reckoned Paul's epistles as being a part of the sacred writings, we need to ask ourselves if Paul felt the same way about his written documents? Did he see a need to collect some of his own writings to be part of the New Testament canon? Was it he who decided to select fourteen of his letters for this purpose, and did he edit them for inclusion in the canon? These are interesting questions, and surprisingly, we can go a long way in satisfactorily answering them. The truth is, Paul was quite aware of his role in helping Peter and John to canonize the New Testament and just before his death his main activity was to accomplish this task. Let us look at the evidence.

Paul had long realized that the words that he was writing to the people had the approbation of God and that they often represented the very commandments of God. "If any man think himself to be a prophet, or spiritual, let him acknowledge that the things that I write unto you *are the commandments of God*" (I Cor.14:37).

Even more than that, Paul proclaimed to the Colossians that he had been commissioned by Christ to fulfill (or to bring to the top, to the very brim) the teachings of God. He knew he had the job of helping *to complete* the word of God for mankind.

> "Whereof I am made a minister, according to the dispensation of God which is given to me for you, *to complete* the word of God; even the mystery which hath been hid from ages and from generations, but *now* is made manifest to his saints" (Col.1: 25,26).

It is interesting that this reference of Paul about *completing* the word of God appears in the text to the Sixth Church within the Pauline body of scriptures. The next book in the canonical collection was the Seventh Church (Thessalonians) which had as its message the main New Testament teaching about end-time events. In other words, in Paul's last doctrinal discourse to the Christian church he said the Word of God was now *complete* and that the next event to occur in the history of the church would be that mentioned in his message to the Seventh Church — Christ's return and the resurrection from the dead! With Paul's discourse to the Sixth Church, the complete doctrinal teachings for the Christian church had been given.

Paul's Last Responsibility

Paul's final appeal to Timothy was that he remain steadfast in teaching the true doctrines of Christ because the outlook for the future was going to be that of teaching fables.

> "I charge thee before God and Christ Jesus, who by his appearing and kingdom shall judge the living and the dead. Preach the word; be urgent at favorable times or unfavorable ones; reprove, rebuke, exhort, with all longsuffering and teaching. *For a time will come* when they will not endure the sound teaching; but, having itching ears, will heap to themselves teachers after their own lusts; and will turn away their ears from the truth, *and turn aside unto fables.* But be sober in all things, suffer hardship, do the work of an evangelist, fully bear the responsibility of your ministry. For I am already being poured out as a drink offering and *the time of my departure is come.* The good fight I have fought, the course I have finished, the faith I have kept. One thing remains: The crown of righteousness which is laid up for me, the Lord, the righteous judge, shall give me at that day; and not only to me, but also to all those who have loved his appearing" (II Tim.4:1-8).

The main desire of Paul was that sound doctrine be continually preached after his death because there was going to be a great falling away from the truth and people would begin to believe fables. These fables were also a major concern of Peter and John. This is why Peter said that in the documents he and John were leaving the Christian church, they were not going to be like the fables that were beginning to be published and taught. Knowing also that his own death (like Paul's) was imminent, Peter said:

> "And I think it right as long as I am in this tabernacle [this mortal body], to stir you up by reminder; knowing that the putting off of my tabernacle cometh swiftly, even as our Lord Jesus Christ also showed me. But I will also give diligence that at each time ye be able *after my decease* to call these things to remembrance. For *not*

by following cunningly devised FABLES, made we known to you
the power and presence of our Lord Jesus Christ, but we [Peter
and John] were eyewitnesses of his majesty" (II Pet.1:13-16).

It was the circulation of fables, and the prospect of more being
published, that convinced Peter, John and Paul (in the last months of
their lives) to do something about the preservation of the true
doctrines of Christ. With this in mind, let us now look at what the
apostle Paul did to play a part in this responsibility.

Paul's Canonization

Realizing that his death was very near, Paul asked Timothy, his
faithful worker in Christ, to urgently meet him in Rome. Paul
considered Timothy's journey to be of utmost importance and he was
urged to expedite it as soon as possible. "With speed come to me
quickly" (II Tim.4:9). Paul was in immediate need of assistance, and
this was especially so since most of his colleagues had either
abandoned him or had journeyed to other regions of the Empire. He
was practically left alone in Rome. "Only Luke is with me" (verse 11).

With this pressing situation in mind, notice the *two requests* that
Paul instructed Timothy to accomplish. For one, he wanted John
Mark (the one who wrote the Gospel of Mark) to come with Timothy
to Rome because he had a *service* [a particular *ministry*] that he
wanted him to perform. And secondly, Paul desired Timothy to
*"bring the cloak I left at Troas with Carpus, and the scrolls, especially
the parchments"* (verse 13).

These two requests were very important to the canonization of
Paul's epistles. Note carefully that Paul urgently needed John Mark
and some important documents that Timothy knew about. Let us
first look at the reason he wanted John Mark to accompany Timothy
to Rome.

John Mark was a very prominent person in the early history of
Christianity. And in the matter of canonization, he significantly
appears at a crucial time. We are told he was a cousin of Barnabas
(Col.4:10), which may indicate he was a Jew with Levitical prestige
(Acts 4:36). At any rate, he occupied a prime social position in the
Jerusalem church and his mother's home was the place where it was

common for the apostles to meet (Acts 12:12-17). And though there was a disagreement between Paul and Mark in their early careers (Acts 15:36-41), this was not a permanent thing and Paul later called John Mark his "fellow-laborer" (Col.4:10,11). And Paul's appeal to Timothy was for John Mark to accompany him to Rome so that he could perform a special service (ministry) for Paul. What was this *service?*

This is where the apostle Peter enters the picture. Though John Mark was often an associate of the apostle Paul in his ministry among the Gentiles, history and tradition attest to his closer relationship with the apostle Peter. In his first epistle, Peter refers to Mark as "my son" (I Pet.5:13). Peter must have been a frequent visitor to the home of John Mark in Jerusalem (that is, his mother's home). Peter no doubt took Mark under his wing while he was a young man and he became a close assistant of Peter. Papias of the late first century said that John Mark was Peter's "interpreter" or his official secretary and the writer of the Second Gospel. As we have pointed out in a previous chapter, the Gospel of Mark really has the earmarks of being the Gospel of Peter. And indeed, it was. This means that John Mark was the one who helped Peter in his literary efforts and other ministerial duties. We find him with Peter in "Babylon" (a cipher for Jerusalem, not Rome or the Babylon on the Euphrates) (I Pet.5:13). But we also find him in attendance with the apostle Paul just a little earlier in time (Col.4:10,11). These indications may show that John Mark was a type of liaison between Peter and Paul — one time he was with Peter and the other with Paul. And just before his death, Paul makes his urgent request for Timothy to bring John Mark with him to Rome. He also wanted Timothy to bring along some important items that Paul called "the cloak, the books, and especially the parchments."

In effect, Paul was asking for Peter's right hand man to come immediately to Rome for a special service. Though Paul did not ask for Peter himself to journey to the capital of the Empire, the fact that he was asking for John Mark was practically tantamount to the same thing! Paul knew that only the apostles Peter and John were the remaining witnesses to the Transfiguration, and this gave them a special commission for the preservation of divine truth which would last the church through the spiritual corruptions which were prophesied to take place in the future.

The Cloak, The Scrolls and The Parchments

Timothy and John Mark were asked by Paul to fetch three important items and bring them to Rome. "When you come, bring the cloak [Greek: *phelonen*] I left with Carpus, and the scrolls, especially the parchments" (II Tim.4:13). It is interesting that the *phelonen*, usually considered to be a heavy outer garment, is mentioned alongside the paper scrolls (actually scrolls made from the papyrus plant) and the parchments (these were animal skins on which permanent documents were normally written). It seems odd that a heavy coat would be mentioned along with literary documents. Most scholars, however, point out that Paul wanted Timothy and Mark to hurry to Rome before winter (verse 21) and that he probably wanted the *phelonen* which he left with Carpus in order to keep himself warm when the cold would set in. This may be the case, but there are some difficulties with this interpretation. The truth is, the word *phelonen* had another meaning in the Greek world at the time, and it is one that is intimately connected with scrolls and parchments.

Vincent, in his *Word Studies in the New Testament,* has this to say about the word *phelonen.*

> "Hesychius explains it as originally a case for keeping the mouthpieces of wind-instruments; thence, generally, *a box.* Phrynicus, a Greek sophist of the second half of the third century, defines it as 'a receptacle for books, clothes, silver, or anything else.' *Phelonen* was a *wrapper of parchments,* and was translated figuratively in Latin by *toga* or *paenula* 'a cloak,' sometimes of leather; also the *wrapping* which a shopkeeper put round fish or olives; also the parchment cover for papyrus rolls. Accordingly it is claimed that Timothy in 4:13 is bidden to bring, not a cloak, but a roll-case. So the Syriac Version" (p.326).

The fact is, the word *phelonen* can mean either a cloak (and it is used that way time and again in Greek literature) or it could mean a receptacle for the placement of scrolls and parchments. It is the context which must determine what the apostle Paul meant by the use of *phelonen* in II Timothy 4:13. Since the word is found right next to scrolls and parchments, the immediate context would suggest a "book cover" a "book case" or "book slip" into which scrolls or pages of books were placed. As Vincent stated, the Syriac Version of the New Testament understood it in that manner. Chrysostom, in the fourth century, commented on this very reference of Paul's and stated that some thought Paul meant a "book case" — a receptacle for books (*Hom. in loc.* vol.XI,p780, ed. Gaume). Even Jerome mentioned this point (*Epist.*36, *ad Damasum*).

What is meant can only be determined by the context, because the word can signify either a heavy outer coat, a book case or some outer cover for books. Even in our modern times we have problems in interpreting similar words unless a proper context is provided. Let me give two illustrations to show the difficulty. In these examples we will consider the modern words *jacket, wrap* and *cover.* Suppose a letter were found in which a woman college student wrote her mother. She said that she wanted her mother to "go to the closet and get out my heavy *jacket* and send it to me. It will provide the *cover* I need from the cold. I am now using the *wrap* you gave me for my birthday and it is not warm enough." If such a letter were found, the context makes it clear that the girl is talking about outer garments in all instances. But what if the following letter were found. "Go to the bookstore and buy the latest fiction book you wrote me about. Take the *jacket* off, because dust *wraps* on the books annoy me. Make sure, however, that the book has a hard *cover* because I don't like paperbacks."

Though these two illustrations use exactly the *same words* they signify opposite things. Obviously, no one would get confused over what was intended in either case, because the contexts are plain as to what was meant. But let us return to our word *phelonen* in II Timothy 4:13. It could mean either a book case, a book wrapper, a book jacket, a book cover, or it could mean a heavy outer garment. Vincent in his *Word Studies* had no objection to it being an ordinary *cloak* because, like many other modern translators, he noted that Paul asked Timothy and John Mark to come to Rome before winter (verse 21). To many scholars this provides the context in which to interpret *phelonen,* though admittedly the reference to winter is eight verses away from the use of the word. On the other hand, the word *phelonen* is found *in the very verse* which mentions the scrolls and parchments that Paul needed. Contextually, it would seem more logical to think of *phelonen* as being associated with literary documents. Indeed, it is even better to consider it that way because Luke was still with Paul in

Rome and surely he could have secured for Paul any protective garment to keep away the cold during the approaching winter. Would it be necessary to fetch one all the way from Troas to keep Paul covered for the short time he was to remain alive? The fact is, Paul's reference to winter (verse 21) is by context too far away for the *phelonen* to mean an actual cloak. But with the word intimately connected with the literary documents which Paul was urgently requesting Timothy and John Mark to bring with them, it seems more probable that the interpretation of the Syriac Version, along with the suggestions found in Chrsysostom and Jerome, happen to be correct. It appears that Paul wanted his important book case (his receptacle for carrying books) to be brought at once to Rome — and the request was one of pressing necessity.

What Was In The Book Case?

It is unreasonable to assume that the book case contained papyrus scrolls or parchments of the Old Testament scriptures. There were always a large group of people with Paul wherever he travelled, and their baggage would no doubt have contained a copy (or copies) of the Old Testament. Besides, Paul could refer to the earlier scriptures by reading them in the various synagogues in the areas he visited. Of course, Paul was in prison when he wrote Timothy and could not attend the synagogues to consult the scriptures. Yet, Luke was with him. Could not Luke have done this for him, or even to have brought the Old Testament to him in prison from the baggage they had? And besides, what would Paul need with the Old Testament in an urgent way just before he was to be killed? Had he not memorized almost all of it over his 35 years of ministry?

But it was of utmost priority that he obtain "*the* book case, *the* papyrus scrolls, and especially *the* animal skin volumes." Note the definite articles in front of each of the three items! Since Paul gave no further description about them, it appears that Timothy and John Mark knew exactly the specific things Paul meant, and they realized that it was important that they be brought immediately to Rome! There is no doubt in my mind that some particular scrolls and parchment documents were being kept safely by Paul in a specially constructed carrying case or book cover. It also makes sense that they were *his own writings* which he had brought together and left in Asia Minor with Carpus. Paul now needed them dispatched to Rome immediately. This must be the reason why Paul requested John Mark to accompany Timothy.

The Role of John Mark

John Mark was Peter's assistant, his right hand man! He was also his secretary and the one who wrote literary documents for Peter. The service that Paul wanted John Mark to perform may have concerned the disposition of some of Paul's writings. This is as good a reason as any why Paul wanted John Mark in Rome. If it was not to take Paul's letters to Peter, then it was to talk over the matter of the letters and have Peter come to Paul in Rome. Since it seems that Paul wrote Second Timothy in the late Summer or Autumn of A.D.65, John Mark's journey to Rome, then back to Jerusalem where Peter probably was, could have been accomplished by late Spring of A.D.66. And with the miraculous events concerning the Temple starting to happen just before Passover, A.D.66 and continued until Pentecost, A.D.66 (when God abandoned the Temple at Jerusalem), it would have been possible for Peter to have reached Rome by the late Summer of A.D.66. If this is the case, Peter's only reason for going to Rome was to see the apostle Paul relative to the matter of the New Testament canonization. This could have been the main reason that John Mark was involved in the issue since he was the literary assistant to Peter. And recall, Paul was urgently admonishing Timothy to bring the written documents with John Mark. The historical scenario that is provided by Paul's last chapter of Second Timothy demands that something of a highly important literary activity was under way.

With both Peter and Paul in Rome in the final weeks of A.D.66 or in early A.D.67, they could have selected and canonized the New Testament scriptures which they had in their possession. It seems certain that Paul even edited his own letters for inclusion into the sacred canon of the New Testament. An example of this are the last three verses of Romans in our present versions. These verses are very close to the writing style of Ephesians and Colossians, and they contain a reference that Paul's teachings were then being called "the prophetic scriptures" (verse 26, Greek). Such a use of the phrase "prophetic scriptures" is a sure sign that Paul's letters were then being considered as sacred and as inspired as were the scriptures of the Old Testament. Recall that Peter and John considered themselves as having "the prophetic word more confirmed" (II Pet.1:18) and this was a reference to their written works as being inspired of God (II Pet.1:20). And now we have Paul saying the same thing about his own writings. They were "the prophetic scriptures" (Rom.16:26). Paul wrote this editorial remark at the end of Romans long after he had composed the actual letter back in A.D.56. This is because he made it clear in the editorial footnote that "all the nations" had now received the teaching of his Gospel (verse 26). This could only have been stated after he had returned from Spain in about A.D.62. This reference dovetails precisely with that which Paul made in the Book of Colossians (written about A.D.64) that the Gospel had now been "preached in all creation that is under heaven" (Col.1:23).

These indications are enough to show that Paul edited the Book of Romans. Since this was done to the ABC book of his collection, he may have done it to others. But what is the purpose for such editing? It is clearly to provide something for a later or different audience, and to bring the earlier documents up-to-date in the teaching of the Gospel. It is sensible that Paul, wanting to make the Book of Romans of universal application, added his brief reference to the advanced teaching of "the Mystery," which he later revealed in Ephesians and Colossians. And importantly, he was now saying that his writings were a part of "the prophetic scriptures" (Rom.16:26). Paul was simply preparing his epistles for canonization.

The Final Act of Peter

Just before Paul was martyred, the fourteen epistles of Paul were placed in their proper order. Along with these were arranged other New Testament works in the hands of Peter and Paul. It was at this time, no doubt, that John Mark wrote his Gospel copying down the words of Peter as he dictated them to him. Peter then wrote his second epistle which mentioned this preliminary canonization and that he and the apostle John were commissioned by God to fill up the books of the sacred canon. Peter then sent by the hand of John Mark his second epistle (along with the books that were collected and arranged by himself and Paul) to the apostle John in Western Asia Minor. This was the particular *service* that Paul wanted John Mark to accomplish (II Tim.4:11). A short while later (probably in A.D.67) Peter himself was martyred in Rome. Tradition has it that he was crucified upsidedown, and there is no reason to dispute the possibility of this. But now, the preliminary books were in the hands of the apostle John in Ephesus to complete his prophesied role of finalizing the canon of the New Testament.

The formation of the canon remained within the responsibility of the apostle John. Not for another 30 years or so would it reach its final and complete status to be positioned alongside the Old Testament to represent the full revelation of God to man. In the next chapter we will show how the apostle John fulfilled his prophesied commission.

19

The Completion of the Canon

The apostle Peter said there were two people who had the authority
from Christ to canonize the New Testament. They were himself and
the apostle John. They were the only ones remaining alive who had
witnessed the Transfiguration of Christ. Peter, in his second epistle,
said this majestic event gave them a special authorization to receive
and to record inspired teachings from God. They had "the word of
prophecy more confirmed" (II Pet.1:19). This gave them the right to
compose or to select any documents they ~~saw fit in order~~ to leave the
Christian church with official documents which would last them
"until the day dawn" (II Pet.1:19). This, in summary, was the
teaching of Peter in the first chapter of his second epistle.

BY INSPIRATION

    The one who carried Peter's selected documents to the apostle
John was probably John Mark. When he left Rome, Paul was dead
and Peter was near death, if not already dead. Certainly, by late
A.D.67, John was the only apostle remaining who had witnessed the
Transfiguration. The responsibility for putting the finishing touches
to the canon of the New Testament fell to him. This was in accord
with Christ's prophecy that Peter was to die a martyr but that John
would continue to live "until I am coming" (John 21:22,23). This did
not mean that John himself would not die, as some began to imagine,
because Christ made it clear that the two Sons of Thunder (John and
his brother James) would be killed for their faith (Matt.20:23). John's
brother was the first of the apostles to be slain (Acts 12:1,2), and
history informs us that John also met his death through martyrdom
(Eusebius, *Eccl.Hist.* IV.31). John, however, was to tarry on earth
until the coming of Christ. As explained in a previous chapter, this
was a reference to John being shown in a series of visions the Book of

Revelation. Though the evidence points to about 56 to 60 A.D. for the first writing of the Book of Revelation, it was revealed again (perhaps with more material added to the original text) in the last part of the first century. Irenaeus who was a native of Asia Minor and one who knew Polycarp, who in turn was a personal acquaintance of the apostle John, said that the Book of Revelation "was seen no such long time ago, but almost in our own generation, at the end of the reign of Domitian" (*Adv.haer.*5.30.3). This reference is powerful evidence that John received the visions (at least in their final form) when he was a very old man. Indeed, Irenaeus said that John lived in the city of Ephesus until the time of the emperor Trajan (A.D.98-117) (*ibid.*2.22). According to Papias, who was Bishop of Hierapolis near Ephesus and a contemporary of John, he was martyred by the Jews.

The fact that John had a long history of living and working in the region of Ephesus is well attested and need not be seriously doubted. Irenaeus also stated that John composed his Gospel while at Ephesus (*ibid.*3.1.1). And since the Book of Revelation was restored to relevance and was canonized as a book about the end-times (as well as written to the seven churches in western Asia Minor), it can be reasonably believed that the center of apostolic activity and authority gravitated to this region of the world. It is true that Jerusalem had its church rebuilt soon after A.D.70, but since there was no longer any Temple in existence and no priesthood at Jerusalem giving proper religious indications regarding the Jewish calendar, etc. that Jewish Christians would have been interested in, Jerusalem ceased to be an important city as far as authority was concerned. Even the ordinary Jews (that is, non-Christian Jews) moved their executive, legislative and judicial center to Jamnia in the plains region near the Mediterranean coast. Jerusalem had lost its influence in both the Christian and Jewish worlds.

As far as it can be determined, Ephesus and the adjacent regions in western Asia Minor had become the *center* of apostolic Christianity. This is the very region in which the New Testament canon arose.

Asia Minor and the New Testament Books

The final New Testament did not have its origin in Jerusalem or in Rome. History makes it clear that it had its formation where the apostle John made his abode for the last 35 years of his life. It came directly out of *Ephesus*. In the first place, well over 80 percent of the writings which make up the New Testament were either directed *to* an area within 500 miles of Ephesus or written *from* that region. When James wrote his epistle to the twelve tribes in the dispersion, it must be recognized that he was not directing his message to the Jews in Palestine, or even to the multitudes in Mesopotamia. In the first century the Palestine/Mesopotamian Jews were acknowledged as a part of the "homeland" of the Jews. James was writing primarily to Jews scattered around the Roman Empire, and the greatest concentration of Jews outside Syria and Egypt was in Asia Minor (Philo, *Embassy to Gaius,* 245,256,281,282).

The apostle Peter was even more specific and wrote his two epistles to the resident aliens throughout Asia Minor (I Pet.1;1; II Pet.3:1). Jude covered the same subject as Peter, so it is sensible that he directed his epistle to the same people. John, of course, wrote his five books in the canon either to or from the region around Ephesus.

And look at Paul. Other than the Book of Romans (which Paul wrote from Corinth which was within the 500 mile radius of Ephesus), the letters to the Corinthians were written from Ephesus and Macedonia (also within the 500 mile zone). The churches of Galatia were located east of Ephesus and well within the radius mentioned above. The prison books of Ephesians, Colossians and Philemon were written from Ephesus and to regions around Ephesus. Those to Philippi and Thessalonica were also within the 500 mile area. The Book of Hebrews went to the same people to whom Peter wrote and its actual destination was no doubt Galatia. In fact, in a few manuscripts, Hebrews is placed (erroneously) next to the Book of Galatians. Though this is not proper to do in the actual manuscript order of the books, it does show that some Christians recognized that the Book of Hebrews was written to people in the central area of Asia Minor — again within the 500 mile zone of Ephesus. The epistles of Paul to Timothy have long been understood to have been written to Timothy while he was in or near Ephesus. Titus got his letter while he was in the island of Crete, again within the central region.

But what about the Gospels? That of the apostle John was written from Ephesus. Luke was the close assistant of Paul and the main area for Paul's ministry in the latter years of his life was Ephesus. John

Mark wrote his Gospel under Peter's direction, and since Peter wrote his epistle concerning the canonization to those in Asia Minor (I Pet.1:1; II Pet.3:1), it is reasonable to suppose that John Mark transcribed Peter's Gospel and took it to the apostle John in Ephesus for final canonization.

The only book in the entirety of the New Testament that does not seem to have any connection with Ephesus (or the 500 mile radius around it) was the Gospel of Matthew. That Gospel seems to have been written to the Jews in Jerusalem and Palestine. However, the principle "to the Jew first" makes it reasonable that such a Gospel (and notably the *first* one) had to go to the Jews of Judaea.

Yet with all other books in the New Testament, the focus is directly upon Ephesus, or within the Ephesian zone. We feel it was no accident that the apostle John decided to spend the final 35 years of his life in that region.

Scholars have seen the importance of this centralized area around Ephesus for the history of the New Testament church at the conclusion of the first century. Professor Thiersch said: "The Church's centre of gravity was *no longer* at Jerusalem; it was *not yet* at Rome; it *was* at Ephesus" (quoted by Godet, *Com.onJohn,* vol.I,p45). And indeed, Ephesus was the new center of Christianity. It is to that region that one must look regarding all matters of authority and canonization within the Christian church between the years A.D.67 and A.D.98! There is no doubt that this is proper.

The Canonization by the Apostle John

John did not create the New Testament on his own. He had helpers. If one will read the writings of John carefully, these assistants can be recognized, and they played a very important part in the overall canonization. References to them are found from time to time cropping up within the contexts of John's compositions.

The best place to start in order to observe this circle of John's helpers is at the very end of John's Gospel. Throughout his twenty-one chapters we find the apostle recording what Christ taught along with the apostle's own comments. But when one reaches John 21:24 (just before the end of the Gospel) there is a remark in the text that interjects what *others* besides John had to say about the Gospel of John. Notice the verse.

> "This is the disciple [John] who bears witness about these things
> (*and WE know that the witness he gives is true*)."

Notice the abrupt change from the third person singular to the first person *plural*. The last part of this verse is introducing further witnesses, other than John (identified only by the pronoun "WE"). Who were these men? In the Gospel they are not identified, but it can reasonably be assumed that the first readers of John's Gospel must have been aware of their identities. They must have represented an officially recognized body of men since they boldly gave their witness to John's written word. "And WE know that the witness he [John] gives is true."

But there is more! The "WE" passages don't stop with the single verse at the end of John's Gospel. They occur elsewhere in John's writings. Notice the short epistle called Third John. John began to speak to a man called Gaius in the first person singular: "I pray that in all things you may be prospering and having good health" (verse 2). Then we find a long string of "I rejoiced" (verse 3), "I am thankful" (verse 4), "I wrote" (verse 9), and "I will call to remembrance" (verse 10). But then, and out of the blue, John introduces a plural intrusion into the text. It says: "In fact, *WE also are bearing witness,* and you know that the witness *WE give* is true" (verse 12). Then immediately the context of Third John returns to: "*I* had many things to write you, yet *I* do not wish to go on writing you with ink and pen. But *I* am hoping to see you directly" (verses 13,14).

It is clear that a body of men, other than John himself, were telling the readers of John's third epistle that *they too* were able to witness to the truth that John was stating. These assistants or editors of John must have been well known to John's readers. All they say is "*you know* that the witness WE GIVE is true." Certainly, these men could reasonably be considered a group of John's right-hand men, known by all, because the editors said "*you know* our witness is true."

There is even more. In John's first epistle we find the insertion of another "WE section." Notice I John 4:11. After John told his readers that "I am writing" (I John 2:1), followed by further references to "I am writing" or "I write" in verses 7, 8, 12, 13(three times), 14(twice) as well as "I write" in verses 21 and 26, there is then interjected into the context:

> "In addition, *WE ourselves* have beheld and are bearing witness that the Father has sent forth his Son as Savior of the world" (I John 4:14).

This shows, once again, an intrusion into the text. This was a deliberate attempt to interpose the witness of a body of men other than the apostle John. And after these men had their chance to include, once again, their witness we find John returning to his "I write you" motif (I John 5:13). These references indicate that there were other men, no doubt known by the original readers of John's Gospel and his first and third epistles, who wanted to make sure that they also were giving their testimonies to the truth of what John was saying.

Who Were These Other Witnesses?

Thankfully, it is possible to identify these men in a general way, but we have not been told their names. Since the "WE sections" in John's Gospel and his first and third epistles are very similar in content and purpose, it can be reasonably believed that they all represented the same group of men who were assistants (or editors) of John. If this is the case, then we can know more about them because in the first chapter of John's first epistle these men are further identified. In fact, the whole of the first chapter gives a rundown of the authority that they had, along with John, in the Christian church. They must have been associated with John during his Ephesian sojourn sometime between the years of A.D.67 and A.D.98. Note carefully the first chapter of First John so that the authority of these men can come into better view. The whole of the chapter needs to be mentioned.

> "That which was from the beginning, which WE have heard, which WE have seen with OUR eyes, which WE have viewed and OUR hands felt, concerning the word of life (and the life was made manifest, and WE have seen and are bearing witness and reporting to you the everlasting life which was with the Father

and was made manifest to US), that which WE have seen and heard WE are reporting unto you, that you may be sharing with US. Furthermore, this sharing of OURS is with the Father and with his son Jesus Christ. And so WE are writing these things that OUR joy may be in full measure" (I John 1:1-4).

The "WE section" continues on through the first chapter of First John. But, abruptly, in chapter two, there is a change to the first person singular: "My little children, *I* write unto you" (verse 1). This continues until 4:14 is reached, and then there is the single verse which again records a "WE section." Once their final witness is recorded, John closes with the usual: "*I* write you these things" (5:13).

Whoever these men were, they figured very prominently in the writing of John's three epistles. But more than that, they were men from Palestine who had been personal acquaintances of Christ and they were witnesses of his resurrection from the dead. This put them into a relatively high position of authority. After all, how many people in the first century could claim such distinction? Even the apostle Paul knew of only about 500 who were so honored. And these men were a part of that group. They may even have been of more esteem in the eyes of Christians at the time. Indeed, if one will look at the very beginning of the Gospel of John, these *same men* gave their own witness (along with John) to the glory of Christ which they had seen with their own eyes. In John's first chapter there is a prominent (and even glaring) "WE section." But strangely, most people pass right over it as though it is not even there. It is time that people begin to pay attention to what the text actually says, rather than hurrying over it in a haphazard fashion to get to the next section. If people would slow down and read what John says, many would be in for some real surprises. Notice an important "WE section" at the very start of John's Gospel.

"And the Word was made flesh and dwelt among us (*and WE beheld his glory, the glory as of the only begotten of the Father*) full of grace and truth" (John 1:14).

Scholars are aware that this interjection is the separate witness of John's assistants or editors (Hastings, *Dict. of Christ and the Gospels,* vol.I,pp.880,881), but the vast majority of readers of the New Testament simply pass over this reference so quickly that they don't even notice the relevance of it. People today are prone to thoroughly avoid the witness that these men gave. It is time to restore their testimony to its proper place—because it is important to do so.

Who were these men who interposed their own testimonies at crucial points in the texts of John? One thing is assured. They were almost certainly Jewish because they were witnesses of Christ in the flesh before his crucifixion and after his resurrection as well. Both the references in John 1:14 and I John 1:1-4 reveal this. The apostle Paul said that more than 500 people saw Christ after his resurrection (I Cor.15:6), and we can be certain that the majority of them (if not all) were of Jewish ancestry! Were some of these witnesses with the apostle John near the end of the first century? An early Christian called Quadratus wrote a short letter to the Emperor Hadrian in A.D.117 saying that he (no doubt in his youth) had talked to some people whom Christ had raised from the dead (Eusebius, *Eccl.Hist.* IV.3). This would mean that about the 90's A.D. there were still some witnesses of Christ's ministry in the flesh still living. They may well have been in Ephesus with John and helping him in the writing of his Gospel and his three epistles. They may even have added a few remarks to John's works after John's death (if they thought it was necessary to do so). After all, the official scribes of the Jews even added genealogical matters to the Temple scrolls down to the time of Alexander the Great (some 100 years after the close of the Old Testament canon). There would be nothing wrong in adding a few editorial remarks to the divine library of New Testament books if the "Elders" who supported the apostle John were still alive after John's death.

These suggestions can make sense. The fact is, there appear to be a number of editorial remarks in John's Gospel, either in relation to the "WE sections" or distinct from them. The King James Version shows some of them by placing their occurrences within parentheses. For example, John 3:13 states: "And no man hath ascended up to heaven, but he that came down from heaven (*even the Son of man which is in heaven*)." Obviously, the italicized words represent a later editorial remark because Christ was certainly on earth when he uttered the first part of the verse, but only after his resurrection was he actually *in heaven.* There is John 4:23. Christ said to the Samaritan woman: "But the hour cometh, *and now is,* when the true worshippers shall worship the Father in spirit and in truth." Christ was telling her that the Temple at Jerusalem, which was the official place in the Old Covenant period where people ought to assemble at special times to worship God, was no longer to be important. Of course, at the time Christ mentioned his teaching to the Samaritan woman the Temple *was still* the proper site for assembly. But the editors (at the time the Gospel was canonized) put in the reference "and now is" to show that what Christ had predicted had come true! Another is John 5:25. "Verily, verily, I say unto you, The hour is coming (*and now is*) when the dead shall hear the voice of the Son of God: and they that hear shall live." The italicized words are a later insertion which could only have been stating the truth after the resurrection of Lazarus and those who were made alive after Christ's resurrection (John 11:1-46; Matt.27:52,53). Another verse is John 13:3: "Jesus knowing that the Father had given all things into his hands, and that he was come from God (*and went to God*)." The italicized words, again, are a later editorial remark. There is also John 17:3. Jesus was talking and said: "And this is life eternal, that they may know thee the only true God (*and Jesus Christ whom thou hast sent*)." And lastly, let us note John 19:35: "And he that saw it bare record (*and his record is true and he knoweth that he saith true, that ye might believe*)."

The Assistants of John

The one thing that becomes evident about the "WE sections" of John is that most of the men who composed that special and select group around John had been Christians from the very beginning! Their remarks in the Gospel indicate that they had seen the glory of Christ firsthand (John 1:14) and in John's first epistle they emphasized their seeing, their handling and their hearing Christ (I John 1:1-4). This may mean that some of them were other apostles or certainly a part of the 500 who witnessed Christ alive after his resurrection (I Cor.15:6). It can almost be certain that they *were all Jews.* and that they later lived near John in Ephesus.

It is essential that it be kept in mind that Ephesus and the area of the province of Asia was, from A.D.67 to A.D.98, the headquarters for apostolic authority within the Christian church. Professor Bartlet, in Hasting's *Dict. of Christ and the Gospels*, summed up the historical evidences for this:

> "There is little doubt that after the destruction of Jerusalem and its Temple in A.D.70, if not before, the Roman province of Asia was the chief centre of Christian tradition outside Palestine. The foundation for this had been laid by Paul, with Ephesus as a base of influence; and hither were attracted not a few of the leading personal disciples of Jesus, including, perhaps, several of the original Apostles. Chief of all, we must reckon John, the son of Zebedee, whose presence at Ephesus for a period of years cannot be explained away by any confusion with another John" (vol.II, p.309).

With the deaths of Peter and Paul in Rome, and Jerusalem not in the state of authority it once was after A.D.70, the principal region for all significant developments within the Christian *ekklesia* (church) was around Ephesus. Many Jews, as we have shown in the previous chapter, had already gravitated to the region after the death of James in A.D.62 and before the Jewish/Roman War. This can account for the reason that John gathered around him a body of men from Palestine who helped him preach the Gospel, to write his works and to help him in canonizing the books of the complete New Testament.

A further record of these men is found in the writings of Papias, the Bishop of Hierapolis, who lived in the end of the first century and the beginning of the second. Irenaeus spoke of him as "a hearer of John and a comrade of Polycarp." Apollinaris, a Bishop of the same city as Papias, but about 50 years after his time, called Papias "the disciple of John." The city of Hierapolis was east of Ephesus but located in the same Roman province of Asia. If Papias was one who personally talked with John (though some later Christian writers thought Papias only saw the immediate disciples of John), then it makes his testimony a valuable one in evaluating what was happening in Ephesus during and just after the 30 years' transition period from the deaths of Peter and Paul to that of John.

Papias makes an interesting comment about the Elders who were the disciples of John and who succeeded him at Ephesus. Since

Papias was in contact with these *Elders* and was interested in their testimonies concerning the early truths taught by Christ and the apostles, his comments are valuable. Note what he said.

> "But I shall not hesitate also to put down for you along with my interpretations whatsoever things I have at any time learned *from the Elders* and carefully remembered, guaranteeing their truth. For I did not, like the multitude, take pleasure in those that speak much, but in those that speak the truth; not in those that relate strange commandments, but in those that deliver the commandments given by the Lord to faith and springing from the truth itself. If, then, anyone came who had been a follower *of the Elders*, I questioned him in regard to the words *of the Elders*—what Andrew or what Peter said, or what was said by Philip, or by Thomas, or by James, or by John, or by Matthew, or by any other of the disciples of the Lord, and what things Ariston and the presbyter John, the disciples of the Lord say. For I did not think that what was to be gotten *from the books* would profit me as much as what came from the living and abiding voice."

This account makes it clear that the apostles were dead by the time Papias made this remark about A.D.115. But, there was still a body of *Elders* in Western Asia Minor that had firsthand knowledge of what many of the apostles had taught. Papias said he even preferred to speak with them about the teachings they presented about Christ than to resort "to the books" which also recorded such things. This seems to make it clear that there already was, within a very few years of the apostle John's death, a set of books which were regularly being consulted concerning the teachings of Christ and the apostles. Indeed, at the same time Papias was making his statements, Polycarp (a disciple of the apostle John who had certainly heard him speak) was collecting the seven letters of Ignatius which Ignatius wrote while on his way to Rome to be martyred (*To the Philippians* 13:1,2). If the seven letters of Ignatius were so important and precious to Polycarp (and to be preserved for posterity and distributed to other churches), then it would seem odd that Polycarp did not possess a complete canon of New Testament books which he would have considered infinitely more sacred. Indeed, Polycarp said in the same letter that the Philippians were "well trained in *the sacred writings*" (which he called "the Scriptures") and then he quoted from Paul's letter to the Ephesians (*To the Philippians* 12:1).

The "Elders" that Papias referred to as being alive just after the death of John might have been the ones who helped John in the final canonization of the New Testament. Were they part of John's select group mentioned in the "WE sections" of John's writings? This seems to be the case. And indeed, some of them may have been a few of the very apostles themselves (and other Palestinian Christians) who came to Ephesus to be with John after the fall of Jerusalem in A.D.70. After all, the first chapter of First John says that those designated by the pronoun "WE" were those who had seen and handled Christ as well as being witnesses of his resurrection.

The Importance of John's Elders

There is another historical reference to the Elders who helped John write his Gospel and his three epistles. It is what we today call the Muratorian Canon named after L. A. Muratori who discovered the document in A.D.1740. It is an account of how some of the books of the New Testament came to be. Though it is written in barbarous Latin, and scholars have argued about its intrinsic worth for years, there are some interesting matters mentioned by the document that refer to the "WE" passages of the apostle John's writings. And because it can be dated very early (to about A.D.180), it provides a reasonable witness of what people believed about the origin of the Gospel of John, and other books, in the last part of the second century. It will pay us to quote an extensive part of the Muratorian Canon. In the section we will transcribe, the main topic was the Gospel of John.

> "The fourth Gospel is by John, one of the disciples. When his fellow-disciples and overseers of the churches exhorted him he said: 'Today fast with me for three days, and let us recount to each other whatever may be revealed to each of us.' That same night it was revealed to Andrew, one of the apostles, that John should write down all things *in John's name, as they ALL RECALLED THEM TO MIND* (or could certify to John). So although various points are taught in the several books of the gospels, yet it makes no difference to the faith of believers, since

all things in them are declared by one supreme Spirit, concerning [Christ's] nativity, his sufferings, his resurrection, his talking with his disciples, and his double advent (i.e. his two separate advents), the first in despised lowliness, which has taken place, and the second glorious with the power of a king, which is yet to come. What wonder then if John so boldly presents each point, saying of himself in his epistle, 'What we have seen with our eyes and heard with our ears, and our hands have handled, these things have we written?' For so he swears as a witness not only one who saw Christ and a hearer of him, but he was also a writer of all the wonderful works of the Lord in order" (emphasis mine).

There can be no doubt that the writer of this early work believed that the Gospel of John, though written under the name of the "beloved disciple" (John), was really a cooperative effort in which several of the apostles took part. And in effect, this is exactly what the "WE" sections of the Gospel of John and John's epistles demand. This makes "the Elders" of John take on an importance that many people have not realized. It indicates that John became the writer for the remaining witnesses of Christ who were still alive at the end of the first century. John's circle of friends included some of the most illustrious luminaries who accompanied Christ in his preaching tours of Galilee and Judaea.

These "Elders" of John were also mentioned by Clement of Alexandria (early third century) when he discussed the method that John used in writing his Gospel. He said:

"But *last of all,* John, perceiving that the observable facts had been made plain in the Gospel [those formerly written], *being urged on by friends,* and inspired by the Spirit, composed a spiritual Gospel" (quoted by Eusebius, *Eccl.Hist.* VI.14.7).

This means that sometime between A.D.70 and his death about A.D.98 (or thereabouts, since John lived to the time of the emperor Trajan), John was asked by his *friends* to write a spiritual Gospel, and in this case they were those who had, with him, seen and heard Christ and had been witnesses of Christ's resurrection. John accomplished the task. And, as it proved to be, it was not the work of John alone but a cooperative effort involving the remaining witnesses who had personally observed Christ and his teachings. Though Peter and Paul had died in Rome (and they had made the first preliminary canonization of the New Testament), it remained for John and his eyewitness "Elders" to complete the final written testimony to the teachings of Christ. And this was accomplished in the last decade of the first century.

There are many reasons to show that the Gospel of John was written last of all the Gospels, and that it was no doubt composed just before John's death. One of the main things to show this is John's appeal that the Holy Spirit that Christ had promised would recall to mind all the essential teachings of Christ.

> "But the Comforter, which is the Holy Spirit, whom the Father will send in my name, he shall teach you *all things,* AND BRING TO REMEMBRANCE, *whatsoever things I have said unto you"* (John 14:26).

Since John was a very old man when his Gospel was written, there were people who were accusing him of not being able to remember the real teachings of Christ. This is why John invoked the witness of the Holy Spirit to counter this. But John was also, in his Gospel and epistles, constantly appealing to the truth provided by competent *witnesses* from Palestine. In his Gospel alone, John stressed the word "witness" (or its cognates) 47 times. This was a most unusual emphasis! Why did John resort to such an appeal? No other writer of the New Testament had to constantly remind his readers that he had many kinds of "witnesses" to the truth of what he was writing. But no other writer was being accused of being too old to remember the truths of earlier times. The fact is, when John wrote his Gospel, there were many people in the world who began to question the accuracy of it, and of the competence of John himself. This is one of the main reasons that John emphasized the fact that the Holy Spirit was promised by Christ to bring back a remembrance of "all the truth" to his apostles (John 16:13), and if that were not enough, John also called on a group of his select friends who were also eyewitnesses to all that he was saying, and they also vouched for the truth of his statements.

It should be recalled that there were many "Gospels" of Christ already circulating by the time John wrote his works (Luke 1:1), and that both Peter and Paul had warned of the fables that were destined to be put forth as the truth (II Pet.1:16; II Tim.4:4). John (even in his old age) felt that it was incumbent upon him to clear the air with the truth. He thus asked the witnesses of Christ's earthly life who were still living to cooperate with him in the production of the final Gospel. This was done just before John's death (about the time he canonized the Book of Revelation). It is for this reason that many features of John's Gospel can be satisfactorily explained. This is why he could record the incident of Lazarus being resurrected from the dead while the other three Gospel accounts did not wish to do so. Since Lazarus was now dead, and this would prevent any harassment from his admirers or his foes, John could tell the story in detail. But John left out things too. There is no mention of Christ's prophecies about the destruction of Jerusalem, to which the other three Gospels paid considerable attention. It would have been unwise to mention matters that had already taken place (and record them as "future" prophecies). And, after all, the Olivet Prophecies had already been adequately covered by the other three Gospels written before the destruction of Jerusalem. John was simply giving a summary of doctrinal and spiritual matters taught by Christ that the other apostles had left out or did not feel necessary to record.

The Transition Period

The time between the deaths of Peter and Paul (which happened about A.D.67 in Rome) and that of John (soon after A.D.98 in Ephesus) was most significant in the history of the canonization. Some of the differences in the contents of later manuscripts can be attributed to this 30 year period. For example, it must be acknowledged that Peter and Paul left with the church at Rome a partial canon of New Testament scriptures, though Peter directed the actual (and final) canonization to his readers in Asia Minor, and most particularly to the apostle John himself. The whole of Peter's second epistle is devoted to this subject. It was to Asia Minor and the apostle John that one must look (according to Peter) for the final canonization, and not to Jerusalem (which was soon to be destroyed), and not to Antioch in Syria, not to Alexandria, not to Carthage, not to

Athens, and not even to Rome. This did not mean that the congregation at Rome was not important. All the *ekklesias* (churches) needed to know what writings were considered canonical to insure proper teaching. It is reasonable to suppose that Peter and Paul left a partial canon with the *ekklesia* at Rome (the same they sent to John) which would last them until John would include his own books and complete the divine library. Since John's Gospel, his three epistles and the Book of Revelation were not canonized for almost another 30 years or so, it meant that the Christian church did not have in its possession a complete New Testament until the last decade of the first century. This period when no full canon was yet available can explain a great deal of the minor (and even major) differences that arose in a few of the early manuscripts. For instance, the original Gospel of Mark which Peter dictated to John Mark in Rome (and that Mark left with the Roman church) probably did not contain the long conclusion (16:9-20) or even a short conclusion of one verse which followed Mark 16:8. Thus, for a 30 or 35 year period some manuscripts were circulating *without* the long conclusion. Yet when John and his assistants finally canonized the New Testament, twelve verses were added to the Gospel of Mark in order to complete it. Even the Book of Acts has come down to us in two distinct types of manuscript versions — one which is more replete with historical and geographical information adding about 10 percent more material to the text. The additions to Acts could also have been made when the final canon was published in Ephesus at the end of the century.

There is also the question of the exact times John wrote his Gospel and three epistles. They were certainly composed during John's residence at Ephesus, but at the beginning, the middle or at the very end? The Gospel seems to be a late production, though John's mention of five porches as seemingly in existence in Jerusalem (5:3) and the reference that Peter "will" be martyred (21:19) might indicate the basic writing of the Gospel was early, even before the destruction of Jerusalem. Prof. J. A. T. Robinson, in his excellent book, *The Redating of the New Testament,* thought this to be the case. John's mention that it was the "last hour" (I John 2:18) would tend to put the original writing quite early—before the apostles came to see that Christ was not coming back in that generation.

While all of this may show an early "first draft" to John's Gospel and epistles, the inclusion of the "WE sections" into their texts makes it probable that their final positioning within the divine canon only became a reality when the Book of Revelation was revealed again to the apostle John not long before his death. Actually, the "WE sections" seem to be editorial remarks which were added by John's assistants (either to buttress the reliability of what John was writing in his old age or to support John's testimony after his death). From our present state of knowledge we cannot know what part of that 30 or 35 years when John was near Ephesus that his Gospel and the three epistles were first written. Certainly, though, they were not canonized as official parts of the New Testament until the last book (Revelation) was accepted again and canonized near John's death.

Conclusion

It is sometimes thought that because the New Testament has come down to us in Greek, that the Gentiles from Greek speaking areas were the ones who had authority to preserve the new canon. There is no scriptural warrant to sustain this belief. Indeed, of the apostles themselves only Peter and John had "the prophetic word more confirmed" (II Pet.1:19). These two apostles along with James the Lord's brother were the "pillar" apostles in the Christian church and even the apostle Paul found it necessary to gain an approbation from them for his work among the Gentiles (Gal.2:1-10). In a particular sense, they were the only apostles specifically commissioned to go to the circumcised (Gal.2:7-9). As far as holy scripture was concerned, it was a well known principle among the Jews that it was they who had been authorized to preserve and protect (and to teach) the Word of God. Paul acknowledged this.

> "What advantage then hath the Jew? or what profit is there of circumcision? Much every way: chiefly, *because unto them were committed the oracles of God*" (Rom.3:1,2).

The word "committed" signifies an entrustment — an official commission. The apostle Paul reckoned that his own ministry among the Gentiles was the same type of authority, and the same word was used in Greek to describe it (I Cor.9:17; Gal.2:7; I Tim.1:11; Titus

1:3). Since the Old Testament had been placed into the hands of the Temple priests for its teaching and preservation (Deut.31:9-11), the apostles must have looked on safeguarding the New Testament in a similar way. There were even early beliefs that the apostle John and his brother James were of priestly descent (Eusebius, *Eccl.Hist.* V.24; Epiphanius, *Haer.* XXVII.14), and these beliefs are compatible to the teachings of the New Testament as we have shown.

At any rate, Peter told the Jewish exiles in Asia Minor that he and John were going to leave them with a New Testament canon and that *only* these two apostles had "the word of prophecy more confirmed" (II Pet.1:19). To accomplish his role in canonization, the apostle John gathered around him in Ephesus a body of Jewish elders who helped him in writing (and no doubt preserving) that canon. No one knows how long the original group of men assisted John, but at the time John wrote his Gospel and his three epistles, those men were still giving witness to the accuracy of John's teaching.

The point that needs to be emphasized is that the center of canonization for the 30 odd years after A.D.67 was Ephesus, and the people who performed the task of completing the canon were Jewish Christians under the direction of the apostle John. It is certain that the New Testament did not have its origin in Jerusalem, in Antioch of Syria, in Alexandria, in Greece, in Carthage, or in Italy. Those areas had to be supplied with the complete New Testament when the final draft of the Book of Revelation was written and canonized. This is why the rest of the Christian world had to look to Ephesus as the central region of canonization. It is from this area that we should look for the emergence of the original New Testament. In the next chapter we will see how the Christians at Rome and other regions came to look on the authority of this region of Asia Minor.

20

The Rejection of the Apostle John

The modern Christian finds it almost impossible to believe that Christians of the latter half of the first century would renounce the apostle John's position of authority within the Christian church, *but they did!* The evidence of this is found in John's own writings as well as historical documents written by Christians who lived within a hundred or so years after John's death. What is so uncanny about this denial is the fact that John was an apostle from the very beginning of Christ's ministry, was specially selected to be a witness with Peter and his brother James to the Transfiguration (which Peter thought so important), was a personal observer of Christ after his resurrection from the dead, was among the select group of apostles who received private teachings and instructions from Christ during the 40 days after his resurrection, was ordered by Christ to take care of his aunt until her death (none other than Mary, the mother of Christ), that he was the one (with Peter) who was instrumental in establishing the Christian church throughout Palestine, was reckoned by Paul as one of the three "pillar" apostles to whom Paul had to submit his teachings for administrative and doctrinal approval, was one so distinguished by Christ that he produced for the church a written Gospel plus three epistles (which are the four biblical books emphasizing *love*), and was permitted by Christ to live beyond Peter's death to restore to respectability and to canonize the concluding prophetic message to the world (the Book of Revelation), but in spite of this, his authority and teachings were rejected by many Christians during the last 30 to 35 years of his life.

People today find it difficult to comprehend why such a state of affairs could have existed while John was alive. But it happened!

This situation has a bearing on the development and acceptance of the New Testament canon. If John's authority to direct the Christian church was being rebuffed at the very time the canon was being formed, it should not be surprising that John's canon itself might be suspect. This is the reason why John's New Testament did not meet with universal approval at first. But John's canon did prevail, at least for the first three centuries among orthodox Christians. This is because of the great influence of people like Polycarp and Irenaeus (in the middle and late second century) who maintained John's authority in essential matters of faith. Both these men were from Asia Minor, and both were governed by the teachings and authority of John. If it would not have been for these men (and others who shared their views), the shift of authority within the Christian church would have gravitated very early away from Ephesus. And, as time went on, the authority did leave the region where the New Testament canon had its origin. Since Rome was the center of political activity, it soon became necessary (so many people thought) that Christian authority should also be moved to Rome. This became an accomplished fact in the fourth century when Constantine assumed the emperorship. Indeed, Constantine created two "Romes." One was the original city in Italy (which finally came to govern Christian affairs in the western part of Europe) and the other was new Rome on the Bosphorus (which governed most Christians in the eastern parts of Europe and Asia).

What region was left in the lurch when the Empire was married to the world Church? It was that which John had established as the center of canonization from the ruin of Jerusalem to his death about A.D.98. Christians ceased to look towards the region that John made his residence and where the New Testament was canonized. And the rejection began to happen very early in the history of the Christian church.

A Strange Set of Circumstances

We must now refer to some historical evidences which moderns find hard, if not impossible, to believe, but what they state actually happened! There remains a genuine letter of Clement, Bishop of Rome, written to the church at Corinth about A.D.95, which contains

excellent moral and ethical teachings reflecting the doctrinal standards of the New Testament, yet the letter fails to mention the apostle
John even once, or that he had any authority to deal with matters then
affecting the Corinthian church. The interesting point that moderns
find baffling is the fact that, in all probability, *the apostle John was
still alive and about to canonize the Book of Revelation* when
Clement composed his letter to Corinth. This is an astonishing set of
circumstances which has puzzled later Christians. Indeed, when one
surveys the words within the 65 chapters that Clement wrote to the
Corinthians, one would not believe that the apostle John was even in
existence or had ever existed.

Strange, isn't it, that Christ's first cousin and one of the founding
apostles of the Christian church was not consulted in matters
concerning the Church at Corinth (about 300 miles away) while the
Corinthians were receiving instructions from Rome (some 700 miles
distant). Look at a hypothetical example of a similar situation using a
modern illustration. Suppose the Catholic community of Lyons,
France wrote to other Christians at Florence, Italy (some 700 miles
away) about straightening up their Christian lives and taking 65
chapters to do it, but not once mentioning the Pope at Rome (who
lived only 300 miles away) as having any authority to decide the
matter! Such a situation would seem almost absurd today. But that is
very similar to what we find in A.D.95 when Clement of Rome wrote
the Church at Corinth. No one considered John's authority at all!

Even more intriguing is the fact that the problems affecting the
church at Corinth about A.D.95 were the same ones that John
himself encountered around Ephesus within his 30 years' experience
in that area. Professor Marsh in Hasting's *Dict. of the Apostolic
Church* summarizes the problems in Corinth.

> "The Epistle of Clement itself supplies complete information as
> to the circumstances under which it was written. Dissension had
> arisen within the Christian community at Corinth, and the church
> was torn asunder. The original ground of contention is not
> mentioned, but the course of the strife is clearly indicated. A
> small party of malcontents (1:1; 47:6) had used their influence to
> secure the deposition of certain presbyters, men duly appointed
> according to apostolic regulations, who were, moreover, of
> blameless reputation and unfailing zeal in the performance of

their duties (44:3). A fierce controversy was raging, and the Corinthian Church, hitherto renowned for its virtues, especially such as are the outcome of brotherly love, had become a stumbling-block instead of an example to the world (47:7). Once before, the Church at Corinth had shown the same spirit of faction (I Cor.1:10,12). History was now repeating itself, but the latter case was much worse than the former. Then, the contending parties had at least claimed to be following the lead of apostolic men, but now the main body of the Church was following 'one or two' contumacious persons in rebellion against their lawful rulers (chapter 47)" (vol.I,p.216).

What a state of affairs. Clement and the Church at Rome thought they had to do something about this dissension. But one thing is conspicuous for its absence. There is no appeal to the apostle John to help the Corinthians in this matter—either to John's writings or to his personal authority. The matter even goes deeper than that. The very things for which Clement was criticizing the Corinthians were the things the apostle John talked about the most in his epistles! Here was Clement complaining about "one or two" taking the preeminence in the church over the constituted authorities, and that very thing is what the apostle John emphasized was going on concerning his authority in Asia Minor. John said:

"I wrote something to the congregation but Diotrephes, who likes to have first place among them *does not receive anything from us with respect.* . . . He goes on chattering about us with wicked words. Also, not being satisfied with these things, neither does he himself receive the brothers [a group of John's representatives], and those who are wanting to receive them *he tries to hinder* and *to throw out of the church"* (III John 9,10).

Why does Clement fail to mention anything of John's experience in Asia Minor? If a similar situation of rebellion developed in any modern church congregation which uses the Bible as its guide, the first section of scripture that a minister would refer to is the one just cited from Third John. After all, it gives (in the plainest of language) a biblical authority to put down such people who want the supremacy against official authorities in the church. But Clement not only *did not* refer to this section of John, he avoided all the writings of John which impinged upon the very problems being faced in Corinth. In Clement's chapters 42 to 47 (inclusively) his emphasis rehearsed the rebellions recorded in the Old Testament and how God dealt with them. Clement also referred to the early schismatics in the Corinthian church whom Paul had to deal with. *But not once does Clement mention John.*

Then, beginning in the middle of chapter 47, Clement recorded a major section about the merits of *brotherly love* (which subject occupies the whole of Clement's chapters 47 to 51 inclusively), yet *there still is no reference to John or his writings.* What is strange is the fact that the very subject of *brotherly love* is that with which the apostle John is most famous in the biblical canon — there are a total of 42 references to "love" in his Gospel, and on 46 occasions John emphasizes "love" in his three short epistles.

Of course, it could be said that Clement may not have had John's Gospel or three epistles in his possession when he wrote First Clement. This may be, but it does not relieve the problem as far as John's authority is concerned. Since John was no doubt still living when Clement wrote [or just recently died, since Clement apparently said that the "pillar" apostles were then dead (5:2), but this may only have meant James and Peter], it is still surprising that Clement made no reference to John or his writings when he was only 300 miles away from Corinth.

One thing Clement does underscore, however, is that the apostles Peter and Paul (who had been intimate with the churches at Corinth and Rome) were the "good" apostles (5:3). This statement implies that John, and the others, were not as "good" (whatever Clement meant by the term) as were Peter and Paul. Clement also called Paul and Peter "distinguished apostles" (47:1-4), but he did not grace the apostle John with such distinction. It is not to be imagined that Clement was repudiating John's apostleship (he could have done that easily had he desired). In the case of the Corinthian problems Clement simply felt it not necessary to convoke that authority. He only called attention to the teachings of Peter and Paul. To the Corinthians both of them were the "good" and the "distinguished" apostles. Still, why did Clement avoid any mention of John when he was no doubt alive and no more than 300 miles away?

The matter does not stop there. About 20 years later, Ignatius, the Bishop of Antioch, was taken as a prisoner to Rome where he was finally martyred in the capital city. He passed by the churches of western Asia Minor and wrote seven letters from or to them. These are valuable documents to show what was happening in the Christian church at the time. But note this. Again, there is not one reference to the apostle John. This silence is as conspicuous as it was in Clement's letter, but it is even more difficult to explain because Ignatius composed letters not only to the Christians at Ephesus (where John had spent some 30 or 35 years of his final ministry and where he wrote his Gospel, three epistles, and the Book of Revelation), but he wrote to Polycarp whom we know to have been an intimate disciple of John. *Yet there is not a single mention of John or his authority in any matter of discussion.* And certainly, by the time of Ignatius' trip to Rome (c. A.D.115) John's writings were then published.

About 20 or so years later (between A.D.140 and A.D.160) Justin Martyr also wrote some major works on the value of Christian teaching yet he only referred to John's works once (and even that may have been a common oral statement that was circulating among Christians) (Justin's *First Apology,* ch.61 referenced to John 3:5). Though many scholars feel that Justin must have been aware of John's Gospel, he does not seem to place any major authority upon it as a witness. This tendency to avoid John in some quarters presents the historian with some intriguing problems.

It should not be thought, however, that everyone avoided a mention of John. There was Polycarp who was his intimate friend. Polycarp wrote a short letter to the Philippians (about A.D.115 since it shows Ignatius still alive, 13:2). In it he quoted from John's canonical letters. Polycarp stated: "For everyone who does not confess that Jesus Christ came in the flesh is antichrist" (*To The Philippians* 7:1). This is a reference to I John 4:2,3 and II John 7. Polycarp even taught that Christians ought to "return to the word *handed on to us from the beginning"* (Philip.7:3) which was what the apostle John demanded in his epistles. Polycarp also recalled the words of Christ in John's Gospel and his epistles: "He that raised him from the dead will raise us also, if we do his will and walk in his commandments, and love the things which he loved" (cf.John 7:17;

14:15; I John 2:6,17; 5:1,2).

This witness of Polycarp is essential. He was the Bishop of the Church at Smyrna (located a short distance north of Ephesus) and was one who personally heard John speak. Indeed, Polycarp had been ordained, according to Irenaeus, by the apostles themselves (Eusebius, *Eccl.Hist.* IV.14). Since Irenaeus as a youth had heard Polycarp speak about his conversations with the apostle John (Eusebius, *ibid.*, V.20), this is powerful evidence that Polycarp was one who had a deep respect for John and his authority.

With this in mind, we should remember an event in the history of the Christian church which might give us some information on why the authority of John was not acknowledged by many within the church. In the year A.D.154, Polycarp made a journey to Rome in order to talk with Anicetus who was Bishop of the city. Though the meeting was friendly, there was one major doctrinal matter that needed to be solved (among a number of minor ones). It concerned the time for completing a short fast period before the celebration of the Eucharist. Polycarp stated most emphatically that he, and the other Bishops of Asia Minor, had been taught by the apostle John to observe the time of the Eucharist on the fourteenth day of the first Jewish month — on the day before the Passover of the Jews. This meant that the time for celebration could fall out to any day of the week. With the Romans, however, they had started, about A.D.140, to keep the Eucharist on a Sunday following the Passover week. Though John had set the example of following Jewish calendar indications in this matter, Polycarp was unable to persuade the Bishop of Rome to abandon the new method of observance adopted by the Romans. This is a clear example of Roman authorities expressing a superiority over the opinions of the apostle John.

There was a reason for doing this, and the change seemed a logical one. Before the Jews in Palestine went to war with the Romans in A.D.132 (which ended in the complete destruction of Jewish power in Judaea by A.D.135), it was common for the beginning of all Jewish years (and consequently their months and holydays) to be determined by the Sanhedrin that had been set up at Jamnia, in the coastal region west of Jerusalem. But when the Emperor Hadrian so disrupted Jewish influence in Judaea after A.D.135, no more official anouncements for determining the beginning of the calendar year were permitted the Jews. This put their calendar into confusion. Consequently, the times for the Jewish annual holydays began to slip out of their normal seasons for observance.

The Jewish year was a Lunar-Solar one. The normal Lunar Year is about 11 days shorter than the Solar and about every three years an extra (thirteenth) Lunar month had to be added to the calendar in order to keep it abreast with Solar time. In a period of 19 years, there were seven extra months added to the calendar in order to maintain the Jewish festivals in their proper seasons of the Solar Year. This was not done haphazardly. In fact, it required an official body of Jewish elders in Jerusalem (when the Sanhedrin was there) and then Jamnia (after A.D.70) in order to accomplish this task. The Jewish community throughout the world was then informed, usually a year or so in advance, when the proper years and months could begin. But after the disasterous war of A.D.132 to A.D.135, the Sanhedrin which had been located at Jamnia was prevented from functioning and Jews throughout the world were denied any official sanction for the beginnings of their years and months. Chaos resulted over the Jewish calendar! It meant that no Leap Months (the thirteenth months) were being utilized! Progressively, the Jewish festivals began to be celebrated eleven days earlier each year. Without the addition of the "Leap Months," by A.D.142 (a short seven years after the Jewish/ Roman War) the Passover was beginning to be observed as early as January (Louis Finkelstein, *Akiba,* pp.236-239, 274). This was an intolerable situation and something had to be done about it. It was accomplished by the establishment of a new Sanhedrin in Usha of Galilee about A.D.142. From then on the Jews were once again provided with official pronouncements concerning the times of the beginnings of their years and months. This new calendar was, unlike the former ones, based primarily on calculations rather than on actual observations of the Moon. This is because the emperor Hadrian forbade any Jew from approaching the city of Jerusalem, and his decree remained in force for another 200 years. This presented a problem to Christians because the new calendar had one feature about it which was offensive to many Christians.

In the 17th year of the Jewish calendar cycle the Passover was observed two days *before* the Vernal Equinox. This was contrary to all tradition of earlier times. In the past it had become a cardinal rule that Passover had to be celebrated *after* the start of Spring. Anatolius, an early Christian scholar, called attention to the fact that all previous Jewish authorities vouched that in the time of Christ the Passover was always held *after* the Vernal Equinox. He said: "This may be learned from what is said by Philo, Josephus, and Musaeus; and not only by them, but also by those yet more ancient, the two Agathobuli, sirnamed 'Masters,' and the famous Aristobulus, who was chosen by among the seventy interpreters for the sacred and divine Hebrew Scriptures. . . . These writers, explaining questions in regard to the Exodus, say that all alike should sacrifice the passover offerings *after* the Vernal Equinox in the first month" (Eusebius, *Eccl.Hist.* VII. 32:14-19). And, *in the very year* that Polycarp went to Rome to inform Anicetus that the Eucharist should be celebrated according to the calendar of the Jews, *that year was the 17th of the Jewish Metonic cycle.*

Anicetus would have none of it! As a matter of fact, when the Jewish calendar began to be in disarray at the end of the Jewish-Roman War (A.D.135), many Christian authorities took it upon themselves to calculate their own Full Moon for the Eucharist ceremonies. And some, notably those at Rome, simply abandoned an association of the Eucharist with the Full Moon and decided to observe it on a Sunday (the day of Christ's resurrection) after the Full Moon of Spring had occurred. Polycarp, however, felt it better to remain with the Jewish calendar determinations on this matter.

Polycarp was not able to convince Anicetus that the Jews should have authority on this issue. He and Anicetus simply observed their own respective Eucharists and parted in a friendly manner. This shows that there were no other major doctrinal differences between the two church communities in A.D.154. But it does indicate that the opinions which came from those who followed directly in the footsteps of the apostle John in Asia Minor had no influence upon the clerics at Rome.

The parting of Polycarp and Anicetus in a friendly way was not the end of the story. About the year A.D.190 another controversy came up over this same matter. This time, Victor, the Bishop of Rome, was not at all pleased with the people in Asia Minor who continued to follow the disciples of John. He brazenly excommunicated those who looked to Ephesus as the center of Christian authority. Irenaeus, who sided with the Roman way of calculating the time for the Eucharist, rebuked the Bishop of Rome for such a unilateral decision (Eusebius, *Eccl.Hist.* V.24). Again it must be recognized that there is no hint that there were *other* major doctrinal differences between the two church regions. For what it's worth, the Jewish convert to Christianity, Hegesippus, mentioned that on a trip from the East to Rome in the middle of the second century he consulted with a number of Bishops about their doctrinal positions and found them all in general agreement (Eusebius, *Hist.Eccl.*, IV.22). And, when one surveys the letters of Clement, Ignatius, Polycarp and Justin it seems that this opinion of Hegesippus' was in the main correct for the orthodox churches. The churches around Ephesus would have been little different from those in Rome on the basic Christian doctrines— except in the matter of celebrating the Eucharist. There was, however, a distinct desire for some Bishops to exercise administrative power over others. Irenaeus considered this wrong. This is why he felt compelled to admonish Victor of Rome not to be so rash in his dealings with the churches of Asia Minor where John's disciples remained! Nevertheless, Rome was slowly beginning to exercise a position of leadership among most Christian congregations.

It was Cyprian the Bishop of Carthage, about A.D.250, who finally stated that Rome had inherited the Petrine authority of primacy (the "keys" being given by Christ to Peter), but even then Cyprian did not think this gave supreme authority to Rome in all doctrinal and administrative matters (Turner, *Catholic and Apostolic,* p.228). In fact, Cyprian even disputed with the Roman Bishop on numerous issues and quoted the statement of Christ (John 20:21ff.) that "all the apostles" had been given a type of equal authority (Cyprian, *Unity of the Church,* p.4). It was not until the Council of Chalcedon in A.D.451 that the Petrine theory of supremacy for the Roman Bishop was finally made "official" in the Empire, and that is when Christ's reference of the "keys" being given to Peter was introduced to prove that leadership (Bruce, *The Spreading Flame,* p.341).

Why Was John Rejected?

The witness of Polycarp and others from Asia Minor make it clear that there were no major doctrinal differences between the churches which had been under John's control and those in Greece and Italy. Also, in Clement's letter to the Corinthians there were no major doctrinal divergences between the Church at Rome and that at Corinth. Even the dissensions occurring at Corinth did not involve doctrinal issues. And with Igantius' seven epistles he revealed a doctrinal unanimity between the churches of Asia and Rome. As a matter of fact, Ignatius was warning the churches about the same Gnostic beliefs that John himself was worried about (believing that Christ had not come in the flesh). Since the doctrinal positions were reasonably stable, why, then, was there a non-recognition of John's opinions by these men in the late first century and up to the last part of the second?

One might imagine that John may have wanted to heed Jewish ways more than those in Greece and Rome (because the controversy over the time for celebrating the Eucharist was whether the church should observe it according to the calendar of the Jews or a new Christian one). True, John may have expressed more attachment to Jewish ways, but anyone who reads his Gospel is fully aware that John had no sympathy with the actual observance of the Jewish Sabbath or their holydays. To John, the Mosaic holydays had become "the Jews' holydays" and he made a plain statement that Christ had cancelled the weekly Sabbath for Christians (John 5:18 see Greek). He even showed Christ's lack of attention to the Mosaic Passover period of the Jews because he records that Christ was feeding the five thousand in Galilee (John 6:1-15) when the Law expressly taught that all able-bodied males should be in Jerusalem for the festival (Exo.23:17; Deut.16:16). Christ also failed to arrive at the Feast of Tabernacles on time though that was required too (John 7:1-17). The fact is, Christians believed Christ to be "the Prophet" of Deuteronomy 18:15-19 and this gave him power to do as he pleased!

And though John emphasized getting back to the Christianity that was given "from the beginning," John was not speaking of keeping the rituals of Judaism. He was making an appeal to return to the teaching which he was presenting in his Gospel. John gave a thoroughly spiritual interpretation to the teachings of Christ and they had nothing to do with the physical performance of keeping Sabbaths, Feast Days, or observing Temple ceremonies. John's teaching was far from Judaism. It was to his Gospel that John was referring when he told his readers that they ought to get back to the teachings of Christ which were given "from the beginning." He did not mean that his readers ought to return to the teachings of Moses! Indeed, John accepted the writings of Paul (which he helped to canonize) and they also made it clear that observing the food and drink laws of the Old Testament and the Mosaic holydays were not required in the Christian dispensation (Gal.4:10; Col.2:16,17).

Actually, when one analyzes the teachings of John in his Gospel and epistles, it becomes evident that he could not have been teaching too much out of the mainstream of Christian doctrines which were then being preached in the world. This includes what was being taught at Rome and Corinth. If one will look at the epistle of Clement to the Corinthians and the seven letters of Ignatius, there is hardly a syllable of doctrinal teaching that varies from that of Paul and Peter—and even that of John himself.

This is an extraordinary thing. Why is it that the main doctrinal positions seem to be the same (or the differences were of no major consequence) and yet the authorities of Greece and Italy (from the records we have available) pay no attention to the apostle John or his authority?

The answer may come from the writings of John himself. In his Third Epistle John said that a certain Diotrephes was one who liked to have first place among those in the church (III John 9). Diotrephes was *not* accepting John's authority, and he was casting out of the church those who wanted to rely on the apostle John. It seems almost impossible for some of us moderns to believe that someone like Diotrephes could continue to call himself a Christian while rejecting the authority of the apostle John to his face. But John records that such a thing was happening. And note this. At no time does John accuse Diotrephes of preaching false doctrines. He may have been, but John says nothing about such a deviation. It seems that Diotrephes simply wanted to have the first place of rulership within the Christian church. This was the same thing that was happening in the Corinthian church when Clement wrote to them. There were no doctrinal issues at stake—only matters involving who was to govern. But why did Diotrephes turn against the authority of John? Why didn't Clement and Ignatius mention John?

We may have an answer to this if we can first recognize a little about the temperament of John! Of all the apostles, he is the one least understood by most modern interpreters. Most have considered him to have been a wishy-washy individual that could only talk about conciliation between peoples and especially a brotherly love among all Christians. True, those things he emphasized but his attitude was far from that of being weak and non-resolute. Just the opposite was the case.

Christ gave John and his brother James (who were both his first cousins) the title "Sons of Thunder" (Mark 3:17). Giving this title signified that they were to be the very spokesmen of God, it meant they would speak the words of God in the manner in which *thunder* would roar from the heavens. This typified the brashness of their attitudes. A good example of showing this was the incident of the Samaritans who rebuked Christ. "And when the disciples James and John saw this, they said, Lord, wilt thou *that we command fire to come down from heaven, and consume them, even as Elijah did?*" (Luke 9:54). Though Christ had to reprove the two brothers for their harshness, this does show the bold temperament that the brothers possessed. With this in mind, it seems to be no accident that it was John who wrote the Book of Revelation. Its theme could well have suited John's personality in the basic sense. It is a book of judgment, of "blood and guts," of punishment for all wrong-doers. Indeed, there is no mercy extended within its pages for those deserving retribution. It describes God's dealing with sin—forthwithly. Was the apostle John selected to record these final judgments against unrighteousness because his attitude blended in with their manner of delivery?

The two Sons of Thunder were also highly ambitious (along with their mother) in petitioning Christ for seats of authority on either side of him (Matt.20:20). The other apostles became angry with these two brothers for their audacious attitudes in wanting to rule over everyone else.

There is another illustration which expresses John's nature. He seemed to be one who would not "give and take" on matters which he considered important. Things had to go exactly the way he thought proper, and he was not considerate of those who would show a deviation from his opinions. Indeed, if anyone taught anything different from John or his assistants, John allowed no one leeway in dealing with such an individual. In his Second Epistle he taught that if any man would come to a person's home and not bring the exact teachings that John was relating then no one was permitted to speak with him (II John 10,11). While such a trait is admirable when matters of essential doctrinal truths are at stake, it may appear a very severe attitude if the opinions involve insignificant social customs or traditions. And this may be one of the things that caused some Christians to have reservations about being in the company of John and his assistants. Scholars have long recognized this. Professor Riggs, in the *Dict. of Christ and the Gospels*, relates:

> "It is commonly thought that John was of a gentle, contemplative nature, and almost effeminate in character. Contemplative he was, and the Gospel is but an expression of his profound meditation upon the character and work of his Master, but a moment's reflexion upon some of the scenes of the Gospels (see Matthew 20:20-24, Luke 9:49,54), in correspondence with which are some of the legends regarding his later life, will show that this Apostle was, at least in earlier life, impetuous, intolerant, and ambitious. Doubtless he was effectively moulded by the Spirit of Christ during his long discipleship, but he was always stern and uncompromising in his hatred of evil and in his defense of truth" (vol.I,p.869).

This temperamental trait of John may well be one reason why many Christians around the world (who wished a more conciliatory approach to Christian ethics and doctrines) found an uneasiness around John and his assistants. But there was more to it than temperament alone. There was another factor in the life of the apostle John that made him to be held in more suspicion than any of the other apostles. Let us now look at the major reason why Christian people were questioning the authority of John in his later years. Many people had reasons not to respect John's opinions.

The Real Reason for Rejecting John

The principal book that all the apostles were relying on to give them a sequential account of prophetic events from their time to the second advent of Christ was the Book of Revelation. That book was written by the apostle John and the information in it purportedly came from none other than Christ himself (Rev. 1:1,2). Almost every chronological indication in that book suggested that Christ would return to earth to perform all the judgments recorded in the Book of Revelation within the generation of the original apostles. Indeed, so soon did the readers imagine the Second Advent would occur that "they also who pierced him" (at Christ's crucifixion) would still be alive to witness his glorious Second Advent (Rev. 1:7). This reference, among several others, suggests that the Book of Revelation (at least its original draft) was written in the early or middle part of John's ministry. We have given reasons for dating its initial composition somewhere between A.D.56 to A.D.60. Prof. J.A.T. Robinson (*Redating the New Testament*, pp.221-253) felt that the Book of Revelation was certainly composed prior to A.D.70, and in this he was no doubt correct. But all the events of the book did not then occur. A great disappointment set in. From the Autumn of A.D.63 onward the apostles were aware that the Second Advent would not happen in that generation. The visions of Revelation were for many centuries in the future.

The reputation of all the apostles, but especially that of John, went down considerably among Jewish Christians. This decline in interest in the prophetic teachings of Christianity was widespread in Judaea in particular. There began to be an abandonment of Christian teachings by these Jewish Christians. There was especially a radical reappraisal of the chronology associated with the end-times. Many of them simply gave up interpreting historical events of their time in a prophetical manner and Peter's Second Epistle deals with this.

While prophetic teaching became highly suspect, the apostle Peter said there was a concomitant reversal in ethical and moral character among the Christian population. This is what Peter and Jude in their epistles were upset with the most. The decline in respect for established authorities (whether human or angelic) became a disaster to the Jewish Christian congregations in Judaea. In a word, all of the teachings of Peter in his Second Epistle were reflecting on the great rebellion which was then developing among Jewish Christians in Judaea. The primitive teachings of Christianity were being substituted by nationalistic ideas. There were widespread teachings that it was perfectly proper to speak against constituted authorities and to resist them in order to obtain a liberty from political oppression.

The main teachings of Peter and Jude in their epistles were to counteract the revolutionary spirit that developed from A.D.63 to A.D.67 among the Jewish Christians in Judaea (and among the ordinary and non-Christian Jewish populations) after the great disappointment took place about the Autumn of A.D.63. Coping with this disappointment was a major theme of Second Peter.

Vast numbers of Jewish Christians in Judaea and surrounding areas then began to flex their political muscles and they joined forces with the nationalists who were wanting to war with the Romans and establish a Jewish state of their own in Judaea. Both Peter in his Second Epistle and Jude in his letter were describing the chaos that was then developing among the Jews of Judaea (and vast numbers of them were Christian Jews who had experienced the great disappointment of A.D.63). They were now well aware that the events associated with Christ's Second Advent were not developing as they expected them to occur. When one reads Second Peter and Jude within this historical environment, a great deal of illumination as to what was happening in Jerusalem and Judaea among ordinary Jews and the great numbers of Jewish Christians becomes available. Their disappointment in the "failure" (or what they considered to be the *failure*) of the end-time events of Daniel and Revelation to occur in their generation caused them to change their minds about the teachings of Christianity itself. They began to consider the apostles as bearing false tidings about prophetic events. They were most especially upset with the apostle John whose visionary experiences reported in what we call the Book of Revelation seemed to be totally wrong for their time.

The apostle Peter reflected the common complaint that was being expressed by the Jewish Christians in Judaea and Peter was trying to stop its spread to other Jews outside Judaea. Note II Peter 3:1,2.

This second epistle, beloved, I now write unto you; in both which I stir up your pure minds by way of remembrance: that you may be mindful of the words which were spoken before by the holy prophets, and of the commandment of us the apostles of the Lord and Savior: knowing this first, that there shall come in the last days scoffers, walking after their own lusts, and saying, Where is the promise of his coming? for since the fathers fell asleep, all things continue as they were from the beginning of the creation.

Not only the people to whom Peter was writing were within an environment of great disappointment, but many of the people were taking up hostile attitudes to the teachings of the earlier prophets and also to the commandments of the apostles of Christ. They had been expecting the *soon coming* of the Kingdom of God on earth (which the visions given to John had taught would last for 1000 years, a period we call the Millennium), but now the majority of Jewish Christians in Judaea were giving up hope that the prophecies would be fulfilled at all. Both Peter and Jude wrote of what was happening to the Christian people among the Jews in Judaea and those two Christian authorities were warning Jews in other areas of the Roman Empire not to follow them in their rebellious behavior.

The Book of Revelation
Presented at Two Different Times

The Old Testament reveals the duality principle of prophetic interpretation in several places and I have referred to it from pages 126 to 130 in this book. And in the Book of Revelation there is the teaching that prophetic events dealing with the time of the end were given to the apostle John in two phases of time. The exact length of time between the two phases is not revealed in the book itself, but it was made clear that the apostle John within his lifetime would experience two periods of time for prophetic revelation. This information is found in chapter ten of the Book of Revelation. Let us notice what it states.

About half way through John's writing of the Book of Revelation, an interlude of time occurs in which the apostle John is informed by an angel that he would experience a second phase of understanding prophetic information at an undisclosed future time. In regard to this, he was told to take a small scroll from the hand of an angelic messenger and eat the scroll. It would be sweet to his mouth but bitter to his stomach. When this happened, the apostle John received further instructions about a future revelation dealing with the end-times that would be given to him. It would involve all nations. "And he said unto me, 'You must prophesy again before many peoples, and nations, and tongues, and many kings'" (Rev.10:11).

The fact is, John had already interpreted the teachings of the sixth trumpet within the seventh seal of the scroll and there was the seventh trumpet still left for him to record as well as the seven last plagues. This future prophetic encounter could hardly have been the present scroll he was interpreting. It involved new information written on another scroll which he was required "to eat." It was something different from the seven sealed scroll that John was then interpreting up to and including chapter nine of our present Book of Revelation. This new prophetic message that John was to have in the future could have been his final visionary experience when he was taken by the Spirit to the Isle of Patmos and where he put the final touches on the complete Book of Revelation. Since John had already interpreted the teaching of the seven seals, it could be that at Patmos he was given the specific messages to the seven churches in Asia Minor (the beginning and the end of our present book).

It is interesting that the time John was told he would be given another prophetic experience in the future, the angel mentioned it within the context of stating that there would be "DELAY no longer" (Rev.10:6 see Greek; like the DELAYING of the Second Advent mentioned in Matthew 24:48 that Christ said in his Olivet Prophecy would cause many to wonder about). The angel telling John of the future prophetic encounter he would have was no doubt explaining this "DELAY" theme that was being mentioned by the angel. And, just as Christ stated in his Olivet Prophecy about the DELAY of his Second Advent, many people in Judaea in A.D.63 began to say: *"where is the promise of his coming?"* (II Pet.3:2). With the DELAY, a great disappointment set in among the people and many began to distrust the teachings of the apostles. The apostle Peter in his Second Epistle said that the Jewish Christians in particular were beginning to revile prophetic teachings, and this would have included the first draft of the Book of Revelation which contained the seven seals.

Because of the great disappointment which happened from the Autumn of A.D.63 to A.D.70, the Book of Revelation had to be brought back into prominence near the end of the first century (with up-to-date additions written by John) in order for the prophecy to be accepted as divine scripture after all.

The truth was, even the first draft of the Book of Revelation, which was given to the apostle John somewhere in the period from A.D.56 to A.D.60, was NOT speaking about prophetic events which were destined to take place in the middle of the first century. They were designed to have their fulfillment in the final generation just prior to the Second Advent of Christ back to this earth. While some people began to understand the truth of this matter, there were still many people who gave up altogether on prophetic interpretations just prior to the Jewish/Roman War of A.D.66 to A.D.73. The great disappointment that happened just before that time provoked many Jewish Christians and ordinary Jewish people into going to war with the Romans. It didn't stop there. There were even hard feelings toward prophetic teachings with those who survived that holocaust.

Even in the period from A.D.70 to A.D.96 (to the time that the apostle John received the final edition of the Book of Revelation), there were survivors of the late war with the Romans that continued to distrust any prophetic teachings whatever and especially to put any faith in an apostle like the apostle John who failed to tell them (or at least he apparently failed to tell them) that the prophecies within his visionary experiences were designed to be fulfilled almost 2000 years in the future. Indeed, even the apostles themselves (apparently to a man) were expecting as late as A.D.61 the *soon coming* of Christ back to this earth. John was teaching nothing more than what the other apostles believed and taught.

Thankfully, however, when A.D.63 came and went without the expected prophecies starting to be fulfilled, Peter and Paul (and no doubt John) began to teach the people that there were yet many centuries ahead for the world before the Second Advent would take place. This is when they began to understand the teaching that the seven days of creation week were analogous to a period of seven thousand years in which God would essentially deal with mankind in teaching his truth to the world. Since only some 4000 years, according to Hebrew chronology, had passed from the first Adam to the time of Christ, it was then realized that a further 2000 years or so were still to be in advance of the world before the Second Advent of Christ and those end-time prophecies could be fulfilled. Early Christians of the first century began to understand this point.

Instead of the "Day of the Lord" beginning to take place in that generation back in the first century, Peter at the very time of the great disappointment began to inform the people not to be weary with their disappointment because "one day with the Lord is as a thousand years, and a thousand years as one day. The Lord *is not slack concerning his promise,* as some men count slackness . . . but the Day of the Lord will come as a thief in the night; in which the heavens will pass away with a great noise" (II Pet.3:8-10).

Since within the context of the third chapter of Peter's Second Epistle there is Peter's reference to the initial creation of God, this shows that he had in mind the first chapters of Genesis regarding the chronology of prophetic events. In Genesis there was the teaching that God created the earth (or at least planned it out) within a six day period. It became common in the first century for Christians to equate each of those days of creation with a prophetic day of 1000 years. This principle was already known 150 years before the birth of Christ (Jubilees 4:30). A document written about the time of Jesus called Pseudo-Philo also states that mankind is destined to dwell on earth for 7000 years (Charlesworth, *The Old Testament Pseude-pigrapha,* vol.II.p.342). This type of prophetic interpretation became the norm in Christian circles after the great disappointment.

In the Epistle of Barnabas (a non-canonical work written just before the close of the first century) is stated the common belief that God had prepared 6000 years for man to rule in his own manner while there remains a further 1000 years (which later was called a Millennium) in which God's kingdom would be on earth and God would then be ruling in power and glory over all the earth. Even later Jewish rabbis took up the theme and adopted it into their prophetic beliefs (*Tamid* 7:4; *San.*97a). Note the teaching found in Barnabas.

He [Moses] speaks of the Sabbath at the beginning of the creation. 'And God made in six days the works of his hands and on the seventh day he made an end, and rested in it and sanctified it.' Notice, children, what is the meaning of 'he made an end in six days'? He means this: that the Lord will make an end of everything in six thousand years, for a day with him means a thousand years. And he himself is my witness when he says, 'Lo, the day of the Lord shall be as a thousand years.' so then, children, in six days, that is in six thousand years, everything will be completed (Barnabas XV:3,4).

This appears to be an attempt by a very early Christian author to properly interpret what the apostle John meant in his earlier version of the Book of Revelation when he stated that Christ would rule for a thousand years after his return. This 1000 year period was equated with the weekly Sabbath day of creation. The author of the Book of

Hebrews about A.D.61 also mentioned that there would remain in the future a "keeping of a Sabbath" (Heb.4:9 Greek) for the people of God after the return of Christ. This was not intended to be understood as a single weekly Sabbath day, but the seventh 1000 year period which we now call the Millennium.

Look what this understanding provides for the prophetic interpreter. If each of the six working days of creation which were mentioned by Moses was also prophetically understood to mean a thousand years in length (as the apostle Peter was indicating in his Second Epistle), then from the time of the first Adam (when our first parent was created and put in the Garden of Eden) unto the start of the Millennium when God's kingdom would be in evidence for a period of 1000 years, there would elapse 6000 years for mankind to "work" at his own form of government and human society.

Since it was evident that Christ and the apostles lived at a time just a little more than 4000 years from the creation of Adam as shown in the Hebrew chronology of the Old Testament, then it became obvious to first century prophetic interpreters that the great anticipation for the commencement of the Kingdom of God on earth in the first century was about 2000 years too soon. This meant that the information in the Book of Revelation (even though it was first composed in its initial draft somewhere near A.D.56 to A.D.60) was really referring to a generation at the time of the end some 2000 years future to the apostles. We ourselves are approaching the conclusion of that 2000 years of time.

Thus we find that the teaching of the apostle John in the Book of Revelation (though much suspicion was cast on it at the time of the great disappointment) was finally redeemed and acknowledged by many early Christians as divine literature after all. This means that the Book of Revelation as well as John's Gospel and his three epistles belong within the biblical canon. Since there were 22 books that were divinely recognized in the Old Testament canon, there were also 22 books placed inside the New Testament canon by John, plus his own 5 books which brought the complete number of books in the final Holy Scriptures to 49 (7 times 7 in number). This represents the complete canon of the Holy Scriptures.

21

The Meaning of Canonization

It is unreasonable to imagine that the apostle Paul (or any of the other apostles) only wrote the letters which we find in the New Testament canon. Paul stated that he had the condition of the various churches constantly in mind (II Cor.11:28). Since he was not able to appear personally to answer their questions and give them spiritual guidance, the only way he could have fulfilled their needs was through correspondence. This could have been done by sending emissaries and/or by writing letters. Paul, and the others, must have written numerous letters. He tells us of at least one other to the Corinthians (I Cor.5:9). And when one considers that most apostles had at least 30 or 35 year ministries, it would not be unreasonable to believe that several scores of letters were written to various churches or individuals.

The point we need to ask is this: What happened to all those letters? Also, what happened to the original autographs of the works that appear in our New Testament? The truth is, not a fragment of the originals or of other letters has come down to us today. Why is there no record of them? This is what we must consider as a concluding thought.

The answer to these questions involves an important point regarding the canonization affected by Peter and finally by John. Consider this. Both apostles had the authority to form the canon of the New Testament. This meant that they were able to refuse or to accept *any* writing that they wished! Obviously, if an apostle had the power to select a book for canonization, it must necessarily follow that he also had authority to reject books. And this is what occurred when Peter and, finally, John canonized the New Testament.

The Codex Form of Book

It is now recognized that the modern form of a book (with leaves attached to a spine and positioned between two covers) had its origin in the last part of the first century. Indeed, the earliest known form of such a book (called a codex, plural codices) is a part of the New Testament. It could be said that it was the creation of the New Testament itself that brought about the modern codex form of book. Previous to the invention of the codex the world's literature was mainly written on papyrus or leather scrolls. But when it became necessary to preserve the canon of the New Testament the codex was adopted. This had definite advantages to it. One Gospel (say Luke's) could be written on one scroll about 30 feet long (and there would have been up to ten such scrolls to contain the whole of the New Testament), but the use of the codex allowed the whole of the New Testament to be written on both sides of the leaves and placed between the covers of *one book*. Not only did this have the convenience of compactness, it also kept the various books in a proper order. Whereas ten or more scrolls could hardly be kept in a consistent order (unless, like the Old Testament, they were in the control of priests in the Temple who maintained the correct arrangement), but if a codex was used, then each book could follow the next and always remain in the same order. With such positioning it would be easy to spot when pages were missing or if extra (and unauthorized) pages might be somehow inserted. It wasn't even necessary to number the pages (though this could be, and was, done on occasion) because it would have been easy to follow the text since the account simply went on from one page to the next. In the earliest codices the Greek words were written in capital letters and there were no spaces between the words. Not only did this economize on space but it was a deterrent for inclusion of unauthorized words or phrases. A further hedge in keeping the New Testament books in order was the fact that each composition was able to end in the middle of a page and the next book could simply continue on the bottom half of the page. And though it must be admitted that no procedure could safeguard the purity of the New Testament text in an absolute sense, the combination of the factors we have mentioned (plus the fact that the apostle John must have seen to it that there was a distribution of the official codices among several of the churches) is a reasonable guarantee that the canonized scriptures which were authorized by Peter and John would be properly maintained. This must have been the manner in which many of the Christian churches received their standard New Testaments.

The canon was finally created in the region of Ephesus where the apostle John spent his last days. And, from the historical evidences we presently have available it seems that the codex form of book had its origin (or at least its practical use) with the formation of the New Testament in the region of Ephesus. Inventing the codex was an outstanding accomplishment of the highest order. The next step in mass communications took place a little over 1300 years later when the printing press was invented. And while it appears that the first codex was the New Testament, the first printed book was the Bible!

It is not unreasonable to suspect that the apostles who saw the need for the New Testament to be canonized (and realizing that they had no official priesthood in a Temple to preserve it properly) resorted to the codex as the method for preservation. It may have been the apostle Paul himself who thought of the idea. Recall that he asked Timothy and John Mark to bring with them to Rome "the book case, the scrolls, and the parchments" (II Tim.4:13). Paul had left these items with Carpus at Troas. The residence of Carpus may be important to the matter. He lived at the port city of Troas (the place for sailing to Europe) and right next door to Pergamus, the center of the "book trade" in the first century (an area just north of Ephesus).

It may have been no accident that Paul's "book case" was in the hands of Carpus. Using such an item may have been the first step in the production of the codex form of book. Imagine Paul using a type of folio case as a protection for single leaves of papyrus or vellum on which he had written important teachings. If there were twenty, forty, or a hundred such separate leaves placed alongside one another in the folio case, and with easy access from an opening on one of the narrow sides, it would have taken but little imagination to see how easy it would be to sew the leaves together at the back, then secure them with hard covers on either side and bind them into a common bond at the back. True, no one can know (at least at the present) if this is what Paul's "book case" was, but still there is no reason to refute the suggestion. Since it is certain that Christians in various parts of the world began to use the codex form of book from near the end of the first century, its creation has to be assigned to the period of the apostles! It is my personal belief that the codex was indeed invented for the express purpose of producing the New Testament for easy distribution and for a more reliable preservation.

The Autographs

There has always been the question of the original autographs. Where were they kept? Or, what happened to them? Certainly, there was only one autograph of each Gospel or epistle (or, perhaps, several copies prepared by the writers). Doubtless each of the books and epistles, when originally written, was in scroll form. It would have been impractical to place such autographs into a codex form in which the New Testament was canonized. The use of the codex, in the first place, was to make it possible to re-produce a number of copies in a convenient form in order to send them to various churches. This is why Peter and John simply had the originals copied (as the early Jews copied scrolls under Ezra when the Old Testament was canonized). The books were copied into codices and sent to several churches for reading and reference. In actual fact, there was no reason for maintaining the originals once the apostle John put his final authority on the contents of the codices.

This procedure also had the effect of telling the Christian church which letters of the apostles were selected to be a part of the divine canon and which ones were not. If, for example, a church or an individual had a genuine letter of an apostle, that letter would in no case be considered as divinely inspired if it had not been selected by Peter and John for inclusion in the New Testament. And indeed, if such a genuine epistle might be found today (which is highly unlikely), it could not be considered sacred literature (no matter how interesting its contents might be) because it was not canonized by the apostles in the first place. On the other hand, if Peter and John had felt it proper to include the story of "Little Red Riding Hood" (assuming such a story existed at the time, and no matter if there was not an ounce of what we call religious teaching in it), it should be accepted today as divine scripture if one recognizes the authority of Peter and John. Actually, this is exactly what Ezra did when he canonized the "Song of Solomon" in the Old Testament. There is not a shred of religious information in that document and the name of God, or its derivatives, is not found once within its pages. More than that, the "Song of Solomon" seems to have, on the surface, an erotic theme that still offends the moral standards of some sensitive religious people.

Of course, Peter and John did not include any "Little Red Riding Hood" in their New Testament canon, but they had the authority to do so (according to Second Peter 1:12-21) had they thought it proper. This right of theirs also extended to the placement of documents within the canon that quoted non-canonical works after the close of the Old Testament period. Jude thought it perfectly proper to cite a section from the Book of Enoch (Jude 14,15), but this did not sanction the totality of "Enoch." The apostle Paul quoted from the Greek classics. The proverb "evil communications corrupt good manners" found in I Corinthians 15:33 is from Menander's *Thais,* ultimately derived from a lost play of Euripides. Then there is "the prophet" of the Cretans (Titus 1:12) who was Epimenides, and Paul's quote is from his work called *Minos.* There are, in fact, numerous illusions throughout Paul's writings to Jewish and Greek works which were circulating in the Mediterranean world at the time. The Book of James has a quote from a source that is totally unknown (4:5), and James referred to it as "scripture." Yet, it is my personal belief that this quote from a lost work only becomes "scripture" to Christians because it is now found in the canon of the New Testament! The apostle Paul also quoted a text from a Greek inscription devoted to "the Unknown God" (Acts 17:23), but it is not to be imagined that Paul agreed with the rest of the text (if it had any) or the theological implications surrounding the use of the inscription.

Really, the inspiration of the New Testament compositions is not so much in the writing of the words themselves (though that was important), but the holiness of the documents comes from the authority of Peter and John to canonize them. The same principle applies to the canon of the Old Testament. We have records of many inspired men of the Old Testament period who taught the Israelites either orally or through writing (and many of them are mentioned in the Book of Chronicles), but the only divine writings which represent the canon for Jews (and Christians) are those selected by Ezra the priest with the help of the Great Assembly.

If this principle regarding the authorization for canonizing the Scripture would be recognized in today's theological world, many of the problems involving the current "infallibility" debate could be resolved, at least in my view. The fact is, many scholars today are more concerned with the *details* which they find within the canonical books (whether they are scientifically and historically accurate) rather than whether the books *themselves* are infallible by virtue of being *in* the canon. To me, Ezra, Peter and John had an infallible commission to produce a canon of Scripture by the infallible Yahweh Elohim (though they of themselves were fallible men). And it is the books *of the canon* that allow the *details* within the books to be holy, and not the *details* themselves.

The present arguments are similar to those of the Scribes and Pharisees who were more interested in *details* of a matter rather than "the matter" itself. Christ upbraided them for saying the gold of the Temple (that is, a *detail* of the Temple) was more important than the Temple which made the gold holy. The gift on the Altar (a *detail* of the Altar) was more significant than the Altar which made the gift holy (Matt.23:16-22). And so it is with the canon. It is the canon itself which makes every jot and tittle within the books of the canon to be holy, no matter how mankind may judge the merits of the *details*. There is a main scriptural example which, to me, shows this principle.

Christ referred to the stone which honest and godly men had rejected from becoming a part of the holy Temple of God (Psa.118: 22; Matt. 21:42; Eph.2:20; *esp.* I Pet.2:4-7). The masterbuilders could observe, without doubt, that the external condition of the stone was in some way "imperfect" and this imperfection disqualified it from being used to make up the stones of the divine Sanctuary. But strange as it may seem, *that* is the very stone which God finally selected to become the chief cornerstone of a new Temple.

In Christian interpretation that very stone which the builders rejected, no doubt because of its outward imperfections, was an example of Christ himself whom Isaiah the prophet had prophesied would be "marred above all men" and one who was not desired of men as handsome and perfect looking (Isaiah 52:13-15 and all of Isaiah 53). Chapter 16 in my book *Secrets of Golgotha* (pages 203-220) shows that Christ while he was a human was sickly in appearance and not at all good-looking. Though the scriptures show that Christ had not sinned once in his life, he was bearing the sins of the world throughout the whole period of his life (not only when he died on the tree of crucifixion) and the consequence of this made him appear as though his sins were causing him to be afflicted. While Christ was able to heal the multitudes, the people looked on his physical frame and stated: "Physician, heal yourself" (Luke 4:23). He looked as though he was burdened with the weight of sin, which indeed he was. As John records: "Behold the Lamb of God who *bears*[Greek present tense] the sin of the world" (John 1:29). This bearing of the world's sins while he lived in the flesh made Jesus appear unhealthy and not full of vigor and vim as most people erroneously imagine him to have been like.

Yet Christ was the stone that the builders rejected who became the head of the corner of a new and spiritual Temple whom all people who experience salvation will have as their chief corner stone. On the surface, however, Christ appeared imperfect to the human eye. People would reject him just like the builders of the Temple rejected one of the principal stones that they could see was marred and imperfect. Christ was not "good looking" at all while he was on earth.

While this is New Testament teaching, what does this have to do with canonizing the books of the Bible? Much in every way. A similar situation involves selecting the books that were to find an entrance into the Holy Scriptures. Let us note the comparison.

Suppose the early builders of the Temple had two stones that appeared identical in every way yet they only needed one stone to finish the Temple. One of the stones had to be chosen while the other was not. Using the illustration of Christ about the stone that the builders rejected, the rejected stone would have remained "unholy" while the accepted stone would have become holy in every way because it became a part of the Temple. On the other hand, if the two stones were switched (after all they were in appearance identical to each other), then the matter of holiness in regard to the stones would have to be switched as well.

But look at another illustration. Suppose one of the two stones was a resplendent and dazzling diamond of great worth in the eyes of man yet it did not fit into the Temple properly as an ordinary stone would.

If the ordinary stone would have been selected as acceptable for the Temple, it would have become "holy" by becoming a part of the Temple while the beautiful and expensive diamond would still be an ordinary stone without the slightest holiness attached to it (though it was of great worth in a monetary sense).

To carry the illustration further, what if there were two stones and one of them was marred and imperfect but for some reason the authorities building the Temple decided to use it to be a part of the Temple while the perfect stone was not selected? Then the marred stone would have become "holy" while the perfect one would have remained an ordinary stone without the slightest holiness.

This is the way it is with books that make up the Bible. Being selected to be a part of the Holy Scriptures makes each book to be "holy." The book at first may not have had any holiness attached to it, but if it was selected to become a part of the divine canon of scripture, then immediately it became thoroughly holy and inspired of God. As an example, look at one of the books of the Old Testament called the Song of Songs (or *Canticles*). It has not the slightest religious sentiment attached to it. The name of God or any reference to deity is not found in its pages. It is reckoned in some circles to be highly erotic and out of character with other books of the Bible. Yet the Song of Songs was selected by Ezra the priest to be a part of the Holy Scriptures and other works that Ezra had in his possession did not find an entry into the Bible. This means that every word of the Song of Songs became inspired.

As mentioned earlier in this book, if the story of "Little Red Riding Hood" would have found a place within the pages of the Bible, its message would be inspired and holy within itself and also holy within the context of other books of the Bible. Of course, "Little Red Riding Hood" does not occur in the Bible, so it still remains uninspired from the point of view of giving divine scripture to the world.

But let us go one step further. Suppose a genuine epistle of the apostle Paul could be found and completely verified as being from his hand, and that it was one of his latest epistles. That epistle, no matter how interesting and valuable it would be from an antiquarian and historical point of view, it could not in any way be considered a part of the divine canon of Holy Scripture. This is because the apostle John did not select it at first to form a part of the New Testament. That newly discovered epistle would be no more holy in the sense of being divine scripture than the writings of Ernest L. Martin.

Moreover, if some books of the Bible do not appeal to some people as proper, because they are within the divine canon, they are all equally holy and inspired of God. One such book that has found numerous critics is the Book of Revelation. That book has some of the most atrocious grammar in it that can be found in any ancient literature. Scholars for generations have chastised the author of the book for his lack of even basic grammar usage. Yet that work is purported to be the very words of Christ Jesus himself (Rev.1:1,2). There is no doubt that Christ could have used impeccable grammar had he wished, but this is not found in the Book of Revelation. Does this make the book uninspired and quite fallible? According to some grammarians they might classify it that way, but because it appears in the divine canon in the manner it does (ungrammatical and all that), it has become inspired scripture and is infallible in regard to the purpose of its messages.

This same principle also applies to certain books that some scholars may deem to have historical, chronological or scientific errors. Men may indeed wish to reject them because of so-called "imperfections" (but some of those so-called "imperfections" which people of the past have thought to be in the books have turned out to be scientifically accurate through our modern scientific discoveries). Yet even the books in the divine canon of scripture, if they contain what we feel to be inaccuracies, all of their teachings are inspired, are holy, and infallible within the biblical contexts in which their messages are given. In similar fashion, all the stones, furniture and artifacts which made up the Temple of God were equally inspired, holy and infallible in regard to the functions which they all had.

Let us put it this way. Some people have asked me if I feel that the Bible and its teachings are inerrant in every way. My answer is this: "I believe the Bible to be completely inerrant, including its errors." Perhaps I ought to say, "including the errors that people think the Bible has." There are numerous kinds of features which some people call "errors." Even errors in language (or historical and/or scientific facts) can sometimes be shown not to be errors at all when one understands the context of the writer and when the words he uses are fully comprehended in the manner the author intended. For example, some modern scientists have criticized the biblical statement that the earth has its foundation on pillars. "For the pillars of the earth are the Lord's, and he has set the world upon them" (I Sam.2:8). There is, of course, no scientific justification for believing that the earth actually rests on pillars. And indeed, even the biblical writers knew that such a statement was a figure of speech. The Bible shows the earth is actually circular in its dimensions (which answers to a sphere) and that it "hangeth on nothing" (Isaiah 40:22 with Job 26:7). Yet, to state that the Lord has set the earth on pillars is an "error" if taken literally. But this should hardly cause anyone to stumble because in the most sophisticated astronomical journals I have found modern astronomers using terms like: "Just after sunset you can see the stars come out on cloudless days." The fact is, any scientist knows that the sun does not actually "set" (it is complete error to state such) and the stars do not "come out" at night ("come out" of what, one might ask?). These are simple figures of speech that are well understood by all literate people though the terms in themselves are presenting absolute errors to the readers. The Bible contains numerous "errors" of such nature (they are figures of speech like we all use today), or the Bible uses standards of measurements that we no longer use or understand which may appear wrong to us.

The fact is, the literature of the Bible was not given to satisfy grammatical, historical or scientific critics and their classifications as to what is proper and what is not. The books of the Bible were intended to give proper messages to people from God in the manner that He thought best. And because a book appears within the divine canon that we might question, that book is still as holy and as proper as any other book in the canon. It is up to us to understand God's reason for putting such books in the canon. It is not up to us to use our own criteria for selecting or not selecting certain books of the Bible or whole sections of books.

What mankind should do is to recognize the authority of God the Father and Christ Jesus to select the books of the Bible. We should then approve of their selections. There is enough information within the biblical revelation itself to show that God picked certain men that He authorized to canonize the Holy Scriptures for us. One of the main criterions for authorizing the special books to make up the divine canon was the fact that the canonizers be priests of the line of

Aaron. It was into their hands (and the elders of Israel) that God placed the authority to select and to maintain the Holy Scriptures (Deut.31:9), and the apostle Paul recognized that it was the Jewish nation that had the priesthood to perform such a job for the Jews and the world. "What advantage then has the Jew? or what profit is there of circumcision? Much in every way: chiefly, because unto them were committed the oracles of God" (Rom.3:1,2).

And for the canonization of the Old Testament, Ezra was a priest and fully authorized to put together the first 22 books of the Holy Scriptures. This canonization by Ezra was fully accepted by Christ himself (Luke 24:44,45). And for the New Testament, Peter said that he and the apostle John were going to leave the Christian family with documents for teaching purposes because they had the "more sure word of prophecy" that was to last until the Second Advent of Christ to this earth (II Pet.1:12-20). It was actually after Peter's death that the apostle John (whom we now know was himself a priest and qualified for the task) finally put all the 27 books of the New Testament together and attached them to the Old Testament. Those 49 books as they are properly numbered for the Old and New Testaments give a remarkable message to people of all nations that the world truly has the divine scriptures that God wishes all humans to have. Those 49 books comprise *His* instruction book for mankind. It is up to us whether we accept it or not. I hope that we will.

Epilogue

There will be some major criticisms leveled at the conclusions reached in this book. The main ones will revolve around my belief that Ezra, Peter and John were the three men commissioned to form the Old and the New Testaments. It is normally assumed by most scholars that the books of the Bible in some way simply "came together" without any rhyme or reason and that no person was in charge of the process. I find this difficult to believe *if* the Holy Bible is truly "Holy" and that it is the authoritative "Word of God." Admittedly, all belief in the holiness of the Bible must eventually rest on *faith*. I have no hesitancy in acknowledging this fact. But in view of the evidences presented in this book, I also see a literary and historical basis for that *faith*. To me, the factors go a long way in showing that the 49 books of the biblical revelation are truly divine. I will now briefly answer four of the main criticisms that may be given.

Criticism One: Martin, are you so naive as to believe that the apostle Peter actually wrote First and Second Peter and that the apostle John was the one who wrote John's Gospel, the three epistles of John and the Book of Revelation? Don't you realize that top university scholars are in dispute over these matters and that you are at odds with them? Surely you can't believe that the apostles actually wrote the New Testament books bearing their names?

Answer: I see no reason not to believe it. There is not a particle of historical evidence that proves otherwise. Prof. John A.T. Robinson of Trinity College Cambridge, England (who died in late 1983 I am sad to say) provided excellent evidence to show that *all* the New Testament books, as far as historical and documentary evidence is concerned, could have been written *before* A.D.70. And he was right! Although it appears to me that the Book of Revelation and the Gospel of John were written (at least in their final form) in the last decade of the first century, Prof. Robinson's evidence vindicates the fact that all the New Testament books could have been composed within the lifetimes of the apostles. Since the books bearing the apostles' names were written to a wide community of Christians (and buttressed by the testimonies of many eyewitnesses), I see no reason for not accepting their authenticity, and there is not a scholar in the world who can prove this appraisal wrong.

Criticism Two: Martin, virtually every New Testament scholar who has studied the development of the New Testament canon feels that the canon was only created gradually and that the 27 New Testament books could not have formed a complete body of books until the late second century at the earliest and early fourth century at the latest. **Answer:** Yes, that is what most scholars attest, and this is exactly where they are wrong! The first chapter of Second Peter makes it abundantly clear from the writings of the apostle Peter himself that he and the apostle John were the responsible ones to canonize the New Testament. They also inform us that a body of Paul's letters were as inspired as are the Old Testament scriptures. To me, it appears utterly absurd that Peter, John and Paul (knowing that they were soon to die and that Christ was not returning in the first century) would have simply *died* and left it to some unknown church members to form a New Testament canon in a gradual and haphazard fashion some 50, 100 or 200 years after the apostles' deaths. This would have been a dereliction of duty of the highest order. Thankfully, we have the Second Epistle of Peter which describes in detail that Peter and John were the authorized ones to canonize the New Testament and I have complete confidence that they did. It is my conviction that scholars should start with what Peter said as the truth and then proceed from that point forward in history in order to find out how the church came to use the canon of the New Testament, not how the church supposedly brought the books together themselves in some unknown and arbitrary way a hundred or so years later. In my view it has been a major mistake for scholars to begin their investigations on the development of the New Testament with the fourth century (when everyone knows the church had the complete canon), and work backwards from that time in trying to discover how the books entered the canon. Just the opposite should be done. We should start with what the apostles themselves said about their roles in establishing the New Testament and then look for the historical reasons why the early Christian fathers until the fourth century failed to mention a few of the canonized books.

Criticism Three: Martin, the scholars who presently work with the texts of the New Testament do not seem to be overly concerned about the disposition of the books. Their interest is primarily in restoring (if at all possible) the actual words written by the New Testament writers by comparing the various manuscripts. Having the proper words is far more important than presenting the manuscript order of the biblical books.

Answer: True, in the scholarly and ecclesiastical worlds today there is little enthusiasm expressed (certainly in a public sense) for a return to the manuscript arrangement of the biblical books, but this does not make the apathy right. And while textual scholars must be commended for their indefatigable efforts to restore as best as possible the original "words" of the apostles, it should also be recognized by them that those "words" require a proper context to be adequately understood. Such contexts are not only found in sentences and paragraphs *but* the relationship of books one to another! Since textual scholars so carefully adhere to the manuscripts in their judgments on what "words" probably made up the original autographs, it is astonishing that an apparent blind eye has (essentially) been turned to the early order of the very manuscripts with which they work. Yet it is easily recognized what the manuscripts show. When the pioneers in the field of textual criticism (Lachmann, Tischendorf, Tregelles, Westcott and Hort) published their resultant editions *for scholars*, they were united in showing *the proper manuscript order* (the one we are advocating in this book). Indeed, even more important to the issue was the appeal by Professor Caspar Rene Gregory in the early part of this century (who is still recognized as an outstanding authority in textual criticism) that *all* New Testament versions today should be published in the original Greek manuscript order (*Canon and Text of the New Testament*, pp.467-469). But to this day his plea has gone unheeded (as well as the clear evidences for the manuscript order provided by the textual critics mentioned above). The general public know none of these facts. (The only New Testament translation of which I am aware that followed the proper order of the books was that of Ivan Panin in 1935. But I know of no complete Bible of the Old and New Testaments which follows the manuscripts in its arrangement of books.) But I feel the time is long overdue to correct this obvious oversight. Many scholars and laity would no doubt agree that the time has come for a change. The present *apathy* which apparently prevails among present publishers of Bibles needs to be changed into one of *enthusiasm* for a return to the original Bible of the manuscripts. Let them publish their *new* translations, *but in the proper order.* The traditional arrangement devised by Jerome in the fifth century with the publication of his Latin Vulgate Version needs to be set aside for the one maintained by the early Greek manuscripts. Such a restoration would have the effect of presenting to the Christian world the kind of Bible that the first Christians were used to. It might also help people understand the biblical messages in a much better way. The rewards would be great indeed.

Criticism Four: Martin, you are exaggerating the worth of such a restoration. The world has got along quite well with Jerome's fifth century arrangement of the biblical books and there is no need to change the situation now.

Answer: The truth is, there is no better time to return to the original Bible! Just because people have been used to the wrong order for the past 1600 years is no excuse for continuing the error. This is especially so because it is now evident (as shown in this book) that the internal evidence from all parts of the Bible supports a manuscript order of both the Old and New Testaments. The present arrangement is clearly sectarian and provincial and is late in origin. It follows the Egyptian order of the Old Testament books and the "Western" advancement of Paul's Gentile epistles over the Jewish epistles of the early Greek manuscripts. This should not be.

But most importantly, look at this. The original manuscript order of the biblical books places the five books of the Christian Pentateuch (Matthew, Mark, Luke, John, Acts) — which are the only books describing the life and times of Jesus Christ, both on earth and in heaven — as the *CENTRAL* part of the whole Bible. This "Torah" of the New Testament in a natural and non-artificial manner becomes the *fulcrum* of all the biblical books as shown by the arrangement provided by the manuscripts. Thus, the *Word of God* (Christ) is the central part in the *Word of God* (the Bible). To show this important and essential truth the world needs "The Original Bible Restored."

APPENDIX ONE

Preliminary Suggestions for the Structure of the Psalms

There are 150 individual psalms comprising the biblical Book of Psalms. There are psalms (or songs) found in other parts of the Bible. Examples: the psalm of Moses (Exo. 15:1-19; Rev. 15:3); the psalm of Deborah and Barak (Jud. 5:1-31); the psalm of Habakkuk — which is pure prophecy (3:1-19). Even in the New Testament there are psalms (Luke 1:46-55; 67-79).

Almost all of the psalms positioned outside the regular Book of Psalms have as their theme the matter of prophecy — usually prophetic teachings regarding the nation of Israel or, sometimes, information about the prophesied Messiah. This prophetic relevance is also found among the psalms located within the Book of Psalms itself. This has not been fully recognized by many people, nevertheless it is true. This can be shown in several ways, but prime teaching on the matter is found in the Book of Chronicles. That book relates that the psalms were sanctioned to be sung within the temple precincts by regularly assigned Levitical singers. These Levites were ordained to "*prophesy* with harps, with psalteries, and with cymbals" (I Chron. 25:1). These special men were consecrated to their tasks by King David and the prophet Samuel (I Chon. 9:22). There were 24 such designated groups to sing specified psalms in a regular order of administration (I Chron. 25:8-31). There were exactly 288 Levites (12×24) who "were instructed in the songs [psalms] of the Lord" (I Chron. 25:7). These 24 divisions were called "wards" and each was accompanied by 12 Levites. This shows that the number 24 (and 12) was important to the arrangement of the singers and the psalms which they sang.

It will be recalled that there were also 24 elders associated with the ceremonies of the heavenly temple as recorded in the Book of Revelation (Rev. 5:8,14; 11:16; 19:4). The Book of Revelation is devoted entirely to prophecy, and the symbolic numbers of 24 and 12 are found in several places in the book. There were 144,000 Israelites ordained "to sing a new song" in the future. Those 144,000 divided by 24 equals 6000 — the number of years which seemingly is assigned to mankind for the period of God's firstfruit activity in His redemption of humanity. At any rate, the singing being done by those saved involves the use of psalms (Rev. 15:3). This shows a distinctive prophetical ring to some of the psalms.

The Levitical singing in the temple, which was established by King David, was certainly prophetical. They "*prophesied* according to the order of the king" (I Chron. 25:2) — they "*prophesied* with a harp, to give thanks and to praise the Lord" (verse 3). One of the principal prophets to King David was "Heman the king's seer [prophet] in the words of God, *to lift up the horn*" (verse 5). Even David himself, who composed most of the psalms in the Bible, was called a prophet by the New Testament (Matt. 27:35). The New Testament also said that Asaph, one of the principal men assigned by David to sing the psalms, was called a prophet too (Matt. 13:35).

We thus have abundant evidence from the Old and New Testaments that the psalms had a prophetic content to them. Many were written by prophets. Indeed, there were more verses quoted in the New Testament from the Book of Psalms which contained prophecies about Christ and of his future role in human affairs, than from any other book of the Old Testament. Christians thought that king David was very typical of Christ. This fact in itself should show that the Book of Psalms is essentially a prophetical book as much as Isaiah, Jeremiah, or Ezekiel. And truly, when one really comprehends what the various psalms mean — and their relationships to one another within the contexts in which they are placed — a prophetic significance can be seen which is very evident.

Let us now look at the 150 psalms within the Book of Psalms. Their arrangement and contexts should be noted. When surveyed properly, the structure and design might open up some outstanding prophetic teaching that many of us may not have seen before.

The Structure of the Psalms

In the original Hebrew apportionment of the Book of Psalms, the 150 psalms are assorted among five major divisions. These five "books" are not discernable in the ordinary King James Version, but they are evident in the Hebrew manuscripts. The five divisions are as follows:

Psalms   1-41 (Book I)
Psalms   42-72 (Book II)
Psalms   73-89 (Book III)
Psalms   90-106 (Book IV)
Psalms   107-150 (Book V)

The fact that there are *five books* is significant. The number has a legal and prophetic symbol attached to it. Actually, the original Ten Commandments were divided into 5 and 5 (not 4 and 6 as some imagine today). The first 5 were spiritual (including the honor given to parents) and the last 5 were social (involving relationships with other human beings). Prophetically, we can see its importance in the Book of Isaiah. The prophet gave some sequential references to the destruction coming upon Israel for their evil. Isaiah gave a 5-fold admonition. [One should note the context in which the 5-fold repetitive clause is given to understand the full message of Isaiah.]

1) "For all this his anger is not turned away, but his hand [God's hand] is stretched out still" (Isa. 5:25).

2) "For all this his anger is not turned away, but his hand is stretched out still" (Isa. 9:12).

3) "For all this his anger is not turned away, but his hand is stretched out still" (9:17).

4) "For all this his anger is not turned away, but his hand is stretched out still" (9:21).

5) "For all this his anger is not turned away, but his hand is stretched out still" (10:4).

This same type of 5-fold prophetic scheme is also found in the Book of Amos. It was intimately connected with prophetic symbolism.

1) "Yet have ye not returned unto me" (Amos 4:6).

2) "Yet have ye not returned unto me" (4:8).

3) "Yet have ye not returned unto me" (4:9).

4) "Yet have ye not returned unto me" (4:10).

5) "Yet have ye not returned unto me" (4:11).

The sequential emphasis of the prophet Amos was to build up God's case for the refusal of Israel to follow Him. God finally gives up trying to reform them by saying: "Prepare to meet thy God, O Israel" (Amos 4:12). In other words, 5 chances were all that God was going to give them.

The Book of Lamentations, which is a message by Jeremiah concerning the complete destruction of Jerusalem and the temple, was also given in a 5-fold arrangement. The first chapter has 22 verses — each beginning with a letter of the Hebrew alphabet, and all the letters are in their regular order. Then the second chapter also has the same 22 Hebrew letters heading each verse. The third chapter, however, has 66 verses, yet the same feature is retained — only this time there are three verses beginning with the first Hebrew letter, the next three verses the second letter, etc. until all 22 letters are used up. Finally, chapters four and five have 22 verses, but for some reason these verses do not begin with the Hebrew letters. Nonetheless, the 5-fold division is clearly seen. The number 5 seems to give the theme of the prophecy a sense of certainty or dogmatism. This shows up in the other sections of scripture where the 5-fold arrangement is maintained.

The Law of Moses was also divided into 5 parts: The Book of Genesis (1), The Book of Exodus (2), The Book of Leviticus (3), The Book of Numbers (4), The Book of Deuteronomy (5). This could signify that all the law that was necessary to govern Old Testament Israel was found within these 5-fold legal books.

And now, back to our Book of Psalms. It was also arranged in the 5-fold scheme. In fact, the ancient Jewish scholars saw a comparison between the 5 books of Moses' Law and the 5 divisions of the Book of Psalms. The early commentary on Psalms 1:1 (called by the Hebrews the *Midrash*) says: "Moses gave to the Israelites the five books of the Law; and corresponding with these David gave them the five books of the Psalms." A good discussion on the resemblance of each of the five divisions is given in the *commentaries* at the start of the Book of Psalms. We show how they tally in the paragraph below.

```
Psalms     1-41 (Book   I) = Genesis
Psalms    42-72 (Book  II) = Exodus
Psalms    73-89 (Book III) = Leviticus
Psalms   90-106 (Book  IV) = Numbers
Psalms  107-150 (Book   V) = Deuteronomy
```

But there is yet another 5-fold prophetic division of the Bible which was designed, like the psalms, to be read in the temple at certain times of the year. These were the 5 books in the original Hebrew arrangement of the Old Testament called the *Megilloth* (Scrolls) to be read at the holyday seasons and on two commemorative days in the Hebrew calendar. The first book was the Song of Songs (to be read at Passover), the second was Ruth (Pentecost), the third was Lamentations (on the 10th of Ab — the day on which the temple was destroyed by Nebuchadnezzar in the sixth century B.C. — see Jeremiah 52:12-14; Zech. 7:5; 8:19), the fourth book was Ecclesiastes (read in the period of Tabernacles), and the fifth was Esther (read on Purim — see Esther 9:20-22).

Since the holyday periods given to Israel are of prophetic relevance, it follows that the 5 books of the Old Testament assigned to be read at those designated times are a commentary on the meaning of the seasons. The Passover season (1) shows the redemption of Israel from Egypt, and in the New Testament it was the salvation afforded to Christians by Christ's death on the cross — which occurred at Passover. The Song of Songs was read at that time. Its theme is that of a courtship and its setting is Springtime. Then, Pentecost (2) shows the beginning of Israel as a nation at Mount Sinai. Within the New Testament, the "church of Christ" began on that day (Acts 2). The Book of Ruth was ordained to be read in the temple and synagogues at that time. It describes Ruth gleaning the firstfruits harvest from the land of Boaz in Judah. The theme of the book fits Pentecost perfectly. The 10th of Ab (3) was the anniversary day for the destruction of the temple back in the time of Jeremiah. [Remarkably, the temple which was rebuilt by King Herod — the one that existed in the time of Christ — was also destroyed on the exact same day, and quite by accident. It makes one wonder if the day is of more importance in the prophetical chronology than at first meets the eye.] The Book of Lamentations was ordained to be read (II Chron. 35:25) and the 10th of Ab was the day selected for its reading. And what a significant book it was! Its subject was the destruction of Jerusalem and the temple. Then came Tabernacles (4). This indicates the time that Israel will be top in the world — under their Messiah. It is a time denoting the Millennium of the New Testament (Rev. 20:3-6). The Book of Ecclesiastes (which describes the peaceful reign of Solomon — a type of the Millennium) was picked to be read at that season. After that is Purim (5) which shows the complete redemption of the nation of Judah — a central tribe of Israel, and the one responsible for dispensing the message of salvation to the world (John 4:22).

Thus, the three holyday seasons and the two main commemorative periods (5 sanctified times) were graced with 5 books to be read that backed up the significance of their themes. These 5 books (and holyday seasons) also compare interestingly with the 5 divisions of the Psalms and the 5 books of the Mosaic Law. Let us see.

> (1) Psalms   1-41 (Book   I) = Genesis   = Song of Songs (1)
> (2) Psalms   42-72 (Book II) = Exodus   = Ruth   (2)
> (3) Psalms   73-89 (Book III) = Leviticus   = Lamentations (3)
> (4) Psalms 90-106 (Book IV) = Numbers   = Ecclesiastes (4)
> (5) Psalms 107-150 (Book V) = Deuteronomy = Esther   (5)

When these three sections of the Old Testament are compared with one another, there is an amazing parallel in many features. It is almost as if an over-all design was intended by the divine canonizers to show a buttressing effect on the messages found in each book. This may well be. To see this in a clear way, let us focus on Book III of the Psalms. This will equate with the Book of Leviticus in the Law of Moses and the Book of Lamentations in the *Megilloth*. The third book of psalms comprises those from Psalms 73 to 89 inclusively. Anyone who surveys those 17 psalms can see quite easily that they generally refer, in the main, to the temple at Jerusalem, and usually to its destruction. Note some particular verses in the psalms of Book III which show this.

> Psalm 73 = "The sanctuary of God ... they brought into destruction" (verses 17,18).

Psalm 74 = "The enemy hath done wickedly in thy sanctuary. . . . they have cast fire into thy sanctuary,
they have defiled by casting thy dwelling place
[the temple] of thy name to the ground" (verses
3,7).

Psalm 75 = "The earth [land] and all the inhabitants thereof
are dissolved" (verse 3).

Psalm 76 = "In Salem [Jerusalem] is his tabernacle, and his
dwelling place in Zion. There [in Jerusalem] brake
he the arrows of the bow" (verses 2,3).

Psalm 77 = "In the day of trouble I sought the Lord. . . . Will
the Lord cast off forever?" (verses 2,7).

Psalm 78 = "He forsook the tabernacle of Shilo [when the
temple was once there], the tent which he placed
among men" (verse 60).

Psalm 79 = "O God, the heathen are come into thy inheri-
tance; thy holy temple have they defiled . . . and
there was none to bury them" (verses 1,3). [The
latter reference is to the Two Witnesses, as shown
in the New Testament. See Rev. 11:9].

More examples from Book III of the Psalms could be given, but this is
enough to show that the theme of destruction is the general context of all of
those 17 psalms. And what is parallel to Book III of the Psalms? In the
Megilloth it is the Book of Lamentations. And, as said before, this book was
ordained to be read on the anniversary of the temple's destruction (Jer.
52:12-14; Zech. 7:5; 8:19). There could be no book more apt for comparison
to the subject matter of Book III of the Psalms. But these two books are
arranged opposite (in their 5-fold structure) to Book III of the Law — the
Book of Leviticus. And its theme? It is all about the priesthood and the
Levites regarding their duties in the temple. It could hardly be accidental
that the books found such an arrangement. The three books support each
other in subject matter.

Now look at Book IV of the Psalms. There are also 17 psalms in this division (Psalms 90-106). Psalm 90 introduces its contextual subject by mentioning a 1000 years (verse 4). A thousand years is, of course, a millennium
of time. And the general teaching of these 17 psalms is millennial — about
the time peace and security will be over all the earth. But before peace can
come to the earth, there is the time of the Great Tribulation that must first

occur. Psalm 91 describes such a subject in detail. Then, it is followed by Psalm 92 — a psalm for the Sabbath day (note its superscription). The Old Testament Sabbath day (the seventh day of the week) also represented the 7000th year period (after 6000 years of human rule) called in the Book of Revelation the 1000 year time when peace reigns throughout all the earth and Satan is bound in chains (Rev. 20: 2-4). And note! It takes only a cursory reading of the rest of the psalms in Book IV of the Book of Psalms to see the Millennial connection. But also, it must be noted that the Judaic authorities consecrated the Book of Ecclesiastes to be read at the Taber-nacles' season. Ecclesiastes described the glories of the Solomonic kingdom (a type of the Millennium) and Tabernacles itself had its spiritual theme as that of the same Millennium.

Book V of the Psalms (Psalms 107-150) is associated with Deuteronomy in the Law. Deuteronomy is called "the second law" or, a recapitulation of the earlier parts of the Law of Moses. And this is what the 44 psalms of Book V denote — a summing up of the subjects from Book I to IV. It is also equalled to the Book of Esther, which shows the complete salvation of the Jewish people. It looks like they will be one of the last nations on earth to finally accept Christ (Rom. 11:25,26). And Book V of the Psalms gives information that could emphasize how God will accomplish this salvation upon those of Israel.

Books I and II of the Psalms are songs composed exclusively by King David. At the end of Psalm 72 is the statement: "The prayers of David the son of Jesse are ended." Of course, there are other Davidic psalms in later sec-tions, but this reference indicates that Book I (Psalms 1-41) and Book II (Psalms 42-72) were all written by David.

Let us now note this interesting feature. The number of the Davidic psalms are 72 (that is 24 × 3). Since King David arranged the Levitical singers into 24 "wards" (I Chron. 25:8-31), it can be seen as being very likely that these first 72 psalms were established to fit a pattern of singing them in order by the Levites who found themselves positioned by David into 24 divisions.

Look at these psalms. In Book I there are 41 psalms. If one reckons the first psalm as introductory, then there are 40 psalms left. The number 40 is a number of trial. This is a well recognized fact by all scholars dealing with biblical symbolism. But in Book II there are 31 psalms. If one allows the first psalm of the second book to be introductory, then there are 30 psalms left. When one adds 40 and 30 together (equallying 70), one has the exact age of David when he died. The age of 70 is also considered in Psalm 90 as the ideal length of man's life on earth (Psa. 90:10). And isn't it interesting that Psalm 71:18 (next to the last psalm in the Davidic collection) records David as saying: "Now also when I am old and greyheaded." Then, the next psalm (the last one of Book II), concerns the glories of the Solomonic kingdom which was to occur at the death of David.

And too, Book I of the Psalms corresponds to the Song of Songs which was sung at the Passover season. The whole of the 41 psalms (1 plus 40) relate to this theme. Note, as an example, Psalm 22 which says that the wicked "pierced my hands and my feet" (verse 16). This reference, in prophecy, referred to the crucifixion of Christ — who died at the Passover! Also, since Israel came out of Egypt at Passover, the 40 psalms of Book I (after the introductory one) probably denote the 40 years of wandering in the wilderness. The 30 psalms of Book II (after the introductory one) may show the 30 years for the establishing of the nation of Israel in the land of Canaan — and this took exactly 30 years from their crossing of the River Jordan to the death of Joshua.

Conclusion

None of us can know for certain why the psalms in the Book of Psalms are arranged the way they are. Certainly, there is a reason behind their positioning because some of the psalms were repeated in other sections. Psalm 14 and Psalm 53 are virtually the same in content, yet one occurs in Book I and the other in Book II. Also, Psalm 70 is parallel with Psalm 40:13-17 and Psalm 60:9-12 with Psalm 108:10-13. In fact, with Psalms 9 and 10 there is an acrostic feature (the use of Hebrew letters at the beginning of verses — like in the Book of Lamentations) which shows that the two separate psalms were at one time *one psalm*. See the *commentaries* for proof of this. This all helps to show that there is a definite reason why the psalms were positioned in the way that they were. It is not the simple message that they give that is all the truth, it is the context in which they occur that makes the difference.

And since it can be shown that the psalms in the Book of Psalms are basically of a prophetic nature, it looks like a prophetic theme is to be found within the 5-fold divisions of the Psalms. We can sum up, succinctly, what it might mean.

The 41 (1 plus 40) psalms of Book I seem to refer to Passover — the beginning of Israel as a nation, and the start of the New Testament scheme of salvation with the death and resurrection of Christ. Book II is equated with Pentecost — the feast of the first-fruits. It shows Israel as a corporate body in the land of Israel, and it also can refer to the creation of the New Testament church and the spreading of the Gospel to the world. Book III is almost totally devoted to describing the destruction of Israel and the temple (both in 586 B.C. and in A.D. 70). This is a subject that parallels the prophecy of the Great Tribulation in the Book of Revelation very well.

Indeed, some of the teachings about that great time of trouble are reflective of verses found within this section of the psalms. Book IV of the psalms shows Israel regathered after their ruin (as demonstrated in the context of Book III). This book concerns the Millennium which is prophesied to happen after the ruin of the Israelitish system in Palestine just before the return of Christ to earth. And finally, Book V is equated with the feast of Purim — the time when Judah (all Israel) shall be delivered — as they were in the Persian period as recorded in the Book of Esther. Book V is also similar to that of Deuteronomy in the sense that it combines all the major features of the first four books.

Since there are 150 psalms in the entire collection (3×50) there may have been a three-year reading plan—a reading of a psalm for each of the 150 weeks to correspond with the triennial reading of the Law and the Prophets in the temple (Acts 13:15). This possibility has been suggested in the *Jewish Encyclopaedia* [1911], Vol. 12, under article *Triennial Cycle*. This could well be one of the reasons for the positioning of the psalms in the manner they are.

The main thing to recognize, however, is that there is far more teaching in the Book of Psalms than at first meets the eye. No one knows for sure just what every detail is trying to reveal. Yet, when one realizes that a consistency of doctrinal and prophetical emphasis is found throughout the Old Testament, it could be that the Psalms are a simple reflection of that fact.

These suggestions are intended as a preliminary survey of the various 5-fold sections which are found in the Old Testament. We should recall that the New Testament also has a 5-fold "Pentateuch" of the Gospels and Acts, and that Matthew's Gospel is arranged in a 5-fold structure. It appears, when one studies them closely, that these designs are not haphazardly formed, but that some kind of message is intended by their application in matters of interpretation. Certainly, further research among scholars and biblical students is needed to comprehend these matters in a better way. Such study, however, would be facilitated if people will retain the manuscript order of the biblical books rather than the arbitrary one that is now being presented to the world. We hope that the information in this book can prove to be an incentive to accomplish this task.

APPENDIX TWO

The Book Of Proverbs — Its Structure, Design, and Teaching

Most people are not aware that the proverbial statements in the Book of Proverbs are really *parables*. They are sayings that use natural and normal illustrations to show comparisons to moral, social, or religious principles. In other words, the use of the proverbs (parables) is intended to portray spiritual truths through the ordinary usage of words and explanations. The intended result, however, may involve the revelation of many "dark sayings" that the ordinary person may be unaware of. Or, to put it simply, there is often more to the proverb than at first meets the eye.

The introduction to the Book of Proverbs in the Holy Bible tells us this very fact. The first six verses are the superscription to the whole book. It says the proverbs have been given in order to show wisdom, instruction, understanding, justice, judgment, subtlety to the simple, knowledge, discretion, learning, counsel, and — "to understand a proverb [parable], and the interpretation; the words of the wise [the word "wise" is plural: "wise ones"], *and their dark sayings*" (Prov. 1:6).

This means that the Book of Proverbs does not only contain the proverbs originated by King Solomon, but it represents a compilation of wise and dark sayings which were associated with the "wise men" who lived before Solomon. Of those mentioned in the Bible there were the sons of Zerah [who was the son of Judah]: Ethan, Heman, Chalcol, and Darda (I Kings 4:31). These four "wise men" (or ancient philosophers) lived in Egypt at the time that Joseph was in power (Genesis 41). And let us not forget the patriarch Joseph himself! When Joseph was able to interpret Pharaoh's dream that a famine of seven years was to grip the Middle Eastern world, Pharaoh admitted that "there is none so discreet and wise as thou [Joseph] art" (Gen. 41:39). [We will soon see that some of the proverbs found within the biblical book are certainly those that originated with Joseph long before the Exodus of the Israelites from Egypt.] Other "wise men" were those "of the east country" (I Kings 4:30) — the people in the land of Edom (Obadiah 8), where the "wise man" Job had his residence (Job 1:1). The land of Uz (Job 1:1) was located east of the Jordan River.

These indications in the Bible show that there were many people of the ancient past who were considered "wise men." And what is the Book of Proverbs? It is basically a compilation of proverbs (parables) uttered by many "wise men" of the past, but brought together by King Solomon (or later editors), in order that the people of God could be instructed in the "dark sayings" and words of wisdom which have been uttered by people who learned the principles that governed life. They represent the "cream of the crop" of ancient philosophical teaching. When really understood, the "sayings" in the Book of Proverbs are no doubt some of the oldest literary statements known to man. It will pay us to understand just what the proverbs are all about, and especially why they have been placed in the order that they have. There is significant instruction awaiting us if we do.

We are told in the Bible that the proverbs accumulated (or written) by Solomon were "set in order" (Eccl. 12:9) — indeed, the proverbs had been "sought out" by Solomon for the express purpose of teaching the people of Israel essential knowledge. They were the words of the "wise ones" (Eccl. 12:11 — the word "wise" is, again, plural, and signifies many wise people of the past that were known by Solomon). The proverbs were "acceptable words" and "words of truth" which were "upright" [full of righteous teaching] (Eccl. 12:10). Since Solomon "set them in order," this shows that the proverbs were not arranged haphazardly. They also must be a selection of some of the better sayings of the wise ones. Actually, Solomon himself "spake three thousand proverbs" (I Kings 4:32). Since the Book of Proverbs contains only 915 verses (and some proverbs take up several verses), it can be seen that Solomon was selective even of his own proverbial creations in order that the whole book could be streamlined to contain the best of many "wise men."

The main ingredient to understanding a proverb, according to the superscription itself, is "the interpretation" behind the words (Prov. 1:6). They may well be "dark sayings," (Prov. 1:6), but they are designed to give enlightenment to those who read. Since this is the case, it will pay us first to apprehend the divisions of the Book of Proverbs and to understand the context in which the various proverbs are placed. This will help us to comprehend what the individual messages are all about.

DIVISION I = Prov. 1:7 to 9:18.

DIVISION II = "The Proverbs of Solomon"
Prov. 10:1 to 22:16.

DIVISION III = "The words of the wise [ones]"
Prov. 22:22 to 24:22.

DIVISION IV = "These also belong to the wise [ones]"
Prov. 24:23 to 24:34.

DIVISION V = "These are also proverbs of Solomon, which the men of Hezekiah king of Judah copied"
Prov. 25:1 to 29:27.

There are yet two remaining divisions to the Proverbs. These final two sections seem to represent individual compositions about two men of whom we have no further information as to their identities in the Bible.

> DIVISION VI = "The words of Agur the son of Jakeh"
> Prov. 30 (the whole chapter).

> DIVISION VII = "The words of king Lemuel"
> Prov. 31 (the whole chapter).

There is a general "story flow" which pervades the proverbs in each of the designated divisions. When this is realized, it helps us to better identify the author of most of the individual proverbs in the various sections and to see why the proverbs were placed in the manner they were. It also gives us the over-all teaching of the theme.

DIVISION ONE: The first six verses of the book are an introduction to the whole of the Book of Proverbs. The very first "proverb," in itself, is found in verse seven.

> "The fear of the Lord is the beginning of knowledge: but fools despise wisdom and instruction."

This sets the theme of the first division, and also to all of Proverbs. "The fear of the Lord," which is the Old Testament way of saying: "Have faith and trust in God," is the very start of wisdom. All else, according to the author of this section, is subsidiary to this main principle. And what is the next step to wisdom?

> "My son, hear the instruction of thy father, and forsake not the law of thy mother: for they shall be an ornament of grace unto thy head, and chains about thy neck."

Paying attention to the teachings of one's parents is the next step to gaining wisdom. Who was the author of this first division? We are not told precisely, but there are some hints. Who was it that respected his father so much that he finally had a "chain of authority" put around his neck? Such a person was Joseph (Gen. 41:42). This first division speaks very much about the "strange woman" (Prov. 2:16-18; 5:3-6; 5:15-20; 6:24-35; 7:5-23; 9:13-18), and of all the early "wise men" of Israel, Joseph was noted for his refraining from an adulterous union with the king's wife (Gen. 39:7-23). Since Joseph was described as being "discreet and wise" (Gen. 41:39) — and lived at the same time as the sons of Zerah in Egypt (I Kings 4:31) — it could well be that he was the main author of the first division (or helped to compose it with the sons of Zerah).

Joseph was also able to interpret Pharaoh's dreams for him in a very judicious way (Gen. 41:25-36) and he recognized that the Sun, Moon, and Eleven Stars represented his father, his mother, and his eleven brothers (Gen. 37:5-11). And what are the proverbs in Division One really about? They are "dark sayings" which need "interpretation" (Prov. 1:6). As said before, they are statements that mean more than at first meets the eye. One must dig beneath the surface to understand the real meaning.

Division One is filled with such "secret" teachings. Note that the main textual subject of this division is Wisdom (1:20; 2:2,6,7,10; 3:13,19,21; 4:5,7; 5:1; 7:4; 8:1,12,14; 9:1). "Wisdom" is personified as a *woman* and rendered in the *plural* (Prov. 1:20ff. Other than the simple use for the meaning of "wisdom," it no doubt refers to something far more — especially since it is put in the feminine gender. The Old Testament was a "man's world," but "Wisdom" and other virtuous attributes are feminine! The holy name for Jerusalem was Zion and it is called a "she" in Psalm 46:5. Israel and Judah are called daughters (Ezek. 23:1). The New Testament body of believers in the Book of Revelation is called "the wife" of Christ (Rev. 19:7). The virtue of "understanding" is also feminine (Prov. 7:4,5), and the chief attitude of all — "love" — is as well placed in the feminine gender (I Cor. 13:5).

But we also find that Babylon, Nineveh, and the evil system condemned in the Book of Revelation are also called "women" (Rev. 17:5; Nah. 2:10; 3:4; Zeph. 2:13-15; Micah 5:6 margin). The subject to whom the proverbs of Division One is directed is "My Son." He is told to have his affection set on Wisdom and Understanding (both expressed in the feminine). Yet he is equally advised to stay away from "the strange woman." Since the proverbs are parables which are "dark sayings" requiring interpretation to understand them, the significance could be intended to show the people of Israel to stay away from the alluring environments of the false "women" of Babylon, Nineveh, and the great woman of the Book of Revelation. But the "true women" are Wisdom and Understanding. There may be more teaching in the Book of Proverbs than one might imagine on the surface!

"Wisdom" is also personified as being with the creator of nature. "The Lord possessed me [Wisdom] in the beginning of his way, before his works of old" (Prov. 8:22-36). It is almost as though "she" were a creator herself (Prov. 9:1) — almost like Christ in relation to the Father (Col. 1:16-18 along with Prov. 8:22-36). There may be far more "dark sayings" to comprehend in this section of Proverbs than many people imagine. Perhaps Joseph (or those associated with him before the Exodus) understood even some of the "secret" things mentioned in the New Testament, though in a veiled way. At any rate, the first nine chapters of Proverbs represent the sayings of ancient "wise ones" — the ones who lived long before Solomon.

DIVISION TWO: The next thirteen chapters of the book are short prover-bial statements made exclusively by King Solomon. The simple title to the section is: "The proverbs of Solomon" (Prov. 10:1). And what is its primary emphasis? Look at the first proverb of this division:

"A wise son maketh a glad father: but a foolish son is the heaviness of his mother."

Whereas in the first division the thrust is mainly upon spiritual things: Wisdom, Understanding, Faithfulness, Duty to God, in this second section it is foremostly the relationships between humans. Of course, the most important association is that of children and parents, and that is empha-sized first. There is nothing especially esoteric about these short and to-the-point statements, yet the order in which they occur could be signifi-cant. Since we are told by Paul that a "root of all evil" is the desire for riches (I Tim. 6:10), it is interesting that the second proverb of Solomon's personal section shows that the "treasures of wickedness profit nothing" (Prov. 10:2).

DIVISION THREE: This is one of the most interesting sections in the whole of Proverbs. One who reads the King James Version would hardly realize that a new division was being introduced — but it is clearly evident in the original text. Division Three actually begins in the middle of chapter 22. The title to it is found from Proverbs 22:17 to 21. Let us look at it. [It must be understood that the verses that now follow *are not* individual proverbs in themselves. They represent a superscription to Division Three.]

"Bow down thine ear, and hear the words of the wise [plural: "wise ones"], and apply thine heart unto my knowledge. For it is a pleasant thing if thou keep them [the following proverbs of Division Three] within thee; they [these particular proverbs] shall withal be fitted in thy lips. That thy trust may be in the Lord, I have made known to thee this day, even to thee. Have not I written to thee excellent things [or, as the Revised Standard Version has it: "*thirty sayings*"] in counsels and knowledge, that I might make thee know the certainty of the words of truth; that thou mightest answer the words of truth to them that send unto thee?"

After this long introduction, we then find the first proverb of Division Three. It is Proverbs 22:22,23.

"Rob not the poor, because he is poor: neither oppress the afflicted in the gate: for the Lord will plead their cause, and spoil the soul of those that spoil them."

There are actually *thirty sections* to this Third Division (Prov. 22:22 to 24:22). The Revised Standard Version, the New English Bible, and most modern translations realize that this is the meaning of the key words in Proverbs 22:20. Why do they know this? The Hebrew of Proverbs 22:20 could be stretched to mean "thirty" from the use of the word "excellent." But there is even a greater assurance that "thirty sayings" is the correct rendering because this section of Proverbs has been found to have existed even among the Egyptians.

There is an ancient document in the British Museum (a writing of the early Egyptian priests) which is a parallel to the Third Division of the Book of Proverbs. [A portion of the text is also found on a writing tablet now in Turin, Italy.] It is called "The Instruction of Amen-em-opet" (or, Amenophis). The date when the original Egyptian work was written has been disputed — some say before the time of Solomon, others afterwards (See *Ancient Near Eastern Texts*, pages 421-424 for more information and the recording of the complete Egyptian text.) The Egyptian version differs in some respects from that in the Book of Proverbs, but there can be no question that the two documents are really the same. And interestingly, the Egyptian version says there are *thirty parts* to it.

If the Egyptian text is earlier than that of Solomon, it could well be that it was a product of the time when Joseph (and the sons of Zerah) were in Egypt and writing many of the wise sayings of the past. It is well within reason that many of these early philosophical works of the Israelites (while they were in Egypt) or of other wise Egyptians could have been maintained for long periods of time among the Egyptians. There is another Egyptian proverbial text called "The Instruction of the Vizier (the chief minister) Ptah-Hotep" that sounds so much like the writing of Joseph — both in its teaching and the subjects of the text — and a historical identification may in some manner be possible. We are told that the time of Joseph and the sons of Zerah was that of much literary activity in Egypt. And since "The Instruction of Amen-em-opet" has found inclusion within the biblical Book of Proverbs (22:22 to 24:22), it may well be that this section of Proverbs may date back to the time of Joseph — as well as Division One (Proverbs 1:7 to 9:18). This would mean that the Book of Proverbs is truly an international collection of many wise sayings from a number of ancient philosophers and sages of the past.

It could be interesting to compare some of the statements in our Book of Proverbs with those found in the Egyptian version. [It must be recalled that there is not exact agreement in every detail. This shows that editing of material was done on a wide scale so that the messages within the Proverbs could be maintained in a particular context.]

In the introduction of Division Three in the Book of Proverbs there is the statement (in the King James Version) concerning "excellent things" (verse 20). There is a vague connection with the word "three" or possibly "thirty" associated with the original Hebrew word. But in the Egyptian version it is clearly "*thirty sayings*." This agreement has even helped scholars to know what the biblical book means. There are other parallels.

The Book of Proverbs	*The Instruction of Amen-em-opet*
"Rob not the poor, because he is poor: neither oppress the afflicted in the gate" (Prov. 22:22).	"Guard thyself against robbing the oppressed and against overbearing the disabled" (*ANET*, p. 421a).
"Make no friendship with an angry man; and with a furious man thou shalt not go" (Prov. 22:24).	"Do not associate to thyself the heated man, nor visit him for conversation" (*ANET*, p. 423a).
"Seest thou a man diligent in his business? he shall stand before kings" (Prov. 22:29).	"As for the scribe who is experienced in his office, he will find himself worthy to be a courtier" (*ANET*, p. 424b).
"When thou sittest to eat with a ruler, consider diligently what is before thee" (Prov. 23:1).	"Do not eat bread before a noble, nor lay on thy mouth [be not gluttonous] at first" (*ANET*, p. 424a).
"Labour not to be rich: cease from thine own wisdom" (Prov. 23:4).	"Cast not thy heart in pursuit of riches, for there is no ignoring Fate and Fortune" (*ANET*, p. 422b).

These are just a few of the parallels that can be found between the biblical Book of Proverbs and this papyrus document found in Egypt. These remarkable points are valuable in showing that there was much interchange of proverbial material among those of the Middle Eastern countries. Indeed, there is an Aramaic work (in the language of the Syrians) which dates to the fifth century before Christ which has a section very similar to that of Division Three of our Book of Proverbs. It is from "The Words of Ahiqar."

"Withhold not correction from the child: for if thou beatest him with the rod, he shall not die. Thou shalt beat him with the rod, and shalt deliver his soul from hell [from the grave]" (Prov. 23:13,14).	"Withhold not thy son from the rod, else thou wilt not be able to save him from wickedness. If I smite thee, my son, thou wilt not die, but if I leave thee to thy own heart thou wilt not live" (*ANET*, p. 428b).

It is not known whether Solomon got his proverbial statements (besides the ones he composed himself) from The Instruction of Amen-em-opet, but it is clear — from what the Book of Proverbs says itself — that he gathered together many of the wise sayings of ancient wise men. It could well be that

Solomon, and later editors of the Bible, simply garnered together the most valuable of what they considered to be the divine wisdom of the ancients. One thing for certain. The whole of Division Three has been found in the literary collections of the early Egyptians. This shows that the Bible is far more in line with the philosophical teachings of many ancient wise men than we may have imagined.

DIVISION FOUR: One would hardly realize that a new section of proverbs was being introduced if only the King James Version were relied on. Still, however, look at Proverbs 24:23. It says: "These things also belong to the wise [the wise ones]." The first proverb of this short division is: "It is not good to have respect of persons in judgment." The whole of the division occupies only twelve verses, but they were thought important enough to include them in the biblical book. The main theme is: *don't be lazy,* and hold your neighbor in esteem. It is really very good advice to anyone, and this section was deemed necessary for the righteous Israelite to hold in importance.

DIVISION FIVE: This section is a very significant one and was designed to muster together various proverbs of Solomon (of the many that he wrote) that would show a king how to act. One person who was intent in learning the wisdom of Solomon on rulership was righteous king Hezekiah in the eighth century before Christ. It was he who ordered his scribes to collect some of the most important proverbs of Solomon which pertained to rulership. And that is what we have in this fifth division (Proverbs 25:1 to 29:27).

> "These are also proverbs of Solomon, which the men of Hezekiah king of Judah copied out."

Now notice that the subject matters of these proverbs are those designed for rulership. Proverbs 25:2 mentions "kings." Verse 3 "kings." Verse 5 "king." Verse 6 "king." Verse 7 "prince." Verse 15 "prince." The intervening verses show how to make judgments between people, how to be wise and honest. Then there is Proverbs 29:2 which has as its subjects "authority" and "rule." Verse 4 "king." Verse 12 "ruler." Verse 14 "rule" and "throne." The division finally ends with a warning for all rulers who have to render judgment — and how to be careful in doing it. "Many seek the ruler's favour; but every man's judgment cometh from the Lord" (Proverbs 29:26).

DIVISION SIX: This section is one chapter (30). It is the literary work of an unknown person called Agur. "The words of Agur the son of Jakeh." He was an agnostic! He had great difficulty in believing that a loving and wise God existed (even though he admitted he did). See verses 2 through 6.

Though it was difficult for him to believe that God truly had an interest in human life, he was compelled to admit it because of the marvels of creation. The rest of the chapter involves the orderliness of animals: birds, fish, insects, carnivores. To Agur, these all seemed to act according to a definite order, but mankind did not. Humans were haughty, they stole, were full of vanity, sensuous, and foolish. And who did Agur consider the most stupid of all? It was himself! "Surely I am more brutish than any man, and have not the understanding of man" (Prov. 30:2). His anguish was so acute that he was asking: "Where is God in all this?" (this is a paraphrase of verse 4). This chapter (and division) ends *without* Agur finding the answer to his quest. His agnosticism was not cured, though he knew there was a God.

DIVISION SEVEN: The last division was that written by an unknown king called Lemuel. "The words of king Lemuel, the prophecy that his mother taught him." Ferrar Fenton tried to identify this "Lemuel" with King Solomon himself. This was done by stretching the meaning of "Lemuel" to signify "The One Who Forgot God." This is a rather fanciful interpretation and little weight should be attached to it. However, we know of no king in the Bible (or in secular history) with such a name. It may well be a cipher for Solomon himself, but no one can be sure of this.

This Lemuel became so distraught with life in the end of his days that he was driven to drink (Proverbs 31:2-9). This could well describe Solomon near his final years (Eccl. 12:1-7). Solomon blamed his downfall on the many foreign women that he had in his harem (Eccl. 7:26-29). The main problem was that they were the wrong kind of women for a righteous ruler of Israel. If "Lemuel" is a cipher for Solomon, it might help to explain why the last part of division seven (22 verses in length) describes the perfect and honest woman — the type Solomon never found (Prov. 31:10-31). He could have discovered such a person if he would have looked in the right places. The trouble with Solomon, he didn't!

AN OVERVIEW OF PROVERBS: The prime reason for compiling these selected proverbs and putting them in the Bible was to show how one can and should "rule" his life. They were placed in order by a ruler himself — by king Solomon. If Joseph was the author of Division One (and perhaps instrumental in composing Division Three), he did so as a king of Egypt (Gen. 41:40-44). Also, it was king Hezekiah who copied out proverbs to help him show justice to his people. Agur appears to have been someone in authority, and finally there was king Lemuel. And recall that in the main body of the book we have shown that all the eleven books found within the Third Division of the Old Testament have a theme of *royalty* associated with them. And the Book of Proverbs is no exception. It was a book designed for those who rule—either those who rule other humans or, more importantly, those who wish to rule their own lives.

Index

Other Historical Research Works by Ernest L. Martin

The Star that Astonished the World. This historical and astronomical work shows the outstanding celestial events that occurred at the time of Jesus' nativity. Astronomers are astounded at the stellar and planetary pageantry that was happening when the Magi (the Wise Men) went to Jerusalem and then to Bethlehem with their gifts for the Christ-child. So spectacular were the astronomical events that over 600 planetariums (as of 1991) are now presenting this new research at their Christmas programs. This book provides new historical research to show that Christ was born in 3 B.C. and the day on which he was born is astronomically determined to within 90 minutes of his birth. It was a prime holyday on the Jewish calendar.

Secrets of Golgotha (The Forgotten History of Christ's Crucifixion). Brand new historical and archaeological evidence has come to the fore which shows the precise place in the Jerusalem area where Christ was buried and resurrected from the dead. For the past 1600 years scholars and pilgrims to the Holy Land have been looking at the wrong place as the site of the crucifixion and resurrection. This new evidence, however, gives positive biblical information that locates the true site. One of the greatest hoaxes ever to be perpetrated against the Christian world was choosing the traditional site of the Church of the Holy Sepulchre. Once this new research is realized a better understaning of biblical events about the crucifixion then emerges.

Select Bibliography

Bruce, F.F., *The Canon of Scripture*, (London:Intervarsity) 1988.

Bruce, F.F., *History of the Bible in English*, (New York:Oxford) 1978.

Campenhausen, Hans, *The Formation of the New Testament*, (Philadelphia: Fortress) 1977.

Collins, R.F., *Introduction to the New Testament*, (New York: Doubleday) 1983.

Filson, F.V., *Which Books Belong in the Bible?* (Philadelphia: Westminster) 1957.

Finegan, Jack, *Encountering New Testament Manuscripts*, (Grand Rapids: Eerdmans) 1974.

Ginsburg, C., *Massoretico-Critical Edition of the Hebrew Bible*, (New York: KTAV) 1966.

Grant, R.M., *The Apostolic Fathers*, (6 vols.) (Nashville: Nelson) 1968.

Gregory, C., *Canon and Text of the New Testament*, (Edinburgh: Clark) 1924.

Guthrie, D., *New Testament Introduction*, (London: Tyndale) 1970.

Henry, Carl F.H., *God, Revelation and Authority*, (4 vols.) (Waco: Word Books) 1979.

McKim, Donald K., *The Authoritative Word*, (Grand Rapids: Eerdmans) 1983.

Metzger, B., *Early Versions of the New Testament*, (Oxford: Clarendon) 1977.

Moule, C.F.D., *The Birth of the New Testament*, (London: Black) 1981.

Robinson, J.A.T., *Redating the New Testament*, (London: SCM) 1976.

Westcott, B.F., *History of the Canon of the New Testament*, (London: Macmillan) 1875.